TO TURN THE SOUL

Essays Inspired by Jacob Klein

TO TURN THE SOUL

Essays Inspired by Jacob Klein

Edited by

Daniel P. Maher

and

Andrew Romiti

PAUL DRY BOOKS

Philadelphia 2025

First Paul Dry Books Edition, 2025

Paul Dry Books, Inc
Philadelphia, Pennsylvania
www.pauldrybooks.com

An earlier version of "European Scholar and American Teacher" by Eva Brann appeared in *St. John's Review* 59:1–2 (Fall 2017–Spring 2018): 22–34

An earlier version of "Jacob Klein's Two Prescient Discoveries" by Eva Brann appeared in *St. John's Review* 52:1 (Fall 2010): 5–19

Cover image courtesy of St. John's College:
St. John's College (Annapolis, Md.), "Jacob Klein Leading a Tutorial, St. John's College, Annapolis, Maryland, circa 1960–1970," St. John's College Digital Archives, accessed April 9, 2024, https://digitalarchives.sjc.edu/items/show/936, SJC-P-0055.

ISBN: 978-1-58988-197-6

Printed in the United States of America.

LCCN: 2024941599

Contents

Preface

DANIEL P. MAHER

The title of this volume refers to the crucial event in Plato's Allegory of the Cave when the soul turns or is turned from looking at shadows or at what is coming into being and begins to develop its native power to gaze at what is (*Republic* 7.518c). The allegory portrays our nature in its education and lack of education, and Socrates contrasts the turn of the soul with a view of education that would amount to attempting to pour sight into blind eyes. Socrates proposes instead that the soul has sight in it by nature, and yet the soul is not rightly turned. We begin to see for ourselves once we have undergone the "turning around" that in Greek is called *periagôgê* or *metastrophê*.

Jacob Klein (1899–1978), who identifies the moment of this turning with the experience of wonder that is the beginning of philosophy, has contributed in various ways to the turning of the souls of the contributors to this volume. Some knew him as a colleague or a teacher at St. John's College in Annapolis, where he taught for forty years, and others have come to know him indirectly through his students or his writings and the stories reported about him. All have been led to wonder and to question and to reflect. To learn from Klein in this way is not to become a follower in a certain school of thought. As Eva Brann writes in this volume, Klein was "terminally disciple-proof."[1] To think under the influence of Klein, then, means to think for oneself; otherwise, one has missed the point.

Klein's influence renders one simultaneously attached to him and independent of him. This sort of tension—or unity of opposites—pervades the understanding of liberal education associated with Klein and, more generally, with St. John's. For example, when he was new to the college, Klein remarked enthusiastically on the *directness* with which St. John's students approached Plato. And yet Klein wrote two book-length commentaries on Plato. His commentary mediates Plato to us, but he wants us to encounter Plato directly. In her essay "Immediacy: The Ways of Humanity," Eva Brann reminds us of Klein's emphasis on directness, which she calls *immediacy*, and of its centrality in the St. John's program.[2] That program incorporates the tension involved in sustaining an *open* conversation about *fixed* texts. And even if the students encounter texts directly, the texts point beyond themselves to the permanent or timeless human concerns the texts are about. Furthermore, our permanent human concerns and our thinking about them seem to be affected by the passage of time, as is reflected variously in the several contributions to this volume: Klein has helped us to think about and explore what Brann calls our "ruptured continuum with Greek antiquity."[3] Several papers in this collection investigate the nature of that rupture, which is simultaneously an effort to recover our continuity with the immediacy of Greek thinking.

A *ruptured continuum* exemplifies the kind of contradiction that inspires or summons thought, as Plato's Socrates indicates in various places, most notably for present purposes in the *Republic* shortly after the Allegory of the Cave.[4] Having established the importance of the soul's turning around, he identifies "the lowly business of distinguishing the one, the two, and the three," that is, "number and calculation," as particularly suited to accomplish this turning because contradictory appearances summon our thought. When something appears as both hard and soft, both big and little, or, more generally, no more one than the opposite of one, we need to begin to think (523d–524e). If we are especially thoughtful, we will ask what is the one being that appears in two ways. The study of number, then, is "in every way apt to draw men toward being."[5] We see the same point reflected in the question Socrates puts to the Eleatic Stranger at the beginning of Plato's *Sophist.* He asks what the people in Elea believe about the sophist, the statesman, and the philosopher: "Were they accustomed to hold all these as one or two, or, just as their names are three, to divide their genera into three as well and attach a name to each individually?" The Stranger responds that it's easy to say "they believed them three. It's no small and easy work, however, to distinguish with clarity whatever they severally are."[6] Listening attentively to the conversation articulating the view held by those in Elea amounts to thinking for oneself about how to use the several names in keeping with the being of things. When we examine the speeches (*logoi*) of others, we are no less engaged with the beings themselves, as Socrates stated in *Phaedo* (see 99d–100a).

The contributors to this volume follow Klein, but we diverge from him and from one another. We look at primary texts, commentaries, and the things themselves in order to try to navigate along the ruptured continuum without prejudging the significance of the differences between ancients and moderns. Despite our not being adherents to a doctrine that could be attributed to Klein, the several papers in this volume reflect our thinking along lines discoverable in Klein's writings. In some cases we engage in exegesis of Klein's work, but more fundamentally we aim to supplement it or to participate in the kind of effort Eva Brann attributes to David Lachterman, who, she says, "carried on Mr. Klein's projects in his own competently ingenious way."[7] We don't claim to be ingenious ourselves, but we do strive to think as competently as we can in the ways suggested to us by "Mr. Klein's projects." In the present collection, our efforts to do this tend to focus either on the nature of genuine education or on the nature of number. As Plato has shown in *Republic* and as Klein has helped us understand, these two concerns ultimately come to the same issue: turning the soul to the things that are.

The Contents of This Volume

Eva Brann has contributed three papers to this collection. In the first, she provides a synoptic view of Jacob Klein's intellectual life as divided between being first a European scholar and then an American teacher. Her singular perspective illuminates Klein's intellectual character both for those who already know his work and those who are discovering him for the first time. In "Jacob Klein's Two Prescient Discoveries," she reflects on two insights Klein developed in the interpretation of two Platonic dialogues. First, in his 1965 book *A Commentary on Plato's "Meno,"* Klein gives a reading of the *Republic*'s Divided Line, which associates levels of being with distinct kinds of human awareness. At the lowest level we recognize shadows, reflections, and images. Plato calls this kind of awareness *eikasia*, which is often translated as *imagination*, but Klein translates it as *image-recognition*, and he shows how this lowest mode of awareness actually pervades all human cognition. The second discovery Brann highlights involves a complicated set of issues the core of which is Klein's "analysis of what it means to be a number and what makes possible this kind of being, and, it turns out, all Being."[8] In a very elementary form, the insight addresses how units, each of which is one, together constitute number, which is not one. That is, how can a pair of units together have a character neither has in itself? Klein initially articulated this analysis and its significance for understanding being in the 1930s in two long articles Eva Brann later translated and published in 1968 as the book for which Klein is best known, *Greek Mathematical Thought and the Origin of Algebra*.[9] With respect to both discoveries, Brann shows how they can illuminate our lives today, especially the problem of pervasive images in our lives and the question of the emergence of properties like conscious awareness from material parts that are not themselves conscious. In her third contribution, "Form Numbers," Brann explores what we should understand by the term *arithmoi eidetikoi*, which Aristotle uses to discuss Platonic views of number. This effort raises the highest ontological questions and requires a close reading of Plato, Aristotle, Klein, and some of Burt Hopkins's work on Klein. She uses this again to revisit the question of emergence and to show how much room there is for further exploration once we develop appreciation for Klein's work.

In "To Flip a Pancake," Julia Klein (no familial relation to Jacob) examines whether Meno is capable of the type of metastrophic questioning Socrates repeatedly encourages him to attempt. Her title draws upon Jacob Klein's characterization of Meno's soul as "flat as a pancake," which suggests that he and perhaps other human beings have no potential for education because their souls have no undiscovered or undeveloped depth. Paul Wilford draws attention to Klein's relationship to his teacher Martin Heidegger and his fellow student Leo Strauss, each of whom is implicated in Klein's essay entitled "Aristotle, an Introduction." Klein had the essay published in a festschrift for Strauss, and in it he references how in Heidegger's classroom he had come to see that he could understand Aristotle and, thus, that he could genuinely reopen the questions animating Greek philosophy. Wilford establishes the importance of Klein's introducing Aristotle's thought by showing him in dialogue with Plato, for this also displays a subtle rejection of Heidegger's historicist approach to ancient thought.

Whereas much of Klein's work laid out the new intellectual orientation that constituted modern philosophical and scientific thought in contrast to the classical tradition, in "Modern Symbolic Unreality" David Lawrence Levine explores the consequences for human beings living on this side of the "ruptured continuum." Our way of thinking estranges us from the world of ordinary experience, which Klein expresses by saying that we conceive things *symbolically*. Levine's paper fleshes out Klein's thinking by unfolding the significance of the arresting claims one discovers throughout Klein's writings, such as, "Mathematical physics is the most important part of our entire civilization and actual life. . . . [T]he principles of mathematical physics are basic to our whole way of thinking and behavior."[10] Levine draws out what it means for us to be dominated in our thought and our actions by this modern rationalism that Klein designates as "symbolic." In "Jacob Klein's Defense of Liberal Education" Antonio Marino López addresses several of these same themes as they arise in relation to the practice of education. He identifies paradoxes or tensions that beset all attempts at liberal education and shows how the character of modern philosophical rationalism exacerbates all three tensions. He uses Klein's several writings to trace out the problem and to articulate how a clear grasp of Greek arithmetic can, even in our circumstances, help overcome these obstacles and achieve the turning of the soul that education in the liberal arts aims to achieve but cannot itself guarantee. The essay concludes with an analysis of Klein's reflections on the several senses of freedom we must distinguish in order to discern the liberation possible through education.

In "Jacob Klein on the Problem of History in Liberal Education," Mary Elizabeth Halper brings together two complementary sides of Klein's thinking in order to inquire into the nature of genuine education. On the one hand, Klein counsels us to "ignore history," by which he means that education should proceed without adopting "the historical sense," that is, the view according to which all things must be understood in historical perspective. On the other hand, she argues that teachers must nevertheless be alert to what Klein, drawing on Husserl, calls *intentional history*, by virtue of which they help students reactivate the original acts of insight that enable them to grasp meaning for themselves through evidence as opposed to encountering technical jargon that packages ideas for them. Teachers who are skilled with this kind of history of ideas can prepare students for the metastrophic moments of genuine education.

The final six papers in this collection deal more directly with Klein's work on the history of mathematics, especially his account of the new concept of number that emerges in early modern thought. Burt C. Hopkins provides a detailed exposition of Klein's account of the distinctive *conceptuality* at work in the modern understanding of number, and in doing so he defends Klein from charges of having used Husserl's doctrine of intentionality to interpret older authors, such as François Viète. Hopkins shows that Klein's term *Begrifflichkeit* should be translated as *conceptuality* and should be understood to refer to the formation of concepts. Indeed, the term *Intentionalität* does not appear in Klein's German text that would become *Greek Mathematical Thought and the Origin of Algebra*, where Klein's *Begrifflichkeit* was rendered as *intentionality*. Hopkins argues that Husserl's account of intentional history was developed in the 1930s *after* the composition of Klein's text and already operates at the level of the kind of symbolic thinking whose origin Klein lays bare. Hopkins defends Klein's argument that the "species" that form the object of Viète's general analytic art are symbolic and thus crucially different from the types of quantity found in the Euclidean tradition.

In "Viètian Magnitudes" Michael Dink carefully investigates Viète's *Introduction to the Analytic Art* and Klein's use of it to determine to what extent Viète respects or ignores the classical distinction between discrete multitudes and continuous magnitudes. He argues that the object of Viète's analytic art is a new kind of general magnitude, which has some features in common with Euclidean magnitudes and some features in common with Euclidean numbers. Moreover, these Viètian magnitudes are conceptual or symbolic in the sense that they are defined by the operational rules of Viète's new system of analysis. Dink both clarifies and modifies the account Klein gives in *Greek Mathematical Thought and the Origin of Algebra.*

Daniel P. Maher's "Simon Stevin and the Matter of Number" examines the argument by which Stevin rejects the traditional conception of number as confused and mistaken. Stevin directly attacks the Euclidean definition of number as *a multitude of units* and the correlative thesis that one is not a number. In doing so, Stevin emphasizes the *matter* of number and thus renders number as a continuous or quasi-continuous quantity, in contrast to Aristotle's view according to which the foundational distinction between continuous magnitudes and discrete numbers derives from the ontological principle of *form* (correlative to matter), which establishes determinate wholes or "ones" in being. Klein regards Stevin and Viète as the two founders of modern algebra, although he gives greater prominence to Viète,[11] and yet the breadth and integration of Stevin's thought reveal him to have a decidedly modern, philosophical attitude.

In "Two Reflexivities" Richard F. Hassing uses the work of Joseph Owens to clarify Klein's account of the symbolic understanding of numbers by showing that the distinction between first and second intentions, widely used in the scholastic tradition, functions differently in the case of Descartes because his understanding of the relation of mind to world differs fundamentally from the "form-receptive realism" characteristic of the tradition. Through first intentions we cognize actual beings in the world, while through second intentions we reflect on our own thinking and produce concepts of concepts, such as *theory* or *species*. Second intentions, then, necessarily involve the mind's ability to reflect on its own activities in knowing the world. Hassing argues that Descartes's understanding of this reflexivity differs from that of the scholastic tradition because he separates mind and world in such a way that we know ideas rather than the world, with the result that there are no first intentions for Descartes. The mind "applies itself" to the corporeal imagination and abstracts intelligible contents, such as mere multitudinousness, which is indeterminate manyness, and then the intellect activates the imagination to symbolize this concept with a particular representation, for example, with the letter *x*, in which the mind apprehends and symbolizes its own conceiving.

In "The Symbolic Space of Descartes's *Geometry* and Its Symbolic Mathematical Underpinnings" Andrew Romiti works to extend Klein's analysis of the origin of modern science and its significance in our lives by exploring the modern concept of *space* as it originates in Descartes before it is picked up by Einstein and others. According to Klein, Descartes's symbolic conception of space represents the real world within the mathematical understanding of nature, and this becomes anachronistically and inaccurately designated as "Euclidean space." Furthermore, "Once this symbolic domain is identified with corporeal extension itself, it enters into Newtonian physics as 'absolute space.'"[12] Romiti uses Descartes's *Geometry*, a text appended to his *Discourse on Method*, to illustrate the symbolic character of the figures of Cartesian geometry and the redefinition of the operations of multiplication and division with these new mathematical objects (lines and figures) that represent indeterminate quantities in their relations to one another. The space in which these and other admissible geometrical objects appear is itself symbolic because everything discoverable in it exists in reference to what Descartes calls *principal lines*, which are themselves indeterminate, symbolic objects.

Whereas other contributors to this volume tend to begin with Klein or with Klein's sources and follow his analysis prospectively, in "Klein and Einstein on Cartesian Space" Joseph Cosgrove focuses on Klein's ultimate aim, which is to address "the conceptual difficulties arising within mathematical *physics* today."[13] He questions the manner in which we should understand Klein's thesis that Descartes identified symbolic and real extension (Klein's "identification thesis") and, in turn, what evidence there may be that Cartesian symbolic space furnishes the conceptual basis of classical physics (his "Newtonian thesis"). Cosgrove argues that Einstein's work on the role of Cartesian space in the development of mathematical physics "confirms" the identification thesis, and aspects of his work on general relativity lend further support to that thesis and to the Newtonian thesis.

• • •

The contributors to this volume have profited tremendously from their engagement with Jacob Klein's work. We hope that others find the papers here shed helpful light on Klein's achievement and entice some to engage with Klein's writings and participate in the further pursuit of "Mr. Klein's projects."

Introduction

ANDREW ROMITI

The legacy of Jacob Klein is wide-ranging in both form and content. Regarding the former, he has had an enduring influence through his writings, through the effect he had on St. John's College as an institution, and through the many individuals who were shaped by coming into contact with him. His writings consist of three books as well as many lectures and essays.[1] As a member of the faculty at St. John's College, he helped define and articulate the goal of liberal education at which the institution is aimed, he left a stamp on the all-required Great Books curriculum, and he served as an exemplar of a life devoted to the love of learning. Among the many individuals influenced by him were friends, colleagues, and students, whose glowing reports serve as a testament to his impact as both a teacher and a man.[2]

As for content, Klein's writings reveal three areas of primary concern: ancient philosophy, the history of mathematics and science, and the nature and practice of liberal education. While Klein's thinking about these subjects is deeply integrated, he has important achievements in each that are worth reviewing individually before outlining their interconnection.

First, Klein wrote two books of commentary on Platonic dialogues, and many of his lectures and essays are concerned with Plato, Aristotle, or ancient philosophical thought in general. Throughout these writings, Klein has a number of valuable accomplishments: he offers deep insight into the character and form of the Platonic dialogues (the "Introductory Remarks" to his *Commentary on Plato's "Meno"* provide excellent guidance on how to approach Plato); he elucidates the nature of Platonic forms and offers a ground-breaking interpretation of Plato's "eidetic numbers" (in doing so Klein believed he had uncovered the Platonic solution to the problem of participation[3]); he details the centrally important disagreement between Plato and Aristotle about the nature of number, which, as the hallmark instance of a one-and-many, has significant implications for understanding their thought as a whole; and he illuminates essential aspects of Greek thought by contrasting them with modern alternatives, as in his exposition of the antithesis between the ancient and modern understandings of the relationship between mind and world.

Klein's contributions to the understanding of the history of math and science are primarily contained in *Greek Mathematical Thought and the Origin of Algebra*, in which he identifies the concept of number distinctive to ancient thought and shows the radical transformation it undergoes in the invention of modern symbolic algebra. According to Klein's analysis, the symbolic concept of number, along with the new mode of concept formation that underlies it, sits at the very core of modern mathematics as a whole and thus also of the modern sciences built upon it. Moreover, because the mathematical science of nature essentially informs modernity as a whole, this new mode of symbolic thinking is foundational to all of modern life. Accordingly, Klein's effort to uncover the character of modern mathematics, in contrast to its ancient counterpart, is directed towards the urgent concern to understand modernity itself and thus also our contemporary lives.

In his writings on liberal education, Klein speaks as both a student and a teacher, a student of the Great Books who has himself taken up the strenuous yet joyful process of educating oneself, and a teacher—or better, guide—for souls who may not know they need to turn away from shadows and escape the shackles of unexamined opinions and unacknowledged commitments. Throughout these writings, he indicates the heights at which liberal education can and should be aimed by delineating various understandings of liberty or freedom; he propounds an ideal toward which educational institutions should strive, while also offering practical guidance for individuals pursuing a life of liberal learning; and he explores the question of the proper form and content of liberal education, making arguments that fly in the face of the conventional wisdom of his time and ours. Klein thus offers an approach to liberal education that can serve as a model for students working to educate themselves, teachers trying to lead others in that endeavor, and institutions aimed at fostering those activities.

Throughout his life's work Klein insisted on the essential importance of studying great books for the sake of wrestling with fundamental questions and ideas, an activity that has both a positive and a negative function. For one cannot access the wisdom of the texts, nor seriously pursue the questions and ideas one encounters in them, without first becoming aware of and confronting the impediments to this enterprise. Klein believed that this process of opening oneself to initially unknowable possibilities is the central work of liberal education and that this work is necessary for any human being who wishes to be free in thought, action, and self-understanding. To become liberally educated, Klein proposes, one must not only seek out answers to the questions one already has; one must seek to uncover the questions that lurk in one's own ignorance.

The interconnection between Klein's three primary areas of interest lies in the project of liberal learning by reading great books. Anyone engaged in liberal education today necessarily begins within the intellectual setting established by modernity, which according to Klein entails certain conceptual presuppositions that are thoroughly suffused within us while also remaining concealed from us, unless we engage in a conscious, sustained, and vigorous effort to make ourselves aware of them. Klein's investigation into the nature of modern mathematics and modern mathematical science has precisely this goal of revealing the hidden influence of the conceptual structure of modern science on our thinking and our lives. Similarly, Klein's work on ancient philosophy stems from an impulse to understand the character of our thinking today by contrasting it with more natural modes that were self-consciously rejected by the founders of modernity. For we understand ourselves better when we have discovered that there are alternatives to the modern ways of thinking that have been inculcated in us by our contemporary cave. Furthermore, studying the history of math and science alongside ancient philosophy allows one to recognize that modern science does not begin from a neutral and objective standpoint but is rather just one of the many attempts human beings have made to understand themselves and their world. The study of ancient thought and the history of math and science are thus complementary in that they shed light on each other and thereby afford us better access to the array of possibilities a liberally educated person must confront. In this way, then, Klein's several areas of interest ultimately converge in the effort to identify and wrestle with fundamental questions and perennial ideas of the utmost consequence to human life.

• • •

The authors of the essays in the present volume have all been animated by Klein's legacy in some substantial way, whether by knowing him personally, having been educated at the institution he shaped, or simply by finding his writings a rich stimulus for thought and exploration. While the majority of the essays are based primarily on the study of Klein's writings, they all share the aim of taking up some inquiry inspired by an encounter with his work, with the goal of deepening or expanding it, exploring its consequences, or traveling down avenues of investigation that

Klein himself pursued and in some cases even initiated. In this way the essays are intended as examples of the endeavor to further Klein's thinking, and they are offered in the hope that they might inspire others to take up this task or aid them in their own attempts to follow in Klein's footsteps. The goal of the present volume is thus to perpetuate Klein's legacy, exemplifying and promoting its development, for the sake of bolstering the very activities to which Klein himself was devoted.

TO TURN THE SOUL

Essays Inspired by Jacob Klein

Jacob Klein

European Scholar and American Teacher

EVA BRANN

The subtitle of my talk might be "Liberal Education: Program and/or Pedagogy?" The reason is that I think of Jacob Klein's life as being an embodiment of that slash in the formula *and/or* and therefore an occasion for asking what seems to me a question the answer to which determines the success, I mean the lively and secure survival, of liberal education.

There is the much more often debated converse to the question: "Is there a specific pedagogy for liberal education?" This is the question: "Is there a specific curriculum for liberal education that goes with the kind of teaching you might call *liberal*?" I won't dwell on the answer today, except insofar as it bears on particular aspects of teaching. I'll just say that I think the answer is that almost anything can be taught liberally—to a point. In particular, the shop crafts are germane enough to the liberal arts (which form one part of liberal education, as I'll spell out later) to serve as a suitable complementary curriculum. To prove it, there's that wonderful book by Matthew Crawford, who is both a student of philosophy and a motorcycle mechanic: it is called *Shop Class as Soulcraft* (and is the much worthier successor of that cult classic, *Zen and the Art of Motorcycle Maintenance*); it shows how fixing things forms souls, just as reading books does.

Let me give my answer to the topic question up front. I'm not a great believer in that mode of talking to my colleagues which attempts to make a whodunit of the telling so that they get to learn my resolution to the inquiry only when they're mostly long adrift in mind.

I am persuaded, even with a certain passion, that liberal education does have its most appropriate program, its preferable matter, and that this matter particularly calls for its own pedagogy. Concisely and thus a little too peremptorily put: You cannot achieve *liberal* education in the mode of a specialized teaching authority, a professor. That is by no means to say that professors who know their stuff inside-out can't sometimes teach liberally—but it will be, I think, in an alternative style for them: *Ex cathedra*, "from the podium," will have to become "in the trenches," on a chair around the table with the other human souls.

I was one of that diminutive number of refugees for whom that little devil Mephistopheles' shamelessly candid admission held: "I am a part of that power that ever seeks evil and ever accomplished good." (It comes from Goethe's *Faust* [I.1336–37], which no German-born person can live through a year without citing thrice.) The Nazi persecution brought me to America, where, with some practical know-how and some luck, anyone who knows how to be happy can be happy, and to St. John's College, where several of my older colleagues were refugees. I came very young and grew very old in Annapolis, so this band of my seniors, including Victor Zuckerkandl, a well-known Viennese musician, and Simon Kaplan, a Kant scholar, who came in middle age, are all gone. Jacob Klein, called Jasha by us all, including by some cheeky students (who are supposed to accord each other and their tutors, as I will do, the honorific "Mr., Mrs., Miss" and later "Ms.") was among them. As far as I could tell—and I observed avidly—they were well appreciated, even well loved by their American hosts who, in their gracious naiveté, admired them for their thorough learning and marveled at them for their pronounced personalities. But Jasha held a special place.

All the refugees that I've known or read of who were fully

adult when they emigrated led a cleft life—a European formation and an American re-formation. Mr. Klein grew up and studied in Slavic and central Europe and fled to the Anglophone West, from the Nazis politically, but psychologically also from an antically tyrannical father. This ogre, however, also came to the States and made Sonoma County, where he turned grapes into raisins, unsafe for habitation. Among the many stories about him that Jasha told me was that of his wedding gift to Jasha and Dodo. Dodo Tammann was the divorced wife of Edmund Husserl's son, and she became a powerful presence at St. John's. The wedding gift was a smallish bag of these raisins.

The years of Mr. Klein's life were split almost exactly between Europe and America: from his birth in 1899 to 1938, his arrival in America—thirty-nine years, and from 1938, his arrival in Annapolis, to 1978, his death while still teaching—forty years. (Winfree Smith, in *A Search For The Liberal College*, gives an indispensable account of Mr. Klein's early years at St. John's, ending with his deanship.)

To me there is, in my mythifying mood, something providential in this half-and-half life. For in Europe Mr. Klein was a private scholar without institutional bonds. He studied, conducted private seminars, and above all wrote his principal book, entitled in English *Greek Mathematical Thought and the Origin of Algebra*. It is a work of enormous scholarship, drawing from primary and secondary works in all the modern and classical languages—oddly not Hebrew; this visibly Jewish man governed by a Jewish fate didn't, as far as I could tell, have a Jewish bone in his body. Let me interject here my understanding of this apostasy. It was not the ordinary assimilation of convenience, still so hotly debated when I was young, but an allegiance that trumped everything, even his love for Russian novels, namely his deep affinity for the Greeks—not the aesthetic Greeks captured in the formula "Noble naiveté, quiet grandeur," which appeared in the first and greatest history of antique art, that of Johann Winckelmann and which dominated that famous German philhellenism. (I myself grew up under its aegis.) What drew Mr. Klein to the Greeks was—let me joyfully risk some political incorrectness—a very masculine view of that Greek grace as sober soundness, as, so to speak, the apotheosis of good sense, a virtue the Greeks call *sophrosyne*, which is translated literally as *soundmindedness*. It was a glory that I, who had spent my post-graduate years as a Greek archaeologist, had never suspected—that behind all those canonical great books, there might be a very specific intellectually handsome togetherness.

Since I've begun to understand something of the *Origin of Algebra*, I've thought that its doctrine was a, perhaps the, principal example of this sense of Greek soundness. The book, after all, traces out a loss, the loss of just this whole-heartedness. Not that Mr. Klein was a modernity-basher. Far from it—he had studied physics and found the revolution on which he was reporting and its modernity (plus, I should say, its extreme realization in post-modernity) irresistibly interesting, and so his account of our condition seemed to me far deeper and more persuasive than the socio-political explanations I was given as a history major in Brooklyn College. There was, furthermore, I learned in time, nothing Heideggerian in his approach to the mode of this loss, no call for the *Destruktion* (mitigatingly translated as "de-construction") for the sake of recovering a pre-traditional ontological origin. But, it seems to me, there might actually be large, sensibly practical consequences from a propagation of the thesis of the *Origin of Algebra*.

Obviously, I should now say as concisely as possible what this thesis, this teaching, seems to me to be. The very subtle, very reliable paragraph-by-paragraph exposition of the thesis in all its complexity is to be found in Burt Hopkin's *Origin of the Logic of Symbolic Mathematics*. I see it, more simply, in this way: The Greeks, meaning the relevant written texts we have (but I think the artifacts harmonize), had a direct, an immediate approach, to beings of thought, what might be called a first innocence, and if you like, even a naiveté, perhaps after all, even of a noble sort. Their direct intellectual sight accorded those beings a fullness, a meaning-fraught concreteness. Their way of regarding numbers is a prime example and probably the most illuminating case—negatively, because for mathematics the psychological element is much reduced so that the intellectual mode stands out, positively because the loss of this immediacy enabled the principal science at the foundation of our epoch, astronomical and terrestrial physics. Greek numbers, *arithmoi*, are collections of *things*, a counting-up of them, in German, *Anzahl*. These counted-up assemblage-numbers undergo, in a long-breathed conversion traced in the book, a reduction to mere symbols, completed by Vieta and Descartes. In the helpful medieval language, they are transformed from *first* to *second intentions*, meaning that a word that once reached for a thing now reaches for the thought-belabored abstraction of the thing. This second-intentionality dominates so much of modern discourse as to be practically a signature of modernity. My favorite example is this: Socrates follows a way, in Greek a *methodos*, "a way gone after" (a good example: *Republic* 596a). We tend to have not a "method" but a "methodology," not a jigged way, but the conception of the jigged way. We talk, very often, in concepts rather than objects. Mr. Klein, a most natural and, I might say, earthy person—and I might also say, like most flesh-and-blood people full of student-delighting singularities, that is, to put it plainly, kookiness—had a gut-aversion to this world of abstractions. He used to expend himself in trying to persuade students that Socrates' forms, the *eidê*, were not "abstractions," literally "drawn-off," life-deprived, thought-ghosts, but full of attractive being.

That brings me to the second half of Mr. Klein's life, the American part, spent almost entirely at St. John's College. He did, to be sure, write two more books in this epoch. The first was *A Commentary on Plato's "Meno."* The *Meno* is to St. John's College something like what the *Declaration of Independence* is to the *United States*, the condition of its possibility; it is our enabling work for freedom from academicism. The *Meno* shows under what conditions learning by inquiry, as distinct from knowledgeableness by study, is possible. Like the Algebra book (as it is, ridiculously, known on the campus of St. John's), the *Meno* book contains some unforgettable insights—unforgettable because as soon as you've read them you think you've always known them. This was the kind of mental plagiarism Mr. Klein chuckled over as a mark of his insights having been understood and adopted. My particular pick is his discovery that the capacity of "image-*recognition*" (*eikasia*: *not* "imagining" or "imagination") attached to the lowest section of the divided line presented in the *Republic* (509 ff.; the commentary on the *Meno* mines other dialogues for relevant illuminations) ranges through all the divisions to the highest, because imaging is the generating principle of the world that flourishes under the "Idea of the Good." Thus our lowest capacity is also our most encompassing. These assimilable insights are life-changing; I'll refrain from personal testimonials, but you can see that at the least the thought of an imagination-ontology will affect your way of reflecting.

The second, late book, *Plato's Trilogy*, on the *Theaetetus*, *Sophist*, and *Statesman*, I could never take to. It is written in a mode that seems to belong to old age: It paraphrases the text with the intention that the reader will extract a commentary from the emphases and deviations. David Lachterman's review of the book helped me to see its accomplishments, one of which is that it really functions as a sort of provocation to reflection on texts left intact by the interpreter. (I might say here that David was, to my knowledge, the most universally learned student who ever came out of St. John's; he carried on Mr. Klein's projects in his own competently ingenious way.)

Most of Mr. Klein's writing was for lectures directed to our students, and these, insofar as they were recoverable, were edited by Robert Williamson and Elliot Zuckerman and published by the college. They have that same quality that he saw in the Greek authors: simultaneously with having grasped it, it grasps you; it sits naturally in the intellect—mine, at least, and many of my colleagues'.

But these published works are not what dominated the second part of his life. In fact, he was almost comically inimical to publication. When I came in 1957 for my appointment interview, he placed me in a chair and, so to speak, danced around me, holding the two publications I had proudly sent with my application between thumb and index finger as if they were some loathsome matter and then tossed them back to me. (Publication wasn't and still isn't a criterion for appointment or tenure at St. John's.) Taking his aversion to publication seriously, I translated the algebra book in secret and confessed only late, because I had questions to ask. Then, however, with splendid inconsistency, he was eager for it to come out into the world, where it first languished, only to emerge slowly and steadily into some fame and influence, particularly, of course, under Burt Hopkins's energetic shepherding.

So now to the point. If the first half of his life, the European part, was under the aegis of learning and scholarly production, the second, American half was predominantly a teaching life, be it as a tutor (our replacement of the title "professor," though it's not used in address) or as dean of the college (1949–1958). As for the latter function, I remember vividly that when the end-of-class bell rang he would issue from his office to stand at the bottom of the stairs of our main building and scan the faces of descending students for signs of life. Once he caught me coming down, maneuvered me into his office, and chided me for having threatened with bodily harm a student who had not been able to inflect the Greek verb "to be."

Here is the serious aspect of Mr. Klein as a teacher in an institution whose faculty had bound itself to an all-required, coherent plan of liberal education, with the consequent abolition of electives for students and specialization for teachers and the replacement of the ways of learning and modes of teaching then, and even more now, current in universities and colleges—less in the latter, since some of these ways are functions of size and consequently of (fantasized) economies of scale.

In my young and ardent years as a tutor I saw in Mr. Klein the incarnation of a teacher in a program which was conceived by its founders, Stringfellow Barr and Scott Buchanan, as a contemporary re-animation of the traditional liberal education that was first set out in the seventh book of Plato's *Republic* and in the eighth book of Aristotle's *Politics* (where the word *liberal*, "belonging to the free" [*eleutheron*] is, as far as I know, first used to distinguish this upbringing from the vocational, utilitarian sort). For Rome, the guiding text was Quintilian's *Teaching Program for Oratory*, and in the Middle Ages Hugh of St. Victor's *Didascalicon* and John of Salisbury's *Metalogicon* (which is, however, concerned only with the verbal arts). These works, to be sure, often concentrate on the specific liberal *arts*, the *skills* of learning, rather than on liberal *education*, which relies on *texts* for reflection.

Indeed, when Mr. Klein arrived in late 1938, for the second year of the college's New Program, it was already fixed in its broad organization into tutorials for the exercise of the liberal arts and seminars for the discussion of great books. The liberal arts were exactly (1) the *trivium*, the three-way of words: grammar, logic, and rhetoric—their correctness, validity, and persuasiveness; and (2) the *quadrivium*, the four-way of things: arithmetic, geometry, astronomy, and music—their countability, extendedness, regular motions, and attendant harmonies. The program of tutorials stuck quite closely to this scheme—reducing it to language and mathematics classes with the modern addition of laboratory. Rumor has it that in the library of those early days physics books were catalogued under music, the study of bodies in ratio relations. Learnedness was required to find the finest working examples for exercises in these arts, taken from the most highly regarded works of language, mathematics, and science. The early faculty had put enticing tutorials together by the time Jasha arrived.

What he also found was a particularly felicitous modern fusion, instigated by Buchanan, of the so-called Great Books with the Liberal Arts, which had long been regarded as ancillary, particularly to the exegesis of Scripture. Canon-establishing lists of Great Books go back to antiquity and forward into our times, so our founders were well-supplied (see especially: Ernst Robert Curtius, *Europäische Literatur und Lateinisches Mittelalter*; Jonathan Rose, *The Intellectual Life of the British Working Classes*). As it seems to me, Mr. Klein's function with respect to the Program's teaching matter was largely to add an additional element of competence and, most importantly, to undergird the programmatic sequence with an intellectual history that put the dawn of modernity found in the mathematical writers of the late sixteenth and seventeenth century at the center of the drama of a break between antiquity and modernity. It was a break mirrored roughly in the discontinuity of our sophomore and junior years; its pathos is that of a great loss of human substance and a huge gain of human power.

Buchanan himself was what is called a charismatic figure, evidently (I didn't know him) full of pedagogically energizing outrageousness—very much the memorable master teacher dominating and drawing the college together—just what it needed in its uncertain, youngest years.

I must say here that the view I am about to offer of Mr. Klein as presenting a model, perhaps *the* model, of teaching best fitting a stable community of liberal learning is my own, perhaps to my colleagues more of a construction than it ought to be, but very plausible to me. It goes along with the conviction, to which I've confessed, that a liberal education that is mindful of its tradition and works pretty well day-to-day, with semi-frequent ascents into sheer glory, has its own proper teaching mode. I think that the delineation that follows fits not only a program of liberal education that has its own institution but also more partial, more tentative efforts. But I should report here that our founders emphatically asserted that the program they were instituting was *not* a curricular experiment. I think that attitude was crucial to our holding together over the years: We thought—how shall I put it?—that if this didn't work out, then there was something wrong with the *world*, not with the Program. And contrary to all pious preaching that urges us not to be too inward-turned but more accommodating to reality, that passionate sense of being, for all *our* flaws, on the right path turned out to be intensely practical. As I recall him, Mr. Klein had a sovereign sense of being in a place that had it right. I might add that I've visited a number of schools where they did things quite differently but had the same sense of "having got it right," and the consequent affect between us was immediate sympathy and potential friendship.

To begin with, then, he had the right *temperament*—a bit of a gourmand (he, who despised academic grading, would grade Dodo's uniformly delectable cuisine at every meal), a little indolent, pipe-puffing (a horrible weed called Balkan Sobranie), amusedly tolerant toward all signs of intellectual effort in the young and overtly repelled by adult intellectualism. In fact, he took delight, not always fairly distributed, in the eager naiveté and good-natured hijinks of the student generation of his first arrival; he had a special affection (which I've inherited) for the scamps. (Our students of the present day, I might say, are more experientially sophisticated and thus more psychologically fraught—but none the wiser for it.)

I say "the right temperament," but I mean *a* temperament; all teachers in the liberal mode need a bit of a personality, both to attract willing attention *and* to repel a too easy familiarity. Mr. Klein had a lot of the appurtenances of personality, for example, the ability to draw perfect circles on the board while facing the class by pivoting his arm behind his back—a source of delight to students studying Ptolemy. But these are gifts that you ape at your peril.

Then there were other traits that were not a gift of nature but the fruit of time. Older, more experienced teachers tend to carry their *authority* with less strain and more élan, to maintain their repose and to intervene with aplomb, even when a learning occasion goes embarrassingly wrong—well, mostly. These ways you acquire more by keeping at it than by having a hero.

Then there were the *bread-and-butter virtues* of any teacher in an institution, enforcing some discipline by mundane means—calling on the silent, administering quizzes, requiring and attending to projects to be handed in. This dutiful fulfillment of institutional requirements *ought* to be supervised by those in charge; in our case that is the dean. Mr. Klein learned meticulous dutifulness, as his wife told me, on the job; his pre-dean nature was to let such things—such mere necessities—go in favor of spontaneous life.

So far I've described a teacher at once too distinctively himself and too ordinarily dutiful to be a very imageable model. I'll now try to say how he came to be the paradigm of a teacher in a school devoted to liberal education.

Let me begin by forfending the imputation that he followed something called "the Socratic Method." Neither Mr. Klein nor we, the *epigonoi* as the Greek say, the successors, do any such thing. On the one hand, it's a contradiction in terms: Socrates had, as I've said, a way, a pursuit, but not a method in the Cartesian sense of a set of jigged procedures for following an inquiry. Mr. Klein used to say that each dialogue was its own world and that in each conversation Socrates goes about his search in a different way, taking into account the character of his conversational partners and of the object in question. So Socrates has his ways which are not a method, and in that respect he is the very incarnation of liberal teaching and our super-model. Yet, on the other hand, this Socrates of the Platonic dialogues is, after all, Plato's marionette, who does as he's told, which means he knows, or Plato knows for him, exactly where he's going. And that we never do know—and we manage to rejoice in that fact.

And here finally begins my positive delineation of a pedagogy specific to liberal education and to Jasha Klein's embodiment of it. It presupposes that liberal education, in its most specific sense, is realized in a curriculum of texts handed to us by the tradition, be they verbal, musical, visual. These works are primary in the order of making or finding and prime in the ranking of quality or worth. Confronted with such works a teacher does well to recede into *equality* with the students, to inquire *along* with them, and yet to be the safekeeper, the tutor of the enterprise. Mr. Klein was a master of the somewhat mysterious art of leading from behind—by solicitous listening, by intimating questions, even by expectant silence. He himself particularly admired a colleague, Richard Scofield, a gentleman of the old American type, for his elegant tacitness.

This *reticence* had its infuriating aspects: The more a young fellow-tutor wanted to be initiated into the deep lore we were sure he possessed, the less forthcoming he was—sometimes, I discovered, because he didn't actually know, but more often because he was terminally disciple-proof; he would tolerantly respond to the admiring affection of beguiled students but would not bind them to him by an inside teaching. It was part of that soundness of his, which did have a Socratic look about it. His most consequential discoveries fit, as I've said, into our own intellects as if there'd always been a place ready for them. Of course, in time the insufficiencies emerged, not such as to undo the insights, but such as to make them the center of a second sort of attention, critical attention.

Playfulness, another Socratic element, is of the essence in liberal learning—playfulness in making the most of the misfiring of the inquiring intellect, playful exploitation of felicitous coincidences and other fortuities, playful extraction of sense from nonsense, playful pinpointing of students' personal ways—the sort that feels to them not like offensive denigration but like gratifying spotlighting. Playfulness, after all, goes with laughter, and surprised laughter is the physical analogue to wonder, the beginning of philosophy. We young tutors, who had just emerged from post-graduate studies, learned something wonderful: Learning has a human face, and a teacher who can't laugh can't be serious.

Seriousness is naturally next. Seriousness is opposed in one respect to levity, for example a leaning some bright students evince toward easily distractible intellectual gadgeteering. In another respect, seriousness is opposed to earnestness, dead earnestness, such as rigidly relentless industriousness. Both evade entering into the "seriousness of the concept" (as Hegel terms it; "Preface" 4, *Phenomenology of Spirit*). "Seriousness" here means not belaboring a thought but letting it work on you, not willfully grasping for insights but letting them come, by giving them room or—as I like to put it—by futzing around. Time-taking patience and messing-about belong to liberal learning, because the works don't open up to strategic invasions.

Serious teachers who join their students in dithering purposefully and procrastinating concentratedly must also sometimes appear in a formidable aspect. Socrates, for example, appears thus formidable just once that I know of, though that leaves its daunting impression—when confronted with a young life going seriously wrong, here that of Callicles, he concludes with an impassioned speech in a tone devoid of any tint of parity or playfulness: He says that he will follow his own account for a life of virtue and bids Callicles and his crowd follow the same rationale of conduct. "For," he ends, "*yours is worth nothing*" (*Gorgias*, end). On rare occasions I've heard that tone from Mr. Klein, a tone utterly distinct from that of powerlessly querulous righteousness sometimes adopted by academics when great perturbations are caused by small differences. These were moments when the stakes were high—our students' souls or our school's survival, particularly its resolute non-careerism—for this is, as I've said, what the word "liberal" in "liberal education" originally betokens.

That brings me to the *protection of the exchanges* that are the life of learning from dangers both within and without the classroom. Of these there are many, of which I'll mention only one: the corruption of *conversation* into debate, into argument, and even into discussion, into all the modes of human communication in which the passion of competition outweighs the desire for illumination. Mr. Klein practiced a pedagogy that incited in students the desire to shine but damped their impulse to outshine each other. I think what made it work was his own sense that some of the greatness of the works we were grappling with magnified us, but also that in the face of this grandeur our gradations, natural or acquired, were minimized. But there was some kindly cunning in it as well: to pretend in the face of much contrary evidence that everyone was genuinely at work and really up to it and to keep pretending it until it—sometimes—came true.

Perhaps I'll mention one more vulnerability of any serious community of young learners: the excitation of friendships formed in the face of deep questions and difficult texts displaces proper preparation and solid learning. For young teachers that somewhat vacuous intensity wears out with time, but some of our students do graduate having had more experience of the love of learning than of learning. Characters like that hung around Socrates, and, as I recall, Mr. Klein didn't know what to do about them either. However, to my mind there are worse ways to waste one's time.

I have not at all exhausted the pedagogical lessons that many of my colleagues and I myself learned from Jacob Klein. Since I can't recall his ever mentioning to me a living model for himself, this conclusion may be justified: What shaped the soundly ingenious scholar of intellectual history that he was in the first half of his life into the devoted teacher's teacher of liberal learning that he became in the second half was a tiny college, St. John's, with an unadulterated program of liberal education, seated in the continent-wide American republic, with a continuous tradition of enabling liberty. This half-European was as American as they come.

I'll finish with a little anecdote to show *how* Jasha was my teacher and my model. When, after his death, Dodo was disposing of his library, she told me to take whatever I wanted. I was simply paralyzed by the prospect of suddenly owning a lot of irreplaceable books. So I went minimal. I chose only his Greek Plato in the Teubner and Oxford editions, multiple volumes, falling apart with use and heavily underlined as well as annotated in his tiny, legible script. Then, nearly two-score years ago, I bound all the volumes up in a broad golden ribbon and never looked inside them again until I was writing this talk. He would have chuckled.

Bibliography

Crawford, Matthew B. *Shop Class as Soulcraft: An Inquiry into the Value of Work*. New York: Penguin Books, 2010.

Curtius, Ernst Robert. *Europäische Literatur und Lateinisches Mittlalter.* Bern: A. Francke, 1948. Translated by Willard R. Trask as *European Literature and the Latin Middle Ages* (Princeton, NJ: Princeton University Press, 1953).

Hopkins, Burt C. *The Origin of the Logic of Symbolic Mathematics: Edmund Husserl and Jacob Klein*. Bloomington and Indianapolis: Indiana University Press, 2011.

Klein, Jacob. *A Commentary on Plato's "Meno."* Chapel Hill, NC: The University of North Carolina Press, 1965.

——. *Greek Mathematical Thought and the Origin of Algebra*. Translated by Eva Brann. Cambridge, MA: MIT Press, 1968. Reprint, New York: Dover Publications, 1992. Original publication: "Die Griechische Logistik und die Entstehung der Algebra," *Quellen und Studien zur Geschichte der Mathematik, Astronomie, und Physik*, Abteilung B: *Studien*, vol. 3, no. 1 (Berlin, 1934), 18–105 (Part I) and ibid., no. 2 (1936), 122–235 (Part II).

——. *Lectures and Essays*. Edited by Robert B. Williamson and Elliott Zuckerman. Annapolis: St. John's College Press, 1985.

——. *Plato's Trilogy:* Theaetetus, *the* Sophist, *and the* Statesman. Chicago and London: The University of Chicago Press, 1977.

Lachterman, David. Review of *Plato's Trilogy:* Theaetetus, *the* Sophist, *and the* Statesman, by Jacob Klein. *Nous* 13 (1979): 106–12.

Pirsig, Robert M. *Zen and the Art of Motorcycle Maintenance: An Inquiry into Values.* New York: HarperCollins, 1974.

Rose, Jonathan. *The Intellectual Life of the British Working Classes.* 2nd ed. New Haven, CT: Yale University Press, 2010.

Smith, J. Winfree. *A Search for the Liberal College: The Beginning of the St. John's Program.* Annapolis, MD: St. John's College Press, 1983.

Winckelmann, Johann Joachim. *History of the Art of Antiquity.* Translated by Harry Francis Mallgrave. Los Angeles: Getty Research Institute, 2006.

Jacob Klein's Two Prescient Discoveries

EVA BRANN

Jacob Klein was in the last year of his nine-year tenure as dean of St. John's College in 1957 when I came as a young tutor. He died in 1978, still teaching. In those twenty-one years that I knew him he was above all a teacher, mine and everybody's. His spirit informed the college. As dean, he had governed as a fierce defender of his conception of this remarkable community of learning. This passion had generous parameters, from smiling leniency toward spirited high jinks to meticulous enforcement of rules expressive of intellectual virtue. As a tutor he shaped the place by lectures that the whole college attended and discussed, by his classroom teaching that elicited from students more than they thought was in them, but above all through his conversation that was direct and playful, serious and teasing, earthily Russian and cunningly cosmopolitan. We all thought that he had secret wisdom which he was chary of dispensing out of pedagogical benevolence, but then again he would tell us things in a plain and simple way that went home as if they'd always been ours. I, at least, always had the sense of hearing wonderful novelties that I'd known all along. He had an aversion to discipleship and a predilection for wicked American kids. He was, on occasion, rousingly infuriating—when one made the attempt to extract definitive doctrines. His reluctance to pontificate was in part indolence ("Jasha the Pasha"), an indolence dignified by his aversion to philosophy carried on as an organized business, and in part pedagogical intention, a conviction that to retail one's thought-products to students was to prevent inquiry. This pre-judgment against authoritative profession is, to my mind, his most persuasive and felicitous legacy to the college and the reason we still call ourselves tutors, guardians of learning, rather than professors, professionals of knowledge.

Nonetheless, there were doctrines and they were published. He had set himself against academic publication, so much so that I had to translate Jasha's great book of his youth on the origin of algebra in secret, though, to be sure, confronted with a *fait accompli* he capitulated quite eagerly. This book is now the subject of Burt Hopkins's acute and careful analysis, *The Origin of the Logic of Symbolic Mathematics: Edmund Husserl and Jacob Klein.*

What I would like to do today is to present two of his chief discoveries from a perspective of peculiar fascination to me: the, to me enchanting, contemporaneous significance, the astounding prescience, and hence longevity, of his insights. I might say that I grew up intellectually within a perspective enforced by our program of studies and reinforced by Jasha's views—forgive the informality; it was universal in his circle—and having its roots in certain continental philosophers, of whom Husserl was the most honorable. It was the guiding notion that modernity is best—if not solely—apprehended as being a ruptured continuum with Greek antiquity, a continuum insofar as the terms persist, ruptured insofar as they take on new meanings and missions. That perspective makes those who view the world from it avid participants in the present—critically *and* appreciatively avid. I will say right away and up front to what issues that I identify to myself as central to our present-day lives Jasha's insights speak: first, to the ever larger share that image-viewing and virtual experiences have in our life; here the question is what degree of "reality" is ascribable to images, and what does life among these semi-beings do to us. Do we lose substance as they lose status? Do originals retain their primary or even a residual function in a virtual world? And second, to the burgeoning of a brain science that tends to ascribe to human nature an ultimately physical being; here the question is approachable in terms of "emergence": Granted that brain and mind are intimately linked, what is the manner in which the latter emerges from, or projects to, the former? How might an entity *emerge*, be it from above or below, that is radically different from its constituents? It seems to me that these are the questions of consciousness—what *awareness* is—and self-consciousness—who we *are*—that should most concern us, because they dominate the public world quite unreflectively. Non-currently stated: Do we have souls?

The two insights are both interpretations of Platonic writings and are set out in *A Commentary on Plato's "Meno"* of 1965 and *Greek Mathematical Thought and the Origin of Algebra* of 1934 respectively. The latter is a very learned book written by a private European scholar for academic readers; the former is a very accessible work written by an American teacher for lovers of Socrates. Of both these notions Burt Hopkins has produced detailed analyses, which have added a new edge to doctrines I've lived with familiarly for half a century. I will, however, feel free here to supplement, embroider, and question Jacob Klein's interpretation of Plato and Burt Hopkins's reading of Klein as I go. I'll do it implicitly, so don't trust this account for faithfulness to the letter, though I hope you may trust it for closeness in spirit. You'll see, I think, what I mean when I speak of Klein's immediacy and naturalness of interpretation: His readings sit well.

The first insight, then, takes off from an understanding of the lowest segment of the so-called Divided Line in Plato's *Republic*, that mathematical image (picture it as vertical) of the ascent to Being and the associated learning. In this lowest segment are located the deficient beings called reflections, shadows, and images, and a type of apprehension associated with them called *eikasia* in Greek and usually rendered ineptly as "conjecture."

Klein's interpretation will start with a new translation of this noun: "image-recognition." The nature of these lowest beings—they are revealed as basic rather than base—is set out in Plato's *Sophist*, so between them, the *Republic* and the *Sophist*, they found the Platonic world.

The second discovery involves a great complex of notions from which I'll extract one main element: the analysis of what it means to be a number and what makes possible this kind of being, and, it turns out, all Being. And again, the great text is the *Sophist*, together with the *Republic*, supplemented by Aristotle's critical account of Plato's doctrine. To anticipate the perplexity that, in fact, *is* also the doctrine: Take any number, say, two. It is constituted of two units; each is one, but both together are two. How can it be that two emerge from elements that are each precisely not two? I might say here that Socrates thinks, and I know from experience with students, that to find this perplexity gripping marks one possible beginning of philosophical engagement.

So now, after these broad previews, to some nitty-gritty. Socrates begins by dividing the whole line mentioned above in some arbitrary ratio and then the two subsections in that same ratio. So if the whole line is, say, 16 units, let the ratio be triple; then one segment is 12, the other 4. Then subdivide the 12-unit segment similarly into 9 and 3 units, and the 4-unit segment into 3 and 1. You now have four segments, two by two in the same ratio with each other and with the first division of the whole: 12:4::9:3::3:1. Whether you want to make the top or the bottom segment the longest depends on whether you assign more length to the greater fullness of Being or the larger profusion of items. It can also be shown that in all divisions of this sort, called "extreme-and-mean" ratio, the middle segments will be equal; Socrates will make the iconic most of this mathematical fact.

So the subsections make a four-term proportion called an *analogia* in Greek—a:b::b:c (9:3::3:1), and they mirror, as I said, the division of the whole line. You can read the line up or down: *Down* is the cascade of Being which loses plenitude as it falls from true originals to mere images. *Up* is the ascent of learning, ending in the direct intellectual view of the prime originals, the *eidê*, the "invisible looks" or "aspects" in Klein's language, usually called the "forms." Beyond all Being there is the notorious Good, the unifying power above all the graduated beings, the principle of wholeness, which I'll leave out for a moment. At the bottom is that aforementioned "image-recognition." Now just as each of the object-realms assigned to the upper sections is causally responsible for the ones below, so, inversely, in learning each stage, each capacity, is needed for the learner to rise. None are left behind; all remain necessary. And so the bottom, the first capacity, is also the most pervasive. Children recognize images early on. Look at a picture book with a two-year-old: "Kitty," he'll say, pointing. "Careful, it'll scratch." "No, it won't," he'll say, looking at you as if you were really naïve. That's image-recognition, the human capability for recognizing the likeness of a deficient order: a cat incapable of scratching.

This capability is as fundamental for Socrates as it is low on the scale of cognitive modes, because imaging is the most readily imaginable, the least technically ticklish way of representing the activity by which the realm of intelligible Being produces and rules the world of sensory appearances: Each decline in the degrees of being is that of original to image, each rise in the stages of learning is that of recognizing that something lower images something higher. Image-recognition must be pervasive.

Just to complete the sketch of the Divided Line, here are the stages of knowledge and their objects in brief: Above images, there are the apparently solid objects of the sensory world, objects of nature and artifice. The acquaintance with these is called "trust," *pistis*. It is the implicit, unreflective belief we have in the dependable support of the ground we tread on and the chair we sit in—the faith that our world is not "the baseless fabric of [a] vision" that melts into thin air under our weight.

This whole complex of dimensionally defective images and taken-on-faith solidity of our phenomenal world is itself an image of the upper two parts of the line. The third part, equal in length to the second from the bottom, contains all the rational objects that look on the way up like abstractions from the sensory world—mathematical models and logical patterns. To these we apply our understanding, a capacity called in Greek "thinking-through," *dianoia*. They are then, reversely, revealed as the types of originals of the sensory world that impart to it such shapeliness and intelligibility as it has. Thus they make natural science possible; they are the rational *counterparts* of the sensory world. Finally, there is the realm of direct knowledge. As happens so often in the dialogues, these upper reaches are named as inverses of the lower ones: "invisible looks" (since *eidos* is from the *vid*-verb, the verb for seeing); they are reached by a capacity for direct insight (which Aristotle will in fact analogize to sensing)—*noesis*. Above and beyond is the very Idea itself, the idea of all ideas, the Good, which produces, nourishes, and unifies all beings, makes communities possible, and grounds all human learning.

Implicit in this ladder of Being is the answer to the question that must matter much to us: What *is* an image, such that we can know it *as* an image? The answer is given in the dialogue on the Sophist, who is in his general person an image incarnate, the mere image of a truly truth-seeking human being. Socrates initially poses the question concerning the Sophist, but he sits silently by as a Stranger from Italian Elea, a follower of Parmenides, finds a solution. I'll venture a guess why he falls silent. In the *Sophist* appears a serious ontological teaching, and ontological *doctrine* is not Socrates' way: He is the man of the tentative try, of *hypotheses*. I'll even venture a—perhaps perverse—appreciation of this mode: His stubborn hypotheticalness, his unwillingness to assert doctrinal knowledge, is the complement of his unshakable faith in a search for firm truth, carried on in full awareness of human finitude.

What then is the Parmenidean solution? I call it Parmenidean, although the Stranger, the intellectual child of Parmenides, calls himself a patricide, since he is about to *deny* a crucial Parmenidean teaching: that Nonbeing is not, is neither sayable nor thinkable. He is a true Eleatic, for he will implicitly *affirm* a yet deeper teaching of his philosophical father: that what counts is being thinkable and sayable. The Eleatic Stranger will show how Nonbeing *can* be thinkable and how speech is in fact impossible without it—as was indeed implicitly affirmed in Parmenides' very denial.

Nonbeing becomes thinkable as *Otherness.* To say that something *is not* is usually to say that it is not this but that, that it is other than something perspectivally prior. (I say "usually," because there "is" also something called "utter non-being," which is indeed, though vocally utterable, insuperably unthinkable.) Relational, comparative Nonbeing, however, is one of the great ruling principles of ontology. It is totally pervasive, since whatever is *a* being is other than other beings. It is the source of diversity in the world and of negation in speech. Has the Stranger really done his philosophical progenitor in? No, as I intimated, he has actually saved him from himself, for he has shown that Nonbeing *is*; it is Being in another mode. Being is still all there is. There is no patricide. Moreover, this Other, a piece of apparently high and dry ontology, turns out to give life to the realm of ideas and to the world of human beings—to inform the one with a diversity of beings and to articulate the other with the oppositions of speech.

Why was this modification necessary in the search for the Sophist? Because a Sophist is indeed a faker, himself a human image of a truth-seeker and a producer of mere images of what is genuine. Otherness, the great genus of "The Other," is the condition of possibility for images, since it has, to be more precise, three tremendous powers: First, it makes possible that some thing *not be what it is.* And that is just what characterizes an image: "It's a kitty," the child says, pointing—but not really; it doesn't scratch. Or people bring out photographs to be in some way in the presence of an absent one, but it's not real enough to assuage longing.

So an image is understood first, and most ontologically speaking, as *not being* what it is, but second as *being less* than an original it represents, for it represents that original in a deficient likeness. (Here arises a huge problem for the fine arts, where an image is often more esteemed than its sitter.) Here is where the second capacity of the Other shows up: There is a defective, a derivative Otherness. And third, it makes that negative knowledge and denying speech possible; we can think and say: The image is—in some specifiable way—like its original, but likeness is *not* identity. The sentence "An image is *not* the original" displays Otherness as negation, articulated as Nonbeing. The ability to utter—and mean—it is specifically human; its loss would be, I think, a serious declension of our humanity. Therefore this complex of considerations, illuminated by Klein in *A Commentary on Plato's "Meno,"* seems to me crucial to coping with our image-flooded world in full awareness.

More particularly: The shaping of our American lives, which is more and more a matter of declining options and refusing temptations, is much in need of suggestive approaches for such coping. What are the truths and falsehoods of images in general? What consequently are the effects of discretionary image-viewing on our consciousness? Do all images in fact have originals, or is it images "all the way down"? And if there are always originals, how can we find our way back to them? What is real within our world, what is genuine beyond it? I'll assert simply that without occasional reflection on such an eminently current issue, our image-immersed lives tend toward going by, in Socrates' words, unlived: "The unexamined life is not to be lived (*abiotos*)," he says in the *Apology* (38a), and that life is, in effect, *unlived.*

I'll go on to a preliminary presentation—call it "tentative" (*peirastikos*; see Diogenes Laertius, *Lives of Eminent Philosophers,*

III.49)—of Klein's second interpretative discovery, a much more technical, but equally future-fraught, construal. (For a fuller treatment see the essay "Form Numbers (*Arithmoi Eidetikoi*)" herein.)

A preoccupation of Socrates—it might be puzzling to readers who haven't yet seen the implications—is often expressed by him in this way: "Each is one, but both are two." To be seized by this odd condition is, as I said, a beginning of philosophizing. The oddity comes out most starkly when we think of counting-numbers, the natural cardinal numbers. Take the first number, two. (For the ancients, one is not a number; it is the constituent unit of which a number is made.) Each of its units is one and nothing more. Yet this unit and another together make up the number two: Neither is what both together are. This ought to be strange to us, because we are used to the elements of natural collection having each the quality that is attributed to them all together: The doggy species subsumes dogs. Whether we think of dogginess either as an abstracted generalization or a quality-bestowing form, each member has the characteristic that names the kind. Clearly, numbers are assemblages that work differently from other classes. Numbers have a unique characteristic, their so-called "arithmological" structure. The recognition of the significance of this situation for Socrates and its bearing on the "greatest genera," the highest forms, particularly on Being, is Klein's achievement.

Let me begin by briefly previewing the kinds of numbers Klein takes into account. He observes—a previously ignored fact—that the first meaning of the Greek word that we translate as number, *arithmos*, is that of a counted assemblage of *concrete things*. Any counted collection—a flock of sheep, a string of horses, a herd of cattle—not *has* but *is* an *arithmos*. If we think as Greeks (as we may, with a little effort), we count ordinally, because we must keep items in order: first, second, third (and then go on cardinally, four, five, six, for verbal convenience). But when we have counted everything we are focused on, we allow it to become a heap-number—a distinct, discriminated group. It is a counted collection that has lost its memory. An *arithmos* is thus a sensory number. It is, for example, a sheep-number, and its units are sheep-monads. To me it seems undecidable whether such a concrete number should be thought of as having an arithmological structure, since in it the sheep are *both* sheepish *and* mere units; as a flock we distinguish them qualitatively, as units we count them quantitatively.

Next come the mathematical numbers made up of pure monads, units that have no quality besides being unities. A mathematical number is defined by Euclid thus: "An *arithmos* is a multitude composed of monads" (*Elements* VII, def. 2), where a monad is a *pure* unit. This type of number has an arithmological structure with a vengeance, and you can see why: A pure unit has *no* characteristics besides unitariness. It's neither apples nor oranges, which is precisely why you can count fruit or anything at all with it. Being thus devoid of qualities, it has mere collectability, but it has no other contribution to make to the assemblage. *Being* two is not in the nature of a monad as a monad, though *adding up* to two is. "Two" appears to emerge from these associable units. If you think this is unintelligible, so does Socrates. It will get worse.

(The difficulty is implicitly acknowledged in one modern definition of number. It begins with *arithmos*-like concrete assemblages. If their elements, when treated as mere units, can be put into one-to-one correspondence, the collections are said to be equivalent. The collection or set of all equivalent sets *is their number.* This definition evades the questions: "*What* number is it?" and "Does the set of sets, the set-number, *arise from the units* assembled of the concrete collection or does this number *bestow on them* their numerosity?" Therein lies an implicit recognition of Socrates' problem.)

It gets worse, for now a third type of number appears. Klein knows of it from Aristotle's critical report in the *Metaphysics* (13.6–9). He tells of "form numbers," *arithmoi eidetikoi.* The highest genera in the Platonic structure of forms are organized in such numberlike assemblages. These are, unlike the indefinitely many mathematical numbers, limited in multitude. (There may have been ten, the so-called root-numbers of the Pythagoreans.) Now the super-genera in the *Sophist* are Same and Other; the highest genus after these is Being consisting of the great forms of Motion (*kinesis*) and Standstill (*stasis*)—this last is often translated as "Rest," but that inaccurately implies that the form is a cessation from, or deprivation of, motion, though the two sub-genera are coequal, positive. Notice, incidentally, that the three kinds of numbers run in tandem with the three rising upper segments of the Divided Line: concrete numbers with the sensory world, pure units with the mathematical domain, form numbers with the eidetic realm.

Each of these forms acts like a monad in an arithmetical collection. However—and this is Aristotle's most pertinent criticism—these high forms are not neutral units. They are each very much what they are in themselves, indefeasibly self-same and other than all others. They are, as he says: *asymbletoi*, "incomparable," literally "not throwable together" (*Metaphysics* 13.7). Thus, unlike pure, neutral mathematical numbers, they cannot be reckoned with *across* their own genus, and so, *a fortiori*, it would be seen that their association *within* their genus is unintelligible. For how can Motion and Standstill be together as the genus Being if they have nothing in common and so cannot be rationally added up?

Klein claims that Aristotle's cavil is in fact Plato's point: The forms are associated in what is the very paradigm of an arithmological structure or, at least, its most radical case—what each is *not*, that they are *together*. Moreover, it is because *they* have a number structure in which unique *eidê* associate in a finite number of finite assemblages that the mathematical numbers are organized into kinds such as odd and even and that innumerable sensory items can collect into concrete countable heaps, be they natural or artificial. Furthermore it is in imitation of these eidetic numbers that we have the indefinitely many mathematical numbers, each uniting as many pure units as you please—though we are left to work out the manner of this descent. For my part, I cannot claim to have done it, though I have tried.

I have mentioned before what is certainly the foremost stumbling block even for well-disposed people in the way of accepting the forms as causes of worldly being and becoming. The perplexity is usually put as the "participation problem": How do appearances "participate" in the forms? These are infelicitous terms, because they imply the least satisfactory answer—that dogs somehow take a part in, or appropriate a part of, the form, a non-solution scotched in Socrates' very early attempt, in the dialogue *Parmenides*, at articulating his great discovery of the forms. To the intellect imaging is at least less awkward logically and more facile representationally than is partaking.

But let me stick here with the familiar term so as to follow Klein in pointing out that the participation problem has two levels: On the lower level, the question is *how the phenomenal world participates in the forms.* On the higher level it is *how the forms associate with or participate in each other.* For unless they do form major assemblages—unless the *genera*, with their constituent elements, the *eidê*, have an organized structure—the sensory world, even granted that it does somehow receive its being from these, can itself have no learnable organization. Crudely put: We can classify the world's beings, natural and artificial, in terms of hierarchies of kinds, such as the genera, subgenera, species, subspecies of biology, only because their causative principles have a prior, paradigmatic structure of associations and subordinations. Only on this hypothesis can sensory heaps be distinguished and counted.

The eidetic numbers are thus intended to be a Platonic solution to the upper-level participation problem. It is, so to speak, a highly formal solution. For while the *type* of association is named—the *arithmoi eidetikoi* with their arithmological structure—the *cause* of any particular association is not given. There is no substantive answer to the question: Just what in a form makes it associate numerologically with a specific order? There *should* be no such answer, because the eidetic monads are, after all, incomposable: Motion and Standstill have in themselves nothing in common; moreover, there is no binding proof that *they* are the sole constituents of Being. And yet, there *must* be an answer, since they are *in fact* composed. One way it fails is that when we count off, in order to reach, say, the number two—"one," "one," "two"—we utter three items. But there are not three but only two items. For two, be it mathematical or eidetic, is not over and beyond the two units; it is just those two together. How two items can become one our reason cannot quite articulate, nor can it say what makes either an eidetic monad (which is a qualitative plenum) or the mathematical unit (which is a qualitative void) associate with others in "families" (that thought-provoking classificatory term from biology) or in "numbers" (those colorless collections that yet have highly specific characteristics).

Here is Klein's novel construal of this very eidetic number Two. Being is named in the *Sophist* as a great eidetic genus. There it is, as I said, composed of Standstill and Motion. Again, neither of these can have any part in the other; Stillness itself is not thinkable as involved in Motion itself or the reverse. Yet there is no thing in the world that is not both together. Our world is one of dynamic stability or stable dynamism, in place and in time. As a duo, these two that are responsible for this cosmic condition are in the realm of forms called *Being*. Being is not a third beside or above Motion or Standstill but just the togetherness of these subgenera. Being *is* only as both of these together, and either can *be* only as part of a pair. As an unpaired monad, neither *is*; both *are* as a couple: Being is *the* eidetic Two. And once more, it is this arithmological structure that descends to and makes possible, is mirrored in, the mathematical number structure of any mathematical two—on the one hand. On the other hand, it makes the phenomenal world as I have just described it: at once stable and moving, variable and organizable. On the way up it might look as if the eidetic numbers are an erroneous levering up of a mathematical notion; on the way down they appear as the not-quite-humanly-comprehensible-but-still-necessary hypothesis for an articulable world, a classifiable *and* countable world. And again, seen from above, Being must—somehow—*bring about* its own division into two, but seen from below, Being *emerges* from its constituents. As in the modern definition of number in terms of equivalent sets it was left unarticulated whether the number set is the ground or consequence of the equivalent sets, so in Klein's exposition of the first eidetic number Two, it is left unsaid whether the genus determines its eidetic monads or the reverse—or neither. It is left, as textbooks say, as an exercise for the reader—a hard one.

I might, before I end, even venture a still formal but somewhat more specific answer to the associability question. In the upper ontological reaches, at least, what might be called extreme Otherness, meaning *at once* contrary (that is, qualitative) and contradictory (that is, logical) opposition, *seems* to be the discernible principle grounding togetherness: Motion and Standstill are as opposite as can be both in their own features and their mutual negation, and *for that reason* they are yoked in Being; so are Same and Other. I will not pretend to have worked through the hierarchy of these five greatest genera. Nonetheless I have a suspicion that Same and Other, the most comprehensive genera, are not only intimately related to each other as mutually defining, but may ultimately have to be apprehended together as prior to and thus *beyond Being*, as a first self-alienation of the One, the very principle of comprehension as well as the arithmological version of the Good. As such, they might even be termed the *negative* Two, but that's too far out. In any case, these Plotinian evolutions are beyond my brief for today—I refer to Plotinus at all only because his One is in fact articulable only negatively and is self-diremptive. (See Addendum 2 in "Form Numbers.")

Now the strange structure of number, in which indiscernibly different yet non-identical elements like pure monads, mere units, can be together what they are not individually, is only a case, though the most stripped-down, clarified case, of what is nowadays called "emergence." Recall that *emergence* is the eventuation of a novel whole from elements that seem to have nothing in common with it. Examples range from trivial through merely interesting to life-changing. Socrates himself points out that the letters sigma and omega are individually different from the initial syllable of his own name, "So," and that this is one new sound composed of two elements unlike it (*Theaetetus* 203c). Two molecules of hydrogen and one of oxygen combine to form water, whose liquidity emerges as an unforeseeable quality. Individuals form communities that evince a might beyond the additive powers of their citizens and whose aspirations may differ from those of its people. The emergent entity is other than, rather than additional to, novel to, rather than inferable from, its elements. In the reverse case, sometimes called *projection*, the elements falling out from a totality are qualitatively quite different from it. This case might be called inverse emergence; an example might be the relation of Platonic forms to their participant particulars.

The most significant problem of emergence is also the most contemporary one. Since it seems indisputable that specific brain lesions lead to specific psychic disabilities, it is claimed by scientists who don't want simply to identify mind with brain that the soul is brain-emergent. Does that make it a mere epiphenomenon? A miracle? "Emergence" names the event as a bottom-up process. But could it be a top-down happening, the above-named inverse emergence? Could the soul shape, or participate in shaping, its physical substructure? Since the soul is understood to have the unity of non-spatial being, while the brain is an extended thing, these are questions recognizable as belonging to the old perplexity the "One-and-Many": One *over*, or *in*, or *out of*, Many? They are questions not asked much nowadays among those dealing with our cognitive nature.

I want to make a claim that should appeal to sympathizers with Jacob Klein's inquiries. When deep human matters are at issue, it helps a lot to have delved into some ontology; the inquiry into Being may not affect our lives materially, yet it illuminates them more directly than does research providing factual information or theory producing instrumental constructs. This is the hypothesis under which Jacob Klein's opening up of two Platonic preoccupations, images and numbers, is of current consequence. Herein lies the prescience, the foresightedness of his Platonic discoveries.

Addendum

I have omitted here, as too complex for brief exposition, a third, more directly global interpretation of the modern condition, which is central to *Greek Mathematical Thought and the Origin of Algebra*. It is an understanding of the basic rupture between antiquity and modernity, of *the* great revolution of the West, as brought about by, or at least paradigmatically displayed in, the introduction of algebra. Algebra works with quantities abstracted from concrete collections (such as were betokened by the Greek *arithmoi*), with "general," essentially symbolical "numbers," such as the variables x, y, z, or the constants a, b, c. These letters are symbols of a peculiar sort: They *represent* neither a concrete thing nor a determinate concept, but rather *present* themselves as the object of a calculation—a mere object, an indeterminate entity. Klein saw algebraic problem-solving procedures, so effective precisely because so contentlessly formal, as emblematic of a modern rage for that second-order, deliberately denatured thinking that dominates as much of our life as is method-ridden. The human consequences of this symbolic conceptuality are great.

Form Numbers (*Arithmoi Eidetikoi*)

EVA BRANN

My attempt here will be to make clear to myself and to possible readers what is meant by a term, bestowed by Aristotle on a Socratic/Platonic notion (*Metaphysics* 13.9.1086a5; 14.2.1088b34), namely, *arithmoi eidetikoi*: "form or formal or kind numbers," "ideal numbers," "idea assemblages," "idea communities," and the mixed version—"eidetic numbers." This attempt will take the form of an explication of a chapter in Jacob Klein's *Greek Mathematical Thought and the Origin of Algebra*, two of whose high points are his understanding of these numbers and his reconstitution of the first of them. I shall also try to fit the eidetic numbers into a schema of Socratic/Platonic ontology (theory of Being), to look for a second and third eidetic number, and, finally, to show that this apparently arcane notion has a broad and immediate application to our American life.

Thus the following headings arise:

I. Interest in eidetic numbers
II. Sources contributing to the study of eidetic numbers
III. Preconditions for counting
IV. Klein's discoveries: understanding eidetic numbers and finding the first eidetic number—Two (Being)
V. Profit from a problem-ridden study
VI. Problems with the eidetic Two

Addendum I.	An attempt to clue out a second and third eidetic number
Addendum II.	An attempt, in the manner of Plotinus, to present the place and principles of the form numbers in a system by extending the "Divided Line" of the *Republic*
Addendum III.	Application to Emergence and Community, bearing of Klein's discoveries on contemporary issues with large human implications

I. Interest in Eidetic Numbers

It might arise from a narrow but crucial unsolved problem in the Platonic Dialogues: How are the "forms" or "aspects," the *eidê* or *ideai* (plurals of *eidos* and *idea*), related to each other? How are their communities achieved, and how is subordination structured? The *arithmoi eidetikoi* are an intended resolution: forms belonging together have the character of *arithmoi*, numbers in the ancient sense, and as a structure of such arithmetic assemblages they form a hierarchy, a graded sequence of priority.

There is also a much wider interest. These numbers bear on the millennial question of *emergence*, to my mind the most engrossing mystery, from its largest down to its smallest instance: How do forty or so thousand Athenian citizens emerge into one city, or three hundred plus million Americans into one republic? How do the letters *sigma* and *omega* form the first syllable, pronounced "so," of Socrates' name? How do two atoms of hydrogen and one of oxygen make up a molecule which in a plurality becomes wet water? And above all, most currently, how, from the electric activity of a human brain, does thoughtful awareness emerge?

II. Sources Contributing to the Study of Eidetic Numbers

1. Plato, *Greater Hippias* primarily, and many passages in other dialogues, especially the *Sophist*
2. Jacob Klein, "The arithmos eidetikos," Part I, chapter 7, section C in *Greek Mathematical Thought and the Origin of Algebra*
3. Burt Hopkins, "Klein's Reactivation of Plato's Theory of *Arithmoi Eidetikoi*," chapter 19 in *The Origin of the Logic of Symbolic Mathematics*
4. Aristotle, *Metaphysics* 1.9; 12.10; 13.1, 6–9, and 14.2

1. The *Greater Hippias* is, to my mind, probably a genuine Platonic dialogue, since it is very clever. The sophist Hippias from Arcadian Elis is even more stupid than conceited, to our advantage. For his stupidity makes Socrates dwell at greater length on a this-worldly observation that underlies the trans-worldly eidetic numbers (300a ff.). In brief: The dialogue's question is "What is beauty?" Hippias clings to this thought: What several are together, that each must be separately. If persons are beautiful as a group than each is beautiful by himself *and the converse* (301a). Socrates, however, gives a counter-example: Hippias and he himself are each *one*, but together *two*, each odd but together even. Hippias is clueless about the significance of this situation—that the collectivity of numbers is radically different from that of sensory things: Each member of the golden kind (*eidos*) is itself golden; each member of a number kind, that is, an *arithmos*, is a one, a unit, a monad, but the number to which they belong is itself Two or Three or what have you.

Two more observations on the preparatory role of the *Greater Hippias*: First, Beauty is the ostensible topic; when embodied, it is here treated as, or at least in analogy to, sensory units which are each severally what all are together: beautiful. (I should point out that in a fleeting, thus particularly significant, passage of the *Phaedrus*—for it is Socrates' way to reveal depths in passing—in sight of eidetic heaven, the *eidos* Beauty is given a name more illuminating than *Beauty*, in fact arrestingly right: *Visibility* (250b); to be beautiful is to be "sightly." So it turns out that the each–all relation need not change even if the connotation of the assemblage name does.)

Second, Socrates assigns himself a curious role in this tricky dialogue. He *doubles* himself, talks to himself as to a close relative and neighbor, and shames himself for conversing ineptly (304d). He seems to me here to embody the "two-making" power, to anticipate the so-called Indeterminate Dyad that must eventually come on the scene in order to complement the unifying function of The Good (see *Addendum 2*, below).

The mention of doubling and dyad makes this the moment to say that *one* is *not* for the Greeks a number but a principle, or even the matter, of number: "A number is a multitude composed of units (*monadôn*)" (Euclid, *Elements* VII, def. 2; one will be ranged among the numbers when the counting numbers are extended by the addition of zero and the negative numbers). Thus an ancient number is a definite *assemblage* of units, either sensory or abstracted, meaning either a material collection of horses, humans, or some other sensible beings or a mathematical collection of monads, purified of sensible matter.

2. and 3. An explication of Klein's chapter, calling to aid Hopkins's extended and justifiably difficult exposition of the chapter, will be my main task.

4. Aristotle, besides naming the notion of *arithmoi eidetikoi*, contributes its most tellingly descriptive adjective: *asymblêtos*, "un-throwable-together," "inaddible" (*Metaphysics* 13.7). The monads constituting eidetic numbers are neither, like sensory units, members of the same kind, for they are precisely themselves kinds; nor are they mathematical units, abstractions "drawn off" from individualizing matter, since they are beings, concretely

substantial. Consequently they are incapable of being simply summed, that is, counted up, into a number. That is because they are incapable of being indiscriminately together in any number whatsoever and therefore of being brought together by the arithmetical computation (*logismos*) called addition within or across any two or more eidetic numbers.

Aristotle gives several arguments why the eidetic numbers are not like mathematical numbers, of which their inaddibility is only the chief feature (*Metaphysics* 13.6–9). He himself distinguishes three kinds of numbers: those constituted of sensory thing-monads, of mathematical pure monads, and of forms. The sensory numbers, for example, a string of ponies, are addible within the string, or from string to string, because they are all of the same kind, ponies. The mathematical numbers arise by the internal addition of pure, that is, quality-less and so compatible monads, and these numbers can be added to each other, again because of the purely quantitative unit-nature of their constituents, thus 1 + 1 = 2 and 2 + 2 = 4. The eidetic numbers, however, are made up of qualitatively distinct, ultimately different, though related, forms. They are terminally *asymblêtoi*, *in*addible. That, Aristotle thinks, makes for an absurd kind of number.

Aristotle is here, be it willfully or nesciently, overlooking the fact that this distinction among the eidetic units is precisely what Plato—I think it is right here to say Plato—values in these eidetic numbers.

I look to Plato's "Seventh Letter" for corroboration. There, having laid out the pedagogic ascent of a lover of wisdom under a teacher, he explains that "weakness of rational speeches" (*logoi*) which will prevent any mindful man from putting "what he has in mind" (*ta nenoêmena*) in writing (343a). And indeed there is no writing by him on the eidetic numbers. The weakness of words is this: What you learn by speech, by accounts, on the way up to Being and beyond, is always involved in "the qualitative" (*to poion*) rather than in bare "being" (*to on*). I think he means that we must speak in subject-copula-predicate sentences even when we really need language that ends—having said something—with the copula: "Being *is*," period. For Aristotle "whatness," quality (*poiotês*) is, tellingly, "the difference of Beingness" (*hê tês ousias diaphora*, *Metaphysics* 5.14); for him "whatness" is not a weakness of metaphysical speech but its strength.

In the Platonic context, however, that weakness is, I think, what makes Aristotle say that the eidetic numbers are an absurdity: each of its units is a *poion*, a qualitatively articulated, thus incomposable, unit. Yet the strength of the eidetic numbers is just that: They display to the student who has ascended to the realm of mindfulness (*noêsis*) a way of superseding "*poiotic*" sentences in favor of *ontic* speechlessness, since their individual quality has been melded as they together constitute one eidetic number that *is*, as I shall try to articulate, without any assignable quality *of its own*.

These consequences follow from regarding the Platonic context: (a) Aristotle's surely devastating critique of the eidetic numbers because of their "*asymbleticism*" is beside the point in focusing precisely on the *intended* failure of rationality; (b) the character of the eidetic numbers has to be explicated as set out, so far as I know for the first time ever, by Klein; and (c) this is probably best done by following his second major discovery: an actual *first* eidetic number. Since one is not a number, this first eidetic number is the Two, and its name is Being.

III. Preconditions for Counting

The obvious prerequisites are the so-called natural or counting numbers, the kind of number, called *arithmos* in Greek, that will provide the—crucially modified—analogue for communities of forms, of *eidê*. Preceding the postulates that establish the rules for and limitations of computation with such numbers, the following cosmic or universal conditions seem to be necessary: The finite places of an ordered *cosmos* (in antiquity) and the non-finite spaces of a law-governed *universe* (in modernity) contain *things*—from peas to planets, nits to nebulae—objects with closed contours that are therefore individually discernible. Most of these, seen from the proper distance, resemble some others and beg to be either *literally laid out in places or spaces*, that is to say as figures and their parts in an Aristotelian place (*Physics* 4.1–6) or as loci in locations of Cartesian space—or made somehow surveyable. So collected and arranged they become countable; they can be *counted up*. Thus the possibility of "laying out" appears to be a precondition of counting up the world's thing-units and laying up the result in a visualizing (quasi-extended) and remembering (quasi-storing) soul.

The actual operation of counting is, in this reconstruction, a computation. A unit having been discerned and thereupon a similarity-group, the former is laid out in place, space, or mind, and counting proceeds by adding one other to the first one, making two, and one more to the two, and so on. It remains to give names to, say, the first ten, and then to devise an easily assignable and indefinitely extensible naming system, a notation that acts as an external memory of the counted sum and its history. In counting, the *one*, the monad, clearly has a double function: it is both the principle of motion and the material constituent of both a counted and a counting number.

This *one* can be material in the ordinary sense when *arithmos* has its basic meaning of an assemblage of things, such as a herd of horses or a string of ponies—a sensory number constituted of *sensory ones*: horses or ponies. Or the one can become progressively more generalized: an equine being, a mammal, and so on. So it can finally be any thing whatever, and as it becomes ultimately general, it is purified of all specificity and reduced (or elevated) to the pure monad of mathematics. As such it is universally comparable, composable, summable. Then in a dramatic flip, it becomes an *eidos*, the exemplar of specificity, and as such, the unit of an eidetic number. Indeed, these are the same three types of monads Aristotle distinguishes (*Metaphysics* 14.3). Those, then, are the factors that make the world a venue of countability: things, similitudes, layouts, notations, remembering souls.

IV. Klein's Discoveries: Understanding Eidetic Numbers and Finding the First Eidetic Number—Two (Being)

Both Socrates' own Hippias and Aristotle in the *Metaphysics* had meant their objection to be devastating. Hippias thinks that the "each one, both two" argument is trivial small talk (*mikrologia* 304b). Aristotle calls the eidetic numbers "concocted, plastic" (*plasmatôdes*), meaning, he says, "forcibly made up to support the hypothesis" (*Metaphysics* 13.7.1082b1–4).

The aim of Klein's chapter is to exonerate these form numbers, to establish them as a major contribution to the solution of the grandest intra-Platonic perplexity (*aporia*, "pathlessness"): the "community" (*koinônia*), the "participation" (*methexis*), the "interweaving" (*symplokê*) of forms that first makes possible the connections wrought in thinking speech, account-giving, and counting (all *logos*), be they silent in the soul or uttered (*Sophist* 259e).

Klein ranks two of these problematic terms, participation and community, by analogy: Participation is on the level of "thinking-things-through" (*dianoia*) what community is on the level of "intuition" (*noêsis*) of ideas. Participation raises the problem of how one form is distributed over many *things*. Community implies the problem of how the various *eidê* or forms or species assembled in an eidetic or form-number, a *genos*, are related to their own genera if not, as will be shown, subordinately, and how these "greatest genera" themselves are related to each other if not, as will be shown, coordinately.

These issues have narrower formulations, some as being soluble problems, some as everlasting questions: First, though sensory participants that are the same in kind share a group name, which denotes what will later be called their "essential" feature, how can it be that idea groups, genera, have different names from their family members? Next, can the eidetic, the specific members of an idea community, ever be comparable with, be thrown together with, members of other idea groups, just as the pure arithmetical units, the "ones" used in counting and calculation, may be? Are all *eidê* summable into some eidetic number? Are there perhaps some respects under which all *eidê* can be thrown together with all? There will arise other questions, of more sophistication but of less scope: What happens to the *eidos* that supplies the *eidos*-name, the eidetic number, as it is distributed over, as Klein will show, its no-longer-subordinate membership? Does it disappear? Are the eidetic numbers numerically hierarchical, the way Ten is incontestably higher than Nine, or are there coordinate numbers? Are there unicorn *eidê*, unique forms that are their own eidetic numbers?

Klein now turns to the *Sophist*. The *Hippias* raised the problem of participation as it goes by in ordinary speech unnoticed by all but Socrates. In the *Sophist*, with Socrates as instigator, but not as a dialectical participant, the solution is implied. We may put it to ourselves this way: Socrates is always with Plato, but a moment has come when Plato takes off on his own, though in the person of a Stranger from the family of Parmenides. For Socrates is about to be condemned to death (*Theaetetus* 210a) and to leave the scene. The fourth part of the Divided Line, the philosopher kings' "highest study" (*Republic* 504e ff.), is about to be filled with actual matter, and ontology is on its way, enlarged by Otherness, by immanent Nonbeing.

The question Socrates has raised in the beginning of the *Sophist* is whether Sophist, Statesman, Philosopher are distinguishable: What is their count? From the very outset the Stranger—I really think one might say Plato—goes about the inquiry in the right way for the future of philosophy. He diagnoses the Sophist as a type (recall that Socrates usually respects the individual human instances) by his debonair making of images, including of himself. Moreover, he *rightly* thinks of images as having a sort of tinsel-being; they are not what they are, they are "counterfeits." ("This," someone might say, showing an image on his iPhone, "is my baby boy." And you would be rude but not wrong to say: "No, it isn't.") Similarly, the Sophist easily makes second worlds by carrying around a mirror, and, himself a confident *sophistes*, he gives a persuasive imitation of a *philosophos*, of one who desires to be a *sophos*. In other words, the Sophist is all but philosophical in trying to hide in Nonbeing. The difference is in motive.

Moreover, the Stranger levers the question into the realm of ideas and their community. Recall that in terms of individuals and their qualities the first part of the dialogue achieves a surplus of definitions, mostly hilarious, of the Sophist—six! It is only when the Stranger ascends to the five "greatest genera" that a deep delineation is formulated (254d). Of these *genê*, the first three are Being (*to on*) and Rest or Standstill (*stasis*) and Change or Motion (*kinêsis*), and the two remaining ones are the Same and the Other.

"Thus the relation of *stasis* to *kinêsis* forms the nucleus" of the *Sophist* and also of Klein's chapter on eidetic numbers (*Greek Mathematical Thought*, p. 88). To be sure, there is, as well, the Other (*thateron*, by crasis, blending from *to heteron*), the most consequential ontological notion that I know of, the drawing of Nonbeing into Being by identifying it with the pervasive Other. Klein will take it up at the end of the chapter, in reference to the doubling power active throughout the forms. (See also *Addendum 2*.)

Klein's exposition will reach its climax in the claim that Being *is* the eidetic number Two (p. 93). There is no ancient report known to me that fleshes out (so to speak) a particular eidetic number, though it is not imaginable that (small) legions of Plato adherents did not labor to discern their matter. (For such an attempt, see *Addendum 1*.)

So then, on the "lowest level of ontological reflection," in fact in the sensory realm, it is *not* demonstrable that two instances can come together as two and yet remain each one—as could mathematical monads. For, take Warm and Cold; when they come together they just become Tepid. But go up in ideality, go to the very greatest genera, Standstill and Motion, and now a new community obtains: These are each one, in fact as opposite and as incapable of being mixed as can be. (In terms of modern dynamics, where rest is simply 0 on the motion continuum, this claim no longer holds.) So each *is* what it *is* and both together *are*, meaning they have Being, belong to the form Being whence they appear to take their individual "is": There *is* Standstill, there *is* Motion—each one, together *two* (p. 87; incidentally, I translate *stasis* not as Rest, as is usual, but as Standstill, so as to avoid the notion that, because it is as opposite as can be to Motion, it is therefore its deprivation, its mere negation; it is a fully positive being, perhaps even superior to Change).

But now something untoward: Standstill and Motion were each one, together two. Now count: there is Standstill, Motion, and the Being that makes us say "each *is*." The count gives Three!

We are now in the higher reaches of ideality. First let me observe that here the question is not the one that is uppermost in the minds of those who first hear about form: How do they emanate, generate, spawn their instances, in short, show some sort of causality such as we moderns brought up in the ambience of Science look for? On the contrary, here the question is the reverse: How do the forms come together, collect themselves under superforms, *genê* (plural of *genos*, "kin groups")? The prior thought is the "wondrous" notion that the many are one and the one many (*Philebus* 14c; cited by Klein on p. 88). The next question then is how this, the one–many condition, works for a genus of forms.

Here enter the *arithmoi eidetikoi*, the "formal assemblages" (p. 89). These genera have the—crucially modified—structure of *arithmoi*, and they are themselves numerable, evidently by their cardinal numbers that are interpretable as the rank-ordering ordinals (second, third, and so on), that are capable of numbering hierarchies.

To begin with, as in the visible world so in the ideal realm, there are both kinships of similarity and complements of opposition (see section III, above). If the alternatives we must consider are that all forms might be related, or none, or some, we find that only the last is actually thinkable—and these assemble in *arithmoi.* Such numbers in their mathematical version, described above, are assemblages of qualityless, "pure" units capable of associating within and over any number. Their eidetic version is precisely *not* associable; each *eidos*-monad is ultimately and radically itself. (I must stop to say here that this poses a great problem, since *the Same* or *Self-sameness* is not in the assemblage with *Standstill* and *Motion.* These forms thus seem to lack the required ultimacy of selfhood. But let that be; I shall continue to point out merely technical difficulties as I go. They may coalesce into some depth.)

At this point Klein turns to Aristotle for the nature and terms of the eidetic numbers (p. 89; see the discussion of Aristotle in section II, above), since they appear explicitly nowhere in the Platonic dialogues. (Klein deals mildly with, even veils, Aristotle's misconceived critique of this major piece of Plato's post-Socratic ontology. To me it seems highly, and not altogether creditably, characteristic: Aristotle's critique allows logical precision to subvert ontological daring.)

The units of the eidetic number are, then, associable but not universally so: Standstill and Motion can be together by reason of their antithetical complementarity, their specific opposition. But they have no kinship whatever with any form above them, for there is none. Nor, as enclosed in their eidetic number, can they give anything to the forms below. (As I'll try to show, not even to so ideal a being as that most archetypal "Ur"-horse—Goethe's coinage, I think.)

Here is the crux of the nature evinced by an eidetic number (p. 90): All the related forms belong to a higher form or genus as its units. But they do not partition that higher genus among themselves. This was a problem young Socrates ran into in his conversation with Parmenides (131c). The resolution is achieved by the fact that the form-assemblage has the character of a quasi-*arithmos*: Just as the number name does not betoken a number that is above and beyond the unit-assemblage—Two is nothing beyond its two units—so Being is not "beside" (*para*) and "outside" (*ektos*), is not additional to, its constituent forms, Standstill and Motion. It is just and precisely their *togetherness*. Since it *is* not separately, it is not distributable either; it has an "untouchable integrity" (p. 90), precisely as being absorbed into its number. Each of the two unique form-monads *is* involved in twoness just insofar as it *is* together with its complement. (Here arises the same problem noted above: I would have said "together with its complementing *other*, but *thateron* is not in this assemblage.) Being is not a third here; it is, in this situation, nothing but the enabler of eidetic togetherness, and together these forms are two, not three.

Then comes the conclusion:

> The eidetic number, finally, indicates the mode of being of the noêton [the object of mindful insight] *as such—it defines the eidos ontologically as a being which has multiple relations to other eidê in accordance with their particular nature and which is nevertheless in itself altogether indivisible.* (p. 91, italics in original)

(It seems to me that within opposite pages [90 and 91] we are here faced with a major perplexity. On the left, the *genos* that gives its name to the eidetic number—here it will be Being—is now said to be nothing "beside" and "outside" the forms it unites, nothing beyond their union. On the right it is said to be in itself altogether indivisible. This eidetic number seems to have gained a strange kind of integrity by losing its separability, its individuality. Its unfracturable integrity is gained from its being indubitably a double, a Two; its separate individuality is lost in its having no essence of its own. This is not Aristotle's irrelevant complaint about the unsummability of eidetic monads, but the question whether the eidetic number can actually be an *eidos*—Being was the candidate—and what its legitimate eidetic name is, since Being itself has now subsided into a mere immanent relation.)

Klein goes on to show that eidetic numbers are the conditions of possibility for counting, with its precondition of division and collection, of discerning things and grouping them (see section III, above). For if the forms did not have an orderly, an ordinally arithmetic structure, neither could the cosmos have it, nor could we discern its order. This structure accounts for the fact that our world harbors definite counting numbers and definite sensory numbers, assemblages of pure units and *arithmoi* in the primary meaning of collections of like *things*—in brief, the fact that it contains both arithmetical and material Twos and Threes and Hexads and Decads. (Plato's badly received Lecture on the Good as a unifying One apparently limited the eidetic numbers to ten; p. 91.)

Eidetic numbers as a whole, then, not only make counting possible, but being themselves a *taxis*, a hierarchically structured order of priority, of superior and inferior, they are responsible for a cosmic ordering, including human ethics (see *Addendum 1*).

I should point out here that this exposition bypasses a major question: Just *how* are eidetic numbers or the individual *eidê* "responsible"? This is the question of causation, the genetic question. To be sure, the English term for an *eidos*, "form," as much as the etymological root of *eidos* in seeing (*[F]id*), points toward what Aristotle will call a paradigmatic and essential cause (*Physics* 2.3), one based both on similarity and on substance-giving; we call that kind of cause "formal." Closely related to the formal cause is the consummating cause (*telos*), which we call "final" and which, in a Platonic setting, would be the "ideal" cause. These are hints for speculation.

The discussion then turns to the failure of the account-giving *logos* with respect to eidetic numbers. Thus the *first* such number, Two—recall that one is not a number, not being a plurality—is called Being (p. 93). But now there seem to be three items: Being, Standstill, and its utterly incompatible other, Motion. Yet it is a twosome; that there should be a third outside these is the "most impossible thing of all" (*Sophist* 250b–d; p. 88)! Yet both participating forms *are*! (Note that the Other has already implicitly turned up—an evidently unavoidable problem.)

At just this point Klein involves the two other "greatest" genera: the Same and the Other. This very active Other—it ranges "through all" *genê*—depends on the stable self-sameness bestowed by the Same; only a well-defined self can be an other to another. (Here the wide application of dialectic to human affairs begins to show clearly; Aristotle will make that the condition of the best friendship—the friend's self-sameness: This person "is of the same mind with himself" [*homognômonei heautôi, Nicomachean Ethics* 9.4.1166a13].)

This means that the Other is, strangely, a bond (*desmos*), connecting every form or form group with every other by articulation: In causing difference, that is, otherness, it establishes distinction, thisness. Meanwhile the Same is, oddly, self-divided since it is every other's other, so other by reason of being selfsame. This dialectic fact, the self-diremption of Sameness and the articulating bonding of Otherness, makes them a communal pair. As such, they enable thinking-through (*dianoia*) to understand the "duplicity" of Being (p. 95) as the conjunction of opposites (by no means a coincidence, an identification, as in Hegelian logic) that is the *coexistence* of "*elements other in kind*" (p. 96).

Once again the question: What survives of this Being, which has been said to have been absorbed in its Two? And to anticipate: Klein's interpretation of the Other, which causes every other to be an other's other, as *the source of duality and duplicity*, is thrown into doubt by the appearance of a "two-making" principle called by Socrates "The More-and-the-Less" and later, by Aristotle, "The Indeterminate Dyad" (see *Addendum 2*). In the *Philebus* (14d) the first name for this "marvelous" notion is "the One-and-Many"; I use "More-and-Less" because it better describes the indeterminate slithering brought about by this cause of the indefiniteness of infinity. Recall that infinity, as later defined by Aristotle, is a principle of *non*-actualization: there is always more in one direction and less in the other (*Physics* 4.6). But as numerically expressed, as a dyadic "doubling," it does turn a single unit into a *discrete multitude* (albeit only of square numbers), whereas, when taken as a comparative increase and decrease, it is responsible for an indefinite change in a continuous *magnitude*. That is, the Indeterminate (or Indefinite) Dyad is a divisive principle that diminishes digital quantities like the unit by fracturing it into two, while increasing numerousness by doubling first the unit, then the double, then its double (4) and so on by successive doubling (2n). In its "more-and-less" version, it increases, in its "more" phase, extended magnitudes such as lines, always approaching but never achieving the infinite, while in its "less" phase it diminishes the underlying magnitude to its least element, never reachable except in thought. For the two-dimensional line, this is the one-dimensional *point*, which Dedekind will take as the pivot providing continuity to the geometric line ("Continuity and the Irrational Numbers," section II).

Finally Klein reports the great discovery in the *Sophist*, the identification of "Otherness" with Nonbeing; as he puts it, it "turns out to be the ontological aspect of 'Nonbeing'" (p. 96). He had emphasized the insuperable incompatibility of Standstill and Motion; they are terminally other. This is verbally articulable by a prefixed "not": Standstill is not-Motion, and—I think this is its simple converse—not-Standstill is motion. But "is not" does not, as I've said, betoken a dead negation; it can be taken as summoning *Non*-Being. Thus Otherness can be interpreted as Nonbeing. On the other hand, Klein showed that Standstill and Motion *are*, have Being, *only* as being together in a community, in the eidetic number called Two or Being. And that means, in turn, that Being is shot through with, inextricably involved in, Nonbeing—whose function is indistinguishable from Otherness. The chief reference is to the *Sophist* (256c–d).

So henceforth the prefixed "not" carries no imputation of the bearer's not-being but rather signifies its—or his—confrontation with an other significant to his nature.

(As before, the difficulty here is the ranging of the Other, be it as non-being or difference, over *all* the forms. This universality seems to breach the eidetic numbers' completeness; they are supposed to be, as mathematicians say, "closed under addition," meaning that any added form must also be *within* an eidetic community—as the Other is not, since it ranges through all.)

The chapter concludes with Klein's identification of The Good with the model, perfect in itself, of any and all wholeness; as such it is the counterpart of the scattered Other (p. 98).

(It is in accord with my claim that Klein's contributions to Socrates' dialectic have a wider than technical application that this view of the Good shows exactly why it is the highest of studies for the philosopher kings of the *Republic*: *The Idea of the Good is the theory of community itself.* As Aristotle, bringing things down to earth, will say: The political community [*koinonia*] called the *polis* is the most supreme and aims at the most supreme good [*agathon*; *Politics* 1.1].)

Klein ends by reminding the reader that the eidetic numbers represent a solution to the issue of the higher participation (*methexis*), that is, the question how instances are related to their forms on a higher level than that of those forms whose instances are sensory namesakes (as copies, progeny, parts, tokens, instantiations, emanations). And finally he emphasizes, as both Plato and his Socrates have all along, that the *arithmoi eidetikoi* are not fully clear. They offer a solution bought at the expense even of ordinary speech. "The horse *is* [an] animal" is no longer a transparent *logos*, capable of being thought through by *dianoia* as a subject, copula, predicate. For that count is three, but the coupling "is" cannot be a third beyond the other two. (Later this problem will reappear as the question: "Is existence a real property," for example, in Anselm, Descartes, Kant.)

V. Profit from a Problem-Ridden Study

I shall append below a list of the technical difficulties from which Klein's remarkable interpretation seems to suffer, and postpone to *Addendum 3* the applications to current life that I discern. Right now the question is: Why is this study—as it appears to me—engrossing?

I do not myself know whether the problems that arise are an intimation of something wrong with the theory or a mark of the ultimate inability of human understanding—"dianoetic" understanding—to be crystal clear or pellucidly rational about the highest study, the dialectic dealing with ontology and *mê*-ontology, with Being and its Beyond. (The prefix, *mê*, translated as "non-," is a more modulated negative adverb than *ouk*, plain "not").

It seems to me, however, that it sometimes makes sense to note but read past even ultimate technical obstacles for the sake of a speculatively illuminating and fruitfully applicable notion. First (but also least) it's good exercise, such as the grand model given in *Parmenides*, where old Parmenides makes young Socrates see the main difficulty with his own incipient theory of ideas; as it happens, this is exactly the problem that, in Klein's understanding, the eidetic numbers solve on the highest level, the problem of participation. Second (and greatest), trying to understand Klein's exposition brings the student to that noetic realm where, for the short time one can stand it, the world turns wonderful (*thaumaston*, *Philebus* 14c). That wondering is said to be the only beginning of the love of wisdom (*Theaetetus* 155d).

VI. Problems with the Eidetic Two

Here is the list of those I have discerned.

1. Does the *genos*, the eidetic number that encompasses the species, the *eidê*, insofar as, in Klein's understanding, it is nothing *beside* or *outside* them, disappear, now reduced to a mere relation?

2. Are the eidetic numbers (Two, Three, and so on) cardinal or ordinal, meaning are they a mere count-up or do they betoken an order, a *taxis*, of qualitative primacy and subordination, such as are expressed in the ordinals "second, third"?

3. Are some eidetic numbers coordinate with others and are some unicorn numbers singletons?

4. The *eidê* under the *genê* are surely self-same, unassimilable with each other, yet the Same is not involved in the first eidetic number, Two. How then do they achieve their inviolable self-sameness?

5. An eidetic number is said by Klein to gain its integrity precisely in losing its separability. If so, is it, as a mere immanent relation, a proper *eidos* at all?

6. There is no account of eidetic causality: How are the eidetic numbers in fact responsible for the cosmic *taxis* Klein attributes to them?

7. The Other, inextricably paired with the Same and pervasively distributed over the whole eidetic realm, is thus unavoidably involved in the Two identified by Klein as consisting *only* of *stasis* and *kinesis*. How else can it exert its power of mutual complementarity? For the eidetic numbers are, as mathematicians say, "closed under addition," that is, *eidê* (somehow) arising within these numbers stay within them, so that for them to participate in Otherness, that form must be *within* Being.

8. Klein identifies the Other as the "two-making," the doubling power, with the Indeterminate Dyad, which neither Plato nor Aristotle appears to do. Is "othering" identical with, or is it not rather distinguishable from, "doubling"?

Addendum I. An Attempt to Clue Out a Second and Third Eidetic Number

Here I attempt to discern a second and third eidetic number, consequent on the Two, Being, which is the first eidetic number. I propose a second and third such number, namely: the Three, Nonbeing, and the Four, Excellence.

This enterprise is highly speculative, even outré. Yet I imagine that in the *Republic* Socrates figured it among the dialectic exercises assigned to the philosopher kings as their most advanced study. In the *Parmenides*, he himself had been introduced to such practices late in his boyhood by hearing the master of all ontology, Parmenides, discourse. Plato's two brothers are near-silently present, as is a person homonymic with Aristotle, who is Parmenides' nominal interlocutor.

I am mindful here of the type of consanguinity eidetic units may show: either similarity or complementarity. The latter may be conceived as direct, that is, simple, "contradictory," opposition at the termini of an abrupt antithesis, such as Standstill versus Motion. Or it may be the "contrary" opposition, one whose termini are connected by an intervening, melding spectrum, such as black sliding to grey and to white, through a mixed middle. Or it may be the complementary opposition of action and passion, such as knowledge receptive to, and thus paired with, its known object.

As for similarity, it predominates in sensory collections. Thus golden things, from pale, matte olive-brown to coruscating, brilliant yellow, are, as sensory objects, all reminiscent of some golden paradigm. Even tables, be they four-, three-, two-, or one-legged, are consanguine through a thoughtful delineation of "Table."

Eidetic numbers, however, are not sensory since they are not constituted of units of sensible stuff, nor are they mathematical since their units are far from quality-deprived, far from "pure." These numbers are therefore like sensory numbers insofar as their monads are each a "what," a *poion*, and thus collectible into similarity groups. Yet they are also like mathematical numbers because in their togetherness emerges a form that no constituent form-monad was individually: "each one, together *Two*."

There are three more structural postulates to be included:

1. The naming form is not over and above the constituting form-monads but is absorbed *in* and constituted *by* them. Thus neither Nonbeing nor Excellence is self-subsisting, but they are what they are precisely in the union of the forms under them: Mere Otherness and unspecified Virtue are vacant.

2. The eidetic numbers are like arithmetic numbers in being sequential, yet unlike in that the sequence is a hierarchy—not a mere colorless serial precedence but ontological priority, an ordering of philosophical poignancy: not mere positional ordinality but significant ontological gradation.

3. The relating principle at work among the eidetic monads in each number, including their relation to the eidetic name, is apt to be different for every number, since the constituents are terminally diverse.

These delineations, then, of eidetic numbers should be realized in proposing them. Plato, in his famous Lecture on the Good, which caused disappointment by being on the One rather than on human goods (Aristoxenus, *Harmonics*, para. 30), may have reported ten form-numbers (*Metaphysics* 12.8). Going even half that far would seem to me folly.

When Klein absorbed the first three of the five "greatest" genera (enumerated in the *Sophist* 253 ff., the section dealing with the "communication," the "interweaving" of the forms), Being, Standstill, Motion (or Change), into the first eidetic number, the two last, Same and Other, remained unaccommodated. It is reasonable to think that they might belong to the second eidetic number, Three.

Of these, the Other appears in two perspectives. It is the positive name of Nonbeing, since whatever is other than a given is a non-this (note well: *not* a not-this, a flat abolishing contradictory). Any "this" is self-same taken by itself, but it never is thus alone; it is always confronted with that negating Other. (This may be the work of a dualizing principle, for which see *Addendum 2.*) So confronted, it turns into the other's other. Thus, as I've noted, the Same is, in community with the Other, also an other. Standstill and Change are apparently of equal power, but Same and Other appear less so; the Other has all the life in this pair; it saves the cosmos from the static, solitary Being of Parmenides and introduces diversity. But above all, it insinuates into the eidetic structure an element so far lacking: *the powers of the soul.* For in its ranging, "all chopped up," through the whole eidetic structure the Other is said to be "just like knowledge" (*epistêmê, Sophist* 257c).

Is knowledge rightly ranged among the *eidê*? Not much later in the dialogue the stranger says that it was "our aim" that *logos* should be "some one among the genera" (260a). Surely *logos* is, or could be, a stand-in for knowledge.

Now it seems that—at least if "Utter Not-Being" (*ouk on*) is to be regarded as truly Nothing—there is no Nonbeing except as Other in relation to Same, and both of these are eidetic units. And these do in fact, in the Stranger's own enumeration, follow after, succeed the *eidê* of the Two. The relating mode, however, of *Knowledge, Same, and Other*, and of this eidetic threesome to its proposed common name, *Nonbeing*, is quite different from that operating in Being, the eidetic Two. If I can articulate this relationship, I will have met my three criteria for being an eidetic number—not, to be sure, a proof of the so-ness of this eidetic Three, but at least of its feasibility.

This relation is altogether relativistic and oscillating. Each eidetic monad has one nature from its own perspective, another from an other's; the Same is Other to the Other. Depending on the inquirer's standpoint each *eidos* has another name; Knowledge confronts the known Other and rejects it, or it takes it in and, in absorbing, makes it its own, the Same; knowledge becomes known. Nonbeing, possibly larger in scope than the Other, since it might include the absolute not-being, Nothing, would then be beyond its eidetic constituents—but as their nonbeing, their other, it is identical with one of the constituent monads, the Other.

The eidetic name I've assigned to this second number, Three, Nonbeing, needs more justification. For Nonbeing was identified in the *Sophist* with the Other (258b). So we have the same *eidos* both encompassing and constituting the eidetic number. That is indeed thinkable, since everything about this second number (Nonbeing: Knowledge, Same, and Other) involves perspective and is equivocal, subjective, and oscillating, whereas the first number (Being: Standstill and Motion) implied a standpoint and was univocal, objective, and grounded.

So, be it among the eidetic units, or between them and their number *eidos*, every relation takes on a different aspect depending on the noetic view. Knowledge and known, as I've said, flip from active to passive: Same and Other appear as objects of knowledge, they act on the knower. But as once received, they accommodate themselves passively to being known; they *become* knowledge. And so for all the relations. The Same becomes Other to its Other, while the Other becomes the Same to that Same it has made into an Other.

Not only that, but the Other is, both as *eidos* within, and as Nonbeing externally, the *eidetic number itself.* Yet further, the three *eidê* and their *genos* itself violate their own "asymbletic," their "unassimilable" character and leak into every unit and number of the eidetic structure, for all must *be*, must be *selfsame*, and must be each other's *other* and so *knowable*, for to be an *eidos* is to be a *noêton*, an object of *noêsis*, of insight.

This paradigm of all Muddle seems to beg for a rectifying Next. That might be *Excellence*. Its four eidetic monads are well known to readers of the Socratic/Platonic dialogues and are often cited by Socrates as generally accepted: *Wisdom, Courage, Moderation, Justice*. Not all of them face amicably in the same direction. In the dialogue *Statesman* one excellence, moderation, is, most plausibly, at variance with another, courage (306a); thus as an eidetic assemblage, these four are united by similarity (so Moderation is for the whole what Justice is for its parts, *Republic* 427c ff.), by opposition (Courage versus Moderation), and by unity (since Wisdom, as identified with Knowledge [428b], is what all the excellences are often said by Socrates to be, namely Knowledge).

The dialogue that most specifically asks "What is excellence?" (or virtue, *aretê*), the *Meno*, comes, I think, *implicitly* to the conclusion that excellence is the desire to *learn*, that is, not to know but to *want* to know. But this is, equally implicitly, a critique of the Athenian quadruplet; this desire is neither among nor above this set. There is, thus, no explicit answer to the question concerning the nature of eidetic number Excellence (and *aretê* surely is a genus), neither there nor anywhere else that I know of. That may be because this popularly known eidetic group would *together* constitute Excellence and would thus leave no definable Excellence beyond, as *stasis* and *kinêsis* left no Being on its own, at least in Klein's understanding. It is a hopeful speculation.

Addendum II. An Attempt, in the Manner of Plotinus, to Present the Place and Principles of the Form Numbers in a System by Extending the "Divided Line" of the *Republic*

In this addendum I realize an irresistible invitation on the part of eidetic numbers to engage in Plotinus-like syste m-making—not that Plotinus would accept the product, but he might just find it interestingly false. I think of this addendum as Plotinean because it picks up on certain intimations to be found in the fifth and sixth *Enneads* that are worked out in Klein's *Greek Mathematical Thought and the Origin of Algebra*. I have, to be sure, found no evidence that Klein, who drew on Neoplatonists for his mathematical exposition, thought of Plotinus himself as a predecessor. Here, then, is a brief summary of these anticipations: the Good is the *One* and only *negatively* apprehensible. Then Being is the *Two*, composed of Standstill and Motion. The Good/One is a productive *over-principle*, which is complemented by a confounding *nether-principle*, the *Indeterminate Duality*, that is responsible for the disordering variety expressed as *matter* in the natural and *deceit* in the human world.

Aristoxenus, as referenced before, reports that Plato thought of the Good beyond Being set out in the *Republic* (509b) as being the eidetic number One. I've put that wrong: One is not a number and, as beyond Being, can't be eidetic, for *eidê* are beings par excellence. Anyhow, Socrates introduced a principle, The Good, that Plato called One, not *monas*, "monad" (the arithmetic term), but *hen*, "one" (an etymologically more aboriginal word). I speculate that this *hen* is meant to name not a unit but a unifier, a principle of unification, in fact imaged by the luminous "understrappings" holding together the cosmos that are described in the Myth of Er of the *Republic* (616c). This One is beyond all beings, thus off the so-called "Divided Line" of the *Republic*, which presents the ideal and the sensory realms in cognitive terms: knowable and knowing. Below this upright line—the diagram of a cognitive ascent, or reversely read, an ontological descent—is a sub-basement not presented diagrammatically but mythically, the so-called Myth of the Cave. It presents a manmade grotto, a place of fire-flickering darkness, enchained amusement, and human-managed illusionistic shadow play. This cave is located, so to speak, below the Divided Line, because its prisoner is wrenched away, turned around, "converted," from his imprisonment; he is dragged out and up into a world of real shadows thrown by the illuminating sun and of real things engendered by it, and these are presented by the lowest segment of the line. Yet below this place of manmade falsity, feeding it, as it were, is the principle that complements, as its antithesis, the Good insofar as it is a principle of Oneness, a unifier of cosmic wholes and of political communities, as well as the distant father of all three types of inner-worldly units, namely the eidetic, mathematical, and sensory.

For Plato, this deep-down principle is the indeterminacy-genus of the "More-and-the-Less" (*Philebus* 24a ff.), a doubly double principle, the one later to be called the "Indeterminate Dyad" (*aoristos dyas, Metaphysics* 13–14 passim; some say it acts conjointly with the unity element [14.2]). This principle, in Aristotle's account, is close to Nonbeing in its extreme opposition to Being (recall that Plato avoided writing of such ultimacies, though a second principle is hinted at in *Republic* 379b: "Then the good is not responsible for all things; . . . it is not responsible for bad things"). Perhaps it is a very low kind of Nonbeing, closer to the above-mentioned "Utter Not-Being" (*Sophist* 237b), distinct from the Nonbeing that is "not the opposite of Being, but only other" (257b; I interpret what follows to say that the particle *mê* belongs to the Nonbeing that coexists with Being and *ou* belongs to a Not-Being that contradicts it).

Aristotle reports attributions of materiality, badness, and falsity to this extreme Not-Being and by association also to the "Indeterminate Dyad," a somewhat more active genetic principle, dually dual, as I said. For it is two-making, "duplicating" (*dyopoios*) in quantity, and deception-making, "duplicitous" in quality. It is both the beneficial base for some otherness and diversity and also the pernicious enabler of image-making and false-speaking. (A neat note: without the aid of the One's units, it can produce no *odd* numbers.)

The next page presents a diagram of the Extended Divided Line.

Addendum III.
Application to Emergence and Community,
Bearing of Klein's Discoveries on Contemporary Issues
with Large Human Implications

Here I apply Klein's treatment of eidetic numbers to two current preoccupations: emergence and community. It seems to me that the problem exemplified by eidetic numbers as explicated in *Greek*

KNOWABLE AND KNOWING:
THE EXTENDED DIVIDED LINE,
Based on *Republic* 508e–519d

	Knowable	Knowing
5	THE GOOD/THE ONE (*hen,* unifying, unity)	
4	*Under the Good* The *Idea* of the Good and Eidetic Numbers: Ontology.	*Noêsis* (Mindfulness, Intuition) by means of Dialectic (Discourse on Being).
3	Logic, Mathematics, Physics: The arithmetical one, the geometric genesis of bodies, the music of motion.	*Dianoia* (Thinking-things-through) by means of *Hypotheseis* (Suppositions).
2	*Under the Sun* Natural Beings and Artifacts (Things).	*Pistis* (Trust: Confident Opinion) by means of *Aisthêsis* (Sense-experience).
1	Images, natural and artificial.	*Eikasia* (Image-recognition) by means of Seeing images *as* images.
½	Grotto: Human deception.	"Myth of the Cave."
0	THE MORE-and-LESS/THE INDETERMINATE DYAD (*aoristos dyas*, duality and duplicity).	

Mathematical Thought and the Origin of Algebra (referred to by aficionados as "the math book") bears directly on problems currently central to (cognitive) *psychology* and to (diversity) *politics.*

In the psychology of cognition, the problem behind all problems is: How does the experience of mentation *emerge* from the activities of the brain? This issue, if it is ever to undergo successfully its necessary conversion from a technical problem to a philosophical question, would do better if practitioners were aware of the spectacularly vivid case of emergence represented by eidetic numbers as understood by Klein. An "emergence," as used in the cognitive context, occurs when a whole arises that is not to be anticipated by an inspection of its subserving parts: When the observed electrical events of a brain do not bear a resemblance, by any articulable transformation, to the reported conscious experience—that is a case of a supervenient emergence. (There are apparently observations of brain patterns roughly resembling pictures shown to macaque monkeys; since direct reports from the subjects are lacking, the experience is an inference.) Here an immersion in eidetic numbers would be useful particularly in order to formulate the likely limits of a solution to the mind-brain problem. Perhaps this is just a long-winded way of saying that at some point science has to descend or ascend to ontology. I call to witness William James: At the very end of his abbreviated *Psychology*, he says, in 1892, that when psychology finally finds its founders as a science, "the necessities of the case will make them 'metaphysical.'" Would that . . . !

The second application of the eidetic number paradigm is, if not deeper, broader. I think that our, the American, exigency now is, and will be for quite a while, how to realize the commitment of our coinage: *e pluribus unum*, "out of many, one." The eidetic number is one sort of community, a way of coming together, that does not result in the emergence of a novel entity and that is, problematic though it be, the more cohesive for it. Note that this way of expressing community directly contradicts the understanding of the first application above, since there the emergence is precisely the supervenience of a new entity. This is a problem to engross the incipient philosopher kings in their final dialectical learning, see IV, end, above: *Is* the eidetic number, the form-number, anything at all, beyond its "informing" function?

Let me imagine a conversational application: It is likely that the quasi-citizens of a "red" republic will all be coopted or coerced into being "reds," and the same for, say, the white subjects of imperial rule. This is the way of a sensory number: All the sensory dog units composing a dog-number (*arithmos kynikos*) are supposed to be doggy, canine; all the members of a red commune are red. The preliminaries to understanding eidetic numbers that I set out above suggest that an alternative is that all members of the community are pure, quality-less units and as such "symbletic," capable of being summed, reassigned, resettled across their own and other communities. That would be a collectivity of denatured nonentities. Then there is the third, *the* polity each of whose participants is an individual (from Latin: "undividable"). Each is a monad (literally "alone"), analogous to the eidetic monad, which is the radically ultimate locus of specificity (*eidos* = *species*), the very incarnation of unique quality. This is, one hopes, how in individualistic democracies like America most citizens see themselves. The community might be best featured as an eidetic number, a community (*koinônia*) that does not *rise above*, emerge, out of its citizenry as a higher entity, but rather *descends into* them, informing them with its nature. U.S. citizens are, in fact, not naturally nationalistic and seem to think of their united continental country in many sensible terms other than those like blood, soil, *Volk*, and ancestral tradition, such as tend to coagulate into a separable hyper-being. Put in terms of our founding charter: How do terminal individuals, who are endowed with their own lives, accorded their own civic freedoms, and encouraged to pursue happiness as a vocation, come together, interweave, make a community, that is *not above but among* them? Like eidetic numbers.

Bibliography

Dedekind, Richard. "Continuity and Irrational Numbers." In *Essays on the Theory of Numbers*. Translated by Wooster Woodruff Beman. Chicago: Open Court Publishing, 1901.

Hopkins, Burt C. *The Origin of the Logic of Symbolic Mathematics: Edmund Husserl and Jacob Klein*. Bloomington and Indianapolis: Indiana University Press, 2011.

Klein, Jacob. *Greek Mathematical Thought and the Origin of Algebra*. Translated by Eva Brann. Cambridge, MA: MIT Press, 1968. Reprint, New York: Dover Publications, 1992.

Original publication: "Die Griechische Logistik und die Entstehung der Algebra," *Quellen und Studien zur Geschichte der Mathematik, Astronomie, und Physik*, Abteilung B: *Studien*, vol. 3, no. 1 (Berlin, 1934), 18–105 (Part I) and ibid., no. 2 (1936), 122–235 (Part II).

James, William. *Psychology: Briefer Course*. New York: Henry Holt and Company, 1892.

To Flip a Pancake

On "the Human Possibility of a Total Conversion"

JULIA KLEIN[1]

In his *Commentary on Plato's "Meno,"* Jacob Klein attends closely to the imagery in the myth of recollection, which endows the soul with depth, and thus the character of what is called in geometrical language "a solid."[2] For a soul that lacks this "inside," this dimension of depth, learning would be impossible. Such is the case for Meno, whose soul, Klein pronounces, is "as flat as a pancake."[3] As if on a long scroll, transcribed on Meno's uncommonly powerful memory are countless words and speeches he has heard others utter—empty pseudo-certainties without substance. And yet, as powerful as it is, Meno's memory alone is insufficient to the task of genuine learning because it is unsupported by a "third dimension"—that is, depth (*bathos*). Unwilling to make the effort to descend beneath the surface of mere memorization in search of real understanding, Meno, Klein ventures, cuts the figure of one who is "totally incapable of learning" (*CPM* 199).

In light of this sorry state of affairs, it is striking to hear Klein say, in a discussion on the character of questioning, "Every one of us (that is, every human being on this earth, without exception) is in some way educated."[4] If all human beings are somehow "educated," then what is the meaning of *education*? And if we all, without exception, have some education, then of what kind of "learning" is Meno incapable? And—to ask a question in the style of Meno—how is this defect acquired? Is it by birth, by habit, by "bad education," or by a bit of bad luck? Last, but not least, how do things stand with the one in the role of the teacher in relation to this hapless fellow?

As Flat as a Pancake

The first thing to consider is Klein's account of Meno's character and his conclusion that Meno is incapable of learning.

To begin with Meno's question: "Can you tell me, Socrates, whether virtue is something teachable? Or is it not teachable, but something that comes from practice? Or is it something neither from practice nor from learning, but something that comes to human beings by nature, or in some other way?" (70a).[5] What strikes me most about this question is that it's a challenge more than a question: It's not about virtue, nor how it is acquired, nor even how Socrates thinks it's acquired, but it's about whether or not Socrates *can tell* Meno something. From the very beginning, Meno reveals his concern is less with genuine inquiry than with the mere acquisition of a catalogue of speeches. On top of this, the tone Meno sets is one of debate, of argument. Klein observes that the very phrasing of the question—with its three classic elements of nature, habit, and teaching—suggests that Meno is up to date on what was the current mode of debate on the subject (*CPM* 39).

Socrates tries to steer Meno toward inquiring first what virtue is (71d), suggesting that one cannot ask the *how* of it without first asking the *what.* Meno's first responses amount to listing examples—virtues proper to men, women, children, and slaves. Socrates urges Meno to confront the question of virtue as a whole, rather than breaking it up into "small change" (79a), referring to "some one and the same form through which they are virtues and upon which one would somehow do well (*kalôs*) to focus one's gaze" (72c). That form, if there is such a thing, would be the very thing signified by the word *aretê*. To look for an answer to the question, "what is virtue," then, is to search by means of speech for something that is itself beyond speech. In rattling off examples, Meno shows only how the word is used; he resists any thinking beyond the mere designation of words.

After Socrates fails several times to get Meno to "make an attempt" (73c) to say what virtue is, Meno's frustration leads him to volley a personal attack: What he has learned from hearsay has now been confirmed, namely, that Socrates induces a paralyzing perplexity in others, assailing his victims with unanswerable questions. He is like a torpedo-fish who renders its prey numb, "in soul and mouth" (80a–b). Socrates gently responds that he is willing to look, together with Meno in friendship, for whatever virtue is (80d). Rather than soften, Meno serves up an addled sort of argument, presumably meant to be thrown like a wrench into their inquiry—which Socrates does the work of clarifying for him: Learning is impossible, for if you seek what you do not know, then you won't know it when you find it, and if you know what it is you are seeking, then there is no reason to seek (80e). Instead of directly attacking this paradox, Socrates recounts a myth he claims to have heard from people wise about things divine. In the myth, we hear that, because the soul is immortal, it has seen all truths before, and it knows the whole of things; what we call "learning," then, is really the soul's recollection of knowledge, which it has forgotten as a result of being born. Learning is possible, so the story goes, because it consists not in acquiring knowledge from without, but in recovering it from within.

According to the myth, learning is an effortful and independent activity on the part of the learner; it requires a deliberate, strenuous search for knowledge deep within the soul. In this way, the myth makes the role of the "teacher" suspect—if by *teaching* we mean the transmission of knowledge into the soul of the learner from without. From this angle, likening learning to recollection draws attention to the learner's inner resourcefulness in recognizing the truth for what it is—as when we dredge up something from memory and recognize it for the object of our searching. On the other hand, the recollection imagery also calls to mind the question of the beginning of such a search: once we have forgotten something—or even if it is merely not present to us immediately—some external reminder seems necessary for us to remember that we have forgotten in the first place. In this way, to liken learning to recollection is to shine a light upon an ineluctable mystery—albeit an unspoken one.

Though Meno shows some interest in this mythical formulation—perhaps in part because of its attribution to people reputedly wise—his pursuit of the question of learning takes on the regrettable form of pressing Socrates to explain to him how what the myth says can be true (82a). Though Socrates refuses to contradict himself by "teaching" Meno—that is, by telling him—that "teaching" is impossible, he will *show* Meno something that demonstrates the truth of the claim, that is, he will *exhibit* recollection "in" Meno's slave-boy. The boy will learn how to find the double of a given square by recollecting from within, rather than by means of being "taught" (82b). Meno is asked to observe and to *see for himself* how the boy learns, just as we are invited to see for ourselves whether Meno himself learns. The demonstration concludes when the slave-boy learns that the side of the double square is the diagonal of the one given. The diagonal's length is "irrational" because it lacks a numerical ratio to the given side. The solution is *alogos*, speechless or unspeakable. It cannot be put into words, but it can be drawn and pointed to. Like the question of virtue, the aim of the geometrical endeavor, even though beyond speech, can nevertheless be looked for and recognized.

Socrates observes to Meno that the slave-boy—unlike his master—did not become paralyzed by offense in the face of his own ignorance. The awareness of it made him better, not worse, for without this, he could not have learned. Further, none of this required any "teaching," but only that the boy be given questions. Socrates merely *elicited* from him the truth he had in himself.

At first, there seems to be some hope that Meno has been persuaded that learning is not only possible, but also that it is good; he assures Socrates that he has followed the demonstration and has seen for himself the truth of the claim that learning comes from within. And yet, after all, he poses again his original question for Socrates—about how excellence is acquired. Meno, Klein says, "has not budged" (*CPM* 184). If he had grasped the meaning of the myth through the demonstration, he would now recognize that learning is not in conflict with what is given by nature, or what is acquired through habit. It was in the slave-boy's nature to be able to learn how to double the square (which is also, one might note, to learn *what* the double square is), but it would still require much time and practice for the boy's learning to yield deep knowledge. As Meno has been asked to see for himself the unspeakable (i.e., irrational) length to which the boy points, so we have been given to see for ourselves who Meno really is. "Meno's unspeakable soul," Klein tells us, "has finally been unveiled. We see [him] now *as he is*, in the nakedness of his soul. And we comprehend *who* he is in relation to learning: a man unwilling to learn and incapable of learning, although endowed with a peculiarly powerful memory" (*CPM* 185).

In the character of Meno's memory, in fact, we find the root of his problem: though his memory may be filled to the brim with opinions, these are not even his own. Even if they happen to be "right," they haven't yet been appropriated and held down fast. Thus Meno's "learning" amounts to the mere memorization of speech. His fixation on hearsay, on the words of others, on being told, points to that absence in his soul of the dimension of depth that would be inscribed by his making an active effort to search himself for knowledge of that to which his speech refers—which is to say, to hunt down his own ignorance, his lack of understanding. Meno's soul, Klein writes,

> is indeed nothing but "memory," an isolated and autonomous memory, similar to a sheet or a scroll covered with

> innumerable and intermingled characters, something of a two-dimensional and shadow-like being: it is a repository of opinions but it cannot become a repository of knowledge. It has no "depth" and no "solidity" at all. (*CPM* 186)

Plato, Klein continues, has a name for this kind of soul: it is a "little" or "shrunken" soul—a *psycharion*—a term appearing in the *Theaetetus* in connection with the description that likens the memory to a lump of wax (195a). "Depending on the quality of the wax in their souls," Klein writes, "men are wise or foolish, slow or quick to learn, in possession of a good or a bad memory. For the quality of the wax accounts for the character of the 'imprints' made on it" (*CPM* 187). Wax that is too hard, for example, can only be made to have very indistinct imprints, since "there is no depth in them" (*Theaetetus* 194e). And if the imprints are made to impinge on each other for lack of space, they become even more indistinct. Klein characterizes Meno's soul as a shrunken *psycharion* lacking depth (*CPM* 186).

Turning Bathos into Bathos

Now that we have heard about the nature of Meno's shortcoming, what can we have learned about the image of depth in the myth? Of what exactly does Meno's memory stand in such dire need?

To begin, Klein regards the image of depth as a metaphor for whatever it is that enables us to learn. Concerning the presence of knowledge in our souls, Plato employs the distinctive Greek verb *en-einai*—literally, "to be in," as held and enclosed within something of *dimension*. Another meaning of this verb hovers just beneath the surface—that is, "to be possible," as when we say, "she has it in her," in order to say that "it is possible for her to do it." Insofar as the myth of recollection images the possibility of learning as involving latent knowledge present in our souls, it suggests a realm of intelligibility that exists behind, or beneath, our words—enabling us to speak, as the realm to which all of our words gesture. Thus on the level of the intelligible, the myth offers a kind of account—or at least, an affirmation—of the possibility of securing answers to our questions. In this way, it justifies belief in the existence of an unknown toward which our questions are directed, as well as the conviction that such an unknown might be transformed into knowledge. So, on the one hand, the image seems to refer to the possibility of gaining access to *deep knowledge*, and the soul who learns is the one that reaches after such depths. To say that one "has it in" oneself to learn would refer, in this light, to the latent knowledge within the soul; to have the capacity to learn is to have an underlying access to the very grounds of intelligibility. The myth's image of the soul's depth, then, gestures toward a past that lies beyond any particular bygone instance of experience—that is, toward the very origin of reasoned human existence.

Insofar as the soul's depth represents an ever-present access to the grounds of intelligibility, it offers a response to one aspect of Meno's paradox, namely, the question of how to recognize the answer one seeks. And yet, to end the story here would be to ignore the *other* aspect of Meno's problem—an implicit but crucial question left dangling even more precariously in Socrates' so-called "solution" to it: Before we rest content in the belief that we'll know the truth when we find it, how can we account for the possibility of beginning the search in the first place? How can we remember that we've forgotten whatever it is we've forgotten?

Alongside the possibility of hitting upon the truth and knowing it as such, the myth also gestures toward some other form of inner resourcefulness, a strong impetus and perdurance, reflecting back the way in which we ourselves are responsible for cultivating and sustaining our own relation to the grounds of intelligibility. Beyond the merely formal possibility of securing answers to the questions we ask, there is also the matter of initiating the effort to secure answers in the first place. Perhaps this effort depends on the predisposition of an individual soul, an acute kind of readiness to acknowledge its own ignorance and to be *moved* by what one finds—or rather, doesn't find. In short, the soul's mythical *bathos* seems to refer not just to knowledge, but also to *desire*. Though the image of depth refers, in the first instance, toward a kind of transcendent past, it also appears to anticipate a possible future experience because it compels attention to the sense of an absence within oneself; that is to say, it awakens desire.

In this light, the dual aspects of the soul's depth—knowledge and desire—begin to merge together, insofar as one can understand the reaching outward and upward to that which one desires to be guided by (or even indistinguishable from) the reaching inward and downward to the ultimate origins of one's thought-full existence. We also see that philosophy combines the two aspects of Meno's problem in one: philosophy aims at the deepest possible knowledge, namely, wisdom, due to a proportionally profound desire, namely, *love*. Yet it is no accident that philosophy must be conceived in this way, that is, as the zenith of that universally human desire to know, since deep desire and deep knowledge seem to presuppose and depend on one another.

Perhaps this tension or apparent contradiction in the soul's depth can help us to understand, in part, *Klein's* ambiguity about the root of Meno's incapacity: On the one hand, Klein says that Meno is unable to descend into the depths because there is, effectively, *nothing* to which he can turn (*CPM* 189). But to say that Meno's soul lacks depth on the level of intelligibility would amount to saying that he lacks the very grounds of possibility of all thought and speech; it would, in short, be to strip him of his humanity. Elsewhere, Klein says that Meno is incapable of learning, because he is *unwilling* to turn and descend into the depths (*CPM* 185). There must be *something* to which he could turn, if only he *would*. We have now to consider the possibility that the "depth" Meno lacks is gotten only by means of the very act of sounding it, as though it owes its being—or at least its manifestation—to the fact of being sought. Perhaps the trying *is* all?

There are echoes of this tension in yet another ambiguous aspect of the recollection myth—one often regarded as a mere *problem*, or at best a Socratic sleight-of-hand: If the myth is supposed to resolve any doubt that knowledge is recovered from within, and not acquired from without, then it fails to do so inasmuch as it doesn't explain how the knowledge latently present in our souls came to be there in the first place. The circularity is clear. And yet, even if we can disregard the possibility that the soul's "acquisition" of its original knowledge took place outside of time (an admittedly hefty "if"), we would still do well to remember that a circle need not always be vicious. If the latent presence of knowledge in the soul represents the capacity to learn, the myth's circularity suggests that, though we may be able to comprehend (or at least assent to) something about the character of the process of learning whenever it does occur, we still can't account for the presence or absence of an individual's capacity for undertaking that process. If we yoke together the two major "questions" Meno poses in the dialogue—first, how virtue is acquired, and second, how learning is possible—and recast them as a single one, we end up with a question to which the myth may be a gesture: "How is the possibility for *learning* acquired?" If there is any acquisition of knowledge that can—indeed, that *must*—be gathered from without, rather than uncovered within, is it not the acquisition of the knowledge of *how to acquire knowledge*? Is not this learning the most radical of all possible learnings? The trying *may* be all, but how might one try for that of which one has no notion?

The image of depth, it seems, is an image of the root of all questioning, in a double sense: it images both that ultimate reality toward which a question is turned *and* that incipient attunement to the possibility of perfection or *growth* or "augment" from or within oneself. The myth of recollection may, in a way, be meant to imbue its hearer with hope in the possibility of hitting upon the answers to our questions; but it does not pretend to dispel that restless penultimacy in the question of raising questions.

As Klein points out, any question, by its very nature, depends upon the presupposition that there is something we do not know and that we nonetheless can know (*ILE* 161). We can't, in other words, actually pose any question without believing in the possibility of answering it. But whereas questions of an everyday, practical, gossipy, or idly curious nature are directed toward unknowns whose reality and accessibility we can alight upon almost effortlessly, we human beings have also been known to ask questions—such as, "what is virtue?"—that lead us into depths and complexities such that presupposing we can answer these questions seems to call for a fairly radical leap of faith. If I were to ask you, for instance, if you happen to know what time it is, there isn't much room for wonder about the kind of answer I seek, nor about the availability of such an answer; if, however, you were to be asked how knowledge is acquired, then this question could be aimed at obtaining an exposition concise enough to memorize and pass along for posterity—or just for the sake of embellishing a debater's bag of tricks—just as easily as it could be directed toward gazing at one of the great mysteries of existence.

To witness the great range in depth from which such questions may be generated, and to which they may be directed, one need look no further than the very first pages of Augustine's *Confessions*—a book in which we also have what is certainly the most well-known image of the soul, and the memory, as a vast inner expanse.

> Lord, grant me to know and understand which is first, to call upon you or to praise you, and also which is first, to know you or to call upon you? But how does one who does not know you call upon you? For one who does not know you might call upon another instead of you. Or must you rather be called upon so that you may be known? Yet 'how

> shall they call upon him in whom they have not believed? Or how shall they believe without a preacher?' (*Confessions* I.1)[6]

Those inclined to view Meno's problem as a mere argument—and rather a bad one, at that—may be hard-pressed to dispel Augustine's version of the same sort of perplexity. In hearing Meno's paradox recast in relation to the prospect of eternal salvation, we feel not only the mysterious recognition of our ignorance, but even more the impetus to be moved by it rather than be paralyzed by hopelessness or offense. Meno is frustrating not because his "paradox" is inherently shallow or quarrelsome, but rather because, if issued from a different cast of mind, it would express what is perhaps the deepest and most searching of all questions, the one that gets to the bottom of our questioning—the absolute mother of all questions. In this light, the myth that Socrates offers in response to Meno's problem appears less a refutation than a call for a kind of *conversion*, an attempt to lead Meno to see the problem as a paradox—a question that, though it may not be strictly answerable, nonetheless incites a deep and searching desire for what is true. In recasting Meno's problem as a paradox, success would consist in Meno's hitting upon its significance by means of the very *act* of trying to ascertain its meaning. In coming to see a difference in *how* the question might be asked, the focus on the question of the *what* begins to recede. So very far is Socrates from wanting to shut down Meno's *problem* that he aims instead to deepen it so thoroughly that it engulfs itself, and the whole inquiry along with it. We have to ask—and yet, we can receive *nothing* that we don't already possess. If Meno's problem inflicts a pause that offers no advance, Socrates wishes to bring him to a standstill of wonderment, in which *advance* is beside the point. Where Meno tries to halt speech in its tracks and turn it to muteness, Socrates attempts to introduce into their inquiry the kind of active silence that describes an attitude of attentive *listen-*

ing. But how can this momentousness or *depth* be brought to one so fixated on words and the saying of them, if it is precisely *the words* that fail to incite this sort of reflection in the first place?

On this note, I look more deeply into the phenomenon of questioning.

On the Question of Questions

I begin with that stark claim of Klein's, that "Every one of us (that is, every human being on this earth, without exception) is in some way educated" (*ILE* 158). Klein goes on to tell us in what exactly this universally received "education" consists—namely, in the assimilation from early childhood of customs, beliefs, opinions, and behaviors, even feelings or second natures, if you will. This "elemental" education by which we become members of families and communities cultivates our humanity at the same time as we are maturing in body. "Ours is a double growth, double nourishment, double ripening" provided by those who inhabit the world in which we are raised, and by means of which we may grow into complete human beings. This education is mostly a passive, receptive kind of learning, more perhaps like a *feeding* than a *leading out*. "Most of the time," Klein writes, "we are not even aware of it" (*ILE* 158).

Within this elemental realm, we do ask questions, though mostly of a practical nature. We want to know whether to turn left or turn right, to know the name of that woman, how to drive this car. We ask because we have to *do* particular things. At other times, we are also wont to ask questions of a gossipy sort, which appear to have little to do directly with action and may spring from passions like vanity or envy. Furthermore, sometimes we ask questions from an idly curious standpoint, not for any practical reason but perhaps only for the charm of trivia. There is yet another kind of question—Klein calls it "exploratory"—in which we give more gravity to our inquiries about things whose certainty we have some significant investment in acquiring, in a trial, for instance, or in travels to foreign places, or about people's characters. All these sorts of questions, Klein reminds us, pay some tribute, in "very, very small coin" (*ILE* 160)—perceptible even in Meno's "small change" inquiry—to the pinnacle of that universal human desire to know that Aristotle mentions at the beginning of the *Metaphysics*.

Beyond this elemental education, our questions can be lifted and transformed, by a conscious formalization, to use Klein's terms, into "formal" education (*ILE* 158). In place of questions generated by the difficulties we find ourselves faced with in our everyday lives, we ask questions on a theoretical level, as we move within a medium of deliberate reflection and of systematic procedure; we require the development of certain formal disciplines, special arts or skills, in order to ascertain what is uncertain, to proceed methodically, to solve theoretical problems. Though this formalizing activity is intrinsically difficult and requires strenuous effort, nonetheless it remains rooted in our practical lives.

While all these sorts of questions arise, as Klein writes, out of the horizon of the familiar, there is yet another kind of question which, "as it were, tends to smash the bounds that limit us."

> We do occasionally stop altogether and face the familiar as if for the first time—anything: a person, a street, the sky, a fly. The overwhelming impression on such occasions is the strangeness of the thing we contemplate. This state of mind requires detachment, and I am not at all certain to what extent we can contrive its presence. We suddenly do not feel at home in this world of ours. We take a deep look at things, at people, at words, with eyes blind to the familiar. We re-flect. Plato has a word for it: *metastrophê* or *periagôgê*, a turnabout, a conversion. We detach ourselves from all that is familiar to us; we change the direction of our inquiry; we do not explore the unknown anymore; on

> the contrary, we convert the known into an unknown. We wonder. (*ILE* 162)

The image of *periagôgê* appears in the famous cave allegory in book VII of the *Republic*, in the moment that the unhappy prisoner is inexplicably freed from his shackles and forced to turn around and thereby to recognize the shadows projected on the wall of the cave as *mere shadows*. All that had been known to him before then is called into question, including what he thought he knew of himself. His blindness at the brightness of the fire he beholds for the very first time is attended by an awareness of another sort of blindness in regard to that which he *does* seem to see clearly.

Though we might be inclined to emphasize how this metastrophic reflection differs qualitatively from all other forms of questioning, Klein explains that it lies at the bottom of *all* possible questions. This ability to detach ourselves from our familiar experiences—"to turn about, to ask the radical question 'why' and to persist in it" (*ILE* 164)—underlies not only theoretical education (when held together with what Klein has called "exploratory" questioning), but also all education as such—that is, all questions. The kind of reflection Klein has in mind "calls myself in question with all my questioning . . . compels me to detach myself from myself, to transcend the limits of my horizon; that is, it educates me" (*ILE* 162). To put it another way: All questions as such "may ultimately derive from the human possibility of a total conversion" (*ILE* 163).

But what does this mean, that they "derive" from it? Must every human being, ever the recipient of elemental education and thus capable of posing all sorts of questions, be somehow already acquainted with the profoundest inward turning around of the whole soul? To put it in terms of the *Meno*: Is recollective learning always going on within each of us, including Meno? If so, how can we understand Meno as incapable of learning?

At this point it might look as though Meno is capable of learning elementally, but not formally. He has not effected the turn of mind that allows him to lift his questioning up to the level of theory. But this doesn't seem quite right, given his demonstrable skill in the art of rhetoric, for one thing. Given Klein's remarkable claim that the metastrophic question may be the basis of all questions, nor can we contend that Meno lacks the *converting capacity* altogether. While formal education arises out of, but remains rooted in, the horizon of the practical and the familiar (*ILE* 164), *liberal* education arises only as a consequence of one's making the metastrophic reflection one's explicit aim and deliberate mode. Learning becomes free and attains its greatest height—which is to say, its greatest depth—when the metastrophic attitude releases us from captivity to usefulness and allows us to abide in awareness of our questioning.

> It is only when we dedicate ourselves to the radical, metastrophic questioning, when we free ourselves from the ever-present concern that the burden of life imposes on us, that formal education becomes liberal education, that the formal disciplines become liberal disciplines or liberal arts. (*ILE* 164–65)

This suggests another turnabout, another conversion, which occurs at a higher level and which leads to a higher kind of learning.

Because truly *liberal* education involves an attitude of study with a view to the enjoyment of *leisure* (as Aristotle says in *Politics* VIII.3), that is, of learning for its own sake, its distinction from "mere" formal education depends on one's inner orientation toward it rather than on any particular content. "It is rather the *way* in which a formal discipline, a subject matter, is taken up that is decisive: whenever it is being studied for its own sake, whenever the metastrophic way of questioning is upheld, whenever genuine wonderment is present, liberal education is taking place." Moreover, only in pursuing this goal is man "really man and really free" (*ILE* 166).

All of this leads toward the possibility that Meno's alleged "incapacity" for learning should be viewed not as a failure to learn by recollection, but rather as a failure to recognize that what he is always already doing *is* learning by recollection. He already possesses within himself the capacity for conversion, which is revealed in the very problem to which the myth is supposed to be a solution. Meno's paradox or question could, if asked in a *different way*, reflect what is perhaps the *most* metastrophic of all possible questions. Maybe Meno lacks not the capacity for learning altogether, but rather the awareness of such a capacity, as well as the desire and the resolve to take his lights by it. As we have already seen, however, to lack an awareness of this might effectively be to lack the capacity itself. Meno has *lost nothing* of his birthright, except insofar as he has failed yet to live up to it, and yet one wonders if and when it becomes too late for remedy.

Perhaps we may learn more about the nature of Meno's problem in light of Socrates' approach to it. Though it might appear Socrates wants Meno to recover some sort of *historical* knowledge, it seems more likely he wants to induce in Meno what Klein calls the "metastrophic reflection" itself. The myth is aimed, in other words, not at getting its hearer to remember something that has been known (or said) in the past explicitly, but rather at getting its hearer to *convert* the known into an unknown, to recover something "forgotten," just *as forgotten.* And beyond this, one must become aware of this movement, and thus engage in it purposively and with effort. If memory is not just the faculty of remembering things past but is also that which, in the present, enables the mind to be present to itself, such that the mind may understand by virtue of its own thought (as Augustine proposes in *De Trinitate* XIV, 11 & 14), then the recollection myth takes aim at what might be called the very seat of attention. This would also hearken back to the second aspect of Meno's "paradox," namely, the question of the beginnings of inquiry. For if the myth is meant to address this aspect, as well as the question of how we recognize the truth as such, then it must address the matter of how an individual soul can become aware of the fact that it doesn't know (has forgotten) something in the first place, which is an awareness very distinctly in and of the *present.* The move Socrates wants Meno to make thus entails at once a presence to, and a leap out of, himself, out of the horizon of whatever he unthinkingly "thinks" he knows, to attend to the *presence* of something *absent* within his own soul. Can we call this the task of the teacher, then? Must the teacher be trusted with somehow inducing metastrophic awareness in the soul of another, thus enabling another to exercise his inner learning capacity? How might a teacher possibly go about such a thing, especially in view of the inward and *ineffable* nature of the end?

On the (Im)Possibility of Teaching

More than any other of Plato's dialogues, the *Meno* makes an explicit theme of the relation between teaching and learning. At first, it appears that the dialogue simply stands to correct a view of teaching and learning that, however wrong, according to Klein, "is ineradicable," namely, that learning consists in hearing and repeating, and teaching in telling and insisting.[7] As we have seen, according to the dialogue, "learning" is much less passive, and "teaching" much less possible, than is commonly thought.

In his *De Magistro* (*On The Teacher*), Augustine presents an extreme form of this demotion of human teachers. In that dialogue, he leads his son, Adeodatus, to the view that the possibility of learning depends not on human teachers but on the gift of divine illumination. Each human being who addresses another in speech intends to "teach" that other something, to convey some particular meaning, that may or may not be taken up (see *De Magistro* 1.1–2). Even if the intended meaning is understood by the one listening, this effect can't have been directly caused by the speaker, any more than a potted plant can be thought to cause directly some intense cerebration on the part of a passerby. The human teacher has no more power to cause understanding than does the plant. In Augustine's view, when it comes to the possibility of meaningful knowledge and speech, one human being is no more than an *occasion* on which another may or may not learn anything of significance. In the closing lines of the *Meno*, Socrates suggests that virtue must be gained by means of "divine dispensation," for those to whom it comes (100b); and perhaps as it is with virtue, so also with learning. The point here is not that we cannot learn by and through the help of others; it is rather that the very possibility—even the *necessity*—of doing so appears to depend upon something that so far exceeds our comprehension and capacity as to deserve no name but God. In the face of what would have many professional teachers understandably up in arms, it's important to remember that not all such *occasions* are equal. Still, however, if a teacher is regarded as one who tries to effect on purpose what might be done by a houseplant, the effect would be humbling indeed. (Perhaps here lies the rub.)

But if "teaching" is not possible, then what, exactly, is it? Beyond the view that teaching consists in telling and insisting, Klein offers two descriptions of what teaching does consist in—namely, "eliciting" and "begetting," where the first approach is more characteristic of Plato or Socrates and the latter more characteristic of Aristotle. All the same, each teacher makes use of each mode (*OLE* 267).

With respect to teaching as *eliciting*, Klein writes: "Through questioning and arguing the teacher compels the learner to pull out of himself, as it were, something slumbering in him at all times" (*OLE* 267). This coheres with the myth's view of learning as *recollection*. For if knowledge is acquired only by means of laborious recovery of knowledge from the dark recesses of one's own soul, then the teacher's task must be to facilitate that process by guiding the learner along an inquiry that compels him to do his own thinking. By this means, when the learner articulates something true, he must—because he *can*—judge *for himself* that it is true. This is the very stuff that Socrates means to show Meno through the "demonstration" in which he leads the slave-boy to recognize how to double the square. Even if Socrates does present "the truth," as it were, to the slave-boy, nevertheless it could not be apprehended as such were it not for the presence in the boy's soul of the proper conditions for learning. Though this sort of activity is often conflated with Socrates' so-called "maieutic" practice—his likening his role to that of a midwife to women in labor—for Klein it is worth noting that this latter art is mentioned only once, in the *Theaetetus*, in the context of conversing about the practice of disburdening others from unexamined opinions that have, more often than not, been "fathered" by others (see *Theaetetus* 157). Though Klein appears to view the consequence of teaching in the mode of eliciting as a positive acquisition, and that of teaching in the mode of midwifing as merely a negative one, what the two share in common is their guidance by the notion that the truth, as Klein reminds us, "according to Plato, has no father" (*OLE* 268).

Klein's description of teaching as *begetting* sounds somewhat more like "fathering" than we may be comfortable with, at least at first glance. Klein writes: "The word of the teacher acts as the form which in-forms the material of the learner's soul, in-forms the capability this soul has, and trans-forms it into a knowing soul" (*OLE* 267). According to this understanding, the act of teaching is a generative one, but not in the sense of implanting truth from without. Rather than leading out into the clear light of day what is already fully formed within the soul of another, the teacher's speech is viewed as giving shape to something hitherto shapeless within the learner's soul. It imbues inarticulate meaning-matter with definition and clarity, and thereby enables the learner to come to *knowledge* for and within himself, whereas whatever was there before could not have rightly been called by that name. This phenomenon, moreover, appears to depend upon some inner orientation on the part of the learner to receive the teacher's words with a view to the desire for what is true—that is, to rise to the occasion in desire for the truth.

In this light, teaching as "eliciting" and teaching as "begetting" appear not only *not* to be at odds with one another, but they even become less easily distinguished. In both cases, the act of the teacher presupposes and his "success" depends upon the presence of something internal to the soul of the learner—whether some kind of knowledge, or some desire, or both. And each approach depends upon some active attitude or apprehension on the part of the learner. In "eliciting" truth from another, the teacher acts in view of the presupposition that the learner has access to truth only from within himself, and not from without. And in "begetting" truth in the soul of another, the teacher depends upon some predisposition within the learner to be formed and shaped. Though a speaker may serve as a planter of seeds in the soul, in the form of significant speech, it is the character of the soul's *soil* that determines whether the seed will grow into some sustaining life form, or remain inert, wither, and finally die.

The responsibility of the teacher—as well as the institution of which the teacher is a member and a guardian—consists in providing the *conditions* that are necessary for learning to take place. Unfortunately, no one fully knows the magic recipe for these conditions. Accordingly, on those occasions when learning does occur, no one can be quite sure to whom to give credit for what—the teachers, the texts, the friendships, or "just plain time passing," to borrow Eva Brann's expression.[8] Still, it seems easier to recognize suitable *external* conditions for learning than the requisite conditions *internal* to the potential learner's soul. The subjective conditions required for the learner would consist in having certain passions, concerns, and attitudes that pervade one's life so thoroughly as to predispose one to notice, believe, trust, and value some things over others. And whence *this* internal condition? Does it belong intrinsically to each individual soul, or only to some by nature, or does it consist in some acquired capacity? Is the potency to become free and god-like innately and equally in us all?

Whether "eliciting" or "begetting," the teacher looks to be no more than an *occasion* on which the learner must do or have something for himself. We must not fall prey to that foolishness of confusing what is merely a necessary condition for an effect with the true cause of that effect (as Socrates enjoins us to remember in *Phaedo* 99b). Nor should we make the mistake of taking the role of necessary conditions too lightly. To provide an occasion includes offering words, but the words themselves cannot be thought to wield decisive power over the critical moment of learning or *not* learning. One can say the same thing until the cows come home, but there's no guarantee it will have any genuine or corresponding meaning for the one who hears it—or even, regrettably, for the one who utters it. One could say, for instance, that teaching doesn't consist in telling or insisting, that learning doesn't consist in hearing and repeating, and that learning happens best in conversation with others. One could say this for years, and yet fail to notice that one is aping another's speech and little more.

But learning *does* happen better in conversation with others, for if it didn't the words would be enough. *Responsiveness* lies at the heart of the learning capacity—not in a passive, deterministic-causal manner, but rather in the manner of attentive awaiting, so as to take up, an occasion for effortful search, for genuine understanding. For cultivating responsiveness to that which is other than, and potentially deeply impactful to, our human hearts and minds, there is no substitute for the living exchange amongst assorted other selves, the cyclical dance between inward and out, and upward and down, the sound of silent thought given flight with winged speech and again retreating, as it unfolds over time. It is no coincidence that our word *conversation* itself derives from the word for turning around, *conversion—conversatio*; for the moment of conversion seems to depend upon a decisive and profound receptivity to that which is beyond us, within, without, above, or beneath, unseen but not unheard. If conversation is where learning lives, then the teacher's task will consist not in talking about, but in actively participating in, genuine conversation, and will comprise an unfolding of active learning in the presence of other would-be learners. If the teacher's task does consist at all in conveying knowledge to the learner, then it would have to be knowledge of a very peculiar sort—knowledge, namely, of *how to learn*. But, as we have gleaned from the *Meno*, the possibility of acquiring this sort of knowledge—that is, the possibility of *learning how to learn*—seems to depend upon an incontestably radical, mysterious, and spontaneous transformation of the soul.

What, then, is a teacher to do? Even if the teacher were somehow to succeed in modeling the activity of learning for the would-be learner, so as to help the learner learn how to learn, this, in turn, depends upon the would-be learner first *recognizing*, and then also *desiring*, that activity for what it is. Even a paragon of learning in action will be utterly useless without an audience whose passions are disposed to see in such an example an object of admiration, inspiration, or love. But if it is the teacher's task, in addition to the modeling, to engage the passions of the would-be learner, this, too, is subject to infinite regress, at least in theory, if not in practice. Like that obscure beginning by which we first become learners, so that primordial moment of desire for genuine learning forever eludes our circumspection. For in respect of the effort to pull and shape some passion from worse to better, there is always something prior that has prepared and shaped the present state of the passions into what they are, in order for them to be plied in some particular direction. But if—as Socrates, Aristotle, and Augustine alike agree—all human beings, wanting to know, must *want* to know *truly*, then all that remains for the teacher to do is present to the learner, with unmistakable clarity, the true and perfect form of learning, and Bob's your uncle: the learner will seize at the chance. Or not.

And so we remain with the difficulty of wondering how learning can happen when teaching is not possible. And yet, whatever Socrates may or may not think about the relative possibility of "teaching" another, nonetheless he lives—and dies—under the auspices of a divine duty to search alongside of others for whatever wisdom and virtue really are.

The Way Up Is the Way Down

"The soul is undiscovered, though explored forever
to a depth beyond report."
Heraclitus, Fragment 71

While the cave allegory in book VII of the *Republic*, like the recollection myth, suggests that souls have depth, it appears nonetheless to paint a very different picture of learning, not only because the movement of learning appears to be outward and up, rather than inward and down, but also because learning appears to be initiated by an external force, over which one has little or no control. Nevertheless, it makes sense to turn to the cave allegory because it emphasizes the decisive pivot—the *periagôgê*—that makes it possible for a soul to learn. With the cave allegory, then, we descend ever deeper into the thicket of *conversion*.

For one thing, the imagery of the cave appears at once both to affirm and to subvert the order in the account we have inherited from the Greeks—namely, the notion that, of all the senses, sight stands closest to the act of knowing. The darkness of the cave, the consequent dimness of vision of its prisoners, and then the eventual dragging of the prisoner toward greater light and vision all appear to confirm the traditional association of vision and understanding. By contrast, Meno's fixation on hearing, on *being told*, suggests he is content with a more passive abiding in ignorance. The shackled prisoners in the cave likewise depend more on hearing than on seeing, for their heads and necks are fixed to look only straight ahead upon the shadows. But if *knowing* is best understood by means of *seeing* imagery, what, then, of *learning*? One reason for the aptness of the analogy between seeing and knowing is that seeing is more autonomous, and less vulnerable, than the other senses, hearing especially. One can force another to hear something, by calling out from behind, for instance, but one can hardly force another to look at something against his wishes. And yet, it is no accident that at the pivotal moment when he is freed in the cave, the prisoner is acted upon by an external force—and *from behind*, at that. The moment of conversion, as we've briefly seen, ultimately depends upon the actions of an *other*, unnamed, unseen, but perhaps not unheard. In any case, what is most intensely active in the moment of effortful *learning*, like that of attentive *listening*, is the resolute awareness of one's capacity for being moved, or for being arrested from movement, for being held captive, or freed from captivity. In short, it consists in an attentive awareness of need or a readiness to receive that which lies beyond one's purview—a need, that is, for that which is hidden from view, but may not be un-hearable. In what is perhaps the paradigmatic conversion story—the *Confessions*—Augustine speaks again and again of an irresolvable tension between his power and his powerlessness, his great responsibility and also his total dependence, when it comes to the decisive turning around of his soul. Learning in general seems to involve a similar kind of tension between responsibility for oneself and receptivity to what is outside oneself—as in an active attitude of listening.

To return to Meno: If hearing is such a fruitful analogy for learning, then what must we make of the fact that Meno's sense of hearing is so well-honed although he is not a good learner? While the relative passivity of hearing to seeing attests to Meno's need for a greater sense of responsibility toward his own education, still his receptivity to what exists outside of him suggests that he may be equipped with at least one aspect indispensable to the movement of learning. But perhaps it would behoove us not to stray too far into the land of the literal, and to keep ourselves close to the metaphorical willows. In that spirit, the fruitfulness of the comparison between one who stands in need of learning and one who needs conversion is concentrated most intensely in the parable of the sower of seeds:

> A sower went out to sow. And as he sowed, some seeds fell along the path, and the birds came and devoured them. Other seeds fell on rocky ground, where they did not have much soil, and immediately they sprang up, since they had no depth of soil, but when the sun rose they were scorched. And since they had no root, they withered away. Other seeds fell among thorns, and the thorns grew up and choked them. Other seeds fell on good soil and produced grain, some a hundredfold, some sixty, some thirty. He who has ears, let him hear. (Matthew 13:3–9 [ESV])

This imagery draws into sharp relief the poetic kinship between *depth* and *hearing* with regard to seeking the truth. Meno's inward expanse appears opaque to himself, which makes it hard and impenetrable—rocky, shallow soil in which only transient things can take root. While the organic matter in the rocky crevices may, to the untrained eye, be mistaken for real fecundity, it will bear plants with but a fleeting life. One might say that, as knowing is to seeing, so learning is to *listening*—an active receptivity with respect to that by which one might be the most deeply affected. Just as Meno's eristic paradox could, from a different turn of mind, express the profoundest and most impassioned of all questions, so his keen sense of hearing might, if inflected somehow differently, be an image of keenness to learn. Meno instantiates incongruity between the objective and subjective conditions that make learning possible. Whereas Meno merely hears, the learner listens; whereas he poses problems to handcuff Socrates, the learner seeks paradox to liberate thought; whereas he finds himself stuck in the mud, the learner pauses in silent, still reflection; and whereas he sates the shallows of his memorial stomach, the learner plumbs his fathomless memory, stretching out beyond a limit that does not cease, but rather incites, an ever expanding longing, an ever more far-reaching search.

For Meno, all is topsy-turvy: up is down, and down is up, though not in the right Heraclitean sense. Though Meno stands in need of a new (or renewed) sense of hope and confidence in his own responsibility and power with respect to knowing, that is, in his radical freedom from professional teachers in his endeavors to know, he also stands to gain the profound recognition of the role of *otherness* in his attempts to learn. That would engender receptivity and humility—and not just with respect to others without, but also with respect to that otherness of the self to itself by which Aristotle would have us learn what it takes to become happy. The way up in knowing, toward the glowing mouth of the cave, is an ascent of the soul, and yet it seems to depend upon the soul's being swayed and then led by someone else. The way down in knowing, toward the primordial origins of our knowledge and our love, is a descent of the soul into itself, and yet it seems to require a sense of transcendent capability, a penchant for the difficult feat of autonomy in arising out of and beyond oneself. To recognize that the way up *is* the way down is to be mindful of Socratic ignorance as more than mere pedagogical artifice. It is to embrace in one's attentive memory the very forgetfulness that bespeaks both the vast emptiness and the expansive fullness that mark the human soul's kinship with the divine. At the same time, one must also wonder whether Socrates' so-called *maieutic* practice isn't perhaps more significant, and more pervasive, than one might have surmised: for what greater gift can one soul give to another than the gift of otherness—both in the form of otherness of self altogether, and so a reminder of that which one has need of seeking, and in the form of awareness of detachment between one's ignorant and one's higher self, which is a need and a boon to the possibility of learning?

On the one hand, we witness in the recollection myth precisely that act in which Socrates attempts to generate an *occasion* for another, Meno, to learn something of utmost significance. The myth appears, as Klein points out, to be tailor-made for its hearer: the introduction of hearsay from reputedly wise people and the reference to the importance of the role of memory serve as enticements that are particular to Meno's specific proclivities (*CPM* 94–99). The emphasis on autonomy, on mystery or paradox, and on seeing over hearing all serve as correctives particular to his other tendencies. For instance, Meno has a penchant for being taught by "teachers," for passive acceptance of others' authoritative speech, for hitting upon clearly articulable (and so repeatable) answers to problems, for using "problems" as weapons against others in attempts at shared inquiry, and for seeing "problems" as hindrances to the quest for truth rather than as profound mysteries that incite correspondingly deep desires within the soul.

On the other hand, we also learn something of the crucial importance of the role of the teacher as an *occasion* for learning. The teacher may not be sufficient to induce learning but may be nonetheless *necessary*. If Socrates hopes to show Meno something about the importance of individual autonomy when it comes to the soul's self-education, perhaps he also means to show *us* something about the need for others to help one become aware of one's own ignorance. To remember a lost coin found is one thing, but to remember that one has forgotten it in the first place is something else altogether. It might call for an external reminder of some kind—a need, a demand, a *question*—without which one would have neither the reason nor the means to incite the search to begin with. The role of others in learning—and so, the deliberate and self-imposed burden of the teacher—consists in reminding another of what one is not and knows not, and in such a way as to let that other desire to *become*. This makes the teacher look rather more important than a houseplant, to say the least. On the other hand, to recognize this power and responsibility is at the same time to acknowledge one's indebtedness to, and dependence upon, others for the same. Even if an individual soul can attain to some self-transcendence and self-sufficiency by cultivating a sort of friendly, internal otherness (as though Aristotle's parts of soul could, in effect, become friends with one another, thereby learning and teaching reciprocally), still there is no ultimate substitute for the otherness that arises by way of selves altogether other, as they dance back and forth amongst themselves in conversation. To abstain from the dance, to profess without passion, is to risk nothing, and so likewise to gain nothing.

The meaning of the myth may be to point us to humility—the very thing that Meno lacks, if not in substance, at least in vision. When Socratic ignorance is read as "ironic" in the sense that it's a condescending cloak, it is often perhaps in part due to the failure to recognize humility for the immensely difficult and desirable task that it is—difficult, but desirable, for out of its unsounded depths arise all questions we regard as perennial. Wherein does recollection end? How can memory reach beyond itself with such force as to move and then to lead us? How can we guard against the refusal of our origins in the transcendent, against the loss of imaginative depth, of the soul in tune with the chords of otherness? How can we cleave to a world that is both too much and not enough, a world in which mystery is beyond, but not contrary to reason? How to endure in a longing that doesn't deny itself an ending in a question mark?

An Introduction to Klein's Response to Heidegger

A Reading of "Aristotle, an Introduction"

PAUL T. WILFORD

Jacob Klein's most important philosophical teacher was Martin Heidegger. In an autobiographical joint presentation with Leo Strauss, Klein credits a seminar led by Heidegger with first teaching him how to "understand something written by another man, namely, Aristotle."[1] Klein's almost complete silence about Heidegger in his published writings is, therefore, somewhat surprising. Given that Klein's lifelong preoccupation with reading old books, uncovering submerged presuppositions, and re-visiting the roots of the philosophic tradition stand in proximity to Heidegger's own investigation of the tradition, why such reticence to speak about his erstwhile teacher? Is it due exclusively to Heidegger's reprehensible politics, or is there also an underlying theoretical reason?

Klein's acknowledgement that Heidegger helped him understand Aristotle makes especially conspicuous Heidegger's absence from Klein's essay, "Aristotle, an Introduction." Although it was first delivered as a public lecture intended to be accessible to students, Klein subsequently revised and published it in a 1964 *Festschrift* for Leo Strauss, entitled *Ancients and Moderns.*[2] We should expect Klein chose this essay as particularly suited to honoring his friend Strauss. As we will see, the essay addresses the friendship proper to philosophic conversation in the Socratic tradition, which Aristotle preserves: "It is in speech, in searching for and finding adequate words, that the λόγος of things, the λόγος of nature (φύσις) becomes audible and capable of being understood" (179). That conversation yields both shared understanding and disagreement, which provides for continuity and conflict within the tradition.

While Klein's essay provides an introduction to Aristotle's thought, it operates simultaneously at much deeper levels. It examines Aristotle's disagreement with Plato concerning "the one immense difficulty within ancient ontology, namely, to determine the relation between the 'being' of the object itself and the 'being' of the object in thought."[3] At yet another level, the essay confronts Heidegger, especially Heidegger's reading of Aristotle. Klein's ostensibly introductory presentation of Aristotle's teaching, we see, raises fundamental philosophic questions that cannot be answered within the limitations of the essay or this reading of it. While my interpretation is intended to be ministerial to the richness and depth of Klein's essay, I will also develop the thesis that Heidegger is the essay's unnamed interlocutor.

Although Klein never publicly articulated the reasons for his break with Heidegger, it seems that, as with his friend Leo Strauss, the break turned on how, why, and on what basis one can read old books. Strauss explains that Heidegger helped give them access to ancient philosophy.

> Heidegger's work required and included what he called *Destruktion* of the tradition. (*Destruktion* is not quite so bad as destruction. It means taking down, the opposite of construction.) He intended to uproot Greek philosophy, especially Aristotle, but this presupposed the laying bare of its roots, the laying bare of it as it was in itself and not as it had come to appear in the light of the tradition and of modern philosophy. Klein was more attracted by the Aristotle brought to light and life by Heidegger than by Heidegger's own philosophy.[4]

In Klein's words: "My studies led me to conclude: we have to relearn what the ancients knew."[5] Strauss goes on to say that Klein convinced him of the need for a return to and recovery of classical philosophy. And so Klein's introduction to Aristotle has at its core the perennial question identified by Aristotle: "'*What* is being (τὸ ὄν)?—that is, *what* is beingness (οὐσίᾳ)?—that is the question of ancient times and the question now and the question always, and always the puzzle one faces.'"[6] In Heidegger's formulation from *Being and Time*, this becomes "the question of the meaning of Being."[7] And as Klein's essay suggests, following both Aristotle and Heidegger, the question of Being is inseparable from the question of λόγος.

Given the immense scope and complexity of such questions, this essay aspires to be nothing more than an introduction to Klein's introduction. If it serves to indicate the essay's philosophical depth and subtlety, then it will have achieved its aim. Given such a caveat, however, let me state the essay's general conclusion: Klein breaks with Heidegger (at least) over the possibility of recovering a natural horizon for philosophic inquiry. In short, Klein's essay on Aristotle is a defense of classical philosophy, understood as the dialogue between Plato and Aristotle. It offers a genuine alternative to Heidegger's analytic of Dasein's radical facticity, the *Destruktion* of the tradition, and the historicity of Being.[8] At the heart of this argument is the status of λόγος. Klein implicitly juxtaposes Aristotle's appropriation of Socrates' second sailing (the turn to speeches in order "to examine the truth of the beings in them")[9] to Heidegger's account of Dasein's "saying of Being" (*Sagen des Seins*). For both of them λόγος opens up possibilities for the study of being, but ineliminable obstacles and limitations remain.

Klein's essay proceeds by contrasting Plato and Aristotle. The complexity in the thought of each of them renders it especially difficult to understand both together. My reading involves an additional contrast of Heidegger with Aristotle or of Heidegger with Aristotle and Plato together. Needless to say, a complete treatment easily exceeds the bounds of a single essay. At the present time, I restrict myself to clearing the ground for a more thorough exposition. First, I will provide a synoptic view of the whole essay, identifying its constitutive parts and highlighting several peculiarities of Klein's presentation, which suggest a profound pedagogic intention at work in the essay. Second, I will focus on the very opening of the essay, especially Klein's decision to begin with facts from Aristotle's biography and from his own, which will provide some evidence for reading Klein's introduction to Aristotle as a confrontation with Heidegger. Although Klein refers to Heidegger in the essay, he refrains from using his name.[10] My goal is not to read Heidegger into the essay, but rather to practice the art of reading as described by Jacob Klein himself.[11]

I. The Structure and Logic of Klein's Essay

Klein's essay is divided into four parts:

- §1 A biography of Aristotle, emphasizing the centrality of his relation to Plato (171–74)
- §2 An account of λόγος that emphasizes the continuity with Plato (175–79)
- §3 An account of five substantive disagreements with Plato (180–94)
- §4 A conclusion or coda that locates man between animals and gods, on the one hand, and in the *polis*, on the other (194–95)

This outline makes immediately evident that for Klein the key to understanding Aristotle lies in his relation to Plato. Although it may seem obvious to the point of banality, I think it is appropriate here to quote Strauss: "The problem inherent in the surface of things, and only in the surface of things, is the heart of things."[12] In this case, the problem on the surface and at the heart of Klein's essay is the dialectic or the λόγος between Plato and Aristotle. Klein's account has a peculiar character in that he contrasts Aristotle both with Plato and with Heidegger. More precisely, he places Heidegger in a tacit confrontation (*Auseinandersetzung*) with an explicit opposition between Plato and Aristotle. Opposed to Heidegger is a dyad, one conversation between two minds. In recovering this dialogue between two philosophers, Klein presents something conspicuously absent from any of Plato's dialogues, namely, a conversation between equals. As Klein recounts, Heidegger himself introduced Aristotle while ignoring his relation to Plato. While that made sense to the young Klein, his independent efforts to understand Aristotle led him to conclude that "we simply cannot ignore" his dialogic relation to Plato; Aristotle's "words bring up the words of another man who was his teacher" (171). The recovery of this dialogue constitutes Klein's response to Heidegger's historicism. The explicit action of the essay—the argument between Aristotle and Plato—points to Klein's tacit argument with Heidegger; for the action of the essay demonstrates the possibility of "acknowledg[ing] Greek ontology without being in the polis."[13]

Rather than juxtaposing Aristotle's teaching on οὐσία with Heidegger's history of Beyng (*Seyn*), Klein points to a mode or manner of philosophizing—one exemplified by the essay itself—that would constitute a response to Heidegger's philosophy. In other words, although the radical disagreement between Heidegger and Aristotle can be stated in terms of their antithetical ontological teachings,[14] Klein does not foreground issues of οὐσία, substance, actuality, or presence (*Anwesen*). Rather, the evident actuality of λόγος in general and of *the* particular λόγος between Aristotle and Plato is foremost throughout Klein's essay. Any ontological argument would need to account for these two perspicuous facts and address the question, what is being such that λόγος is possible?

Bracketing the introduction and conclusion for the moment, I turn to the two central parts of the essay to highlight the peculiarity of Klein's approach to Aristotle, which does not attempt "to encompass in a brief statement the whole of Aristotle's philosophy," but only to "point to, or rather hint at, some of the fundamental features of [that] vast edifice" (174–75).

Klein begins with a somewhat peculiar table of terms, noting that they are common Greek terms, which, although not originally Aristotelian, come to have "to a large degree an uncommon and unambiguous significance" in Aristotle's philosophy (175).

φύσις (*nature*)	ζωή (*life*)			
ψυχή (*soul*)	νοῦς (——)	ἄνθρωπος (*man*)	τέχνη (*art*)	λόγος (——)
τάξις (*order*)	κόσμος (*world*)			

I highlight three oddities. First, Klein does not include any term pertaining directly to the question of being, such as τό ὄν, τὸ τί ἦν εἶναι, οὐσία, ἀρχή, αἰτία, or τέλος, not to mention ἐνέργεια and δύναμις, which pervade Aristotle's philosophy. Indeed, Aristotle's relation to Plato turns on the distinction between ἐνέργεια and δύναμις, which becomes clear in the third part of the essay where Aristotle uses these terms to articulate differences in the mode or manner of something's being.

Second, the list includes no direct reference to man's political nature. While φύσις and κόσμος are present, πόλις and νόμος are conspicuously absent.[15] If, as Klein asserts, Aristotle is in a certain fundamental agreement with "Platonic—and Socratic—philosophizing" (174), how can the political be justifiably absent from Klein's account? Elsewhere Klein asserts the centrality of political concerns in philosophy:

> Almost the entire body of traditional philosophical terminology is derived from the language of political life, and especially the language of the courts. This shows the general preponderance of political interest in all of our thinking. It was primarily the questioning of political patterns and habits which gave rise to an inquiry into the nature of things.[16]

Third, Klein does not explain the ordering or arrangement of the terms. He does not tell us why he divides them into two columns, nor the principle governing the selection of the three pairs of terms, nor the meaning of the juxtaposition. This suggests Klein has adopted one of two strategies he describes for writing so as to be understood. One strategy is "to say *explicitly all* that is *necessary* for the meaning to be grasped," but there is another way:

> Here the most important and decisive is *not* said explicitly at all. Compositions of this kind tend to articulate the whole in such a way as to make us wonder why the parts are arranged as they are. We are compelled to raise questions about the link that holds them together. . . . [W]ritings of this kind taunt us [with] . . . the taunting presence of a hidden answer, yet of an answer within our reach.[17]

This last oddity helps us recognize the sort of introduction Klein is writing. "Aristotle, an Introduction" is not so much a conventional, simplified, and pre-digested summary for the beginning student, as it is an attempt to *induce* the reader into the heart of Aristotle's philosophizing.[18] Accordingly, the essay continually raises (or points to) questions that it does not answer. In this manner, we come to learn by the end of the essay that this chart is not so much a synopsis of Aristotelian terminology, as a set of phenomena in need of explanation. These are the objects of Aristotle's wonder and are thus the primary concepts (*Grundbegriffe*) of Aristotle's philosophy.[19] The question of the relation of the two halves of the table turns out to express the central question of the essay, which Klein seems to think is also the central question of philosophy as such: What is the condition of the possibility of philosophy? Or, how are things intelligible in the first place?

Klein proceeds to dive right in, declaring that "unavoidably, we have to begin with λόγος" (175). The commonsense, everyday understanding of λόγος as audible discourse between a speaker and a hearer who share some understanding quickly leads to a question about units of shared meaning or νοητά that pass back and forth between interlocutors in conversation. The question of the referent of the νοητά leads to the question of the relation between "human speech" and "the language of the things themselves," which Klein connects to Socrates' second sailing (176). Klein concludes this second section of his essay by underscoring Aristotle's continuity with the Socratic turn to speeches in order to find "the reasons for things being as they are," arguing that for Aristotle no less than for Socrates, "it is in speech, in searching for and finding adequate words, that the λόγος of things, the λόγος of nature (φύσις) becomes audible and capable of being understood" (179). For present purposes, I want to highlight the doubly directed character of λόγος, or what might be termed its dual mediating power: Speech is the medium in which we grasp the intelligibility of beings, and it is the medium in which we understand one another.

Λόγος means principally intelligible speech. "In a manner which, itself, is hardly or not at all understandable, the sounds [of which our speech consists] carry with them—or embody or represent—something else, precisely that which *makes* us understand, whenever we understand." Speech trades on the possibility of shared intelligibility, even as all speech risks being misconstrued. Such misunderstanding, however, is possible only if speech is in fact intelligible. Misunderstanding, as well as the humorous pun or ironic remark, plays on the possibility of polysemous speech, on the possibility of the same sound conveying a multiplicity of possible meanings, a plurality of possible referents. Despite such ambiguities, the primary function of speech consists in the communication of an intended meaning between two or more persons. "The speaker transposes what he means into sounding words, and the hearer who understands reverses that process in reaching back to the intended meaning. The intended meaning is what the Greeks call τὸ νοητόν . . . a verbal adjective of νοεῖν." Λόγος is inextricably bound up with τὸ νοητόν; that is, speech is bound up with understanding. Λόγος, hence, means "inseparably both speech and that which can be and is being understood *in* speech" (175–76).[20] Though Klein does not highlight the connection, he has passed from the right side of the table to the left, for νοεῖν is derived from the noun νοῦς. Λόγος is the manifestation of soul possessing νοῦς;[21] νοῦς appears in the world as λόγος. Λόγος is first and foremost that which passes between two human beings, so much so that the Stranger from Elea in Plato's *Sophist* can assert that "thought [διάνοια] and speech [λόγος] are the same," only that διάνοια is "a *silent inner conversation* of the soul with itself,"[22] which raises the question of whether the exchange of νοητά in audible speech is somehow more primary than private thought.

Both private thought and public speech are directed at something other than themselves, which Klein describes as intentionality. But how the sounds we make convey meaning may be "not understandable at all" (175). Clearly we use speech to convey intended meanings, as though speech were something in one's possession like a tool to be deployed at will. And yet speech draws much of its power because the λόγος conveyed in sound is not simply dependent on our will. Consider the almost proverbial injunction Socrates issues to his interlocutors to follow the λόγος where *it* leads.[23] Klein emphasizes the wondrous character of discourse, trying to help the reader see that what is wholly familiar, because constitutive of every possible mode of our being,[24] is in fact passing strange. We cannot follow Klein's introduction to Aristotle without first being struck that "The power of discourse is the power inherent in human speech," which is perhaps the "greatest marvel . . . under the sun."

Klein's stress on understanding and human speech culminates in a description of man as the animal possessing speech that sounds almost Heideggerian:

> It is in *man* and through *man* (ἄνθρωπος) that λόγος manifests itself conspicuously, so much so that Aristotle is able to say: 'Man is a living being possessing speech,' and that means possessing the ability to *understand* the spoken word (ζῷον λόγον ἔχον). (176)

Klein's stress upon man as the locus of λόγος's self-manifestation is striking. Klein subordinates man to speech; rather than being the progenitor, master, or even artisan of λόγος, he is its conduit or home, its dwelling. The emphasis on λόγος as the subject and man as the medium is highlighted by the unusual locution "speech 'bespeaks' . . . everything man is familiar with," which includes earth and sky, living beings and artifacts, and the customs and institutions that shape human life "in misery or happiness, in friendship or enmity, in praise or blame." "That is what his speech and understanding are *mostly* about" (176).[25] Klein elsewhere insists on this point: "It is in *man* and, to repeat, *only* through *man* that λόγος manifests itself conspicuously. Neither birds nor porpoises nor seals have λόγος, though they are able to 'communicate' with each other and even with human beings."[26] Man's speech implies not only dependency on the world and its relations, but also a privileged access to them; the priority of the world with its τάξις that man experiences as intelligible through λόγος seems to be the condition for audible λόγος to convey τὰ νοητά. This would imply that the items named on the right side of Klein's table depend on those identified on the left. Our speech and its νοητά do not appear to originate from within us but rather from the intelligibility of the beings themselves. In Klein's presentation, the question about what has to be the case for thinking to be possible ultimately leads to cosmological speculation and the postulation of the eternity of the cosmos.

The common commitment to the investigation in speech of the beings themselves nevertheless leads to at least five interrelated, Aristotelian modifications of the Platonic-Socratic teaching (179). The details of this complicated analysis cannot be considered here, and yet it is important to note that each is explored through considering the distinction between ἐνέργεια and δύναμις, especially in relation to εἶδος and ὕλη. The thread running through this section—from Klein's treatment of Aristotle's account of γένεσις to his presentation of Aristotle's description of νοήσεως νόησις—is the problem of the relation between the εἴδη and the νοητά, between what makes the beings what they are and what makes the beings intelligible. How are the εἴδη both being-at-work in the world and being-at-work in our understanding? As Klein states in *Greek Mathematical Thought and the Origin of Algebra*, "the one immense difficulty within ancient ontology, [is] to determine the relation between the 'being' of the object itself and the 'being' of the object in thought."[27]

II. The Peculiar Circumstance in Aristotle's Life[28]

In 1959, a few years before Klein revised his lecture for Strauss's *Festschrift*, Strauss composed some brief remarks on the occasion of Klein's sixtieth birthday. Other than some playful teasing about Klein's abhorrence of "the limelight," Strauss focuses almost entirely on Klein's relation to Heidegger. After noting the profound effect of Heidegger on the "lasting directions" of their thought, Strauss states the challenge of Heidegger succinctly:

> Heidegger, who surpasses in speculative intelligence all his contemporaries and is at the same time intellectually the

> counterpart to what Hitler was politically, attempts to go a way not yet trodden by anyone or rather to think in a way in which philosophers at any rate have never thought before. Certain it is that no one has questioned the premise of philosophy as radically as Heidegger.[29]

Strauss does not explain what he means in describing Heidegger as "intellectually the counterpart" to Hitler, but in what follows Strauss emphasizes the radicality of the innovation, the revolutionary nature of the project, its destructive dimension, the totalizing nature of the ambition, and the fact that one individual overwhelmed Germany.[30]

The magnitude of Heidegger's influence on the generation of German thinkers that came of age between the wars can hardly be overstated. Hannah Arendt and Hans Jonas would later recall how even before the publication of *Being and Time*, Heidegger's reputation as a teacher spread amongst students of their generation who, dissatisfied with conventional academic offerings, were in search of something commensurate to their sense of dislocation.[31] As Strauss recalled, "gradually the breadth of the revolution of thought which Heidegger was preparing dawned upon me and my generation. We saw with our own eyes that there had been no such phenomenon in the world since Hegel."[32] The famous 1929 Davos debate between Heidegger and Cassirer "revealed the lostness and emptiness of . . . academic philosophy to everyone who had eyes."[33] Against this background we appreciate Strauss's praise of Klein:

> While everyone else in the young generation who had ears to hear was either completely overwhelmed by Heidegger, or else, having been almost completely overwhelmed by him, engaged in well-intentioned but ineffective rearguard actions against him, Klein alone saw why Heidegger is truly important: by uprooting and not simply reject-

> ing the tradition of philosophy, he made it possible for the first time after many centuries—one hesitates to say how many—to see the roots of the tradition as they are and thus perhaps to know, what so many merely believe, that those roots are the only natural and healthy roots.[34]

These general remarks accord with Klein's autobiographical reflection in "A Giving of Accounts." Recalling his studies, including his doctoral dissertation ("which is not worth the paper on which it was written"), Klein states, "I always felt that I could not really understand anything outside me, could not understand anything uttered or written by another person. I felt that I was in a kind of vicious circle out of which I could find no escape."[35] Tempting as it may be to dismiss this as an instance of Klein's self-effacing modesty, it is extremely important that Klein highlights *this* deficiency in particular. For an individual who would devote his adult life to conversation, to trying to understand the words of other human beings—both spoken and written—and who emphasizes in his own writings that "λόγος cannot help moving in the medium of the immediately understandable" (176), it is a remarkable admission. While Klein may be exaggerating for pedagogic purposes, his self-description as suffering a condition bordering on solipsism highlights the transformative effect of hearing Heidegger's exposition of Aristotle: "I was struck by one thing: that he was the first man who made me understand something written by another man, namely, Aristotle. It broke my vicious circle. I felt that I could understand. Then I began studying seriously, for myself, seriously, not superficially."[36] Klein's debt to Heidegger is encapsulated in that experience of understanding Aristotle making possible serious as opposed to superficial study.

Klein does not elaborate here on the difference between superficial and serious study, but a plausible interpretation is that it parallels the distinction he makes elsewhere between two types of questioning: that born of idle curiosity and what he terms "metastrophic questioning" in which "we detach ourselves from all that is familiar to us; we change the direction of our inquiry; we do not explore the unknown any more; on the contrary, we convert the known into an unknown. We wonder."[37] We ask "Why is that so?" not in search of factual information or to learn about a specific operation, process, or event. Such questioning "does not lead to any discovery or recovery. It calls myself in question with all my questioning. It compels me to detach myself from myself, to transcend the limits of my horizon; that is, it educates me. It gives me the freedom to go to the roots of all my questioning."[38] Metastrophic questioning frees one to examine the grounds of one's questioning activity and to look upon such grounds with wonder.[39] It liberates from one's own idiosyncratic particularity and from all historical parochiality: metastrophic questioning is simultaneously the condition of the possibility of self-knowledge and the answer to the hermeneutic problem.[40]

If the setting of Klein's *periagôgê* was Heidegger's Aristotle seminar, the proximate cause was the theoretical plausibility of the de-sedimentized philosophy of Aristotle. Strauss accounts for the novelty of Heidegger's presentation of Aristotle first by observing that "Heidegger was the first great German philosopher who was a Catholic by origin and training" and so possessed "a premodern familiarity with Aristotle [and] thus was protected against the danger of trying to modernize Aristotle." Nevertheless,

> as a philosopher Heidegger was not a Christian: he thus was not tempted to understand Aristotle in light of Thomas Aquinas. Above all, his intention was to uproot Aristotle: he thus was compelled to disinter the roots, to bring them to light to look at them with wonder. Klein was the first to understand the possibility which Heidegger had opened without intending it: the possibility of a genuine return to

> classical philosophy, to the philosophy of Aristotle and of Plato, a return with open eyes and in full clarity about the infinite difficulties which it entails.[41]

One product of Klein's turn "to the study of classical philosophy with a devotion and a love of toil, a penetration and an intelligence, an intellectual probity and a sobriety in which no contemporary equals him" (and so the ultimate fruit of his encounter with Heidegger) was *Greek Mathematical Thought and the Origin of Algebra*.[42] While the focus of the present essay precludes even a cursory engagement with this remarkable work, it is important to note that this book is not just about mathematics but about the conditions of science, that is, the intelligibility of being, and about the possibility of recovering a pre-modern outlook, or in Hegel's formulation, the perspective of "natural consciousness."[43]

Let us now turn back to the opening of "Aristotle, an Introduction":

> Many, many years ago, I attended a series of lectures on Aristotle's philosophy. The lecturer began his exposition as follows: "As regards Aristotle himself, as regards the circumstances and the course of his life, suffice it to say: Aristotle was born, spent his life philosophizing, and died." (171)

These remarks refer to the 1924 course Heidegger gave entitled *Grundbegriffe der aristotelischen Philosophie*.[44] In the audience were some of the most preeminent figures of twentieth-century philosophy, including Hans-Georg Gadamer, Helene Weiss, Hans Jonas, Leo Strauss, and Karl Löwith. Heidegger's introduction was memorable, not only for Klein. Arendt, for example, would recall many years later almost exactly the same words when describing the relation between philosophic thought and the accidental features of mind's embodiment.[45] Heidegger's avowed purpose in the lecture course is to "see the *ground* out of which" certain basic Aristotelian concepts have arisen and, thereby, enable us to consider the basic concepts "in their *specific conceptuality*" and by understanding "the basic concepts . . . with regard to their conceptuality" gain "*insight into the fundamental exigencies of scientific research.*"[46] Heidegger's reading of Aristotle is therefore intended to be pertinent to all scientific investigation insofar as Aristotelian conceptuality continues to rule over the Western conception of the essence of science (*Wissenschaft*). As Heidegger states explicitly, the selection of Aristotle for such careful examination rests on the presupposition that to Aristotle "belongs a distinctive position not only within Greek philosophy, but within Western philosophy as a whole."[47]

Indeed, it would be hard to overstate the importance of Aristotle for Heidegger, and this lecture course is but one of Heidegger's many treatments of Aristotle. As is commonly remarked, Heidegger's early engagement with Franz Brentano's *On the Manifold Sense of Being in Aristotle* helped determine the direction of Heidegger's thought. Subsequently, Aristotle proved decisive as Heidegger broke with Husserl through (according to Heidegger) a radicalization of Husserl's own phenomenological method of inquiry.[48] From the 1920s onwards, Aristotle's significance to every dimension of Heidegger's thought is evident. Although discriminating amongst various aspects of Heidegger's thought is problematic, for the sake of presentation we can identify six axes of confrontation: (1) philologically, as one sees in all the lecture courses of the 1920s leading up to and culminating in *Being and Time*, Heidegger was developing his own distinct philosophic lexicon in relation to Aristotle's Greek; (2) hermeneutically, Heidegger would return again and again throughout his career to Aristotle as the quintessential expression of the Greek way of thinking being;[49] (3) anthropologically, Heidegger would oppose the designation of the human being as Dasein to the definition of man as the rational animal;[50] (4) logically, Heidegger would attempt to overthrow the Aristotelian presupposition that assertoric logical statements are the primary form of λόγος—an endeavor that would require overturning Aristotle's commitment to the principle of non-contradiction as the fundamental rule of thought and meaningful speech; (5) ontologically, Heidegger argues that the tradition of classical metaphysics—with its emphasis on being as presence and being as what always is—is definitively determined by Aristotle's doctrine of being as οὐσία; (6) theologically, Heidegger takes Aristotle's identification of eternally active νοῦς with god as the quintessential expression of onto-theological metaphysics (that is, Being is understood as a being, even if it is the highest being, thus obscuring the ontological difference).[51] For Heidegger, the nerve of Western metaphysics is the errancy of the onto-theological interpretation of being, an interpretation of the being of beings as determinate actuality that is first rendered systematic in Aristotle.[52] If Aristotle is the beginning of the decline of the West, the decline into *Seinsvergessenheit* (the forgetting of Being), it is because he is the end of the Greek beginning or inception (*Anfang*), both insofar as he is the final expression of a mode of thought and insofar as he is the *telos* of that line of thought—the *non plus ultra* expression of its presuppositions.[53] Without exaggeration, one can say that, for Heidegger, the fate of Western metaphysics is contained in Aristotle's teaching.[54]

Thus, by directing our attention to Heidegger at the beginning of his essay on Aristotle, Klein subtly indicates the scope of his inquiry and the significance of the possibility of understanding Aristotle as he understood himself.[55] Klein notes that at the time he thought Heidegger's beginning entirely appropriate—cutting through philological pedantry and the historico-critical baggage common to academic scholarship—for all we really have access to are Aristotle's philosophic works; everything else is incidental to the thought and so can be bracketed. But Klein came to realize this was inadequate; for in every attempt "to understand what Aristotle is saying," we find "that his words bring up the words of another man who was his teacher" (171). Klein concludes: "There is no alternative: we have to face that peculiar circumstance in Aristotle's life" (171). Thus Klein's rejection of Heidegger's approach is not really a turn to Aristotle's biography in the conventional sense (for example, there is no mention of the sort of details usually included in an account of Aristotle's life such as being the son of a physician) or a historical contextualization (besides the brief remark about Alexander, there is no explicit discussion of politics save for the politics of philosophy). It is rather an attempt to bring into focus the principal foil required for understanding Aristotle, namely, his dialogical partner.

With this justification that throughout Aristotle's corpus one always encounters echoes of Plato, Klein offers a brief chronology of Aristotle's life, noting when Aristotle would have been in Athens, studied under Plato, moved abroad, and returned to found the Lyceum. This is followed by a discussion of the nature of the texts that have come down to us as well as when and where they might have been composed. Klein concludes that regardless of all such questions, the Aristotelian writings we possess

> bear an unmistakable stamp: the language and peculiar terms in which they are written. Whatever the degree of incoherence or coherence in the body of Aristotelian writings, their language has always the same characteristic mold. And, what is more, the shadow of Plato is always perceivable in them. (173)

A brief account of when Aristotle might have composed various writings seems sufficient for Klein's purposes, yet he goes out of his way to address explicitly a tendency in classical scholarship to try to date Aristotle's works in a manner comparable to the task of finding the correct chronological sequence for Plato's dialogues.[56] Klein notes that philologists have attempted to construct "the development of Aristotle's thinking and to distinguish a 'Platonic period' in Aristotle's life from a post-Platonic, and finally an anti-Platonic phase" (173). However, before concluding that the evidence for establishing such stages in Aristotle's thinking is woefully insufficient—not to mention the fact that interpreting the chronology of a philosopher's writing as "mirroring the development of [their] own thinking . . . is a sign of considerable naïveté or of no less considerable rashness"—Klein appears to make something of a concession to those enterprising philologists. For he acknowledges "that Aristotle's thinking must have had a history," and he grants "that what we call his philosophy did not spring out of him as Pallas Athena did out of Zeus' forehead" (173–74). This seemingly off-hand remark—within a philological discussion that is itself set within Klein's biography of Aristotle and opposed to Heidegger's immediate entry into philosophical questions—is worth considering more closely. For Klein's metaphor serves not only to admit the temporal conditions of human thinking but also to highlight the difference between wisdom as a god would possess it and wisdom as a man might pursue it. One might say that it playfully points at the serious question about the relation of thought to history or the diachronic dimension of human thinking. In other words, the philological endeavor that Klein criticizes surreptitiously presupposes a particular view of the relation of history and thinking. Insofar as historical science obscures the philosophic foundations of its method, its attempt to uncover origins is in fact a further sedimentation of the fundamental question. That is, the conventional approaches to the history of philosophy tend to supplant philosophical inquiry into the grounds of λόγος, that is, inquiry into the relation of the νοητά in λόγος to the εἴδη. Nevertheless, one cannot simply dispense with philology, precisely because human thought does not spring from Zeus's forehead. Thus we can understand Klein's digression as a brief indication of the "infinite difficulties" that confront an attempt to recover the Platonic-Aristotelian dialogue.

To reiterate, the philological aim of dating Plato's dialogues or Aristotle's works rests on the assumption that one gets purchase on the challenge of interpretation by transforming a philosophical question into a historical question. Yet this effort presupposes that history decisively determines or conditions thought. Moreover, the attempt to classify Aristotle's thought into different stages overlooks and obscures the conspicuous phenomenon that should be the beginning of inquiry into Aristotle, namely, that every stage of Aristotle's thought is marked by his engagement with Plato and that what is at stake in that engagement is what Aristotle takes to be true. In Klein's words:

> Aristotle's relation to Plato is a supreme example of the true pupil-teacher relationship: the pupil's unswerving loyalty to his teacher manifests itself in the pupil's commitment to Truth, even if that commitment makes the pupil reject the teacher's teaching. (174)

Citing Aristotle's remarks from the *Nicomachean Ethics* regarding the "men dear to him (φίλοι ἄνδρες)" who introduced "the doctrine of 'ideas' (τὰ εἴδη)," Klein identifies the nub of contention, namely, the being of the εἴδη (174). But at this stage in the essay, Klein does no more than hint at the sedimented character of our approach to this ostensibly familiar piece of terminology. Rather, Klein highlights something even more familiar, namely, friendship, which Aristotle himself spends two books of the *Ethics* demonstrating is integral to the good life for a human being. Yet the loyalty at the heart of a philosophic friendship cannot supersede the love of wisdom; for that would undermine the ground of communion. Accordingly, Klein quotes Aristotle as saying, "But—for those pursuing philosophy, at least—it would seem that it is probably better and, to safeguard the truth, even necessary to go against the grain; for, both one's friends *and* the truth being dear to one, it is right and proper to give greater honor to truth" (174).

Without further elaboration or comment, Klein reminds the reader of two further "historical" facts, two pieces of evidence that lie outside of Aristotle's texts, which one might overlook if, with Heidegger, all there was to say was that "Aristotle was born, spent his life in philosophizing, and died" (171). First, "The companions in the Academy called themselves 'friends' (φίλοι)." Second, in a fragment of an elegy, "Aristotle speaks of an altar dedicated to 'holy Friendship' and unmistakably refers to Plato (without naming him) as a 'man whom bad men have no right even to praise'" (174). Klein's apparent response to Heidegger is then an insistence on one feature of Aristotle's life: his relation to Plato, as teacher, friend, and interlocutor—a relation governed throughout by love of truth.[57]

Klein concludes this introductory section with an exhortation: "Let us, then, keep in mind this exemplary relation of Aristotle, the pupil, to Plato, the teacher, in trying to understand Aristotle's own way" (174). As with the model pedagogic relation, understanding does not mean agreement, just as learning is not repetition. Taken in conjunction with the first words of the essay, Klein's hortatory subjunctive suggests how fraught Klein's relation with his own teacher must have been. Although Klein does not mention him at this point, Heidegger was in spite of everything the catalyst for Klein's return to Aristotle. For all their disagreement and for all Heidegger's moral betrayal, there is the debt of the "peculiar circumstance" that made Klein's own philosophic quest possible. Yet the contrast is no less telling, for there was no friendship with Heidegger, let alone anything akin to that love Aristotle expresses for Plato. Perhaps the beginning of Klein's response to Heidegger is already contained in the question: what is philosophic friendship? It is altogether fitting that Klein poses such a question in his *Festschrift* essay for Strauss.[58]

Modern Symbolic Unreality

or Mr. Klein's Question: Who Lives Symbolically?[1]

DAVID LAWRENCE LEVINE

"Everything is being transcended continually in thought and action."

Goethe, *Letter to Zelter*[2]

"The idea of a *mathesis universalis* determines the whole orientation of our lives. Our rationalism is a symbolic one."

Jacob Klein, *Modern Rationalism*[3]

"The proposition that an abstract idea like *number* is subject to historical change strikes at the heart of the most basic proposition of the conception of science, that its basic concepts are essentially *a priori*, timeless, or at least invariant through time."

Burt Hopkins, *The Origin of the Logic of Symbolic Mathematics*[4]

"Everything that frees our spirit without giving us mastery over ourselves is pernicious."

Goethe, *Maxims and Reflections*[5]

1. Prologue

Readers of Jacob Klein's major work *Greek Mathematical Thought and the Origin of Algebra* are left with this question: What are the *human implications* of the monumental structural change in human thinking of which he gives an account? The work itself focuses on the incremental changes that human thinking undergoes from the early Greek philosophers to the seventeenth century. In his later essays and lectures, however, he gives clearer formulation to the greater implications, presuppositions, and consequences of this change. And they are significant.

In particular there are occasional stunning claims throughout these later writings that seem to be the implications of his early work but which remain isolated and underdeveloped. This major development in human thought has led, he says, not just to new conceptual tools for the new sciences but to "*an entirely new way of thinking*,"[6] one that marks a major break with the earlier traditions, or, as he says, entails "*a characteristic modification of every ancient concept*."[7]

This new way of thinking, moreover, has the following perplexing results: on the one hand, he says, "*[e]ven our simplest acts [have] become incomprehensible [to us]*,"[8] and on the other, "*our own life does not [any longer] belong to us*."[9] Our acts are "incomprehensible," our lives no longer ours. How these might be thought the consequences of the conceptual revolution is my task here.

2. Introduction: The Clouds (Head-in-the-Cloudness or the Problem of Conceptual Envelopment)

"[The Clouds] become all things that they wish."

Aristophanes, *The Clouds*[10]

Philosophy has long been characterized, if not caricatured, as an activity remote from human things. Thales, the first philosopher according to some, left us with the memorable, if disorienting, image of the philosopher so absorbed in observing "the things above" that he or she doesn't see what is in front of his or her feet and thus falls into a ditch. Aristophanes even portrayed the philosopher or "sophist" Socrates suspended high up in a basket, remote from our everyday world, that he might be closer to the things to which he truly aspires—the Ideas (*eidê*)—there portrayed as "clouds." Goethe's Faust worries about the inhumanity and human relevance of his philosophical studies. And we still say, colloquially, of someone absorbed in hyper-theoretical matters that he or she has his or her "head in the clouds." To be honest, there is some truth to this.

With Aristophanes, I wonder whether we might not suffer from an acute case of "*nepholopsia*" (a neologism coined by Oliver Sachs), that is whether we too might be "enveloped by clouds." But I wonder too whether Aristophanes' picture might not be too broad-brushed. Might there not be different sorts of theoretical absorption, with different degrees and kinds of "head-in-the-clouds-nesses"? Might there not be reason to make important, internal distinctions about *modes of philosophizing*? And might there, then, not be reason to revisit the ancient distinction between kinds of constitutive mis-thinking (sophistry) and that self-critical thoughtfulness that seeks to think well (philosophy)?

3. Greek Mathematical Thought and the Origin of Algebra (A Major Transformational Change in European Thinking)

I raise these questions because such questions arise concerning modern thought in Mr. Klein's works.[11] For those not familiar with him, let me say a few words. Mr. Klein was a long-time tutor on the Annapolis campus of St. John's College, also a dean, and a person of considerable intellectual influence. In a deep sense, he was a second-generation "founder," that is "re-founder," of the Program of study at the college.[12] If my memory serves me right, Mr. Klein wrote his dissertation on Hegel. He came to the college in the late 1930s from war-torn Europe, after nine-plus years of independent study, where he had the good (if mixed) fortune to have studied with Husserl and Heidegger.

Under their mutual influence, he wrote his book on *the major transformational change* in European thinking that marks the early modern period. It bears the daunting title (as translated into English by Eva Brann): *Greek Mathematical Thought and the Origin of Algebra.* But what, we might ask, have developments in modern mathematics to do with the way *we* think today? There may be new developments in a science, but do they necessarily affect the way *we* think more generally? Here is Mr. Klein's contention (shared with other phenomenologists[13]): that this transformation is of such depth and consequence that it affects not just "mathematics," but *our* "thinking"—"the mentality of present day Europe," he calls it[14]—and, as a result, further still, affects *our whole lives.*[15] It is this change in *our mode of being in the world,* most pointedly, that *we* inherit and that characterizes us still.

He claims that we can see this fundamental re-orientation of Western thought most clearly—most "clearly and distinctly"—in the mathematical revolution of the early modern centuries, a change that would be less visible to a reader, say, in a complex philosophical work. Through the "simple" notion of "number" (*arithmos*) and its transformations we can see the effective reconsideration of what it means to be a "one out of many" or a complex whole (that is, a number), and with that what it means to have and to be an object of thought.[16] Herewith, the way we've come to take the world to *be*—ontological change—is revealed through these mathematical developments.

But more, Mr. Klein had to re-think what was at stake, what was most fundamental in the minds of each of the thinkers who were instrumental to this change. In so doing, he sought to reawaken the original character and evidence of ancient and modern thought. For example, Plato. Mr. Klein came to see deeply the "natural" ontological origins of Plato's thinking at its highest and the genuinely philosophical nature of Plato's presentation of the "forms" or "ideas" (*eidê*). He articulated an ontological (arithmological), not an epistemological, understanding of the "ideas," returning us to Aristotle's elusive and puzzling insight that the ideas were "eidetic numbers."[17]

In another respect, Mr. Klein's reading is indebted to Aristotle, namely, to the latter's remark in the *Poetics* that the Platonic dialogues are "mimes." This brings Mr. Klein to open up the dialogues anew. They are not ornamented philosophical treatises, nor logical exercises, but—and here is his great insight—*the dialogues always in some way themselves embody the question they attempt to explore.* They are mimes. The bases for these re-readings are further exemplified and explicated in his two other books: *A Commentary on Plato's "Meno"* and *Plato's Trilogy: The* Theaetetus, Sophist, and Statesman.

In addition for those of us at St. John's, as inheritors of his re-founding, this has meant that the mathematics tutorials, and with them the laboratories, as well as our modern readings more generally, are to be seen in this renewed light as having additional, deeper dimensions to be explored and revealed. And this meant that the study of the freshman year (though not only that) was reinvigorated—that is, no longer to be taken for granted as "given" or as already "known"—such that there is much still to discover about the foundational insights and influence of Plato and his student, Aristotle, for the tradition and for us.

4. "Even Our Simplest Acts [Have] Become Incomprehensible" (The Fundamental Premise— The Paradoxes of the Two Substance Doctrine)

Let us begin with what Mr. Klein claims is *the founding premise* of modern thought. The way we have come to think, our "modern symbolic rationalism" as he calls it,

> is the true *result* of the Cartesian distinction between "mind" and "external world." It is the true expression of

> the *paradox* . . . that the mind, which is supposed to be sufficient to understand the world, is preconceived as a mind *alienated* from this same world. We approach the world *not directly* but by means of concepts which are abstractions of abstractions and which at the same time we interpret as being in *direct* contact with the world.[18]

One might call this "the world paradox" of modern philosophy. That our modern symbolic rationalism is said to be "the *result* of the Cartesian distinction" is especially unexpected, since Mr. Klein had also argued in his earlier work that our symbolic rationalism *had its beginning* earlier, as revealed in the conceptual revolution in mathematics. How, then, are we to think of this twofold claim?

Let us begin by thinking about the Cartesian distinction. At its heart, *the fundamental premise* of the new thinking is *profoundly paradoxical.* It involves a radical break from the previous traditions of metaphysical continuity. To put it strikingly: The new thinking is worldless, alienated, isolated, "solipsistic," "monadic," or in Mr. Klein's words, the new thinking is "shut up within its own cell."[19]

To illustrate this, Mr. Klein refers to Descartes's foundational and exclusive distinction between *res cogitans* (the inner experience of a "thinking being" or substance) and *res extensa* (the thinking about our external experience as extended substance).[20] The implications of this distinction are also visible in Descartes's surprising reluctance in *Meditations III* to associate the "images in his mind" with anything real in the world, "outside" him. We makes mistakes when we presume such a connectedness, he says. In Descartes's language: "*The principal error and the most ordinary which we may meet with in [our judgments about ideas] consists in my judging that the ideas which are in me [en moi] are similar or conformable to the things which are outside me [hors de moi].*"[21] This discontinuity and reluctance is the unavoidable conclusion of what, in Mr. Klein's era, was called "the psycho-physical problem." The worldlessness of the new knowledge follows unavoidably from any attempt to explain our "psychological" experience of consciousness "physically," that is, *res cogitans* as *res extensa.*

To illustrate the problem: If a wooden box, for example, is thought to be out there in the world, then how does it come before our attention "in our minds"? We say it is material—wood [Knock, knock]—but our minds are not wood. How then are they connected if they are so different in nature?[22] Nowadays physical scientists (heirs of Descartes) try to account for this discontinuity by offering an elaborate chain of causality.[23] They say that light (not wood, but sub-visual energy waves measured in angstroms) is reflected off the wooden box and received by our eyes whose inner faculty in our retinas (rods and cones) converts the light waves into electro-neural impulses—not wood, not light, but electricity—that are then conveyed to the brain, whose function in turn is to convert the impulses into psychological images, that is, into "perceived images" (not wood, not light, not electricity). These end-images are themselves *not anything like* the intermediary mediums of transmission nor, as a result, like any supposed original world. We cannot guarantee "the chain of custody," so to speak.

"The question immediately arises," Mr. Klein observes, "how the external world can be known through the intelligence, how the thinking substance and the extended substance can get in touch with one another, since they are *totally alien* to each other."[24] For example, how can a "wish" raise my hand? And if I were to ask you to raise your hand—go ahead, raise your hand—how did you do that? How can my "weightless" intention be translated into a word that is then carried as sound waves to you and "heard," and then converted into an image or thought that in turn is converted into an intention on your part to make the physical effort to raise the weight of your arm? Intention→word→sound→electro-neural impulse→image→intention→act. If mind and body "are *totally alien* to each other," "how can a *wish* . . . initiate . . . a movement [that] belongs purely to the 'extended substance'?" Mr. Klein's conclusion: "*Our simplest acts become incomprehensible*"[25] and, by extension, one might add, our conscious life as a whole is unintelligible in physical terms.[26]

In other words, how can anyone be confident that the psychic experience of the image bears any resemblance (not to say efficacy) to some purported worldly box?[27] Descartes and modern philosophy say we *cannot.*[28] Hence all we can ever claim that we know, all we actually "know" in this view, is our own restricted or, as we have come to say, "*merely* subjective" psychic experience. The "phenomenal world" (in the modern sense) is herewith born. No further ontological claims are possible.[29]

At this point the question arises of the status of what we have all along been calling *knowledge*. We have now to rethink the character and status of a mode of thought so re-conceived, *in* the mind, *of* the mind, alienated, worldless, solipsistic, or "subjective." The new modern discipline of epistemology[30] arises to address these new profound perplexities (an episteme-odicy?). Accordingly, "epistemology" replaces "ontology" as the depth exploration of what is knowable, and hence fundamental.

So striking is the reorientation that "knowledge" can no longer be thought of in traditional terms as "*conformable* [co-formable] to a world," or as "*corresponding* to its correlative object," or as "*adequate*" (from *adaequatio*) to any objective world other than itself.[31] How then are we to assess what we think we know?

New and very different measures are needed. The traditional, "objective" conceptions have now to be replaced by new criteria of immanent or internal assessment, with categories of evaluation such as "simplicity," "inner consistency," "non-self-contradictoriness," "innate ideas,"[32] "clarity and distinctness," "certainty," "universality and necessity," and so on. These are the new measures of "objectivity," that is, rather, of *our subjective experience of objectivity* (Kant: "subjective universality").

This inward turn to consciousness is the result of "*an entirely new way of thinking*" that began to emerge centuries prior to Descartes and that Mr. Klein calls "*modern symbolic rationalism.*" This "entirely new way of thinking" the founders of modern thought well understood would "turn us around," that is, be "revolutionary."[33] This will be explored further, but first one added conundrum.

5. We Have Become "Blind with Seeing Eyes" (Real vs. Imputed Qualities—The Loss of the Natural World)

> "In the knowledge of nature is always the authoritative evidence of the senses as to each fact."
>
> Aristotle, *De Caelo*[34]

> "The learned have a way of being so clever as to contrive to render themselves blind to things that are in their own nature evident."
>
> Descartes, Rule XII[35]

> "Seeing and Hearing has been lost to consciousness."
>
> Hegel, "Force and the Understanding"[36]

This rethinking involves yet another schism, equally consequential. For the doubts about the status of images "in *me*" led to the search for what, if anything, is reliable, not to mention "knowable," about these inner or subjective images of *mine*. To use Locke's language (who follows Descartes), the new break is between the "original or *primary* or real" qualities which are taken to exist in bodies and thought to give rise to corresponding ideas in us (such as bulk, figure, number, and motion), and the "*secondary* or imputed" qualities (such as warmth, pain, and color). *Real vs. imputed qualities.* Concerning the latter he says, "there is *nothing* like our ideas existing in the bodies themselves."[37] "[L]ight, heat, whiteness, or coldness [secondary qualities], are *no* more really in them [that is, in bodies in the world] than [are our personal experiences of] sickness or pain."[38] "Whatever reality we by *mistake* attribute to them [the secondary qualities] are in truth *nothing* in the objects themselves, but powers to produce various sensations in us."[39] In short, our experience of our world, according to these thinkers, is often misconstrued and *mistaken*.[40] Paradoxically, a connectedness is presumed all the same in order to explain our mis-represented connectedness. Descartes concurs.

In sum, the new and radical break is between the quantitative aspects of these ideas (real or primary) and their sensuous aspect (imputed or secondary), the latter thereafter demoted as "merely subjective," *merely*. Both Descartes's and Locke's accounts have physiological bases.[41] To this Descartes adds that this distinction is also truer to our conscious experience. He objects that our sense images in our minds are often unreliable. For example, we mistake the true size of the sun and moon; they look small but really aren't. In short, what we *think* is truer than what we *see*. Hence we are told that we have to turn *away* from our everyday conscious experience and turn within, taking our bearings now by our "*inborn light*," that is, the "intuitions of reason."[42]

But this divide leads to a very curious state of affairs also characteristic of modern thinking. Perhaps an analogy would be helpful. In certain cases, after a major accident, for example, it sometimes happens that people lose their capacity to see or experience some part of their visual field. This is called "*agnosia*."[43] It would appear that we have been asked by these philosophers to accept something comparable, though in this case to deliberately and self-consciously *deny* part of our conscious experience, not as a result of an accident, but on behalf of the newly reconceived, restricted notion of reason. We are asked to demote, ignore, downgrade, overlook, discount, what had previously been taken as immediate, generally reliable, indeed as our natural world. We might call this a *deliberately self-imposed agnosia*.[44] In this way, we have "lost our senses," or have become, in Goethe's wonderfully revealing phrase, "blind with seeing eyes."[45]

Indeed what is asked of us is "extravagant" (Locke's term).[46] This distinction asks us to deny ourselves what for us is the real world of our experience, what humans have always thought their natural home. You see and hear me; I see you. No problem. However, we are told that there is a serious problem. Should we not, then, re-cast Aristotle's question of old and ask: How can we attain to what is *first in itself*, if we begin by relinquishing (denying) our connectedness to what is *first for us*?

6. "An Entirely New Way of Thinking" (Losing Sight of the Difference—Concepts of the Mind and Concepts of Experience)

> "[The book of the world] is written
> in the language of mathematics."
>
> Galileo, *The Assayer*[47]

In addition to these curious consequences, it is Mr. Klein's contention that our modern way of thinking—our "modern symbolic rationalism"—had a *long history* that culminated in Descartes's radical distinction. Here is where developments in mathematics help to *illustrate* the change that characterizes the new thinking. In his long and elaborate account, Mr. Klein documents the fundamental shift in our thinking that began to emerge in the fourteenth century and has been dominant ever since. What becomes plain is not only that "concepts" are of different kinds but also that our "concept of concept" changed.[48]

Some concepts name the things of our experience: dog, red, wet nose. Others are concepts of other concepts, concepts about the way we use and refer to them: an "adjective," a "theory," a "transcendental concept." To help us understand this fundamental difference, Mr. Klein re-introduces a medieval distinction. Scholars (specifically Albertus Magnus) had distinguished between concepts of the "*first intention*"—those that name and refer *imme-*

diately to the things of our experience—that we might call "concepts of experience," and another type of concept, concepts of the "*second intention*"—those that refer *internally* and reflexively, so to speak—that we might call "concepts of the mind" or "beings of reason."

This distinction, Mr. Klein cautions us, "has nothing to do with *abstraction*" per se[49] (a mistake I originally made). Every concept is, after all, in some sense abstract. Following Aristotle (and the tradition), Mr. Klein speaks of concepts as "drawn, [that is] abstracted, from individual objects," and therefore as general in themselves.[50] So too concepts of the mind. They are drawn from other concepts. The important point, rather, is that this fundamental distinction comes to be *re-cast* ("handled" or "dealt with" differently) and therewith an "intentional shift" occurs in our mode of thinking.

Mr. Klein uses the term *abstraction* generally (as does the tradition), both for the initial receptive experience of kinds of things (that Aristotle called "induction" [*epagôgê*][51]) as well as for the subsequent active and selective apprehension of particular features (that Aristotle called abstraction proper [*aphairesis*: taking away or removal], most notable in this context being the reductive abstractions of mathematics). While Aristotle made this distinction, the word *abstraction* has developed a general meaning over time. In Mr. Klein's use of the term, the first mode of abstraction emerges out of our simple experience of the kind-character of things of our experience (*eidê, genê*). In this view we have a rich, complex, and articulated world amidst which we live. The second mode of abstraction arises when we abstract some feature from out of these abstractions (that Mr. Klein refers to as "abstractions of abstractions").[52] As long as we can keep this distinction clear, there's no mix-up.

According to Mr. Klein, the worldliness and groundedness of the first mode of abstraction changes with the emergence of the new thinking.[53] In particular, a new species of concept comes to the fore that brings us to think about the above distinction differently: "*symbolic abstractions*," such as those we find most conspicuously (though not only) in algebra. Let us take Mr. Klein's example: In algebra we see sentences such as $(\alpha + \beta)2 = (\alpha2 + 2\alpha\beta + \beta2)$. How did we get here? *Considerable conceptual re-constitution was necessary*, to such a degree that Mr. Klein claims that what has evolved here is "*an entirely new way of thinking*." This new symbolic language is so different in kind from natural language that they are *not transposable* the one into the other. "It is a common mistake," he says, "to believe we can translate the theorems of [the new thinking] . . . into ordinary language."[54] How are we to understand this?

We tend to think that such all-too-familiar algebraic formulations are merely indifferent "tools" or "languages" used to express our new discoveries but that they don't otherwise reflect the way we think more fundamentally. This is misleading, Mr. Klein claims. "The mathematical method of our physics is inseparable from the very nature of this science"; indeed, he stresses that this mathematical method "represents . . . the most important character of our general frame of mind."[55] In other words, it defines not just a disciplinary but *a new "general" frame of mind*, one that defines the way we still think today. *We* came to think, in short, as modern mathematicians came to think.

Let us look at the elements of the above formula. What, for example, is "α"? What does "α" stand for and intend? What is the conceptual difference between the "α" in the above equation and the "two"? And is there a difference between the "two" as used here and the "two" as an ancient thinker might have used it? What Mr. Klein's analysis makes apparent is that *both* the "α" *and* the "two" now entail *a new and curious kind of non-specificity or generality. Both* are *indefinite or indeterminate. Both* are without reference to a specific object. The founders of this new mathematics used the word "symbolic" to name this new order of *indeterminate generality*.[56]

Curiously, the notion of "symbol" itself is subject to this recasting. It is itself symbolic in this new way. Previously, symbols were always *of* something. A badge is a symbol of the law, for example. The new symbolic abstraction, however, has lost its representational property and "no longer refers directly . . . to an object," Mr. Klein says.[57] These symbols are no longer *of* anything in particular, and precisely for this reason they stand for nothing other than themselves and hence themselves become objects for us. One might call them *abstract symbols* or *non-symbolic symbols*, or *non-representational symbols*, if these are not contradictions in terms.

By contrast, the Greeks thought differently. For the Greeks a "number" (*arithmos*) is always grounded, always something definite, *both* in number and kind, "a definite number of definite things" (*pas arithmos tinos esti*).[58] A group is thus unified, not just by some common quality like number, but, more specifically, by the *kind of things* numbered, their genus or *eidos*.[59] In this view what makes it fundamentally whole is its *kind*. Thus there are, to begin with, different kinds of "natural twos," for example, two apples, two oranges,[60] thereafter two kinds of "fruit," and then two "pure units," but always class-specific, however general.[61]

In our algebraic formula, however, the "α" doesn't intend an object of any particular number or sort (not even "pure" units), but rather intends, as Mr. Klein points out, "the [very] concept of number as a *multitude* [as such]." *This marks a different level and kind of conceptualization.* Now we'd say that what makes a group, its unity, is its multitude, indifferent to the kind of things in question. Moreover, this new kind of number has become an ontologically *prior* category (as Descartes argued), not just one among many categories (as in Aristotle). This constitutes a very different sense of relating to the things of our experience, hence a different sense of the whole. A different "world" therefore emerges before us, one with which we are less immediately related, less engaged with the natural kinds that present themselves, but where we are *trans-focused* on the generality of things that, from the perspective of the prior traditions, are underspecified and indeterminate.[62] As such this marks a different orientation in and to our world. Our mode of being-in-the-world has changed.

Hence the elements of the modern equation are not what they might at first seem, not what early arithmeticians consider natural numbers. This change in conceptuality (or "mentality") is not, as we saw, restricted to the new abstract and indefinite "unknown Xs" but extends even to what we might at first think is most known and most familiar. Here even "number" is taken "apart from the things counted." It too has become "symbolic" in this new sense (unconnected, dissociated).[63] And so have *all* of our ideas. We're moderns.

Perhaps now we are starting to get an inkling of what Mr. Klein means by the "*new general frame of mind*," the new thinking that entails a "characteristic modification of *every* ancient concept." Even the most familiar is recast. Even the new is now taken as if familiar.

7. As if Thinking (Lingering Ontological Questions about the New Knowledge)

"What remains *questionable* . . . is a closer relation of the mathematical . . . to the intuitive experience of given things and to these things themselves."

Heidegger, "Modern Science, Metaphysics and Mathematics"[64]

Once again the medieval distinction might help. One might think that such "an abstraction of an abstraction"—multitude as such—belongs to the second class of concepts. However, modern mathematicians come to "*deal* with 'α' [and such expressions] in exactly the same way that *arithmetic* deals with ordinary numbers," *as if* they are simple, first-intentional objects.[65] "In other words," Mr. Klein says, we have come to use "concepts of the second class *as though* they were concepts of the first class," such that they are no longer distinguished as before (hence "inseparable").[66]

Let's think about this. Let's think about this "*as if thinking*" for a moment. We now "use concepts of the second class *as though* they were concepts of the first class." This is a new cognitive intent. What was once thought different is now used ("handled" or "dealt with") *as if* it were, for all intents and purposes, the same. In the above distinction, a concept of the mind refers only to other concepts, hence it is "internal," so to speak. But to use them now *as if* they were of the first class is to treat them like concepts that have a reference apart from themselves, a reference to objects of experience. Concepts of the mind thus *lose their dissociation and therewith their distinctiveness* and are now thought *as if* they too are somehow like *all* other concepts. Once thought of as having a different ontological import, they are now thought of *as if*, for practical purposes, having the same ontological import. Hence the separate becomes inseparable; the distinguishable becomes indistinguishable; the intermediate becomes immediate; the indirect direct; and the abstract is considered *as if* ordinary and natural. To put the question simply: Does this mean that "concepts of the mind" are "real?"

Many things are embedded in Mr. Klein's claim of an "intentional shift" (a shift in conceptuality: *Begrifflichkeit*).[67] The ontological standing of *both* our "first-intentional concepts" *and* "second-intentional concepts" changes. The new "*indeterminate generalizing shift*" in understanding impacts both types of concepts. If "concepts of the mind" are now thought of as "concepts of experience," then both are somehow conceived of as firsts, worldly, "real." But since concepts of thought have no reference outside themselves, we find ourselves in a paradox: concepts which have no objective reference are taken, that is mis-taken, *as if* they do. And given the world paradox, where firsts lose their natural reference, all our concepts are worldless and therewith ontologically puzzling. All are "modern ideas" (idealism).[68]

In summary: To take a concept of thought *as if* it were a concept of experience means to *lose sight* of its original ontological distinctiveness.[69] To quote Mr. Klein: "The *whole complex of ontological problems* which surrounds the ancient concept of number *loses its object* in the context of the symbolic conception, since there is no immediate occasion for questioning the mode of being of the 'symbol' itself."[70] The symbolic interpretation of number in modernity permits arithmetic to become a universal science of "algebra as a general theory of proportions and ratios."

> The 'material' of this universal and fundamental science is no longer furnished by 'pure' units whose *mode of being* may be subject to dispute . . . ; the 'material' is now rather constituted by 'numbers' *whose being no longer presents any problem* since, as the products of symbol-generating abstraction, they can be immediately grasped in the notation.[71]

In short, their *ontological ambiguity* is eclipsed, disappearing in our new *conceptual facility*.[72] Here we have an example of what Husserl and his students call "sedimentation," that is, that we lose sight of the *original evidences* for our ideas, the result of the passage of time and the rethinking of generations.[73]

With characteristic understatement, Mr. Klein thus concludes: "it is *by no means easy* to determine [the] true character [of concepts],"[74] and, as we've seen, of the modern concept of number in particular. We are thus left with questions. First, is to take a "concept of the mind or thought" as a "concept of experience" to *mistake* the one for the other? Second, does this thought-conflation become an *unthinking substitution* and in turn a *thought distortion*? Third, is to think of a thought thing *as if* "real," *as if* grounded, *as if* derived from the world, to misjudge the fundamental nature of our thinking? As a result of such questions Mr. Klein names this peculiar modern ontological ambiguity "*symbolic unreality*."[75]

Un-reality. In this view, it is modern thought, not ancient philosophy, that is remote from human things.

The net effect of these transformations, to quote Mr. Klein, is that a "complicated network of sedimented significances underlies the 'arithmetical' understanding of geometry." Moreover, "our actual interpretation of the world, as expressed not only in our science but also in our daily life," rests upon that sedimented network of conceptual amalgamations.[76] There is thus no "clarity;" their "interlacement"[77] obstructs their original ontological standing. Hence "un-reality."

Mr. Klein's project can thus be stated simply: He seeks to *re-raise* for us the ancient ontological concern. What does this new mode of thinking in fact "understand"? *"Of what" (tinos) is this new mode of thinking* really? What, then, of our presumption "to know?"

8. Making Our Way through Our Encumbered History

So far our story has been long. Let me provide an overview.

§1. We began with a metaphor, adapted from Aristophanes: *head-in-the-cloudsness.* This introduced us to the problem of conceptual envelopment, or in the case of modern conceptuality, mutually incompatible orders and treatments of ideas intermingled, hovering about one another.

§2. We have all inherited and are now "enframed" (as Heidegger would say) by this change in our Western mode of thinking begun centuries ago, which affects not only our most abstract concepts but even our most familiar ones. Simple things like number, though not only that—even our general sense of what an "object of thought" is as such—have changed fundamentally.

§3. How are we to understand this? In one sense, it goes back to the fundamental premise of modern thought and philosophy: *the world paradox.* We have inherited a rather odd, deeply encumbered (enveloped) way of thinking. It was proposed that there are fundamentally two thought substances—the mind and the world—and that these are somehow exclusive. Yet it is presumed at the same time that the one has access to the other. How this is possible, we saw, is deeply problematic. Is a box a figment of our minds *or* in the world? And if it is but a thought thing, how are we to assess its being and truthfulness? Truth thereafter comes to mean "what is clear and distinct *to us*" (Heidegger: subjective metaphysics).

§4. To this was added another conundrum, one that makes our conscious life even more puzzling (incomprehensible). For we now had to ask "what is knowable" about these newly reconceived "images or ideas." Some were said to be clear to us, others not, and it was urged that, if we want what is "most true," then we should attend principally to the former. Only the "real or primary" aspects of our experience, not the "imputed or secondary" ones, are to be thought so. Because of this deliberately self-imposed *agnosia* (as we called it), the "natural world" was replaced by the new "true world" of modern thought.

§5. We then tried to get a better sense of this "entirely new way of thinking." How did it arise? Our "concept of concept" changed. The traditional distinction between first- and second-intentional concepts—between "concepts of experience" and "concepts of the mind"—was conflated. From then on they are undistinguished (or "inseparable," as Mr. Klein called it). Hence, the one can't be explained in terms of the other (it is no longer "translatable"). We now have generalized, objectless concepts of no particular kind merged with the common objects of experience.[78] But not only the new symbolic abstractions, even—perhaps especially—what is most familiar also exhibits this "characteristic modification of every ancient concept"[79] pervaded by this indeterminate generality. This intermixing, moreover, has become a matter of philosophical indifference.

§6. By *merge* Mr. Klein means that second-intentional concepts are dealt with *as if* they were firsts, dealt with, in the case of the mathematical formula, as part of any arithmetical treatment. In short, the new mathematics *bypassed* the fundamental, philosophical distinction and incorporates the new kind of conceptualization into its practice. But as such, Mr. Klein says, their philosophical presuppositions remain "unclarified." We are thus left with this fundamental question: "*What is this new knowledge 'of'?*"

9. "Our Own Life Does Not Belong to Us" (The Human Consequences of the Conceptual Shift)

> "No one knows himself any longer; No one can grasp the element in which he lives."
>
> Goethe, *Letter to Zelter*[80]

> "[The frame of mind of] mathematical physics is the most important part of our civilization and actual life."
>
> Jacob Klein, *Modern Rationalism*[81]

With such ontological perplexities hovering about us like clouds, the question that follows, for Mr. Klein and for us, is what this all means for *our* being-in-the-world. It is his greater contention, we remember, that this revolution in thought affects our "*whole lives.*" So, to bring us back to the prior question, let us look at another of his surprising claims: "*Our own life,*" he says, "*does not belong to us.*"[82] What could he possibly mean by this? And how is this an implication of the foregoing?

To this point we've seen several things that might help us understand this unsettling claim. We remember that (a) the attempt to explain even our "simplest acts," indeed our conscious life as a whole, by means of a physiological account placed us amidst *paradox*, or more strongly, as Mr. Klein says, made "our simplest acts . . . incomprehensible" to us. To this was added yet another paradox, namely, that (b) the two-substance presupposition of modern thought led us to be unsure of any natural continuity between our personal experience and the world that we used to think was our own (hence modern anomie, estrangement, alienation).[83] And then when we considered what this new mode of thinking asked of us, we again saw that (c) our sense of our inner world changed; our very way of conceptualizing ideas changed (our concept of *concept* changed). No longer did we distinguish between concepts of the mind and those of experience (they were conflated, "inseparable"). But more, even our most familiar concepts were recast. Even our twos, indeed *all* our concepts of experience lost their distinctive groundedness in the real, their worldliness (hence idealism). We also remember that (d) we were asked to strip down our sense of the whole to its barest, skeletal minimum such that the things we touch, hear, smell, and see no longer are credited with being real (modern *agnosia*).

We were thus left, not with answers, but with *fundamental questions*: Figments of our conceptualization? Hypotheses? Hyperbolic reasonings? Presumptions? Projections? In short, our modern search for "clarity and distinctness" has only led, in Mr. Klein's view, to ontological unclarity and indistinctness. Mr. Klein's forecast: persistent "cloudiness" for many days to come.

All these lingering questions, perhaps, give us a better sense of what he meant by our world somehow now being "*symbolically unreal.*" We too had learned to think and experience the world as the mathematicians did.[84] The basic principle: "*The directness of our contact with the world,*" Mr. Klein says, "*is of the same symbolic character as the concepts we use to understand it.*"[85] Simply put, we are "enframed" by this new mode of thought. As in Plato's cave, we see the world through the machinations of the opinion-makers that are at work "behind our back" pre-filtering the way we are to see the world. Such is our modern inheritance. Such is Mr. Klein's conclusion: "[modern symbolic] rationalism is that approach to an understanding of *human behavior, history and the world around us* [that is to say, to *all* of our experience] implied by the premises of mathematical physics."[86] Thus we can answer the question posed by the subtitle of this essay: "Who lives symbolically?" It is *we* who live symbolically.

So what does it mean to live in such a modern world, a world experienced through the *prism* of symbolic rationalism? What does it mean to *live symbolically*? How are we to take our bearings in such a post-natural world without signs and senses?

The transformation of reason that emerged from the revolution of the early modern period, we learned, is of a very particular kind. It seeks to be "clear and distinct" and universal (*mathesis universalis*), with the result that we now seek such extreme, *reductive* (mathematical) *clarity* in all things. As Mr. Klein saw, we now "rationalize" everything in this new way (the rationalization of *all* human life[87]), seeking for everything a "method," a "systems approach," an "algorithm," a "procedure," a "formula," all modeled after the new thinking such that their *selective and efficient truths* will be revealed. In short, the world and our experience thereof have been re-made after its image.

And now Mr. Klein's most puzzling claim: He says "our life is not our own" in another important respect. For the most part, we've addressed the "objective" side of this unsettling new truth. But what about the other? The new thinking strives to be universal and therefore is applied to *ourselves* as well. We think about ourselves now as if we too were but "thought things." In the words of another philosopher seeking to understand this radical change, Hegel, the new self "no longer has any [specific] content, possession, existence, or outer extension."[88] It is a mere content-less, predicate-less, character-less, thinking thing (*res cogitans*), the modern "self," "I," or "ego". But is this who and what we are?[89]

"Our life does not belong to us." In our new way of taking the world, we've seen: (a) we can't understand *our own* acts; (b) we can't be sure of *our own* world; (c) we're unclear about the signification of *our own* thinking (such that Mr. Klein went so far as to call it "symbolically unreal"); (d) a pre-decision decides for us what is the "truth" of *our own* experience; and (e) we know ourselves as but the remnant of the same reductive methodology. Mr. Klein thus rightly wonders: In the "true world" of modern thought, how can we "know ourselves"? In such a "true world," how can we "belong to ourselves"? What we think about our *lives*, what we think about *ourselves* has become "cloudy."

Let me end with this provocative summary of Mr. Klein's major work: The greatness of modern thought and modern science has, in part, to do with its concealing the fullness of being (as *res extensa*) and in alienating us from our ownmost natures (as *res cogitans*). Such is the immense formative influence of the "mathematical" revolution on our thinking and on our lives.[90] *Res extensa, res cogitans*, that's us.

Jacob Klein's Defense of Liberal Education

ANTONIO MARINO LÓPEZ

> It is not self-forgetting and pain-loving antiquarianism nor self-forgetting and intoxicating romanticism which induces us to turn with passionate interest, with unqualified willingness to learn, toward the political thought of classical antiquity. We are impelled to do so by the crisis of our time, the crisis of the West.
>
> Leo Strauss, *The City and Man*[1]

Jacob Klein undertook the defense of liberal education with full knowledge of the obstacles to be overcome; these may be gathered under one fundamental theme: our need to recuperate Socratic philosophy as the only means to surmount the crisis of modern philosophy, the crisis of our time. He went about this task, however, without the fanfare and jeremiads characteristic of the preachers of postmodernism. His defense was more practical than theoretical insofar as he devoted most of his energies to designing and pursuing the program of liberal education at St. John's College, whereas he wrote only three books. By choosing this road he showed in deeds that, even in our modern, capitalistic world, a college dedicated to liberal education is possible. Despite the primacy of the practical in his life, Klein still wrote several essays and delivered several lectures in which he expounds the theoretical defense of liberal education, many of which were collected and published posthumously in a book entitled *Lectures and Essays*.[2] Following the thread of this overarching theme as it appears in these works will, I hope, allow us to see the full scope of Klein's defense.

Implicit in the idea of liberal education there lurk three fundamental paradoxes that need to be made explicit in order to show why it needs to be defended. The first paradox appears when we reflect on its most superficial sense. Liberal education differs from traditional education because its aim is to free the student from the traditional dogmas of his society, whereas traditional education aims to mold the student's mind in conformity with society's most cherished values and laws. The opposition of the aims of these two types of education could not be more radical. And it is by no means self-evident that fostering freedom of the mind is desirable in a society, even if it is restricted to a select few. Athens' condemnation of Socrates for corrupting the young is the classical paradigm of this opposition. Freedom of the mind appears to the city as subversive heterodoxy.

The second paradox is made evident by reflecting on the internal contradiction of the concept "liberal arts," which are the studies necessary for the liberation of the mind. The arts are developed in the realm of necessity. Man invents arts in order to wrench his livelihood from meager nature and to protect himself from its inclemency. The city is impossible without the proliferation of the arts. Thus, the arts—whose essence is being useful—far from freeing man from the needs of the city, bind him ever more strongly to them. The need for the arts is inherent in the human condition, therefore a type of art that aims at freeing the mind from the needs of the city, as understood by the city, is essentially paradoxical if not nonsensical. One could object that not all the arts are dedicated to the satisfaction of bodily needs, as is shown by the existence of the fine arts. But traditionally the aim of the fine arts is not to liberate the citizens from the laws and customs of the city; until modern times, the fine arts were subordinated to the religious life of the cities. To overcome this second paradox and begin to see that "liberal art" is not an oxymoron, we must notice that despite being determined by their usefulness, the arts as such are not determined by the dogmas of each particular society. Whether we think of building houses or computers, their "technical" aspect, as we say, is the same everywhere. This universality points to their possible use for liberating the mind. But even if we grant that there is no internal contradiction in the concept of a liberal art, it would still be necessary to ask if the pursuit of such arts is good for the city and for man. Mathematics is the prime example of an apolitical knowledge, but it is not self-evident that a mathematician wholly indifferent to the affairs of the city may nonetheless be a good citizen.

The third and most perplexing paradox concerning liberal education appears when we consider that its final goal is to prepare the student for the philosophical life. According to Socrates, philosophy is the life-long and unending pursuit of eternal truth, and the liberal arts (arithmetic, geometry, astronomy, and music, as defined in the *Republic*) are needed to induce the turning-around (*metastrophê*) of the soul towards the eternal ideas and the idea of the Good. But the dual nature of the arts—they are both useful and universal, inherent in the needs of the city and independent of them—implies that studying them need not bring about the turning-around that makes them liberal arts. Indeed, they usually do not have such an effect, as may be seen in the fact that there are many more mathematicians than philosophers. Furthermore, these arts are eminently teachable (as the etymology of "mathematics" shows), but their liberating effect cannot be taught. Thus, insofar as they are arts, they are not liberating, and insofar as they turn the soul, they are not arts. And, once again, even if we grant that the liberal arts are possible and that they may bring about the reorientation of the soul needed by the potential philosopher, there remains the question of how he or she may benefit the city. In its most general form this is the problem of the relationship between theory and praxis. This should remind us that the idea of liberal education is first proposed by Socrates in the *Republic* as an answer to the following perplexity: Does the contemplation of the universal and eternal ideas prepare the philosopher to be a good king? Although the "answer," in fact, is the complete argument and action of this dialogue, it is readily evident that the defense of liberal education is inseparable from the defense of philosophy. Liberal education is the best education only if the philosophic life is the best life. But it remains an open question whether the philosopher-king is possible, and if he isn't, or is extremely unlikely to ever exist, can liberal education still be the best?

An additional and no less formidable challenge to liberal education is posed by modern philosophy. Its opposition is rooted in a fundamental change in the understanding of scientific knowledge that necessarily implies a revision of the purpose of philosophy and its relationship to the city. These fundamental changes may be outlined under the headings of the three paradoxes we have examined. Regarding the first one, modern philosophers agree that there is a radical opposition between traditional education and philosophical education, but they understand "traditional education" as the product of Greek and Medieval philosophy. They therefore aim to bring about a twofold liberation: from Christianity and from the false or primitive sciences of the ancients. Accordingly, modern philosophy understands the liberation it wants to bring about as affecting the whole city and not only the philosophers. Thus, although modern philosophy seems to replicate the opposition between traditional dogmas and philosophy, in fact it is both more and less radical than Socratic philosophy: more radical because it seeks to subvert the traditional order of the entire city, and less radical because it nevertheless promises to satisfy what all cities have always in fact desired, namely, empire and wealth. And it dares to promise this because it has founded a new science based on truly solid foundations and capable of conquering nature for the benefit of mankind. Regarding the second paradox—the apparent incongruity of freedom and art in the liberal arts—the modern teaching resolves it by transforming both terms. The traditional liberal arts are no longer seen as the means to turn the soul towards the eternal ideas. Instead, their substitute, the new mathematical physics, is both apolitical and subservient to the city. It is apolitical insofar as its truth does not depend on the opinions of the city, but it submits to the city's ends insofar as it is the foundation of technology. Thus, it can be both theoretical and useful. Meanwhile, the turning of the soul assigned to the liberal arts is now attributed to the methodical doubt which opens the way towards the new philosophy. Thus, modern freedom is produced by modern science, the freedom of the conqueror of nature. Finally, the third paradox is removed by the modern philosopher's philanthropic intentions. But his philanthropy requires the unending progress of the new sciences and their concomitant technologies. From the point of view of modern philosophy, the liberal arts are regarded as the propaedeutic for scholastic philosophy, and consequently as the kind of studies that should be replaced by the "new organon" (Bacon) or the new method (Descartes). The modern objection is both theoretical and practical. The theoretical rejection is a consequence of modern philosophy's critique of scholastic philosophy's "Aristotelian" metaphysics; the practical rejection follows from the utilitarian aims of modern science. Liberal education is thus rendered one of the components of traditional education that must be replaced by the modern sciences. This change has been most thoroughly carried out in schools and universities throughout the world.

"Modern philosophy," however, is a large mantle that does not fit properly each particular modern philosopher; nevertheless, the general characterization just outlined is sufficient to bring out the need for a confrontation with modern thought as an unavoidable part of the defense of classical liberal education. Fortunately, Klein takes up the characterization of modern philosophy in an early essay entitled "Modern Rationalism," and we can learn directly from it how he conceives the essence of modernity and its consequences for modern man. A close reading will show that this essay contains all the elements necessary to elucidate the relationship of his interpretation of modernity to the need for liberal education. I will therefore use it as a general introduction to his defense. After this, our attention will be directed to his fullest statement about liberal education, entitled "The Idea of Liberal Education." In this essay, Klein focuses on the central role assigned to the liberal arts, especially to Greek arithmetic, as the means of turning the soul (the *technê tês periagôgês*) towards the Idea of the Good. We shall have to pay special attention to his claim that this turning of the soul is the key event in the liberation sought by liberal education and to how this connects to the overcoming of modernity. In the third part of this essay, I shall explore Klein's lecture entitled "The Problem of Freedom," for in it he delves into these fundamental questions: how does the modern conception of freedom differ from the idea of freedom implicit in liberal education? And why is the freedom of thought sought by liberal education different from freedom in its modern version?

I

Klein expresses his central thesis concerning modernity in these words:

> Mathematical physics is the most important part of our entire civilization and actual life. This is true not only in respect to the technics so inseparable from our modern life, not only because it determines our own understanding of the world, but also because the principles of mathematical physics are basic to our whole way of thinking and behavior. In a broader sense rationalism is that approach to an

> understanding of human behavior, history and the world around us implied by the premises of mathematical physics. (57)

This is certainly a startling claim, and it becomes all the more startling when we learn that the advent of mathematical physics was prepared by a change in the concept of number, which occurred between the fourteenth and seventeenth centuries, along with its consequences for the understanding of mathematics (54). But the "physics" of mathematical physics also suffered a radical change. Klein argues the new conception of number can be used to develop a new universal science (*mathesis universalis*) when joined to Descartes's distinction between two kinds of being: *res cogitans* and *res extensa*, the thinking substance and the extended substance. The absolute difference between the two substances leads us immediately to ask "how the external world can be known through the intelligence, how the thinking substance and the extended substance can get into touch with each other, since they are totally alien to each other" (56). Klein points to Descartes's answer in these words:

> [n]o matter what the procedure might be by which we attain knowledge, one condition according to Descartes is indispensable: that the thinking substance have within it such qualities as correspond to similar qualities of the external world. . . . he calls the qualities of the mind . . . innate ideas, which guarantee the possibility of a perfect knowledge of the external world. They are (apart from the idea of God) number, magnitude, figure, space, time and movement. (56)

This implies that the new universal science only deals with the external world insofar as it can be related to the six innate ideas, which are the domain of mathematical physics. Whatever cannot be known by means of them is not the object of scientific knowledge. Klein emphasizes the peculiarity of this new science, remarking that it

> presupposes the distinction between thought and the external world as totally disconnected entities. All efforts to bridge the two and claim that intelligence is sufficient to grasp the external world (as in mathematical physics) must not make us overlook the fundamental fact that this dichotomy involves a profound distrust of the reality of the world. (57)

The fact that the dichotomy is inherent in the modern conception of man and world means that modern man is essentially alienated from the world by the very power he attributes to his rationality. Although awareness of this problem was readily voiced by many of the critics of modern rationality from Pascal onwards, it was Klein who, as Richard Kennington put it: "was perhaps the first in this century [Twentieth] to reopen the quarrel of the ancients and the moderns from the side of the ancients; he was certainly the first to reopen it from the standpoint of ancient mathematical and natural science."[3] His quarrel's centerpiece is the transformation of the concept of number, which is the theme of his book *Greek Mathematical Thought and the Origin of Algebra*. Although it is beyond the scope of this essay to go into the details of this work, we can get a sense of what the transformation of the concept of number entails from the explanation Klein offers in "Modern Rationalism."

Modern man's peculiar alienation is described by Klein as being the consequence of the change in the relationship between concepts and their objects produced by the symbols used in algebra. In order to explain this, he first elucidates the difference between concepts by which we refer to objects (first concepts or *intentiones primae*) and those by which we refer to other concepts (*intentiones secundae*). Examples of the first type are "dog" or "cow," which indicate individual objects, whereas if we say "Red is an *attribute*" or "Idealism is a *theory*" we are using concepts of the second type (60). The concepts used by the universal science are of the second type because "the step to the symbolic notation of algebra and, therefore, to the conception of mathematical physics involves an entirely new way of thinking, presupposes an entirely new way of handling concepts" (61). The novelty may most readily be seen by comparing the Greek concept of number (*arithmos*) with the modern concept. "For the Greeks, number (*arithmos*) meant precisely a definite number of definite things, for instance, four chairs, ten dogs, fifty people" (62). They are concepts of the first type and therefore they presuppose that thinking can relate to the things in the world by counting them. (Why and how this is so is an extremely difficult question which cannot be explored in this essay.) The modern concept of number does not direct us to things counted, as can be seen by considering an algebraic expression such as $a + 2ab = c$. Klein explains that "a" does not mean

> certain objects, namely units, the multitude of which it indicates, but rather the *concept* of the number as a multitude of units. So, at first glance, "a" belongs to the concepts of the second class which are applied not to individual objects but to concepts themselves. This, however, is only the first step. Actually, we deal with "a" and with all such algebraic numbers in exactly in the same way arithmetic deals with ordinary numbers. In other words, in algebra we use concepts of the second class as if they were concepts of the first class. We identify, in the process of algebraic thinking, concepts of the first class with concepts of the second class. What we call a symbol is nothing else but a concept of the second class interpreted as a concept of the first class. Therefore, we can now state that the "peculiar kind of abstraction" used in algebra is a symbolic abstraction. This is the peculiar kind of generalization involved in

> the idea of "universal science", which has developed into our science of nature, or mathematical physics. (62–63)

The most important consequence of this "peculiar kind of abstraction" is that by using concepts of the second class as if they were concepts of the first class, we no longer need to ask how the algebraic equations and mathematical physics in general relate to the external world. Their truth no longer depends on the correspondence between concept and thing intended, as the truth of a pre-modern proposition would. *This is a dog* expresses what I know about the world and must correspond to the world in order to be true. By contrast, the truth of the equations of mathematical physics depends on their coherence as symbols that follow the rules of construction of symbolic mathematics. This implies that the dichotomy between *res cogitans* and *res extensa* remains intact. Scientific knowledge is obtained through the method or procedure of generating symbolic abstractions expressed by algebraic formulas. No matter how sophisticated and extensive, the edifice constructed by the *mathesis universalis* cannot overcome the alienation of man and world. In fact, as modern science and technology become the dominant and authoritative modes of knowledge of man and world, it becomes ever more difficult to see that they are at the root of modern alienation. In Klein's words:

> Our rationalism is a symbolic one. It is the true result of the Cartesian distinction between "mind" and "external world." It is the true expression of the paradox of which we have spoken, that the mind, which is supposed to be sufficient to understand the world, is preconceived as a mind alienated from this same world. We approach the world not directly but by means of concepts which are abstractions of abstractions and which at the same time we interpret as being in direct contact with the world. (63)

Initially, it is difficult to understand what this alienation means for us in our daily lives. That a change in the concept of number is one of the roots of modernity's most fundamental maladies, which is the same as to say that modern philosophy has indeed succeeded in doing what Marx claimed it had never done—changing the world—is of momentous importance for our self-understanding. In the closing paragraphs of his essay Klein explicates how this alienation has affected our daily lives and indicates how it may be overcome:

> Thus, our own life does not belong to us. We appear to be in the most direct contact with the world around us, but in reality, the vast machinery of our society permits us to perceive the world only through generally accepted views. The directness of our contact with the world is of the same symbolic character as the concepts we use to understand it. We can comprehend how our whole social and economic system, which we term Capitalism, and which is, in its origins, closely connected to the modern idea of knowledge and science, has acquired such symbolic unreality.
>
> There may be many ways to overcome this symbolic unreality. One of these ways is to understand how ancient science approached the world. (64)

If we accept that we live in a "symbolic unreality," we also have to accept as necessary the task of finding our way out of it, for, as long as we stay immersed in it, we remain indeed men without world. We need to understand how ancient science approached the world, but in order to do that we first have to be liberally educated.

II

The essay entitled "The Idea of Liberal Education" (published in 1960) is Klein's most comprehensive discussion of the liberal arts. He also wrote three other lectures bearing directly on them: "The Problem of Freedom," "History and the Liberal Arts," and "On Liberal Education," but I leave out the third because it is very similar to the first, and the second I omit for reasons of space.

"The Idea of Liberal Education" begins with an ironic remark about lecturing on education: "The volume of noise made about education all over the country for many years now has, in recent months, increased to such a crescendo that no man with a sane mind should try to add a note to it. Yet this is what I am doing" (157). Although one could see this as no more than a humorous way to open a lecture, there is a serious question implied in it. Since the "volume of noise" he refers to has grown to a full-blown cacophony in our own time, the question as to why anyone would bother to contribute one more note is as important now as it was then. The implied answer, then and now, is that, despite the cacophony produced by all kinds of "experts" on education, it is possible to reach the ears of those willing to listen if one shows in simple terms the perennial nature of education. Klein says: "I shall use simple terms at the risk of being trite and saying things that everyone seems to know anyhow. All I want is to remind you of things that you do know" (157). His Socratic vein is evident, and it points to the fact that, concerning education, there has always been a lot of ambient noise.

The lecture begins by reminding us that all human beings are educated in some way: "everyone assimilates from his early childhood sets of customs, beliefs, opinions of all kinds, ways of behavior, and even ways of feeling and reacting" (158). This is our natural situation, which throughout human history has been determined by the particular community into which we are born. One may wonder to what extent the horizon of each political community has been altered by the homogenizing forces of modernity and its pedagogic techniques applied in "mass education," but enclosure in it would still hold true even if all the children of mass-educated parents were educated in the same way in a universal homogeneous state and only one universal *nomos* prevailed. That would probably make the chains of the global-cave dwellers all the more adamantine. There is, however, what may be regarded as a "natural solvent" to erode the chains. No matter how deeply the dogmas of our community entrance us, the problematic, unexpected aspects of life and the mistakes we make attempting to overcome them lead us to reconsider what we have always regarded as true beyond doubt. Experience is obtained by trial and error, and it is the natural stimulus to loosen the chains. Klein says: "When we invoke experience, we mean mainly disappointments, difficulties, troubles, obstacles, sufferings, and catastrophes that we have encountered, succumbed to or overcome, and keep anticipating. We become wise (not all of us, to be sure) through such adverse experience" (158). The first or elemental education is dialectically related to the second in such a way that experience may prove to be liberating insofar as it forces us to reflect on our elemental opinions and beliefs. I take this to mean that the various and unforeseeable circumstances of life are, as it were, "natural teachers." We may wonder, however, whether, having solved so many problems with technology, human life can become so "automatic" that experience in this sense may vanish.

A third level in the education of man is prompted by the need to solve the problems encountered in experience. This is

> the medium of deliberate reflection and of systematic procedure. In this medium the troubles and obstacles are lifted, by a process of conscious formalization, to a new level, *the theoretical* level. They become problems. How to solve them has to be learned: formal disciplines are required to bring a problem into focus; that is, to disentangle the kernel from the shell, to proceed methodically, to aid our memory, to make visible what is obscure. (158, emphasis added)

The emergence of the theoretical level is presented here as a natural consequence of the problems encountered in daily experience.

Klein stresses the fact that "formal education . . . grows out of our elemental education and remains rooted in it" (159). Because they remain rooted in it, the formal disciplines, such as arithmetic and geometry, are not wholly freed from the aims of elemental education. Architecture, for example, has a theoretical basis (arithmetic and geometry) but its aim is to construct the kind of dwellings suitable for the needs and tastes of human beings. Mankind built houses long before architecture became a formal discipline, but even if their dwellings remained standing for centuries, they ignored the general principles of construction. At the theoretical level, the formal disciplines develop a universality which seems to liberate them from the particular societies in which they may appear. That this is not unqualifiedly true is sufficiently evident when we consider that no architect can design (and obtain remuneration) completely ignoring the tastes and dogmas of his patrons. Architecture as such is not a liberal art.

In the second section of his lecture, Klein "digresses" from his examination of the relationship between elemental education and formal education in order to take up the phenomenon of questioning. This digression is necessary because, as he will explain, the kind of knowledge we obtain depends on the kind of questions we ask, which in turn depends on what drives us to ask them. Most questions are of a practical nature, originating in the need for knowledge in order to solve problems in daily life, but there are others, which Klein classifies as "gossipy", stemming from our passions, perhaps numerically even larger than the previous type. He also distinguishes questions that arise from idle curiosity from serious questions, the answer to which is important to us. The latter type he also calls "exploratory questions."

Klein emphasizes once again that all our questions

> originate within the horizon of our daily lives, a horizon that includes the familiar and the surprising, the routine and novelty, that which has precedents and that which has

> not. . . . The unexpected is still woven out of the texture of the expected. And it is this frame of the fundamentally familiar that actually allows us to formulate our questions. (160)

We may thus appreciate the direct relationship between the kind of questions we ask and the different levels or aspects of education. That "[t]he unexpected is still woven out of the texture of the expected" may be understood in two senses: on the one hand, it implies that we never really break with the horizon of our societies, or, to put it in more general terms, that all our questioning is historically determined; on the other, the unexpected may be radically so and therefore it may entail a true break with the expected. The dialectic of both senses is expressed by Heraclitus thus: "He who does not expect the unexpected will not find it, for it is both unfindable and aporetic."[4] Liberal education is only possible if the break with the expected is possible.

Klein also underlines the fact that language is what makes our questioning possible: "Our questioning is guided by language itself, which is oriented toward the world around us as we know it, including those parts or elements that in some way remain hidden to us" (160–61). But the guidance of language is possible because, as Aristotle has shown, "the various modes of being which determine the structure of what we call a world, our world, . . . are prefigured in the various forms of our questioning" (161).

Next, the examination of the phenomenon of questioning points to the fact that although we desire knowledge, the answers we give for the most part are opinions. Klein directs our attention to what may be regarded as the natural relationship between opinion and knowledge: "We live, for the most part, in holding and meeting opinions. But the important thing about opinions is precisely that they cannot avoid putting on the cloak of knowledge. The possibility of our having opinions rests on the possibility, at least, of our having truth" (161). We have to examine our opinions in order to see if they are true or not, but examining them is not what we normally do. For the most part, we take opinions as knowledge. This is what keeps us from raising questions. Asking questions is a natural human disposition that points to the possibility of truth, but it does not, by itself, turn us to its quest. We are not philosophers by nature, yet philosophy is not against nature. There is only one type of question that requires the examination of our opinions, but we are only able to ask it when we experience what Klein, following Plato, calls *metastrophê* or *periagôgê*—a turnabout or conversion of the soul towards the eternal ideas. We ask this type of question when we undergo the experience of *thauma* (wonder), described by him in these words, which I quote at length because they are crucial for the idea of liberal education:

> This state of mind requires detachment, and I am not at all certain to what extent we can contrive its presence. We suddenly do not feel at home in this world of ours. We take a deep look at things, at people, at words, with eyes blind to the familiar. We re-flect. We detach ourselves from all that is familiar to us; we change the direction of our inquiry; we do not explore the unknown anymore; on the contrary, we convert the known into the unknown. We wonder. . . . [This kind of questioning] does not lead to any discovery or recovery. It calls myself in question with all my questioning. It compels me to detach myself from myself, to transcend the limits of my horizons; that is, it *educates me. It gives me the freedom to go to the roots of all my questioning.* (162, emphasis added)

Klein distinguishes the kind of knowledge obtained by the metastrophic questioning from the kind sought by what he called "exploratory" questions, which seek either what we do not yet know (discovery) or what we have once known (recovery). He characterizes the primordial form of the first as prophecy and divining, and that of the second as mythmaking. Science and history he regards as derivative, correspondingly, from the first and the second primordial forms. It is important to notice that neither of these primordial forms or their derivatives properly makes us free. By means of scientific research we discover what we did not know, and, in this sense, science is akin to prophecy and divination because they both answer exploratory questions. What is discovered is the answer to our exploratory question, and, for as long as we accept it as a valid answer, we are not compelled to continue raising the same question. In the first book of the *Iliad*, once the seer Kalchas tells Agamemnon the cause of the plague, however much the king dislikes the answer, he no longer keeps asking about it. Once scientists discover that bacteria cause infections, no one keeps asking if they do. And insofar as history is rooted in questions about the past, questions about what we once knew, our attempts to recover it are limited by our memory. We can know nothing about societies that left no records, or events about which there can be no memory, such as the origin of man. Our questions aiming at recovery are necessarily answered mythically, by someone claiming to know what and why something happened in the past. Both scientific and historical knowledge arise from the type of questions asked; both increase our knowledge. The metastrophic kind of questioning differs from both of them because it forces the questioner to relinquish his most cherished dogmas and question his own questioning. Such questions lead us to face our own ignorance.

In the third section of his lecture, Klein takes up again the explication of the genesis of formal education out of elementary education. He directs our attention to the emergence of grammar and arithmetic as a consequence of our asking about the basis for two everyday experiences: conversing and counting. We talk, understand, and misunderstand each other. If we investigate how this is possible, we discover the structure which underlies all our speeches and this knowledge grows to become the science of grammar and, one may add, logic and rhetoric, that is, the trivium. But "the act of speaking presupposes the distinguishing of one word from another and the relating of one word to another. It presupposes, that is, counting. For counting is distinguishing and at the same time relating one thing to another" (164). Reflection upon this produces the formal discipline of arithmetic and the other disciplines of the quadrivium. Understanding how these formal disciplines become the sources of the liberal arts requires that we notice that they are both theoretical and practical before being liberal or metastrophic arts. Reflecting on the nature of language, asking why and how it is that we can communicate, is theoretical insofar as it is not motivated by the desire to solve some practical problem, but it also has practical consequences because learning grammar helps us to communicate more effectively and clearly. The same can be said of the inquiry about the presuppositions of arithmetic. Klein describes the whole situation as follows:

> The formal disciplines come into being as the result of our human ability to detach ourselves from our familiar and conflicting experiences, to turn about, to ask the radical question "why" and to persist in it, pursuing at the same time the exploratory questioning within the horizon in which we live. That is why the theoretical level thus reached always remains a two-sided one: the formal disciplines and sciences can also be applied disciplines and sciences; theoretical problems have or can have direct relation to our doing and making, to our practical life. *It is only when we dedicate ourselves to the radical, metastrophic questioning, when we free ourselves from the ever-present concern that the burden of life imposes upon us, that the formal education becomes liberal education, that the formal disciplines become liberal disciplines or liberal arts.* (164–65, emphasis added)

Klein's emphasis on the origin of theoretical or formal disciplines in the everyday world may be understood as an indication that the liberal arts need not turn their practitioners into detached inhabitants of the ivory tower who do not know if their neighbor is a man or a beast. Liberal arts do not lose their usefulness, but they are not guided by utility. Because even the theoretical aspect of the liberal arts is guided by questions aimed at discovery, that aspect does not make them capable of freeing the student. By contrast, the metastrophic question directs its attention to its own foundations or roots, for instance, to asking about the ontological roots of arithmetic. The difference with modern sciences is forcefully shown by Klein in "Modern Rationalism":

> In modern science there are no definite borders between pure science, on the one hand, and the so-called applied sciences and technics on the other. Modern science, as a whole, is not only applicable to certain procedures, the result of which is technics, but is itself technical. Despite its heritage of the idea of ancient science, modern science is not so much the understanding of nature as the art of mastering nature. (60)

As we have seen, the liberation is due to the kind of questioning which guides the inquiry.

The relationship between the liberal arts and leisure (*scholê*) is the main theme of the fourth section of "The Idea of Liberal Education." Klein reminds us that leisure was the prerogative of free men—those "not under compulsion to do servile work" (165). These were the men who could engage in liberal education:

> To study for the enjoyment of leisure and in leisure means to be engaged in liberal education. . . . This kind of education does not look for some goal or good beyond itself. It is in itself its own end. Long before Aristotle and long

> after him, even under totally different social conditions, this statement defined liberal learning and liberal education. (165)

The relationship between leisure and liberal education is a thorny issue for modern sensibility because it presupposes a leisured class as distinguished from a working class. And a society in which this distinction obtains is non-egalitarian and therefore, according to modern thought, unjust. It would seem, then, that the necessary conditions for liberal education are found only in unjust societies: if freedom of the mind is available only to those who are free from work, liberal education depends for its existence on the presence of a fundamental injustice in society. We can now see that the traditional opposition between the city and liberal education is rendered even more acute by the egalitarian basis of modern political thought. Klein seems to think that the difference between rich and poor, leisured and worker, in modern societies may be ameliorated if governments design a proper educational policy, along the lines that Jefferson suggested to John Adams in a letter. The proposal was that the state should offer free public education and select annually the best students in elementary schools, send them on to high school and eventually to the university: "Worth and genius would thus have been sought out from every condition of life and completely prepared by education for defeating the competition of wealth and birth for public trusts" (quoted by Klein, 168). Thus, a modern republican government can provide the leisure needed for the study of science while at the same time providing for the formation of an aristocracy of the mind within a democratic republic. Klein is quick to note that Jefferson's primary intention is to promote the study of useful modern sciences, not the liberal arts or ancient philosophy. Although one could argue that the education offered by the arts of the trivium would be beneficial for those pursuing careers in politics, it would still be true that their aim would be practical.

We shall further explore the modern opposition to liberal education from the perspective of the concept of freedom in the last section of this essay. For now, it may suffice to note that modern man finds his essence in work and regards leisure as the unjust remnant of the type of society modernity is meant to abolish. Opposition to liberal education is profoundly engrained in the modern spirit.

Without in the least belittling the enormous tension between the modern commercial republic and liberal education, it remains true that liberal education depends crucially on the kind of questioning that guides it, metastrophic questioning, which does not depend on the particular social conditions of the questioner. This theme is taken up by Klein in the last section of this lecture, which begins with this statement: "Liberal education is a precarious and even perilous kind of business" (166). Klein used the same expression ("precarious and perilous") at the end of the third section, which, in a writer as careful as he is, must certainly catch our attention. It is a precarious business because it can easily be derailed, and it is dangerous because metastrophic questioning puts the questioner at odds with his community—Socrates being, of course, the paradigmatic case. Klein collects the obstacles under three headings: (1) the learning situation itself; (2) the intellectual tradition; and (3) the political community. He considers these obstacles as "rooted in what is specifically human in man, and it is not possible not to meet them" (166). These three obstacles certainly throw cold water on any prospects for universal enlightenment.

Under the first heading, he points to two fundamental aspects of all learning and teaching: it requires teachers and students, and it requires institutions where education takes place. Regarding the relationship between teacher and student, the most important threat is that teachers usually want their students to accept their doctrine as true. It is very difficult to teach without indoctrinating the students, and indoctrination is inimical to the arousing of *thauma* or wonder. Usually, students imbibe the doctrine and are happy to become acolytes. What Klein calls the "paraphernalia of academic life" (classes, schedules, examinations, degrees, etc.) is necessary for the study of the formal disciplines—rooted in the exploratory kind of questioning—but it often obstructs and discourages metastrophic questioning.

The transmission over time of the teachings of the teachers forms the traditions or "schools of thought," and in them knowledge becomes sedimented or petrified. In this case, the difficulty is due to the nature of *thauma* and the causes of sedimentation. *Thauma* is what we experience when, prompted by metastrophic questions, we have to admit that we cannot explain something we have always believed we knew. We must first experience the aporia and recognize our lack of resources to answer the question. If we persist in the inquiry, we may move towards an answer, but in order for genuine learning to occur, we must see by ourselves the truth of the answer rather than accept it on the authority of the teacher. What a teacher is trying to teach may indeed be something he truly knows, but if the student cannot grasp the evidence in which the teacher's propositions is grounded, he is only acquiring an opinion. This problem becomes more acute as it is transmitted without making the fundamental evidence available, or at least pointing to the insufficiency of the grounds for the claims made. It is in this sense that knowledge becomes "sedimented" by its transmission. The task of liberal education is to promote the questioning that, by removing the sediments, allows the original evidence to appear. The classical example of such an education is the Platonic dialogue, when properly read.

Klein considers the political obstacle to liberal education as the most serious. "Man conceived as a political animal and man conceived as being desirous to know are not necessarily identical" (168). The cities or political communities formed by the political animal must—or should—pay the highest attention to the education of their members, for their very permanence depends on the coherence between the type of regime under which they live and the ends pursued by their educational institutions. Man "conceived as a being desirous to know," however, as a philosopher, pursues an education that is not guided or limited by ends at which his city aims. In a military regime, for example, education seeks to form the best soldiers. In a commercial republic, education aims at providing the skills necessary to succeed in becoming wealthy. No political regime has wisdom as the aim of its education. Hence the philosopher is necessarily at odds with all political regimes. In Klein's words:

> The demands of the political community to which we belong are indeed inexorable. It is important to understand, however, that the idea of liberal education cannot be easily reconciled with those demands. It is important to see that there is a definite tension between the exigencies of political life and the self-sustained goal of liberal education. This tension is very great. (169)

Awareness of this very great tension, of the fact that liberal education is a "perilous business," is a necessary condition for its defense. Liberal education is a preparation for the pursuit of wisdom, but the pursuer of wisdom cannot lose sight of the antagonism of the city. The defense, in sum, must rest on the conviction that the unexamined life is not worth living, that philosophy is the best life, even if it is perilous for the being desirous to know.

III

A defense of liberal education must include, inexorably, an explication of the freedom sought by it. In his essay entitled "The Problem of Freedom," Klein provides us with such an explication. Although the connection to liberal education is not thematized in this essay, it contains ideas that are immediately relevant for its defense. The key question to ask is if the modern understanding of freedom is incompatible with the freedom of thought at which liberal education aims. Before going into the details of the problem of freedom, it is important to emphasize that for Klein the modern concept of freedom is the second pillar of modernity, rivaling in importance the conception of a mathematical science of nature (122). We may infer that just as mathematical physics pervades all modern thinking and life, so does the modern concept of freedom. We may also anticipate that the modern solution to the problem of freedom may in fact produce novel conditions of unfreedom that must be faced by liberal education.

Klein's argument is organized around the three fundamental freedoms: freedom of thought, freedom of the will, and freedom to act or do, that is, political freedom. Each one of them is opposed by something that must be overcome—they are freedoms from. Regarding freedom of thought, what opposes it is the world we live in. He describes the opposition in these words:

> We do not think about the world we live in, it has been thought through for us by others. *We* do not think, *others* think for us: customs, current opinions, lawgivers behind some screen, determine what we think and how we think. Moreover, passions obscure any clear vision. They are as much the masters as customs and current opinions are. The world rules tyrannically over our thinking. We are its slaves. (118)

Freedom from this tyranny is obtained by means of liberal education, in which, as we have seen, the key is metastrophic questioning. We obtain this freedom when our souls turn around and begin the arduous ascent towards the exit of the cave and we are able to contemplate the truth and the idea of the Good. But the freedom from the tyranny of the cave or world seems to lead to a new tyranny, the tyranny of the truth. "This is what has bothered 'free thinkers,' the 'free minds' of all ages. It does not seem enough to shake off the chains of the cave. No other authority can be tolerated, if we want to be really free" (119). The full import of this statement will only become evident after we have considered the nature of modern freedom. At this stage of his argument, however, Klein wants to direct our attention to the fact that accepting the authority of the truth is necessary for freedom of thought, but the acceptance comes from the will. Freedom of thought is limited by the authority of truth and our willingness to accept this authority. Why this is the case is not fully argued. It would seem that once we have seen the truth of some proposition, for instance of a Euclidean theorem, it is no longer up to us to will not to see it. To regard this as an impingement on our freedom of thought seems far-fetched, but if freedom is understood as self-determination, it is a defensible claim. In order to elucidate this question, it is necessary to examine in what sense the will is said to be free. There is, however, one aspect of Klein's argument that can be grasped at this point: the concept of freedom is problematic because it cannot be neatly divided into the three types mentioned. Freedom of thought is necessarily bound to freedom of the will; without both, neither of them would seem to be possible.

Klein's discussion of freedom of the will is very brief—three paragraphs (119–20). The main point is that freedom of the will, like freedom of thought, also must submit to an authority beyond itself, in this case, the authority of the Good. He first recalls the Stoic teaching:

> To make the will free, i.e., to make our own will the very origin of our action or inaction, of our thinking and not thinking, amounts to finding in ourselves something that nothing and nobody can challenge or suppress. I am free when I follow nothing but my own will. I might *appear* a slave but *I am not* a slave. I enjoy sovereign independence.

> It is within my power not to be touched by feelings of misfortune, by anger, envy or jealousy. It is within my power, my sovereign power, to be like God. (120)

We should notice the abundance of political terms in this description because, as Klein emphasizes, most of our vocabulary regarding freedom has its origins in the vocabulary of politics. The importance of this observation will become evident in the discussion of modern political freedom. Besides the Stoic teaching about the freedom of the will, Klein also mentions the Judeo-Christian and the Epicurean doctrines. In both the Stoic and Christian versions of freedom of the will, "[t]he authority of the Good determines whether the will is really free or unfree" (120). The will is free when it wills what it ought to will. Although there is a "profound and unbridgeable difference" in the understanding of the will in the Stoic and Christian traditions, they share being subordinated to the authority of the Good; in both instances they are bound by "golden chains" which are nonetheless chains (120). Klein ends this discussion with two rhetorical questions: "May we conclude then that freedom of the will is the freedom to accept the authority of the Good? And are we not then enslaved again?" (120).

In order to see better the drift of this argument, it may be helpful to anticipate where it leads. Klein has shown that neither freedom of thought nor freedom of the will is an absolute freedom because each one is subordinated to something outside itself, the truth in one instance and the Good in the other. Insofar as they are limited, they both subject man to a principle other than himself. In this sense both freedoms are premodern and imperfect. But this judgment has as its basis the modern understanding of freedom, and Klein's intention is to show that the latter originates in the realm of politics and therefore its use as the foundation to understand the whole of freedom may be deeply questionable.

The explanation of political freedom follows the same logic as those of the other two freedoms. First Klein shows how the problem of freedom arises in every society and what the main solutions found for it are. Next, Klein argues that the best solution does not offer absolute freedom because man is subject to an authority that limits his freedom. In the second part of the argument Klein maintains that the political problem of all ages was actually solved by the political philosophers of the seventeenth and eighteenth centuries. The solution found is the modern concept of freedom. This achievement, as noted above, he deems to be as important as the conception of mathematical physics. Let us examine the details of each part of the argument.

In every society there are three types of possible relationships among men as they pursue their diverse goals. They may act under absolute compulsion, as in the relation of Master to Slave, where one man or a group of men has the power of life and death over the others. A second type of relationship obtains when men collaborate out of friendship, but it is of limited power in securing freedom. The third type is found when the relationships are based on mutual agreement or contract. But in order to secure observance of the agreement it is necessary to have sanctions and penalties which are set by law. The rule of law and the sanctity of law are the solution to the political problem of freedom from tyrannical rule. "But," Klein asks, "is not the Law a new kind of tyrant? Cannot laws rule as tyrannically over us as despots do? Was not even slavery a lawful institution?" (122). It should be noticed that the problem is not that laws may be good or bad but that, insofar as they are laws, they limit freedom. Political freedom, then, is freedom to obey the law, just as freedom of thought is freedom to accept the authority of the truth and freedom of the will is freedom to accept the authority of the Good.

The modern solution to the problem of political freedom is the social contract:

> The people as a whole makes a contract with itself to observe certain rules. By this very act *Law is generated.* It cannot henceforth be understood as imposed upon men—

> it is self-imposed. I obey the law because I participated in the lawgiving, I gave it to myself. . . . This primordial political act of lawgiving, in constituting the social and political body, establishes once and for all political freedom. (122)

This "theory of lawgiving," as Klein calls it, solves the problem of freedom because it removes the limitations inherent in the concept of freedom of thought and freedom of the will. "Freedom appears as a free creation of man" (123). There is, however, a very serious difficulty in this conception because it changes the emphasis from the content of law to the procedure by which law is generated. As a consequence, "The content of the law, its goodness or badness in terms of human welfare, in terms of the common good, is not the ultimate concern" (123). This novel conception of freedom eliminates the authority of the Good as something to which our will must submit. As long as the procedure by which a law is approved is constitutional, it is valid and presumably good; however, because constitutional approval is the procedural guarantee that a law has been freely accepted it cannot be regarded as tyrannically imposed. Instead of the common good which guides the art of politics in the premodern sense, we have the general will. The content of law is no longer understood as the product of some wise legislator; laws are produced by trial and error as the outcome of tactical maneuvering for votes, for parliamentary advantages and bargaining. Thus, political freedom as a free creation of man requires the cancellation of practical wisdom or *phronesis* as the highest virtue in the realm of politics. Klein acknowledges that it may be objected that the world has always been ruled with but scant wisdom (126), but this would suggest that the new understanding of law is just as unable as the premodern understanding to guarantee the justice of its laws. The paradoxical conclusion seems to be that the modern solution to the fundamental political problem—how to avoid tyranny—is no more capable of achieving it than the classical solutions. This suggests that modern political theory is in fact inferior to classical political philosophy due to the supposition it makes that the new concept of freedom can free modern societies from the threat of tyranny, which only makes us oblivious to the persistent danger.

In order to relate this discussion of the problem of freedom to the defense of liberal education, we must now consider what Klein calls the "fascination" exerted on us by the modern solution (124). This fascination may be considered the political parallel to the symbolic unreality produced by mathematical physics, as it makes the modern concept of freedom the paradigm for the understanding of freedom of the will and freedom of thought. Mathematical physics, as we saw, brings with it a change in our understanding of the relationship between concepts and their objects, or, more generally put, between thinking and nature. The modern concept of freedom "show[s] the way to a re-interpretation of the relation of the will to the Good. . . . If the Good is not given to the will from the outside, as it were, but set by the will itself, man as a willing being, as a moral being, can dispense with those golden chains, can be completely free, completely autonomous" (124–25). Becoming fascinated by this concept of freedom, we extend it to an understanding of the will as setting its own goals and determining as good whatever it wills. Under its spell, we come to see the world as a multicultural mosaic in which we can no longer distinguish barbarism from civilization. This same fascination transforms our understanding of freedom of thought. When applied to the relation between thinking and truth, it produces the notion that truth is a human construction (125). This is at the core of the postmodern attempts to abolish "logocentrism." Both effects of the fascination would seem to render liberal education purposeless. In the closing paragraph of this lecture, Klein offers his rejoinder:

> We have gone far beyond the realm of natural life lived by our ancestors. Once again, it seems to me, we should examine our assumptions, try to discover at what point our

> thinking and willing enter the mechanism and automatism of our political practices or are subjugated by them. Once again, we have to face the immense task of education which such an exploration entails. Once again, we have to picture ourselves in a cave, perhaps a deeper and vaster one than our forefathers ever imagined. The freedom we enjoy has perhaps created more chains and chains of a novel nature that hold us down. Once again we have to try to disentangle ourselves. We might fail in this enterprise, of course. But in failing we would still be exerting our freedom. (126)

IV

As I hope to have shown, Klein's defense of liberal education confronts directly the three most formidable challenges to its desirability and its possibility. One of these, the political challenge, we may regard as perennial because each political community sees itself as the rightful horizon for all human activities; it unavoidably sees the questioning of its fundamental opinions as subversive and inadmissible. But the variability of its *nomoi*, in both senses—custom and law—sooner or later awakens the need to question their truth. The city needs liberal education even as it rejects it. The possibility of liberal education, however, is rooted in man's nature as a being with speech who desires to know; therefore, it may flourish even in very inimical political situations. As long as man is capable of metastrophic questioning, liberal education is possible. The other two formidable challenges are peculiar to modern societies. One is the outcome of the conception of mathematical physics and the other of the modern conception of freedom. Each of them adds new and vaster galleries to the cave, forging novel and sturdy chains. To use this metaphor to represent modernity is to reopen the quarrel of Ancients and Moderns by raising doubts about the truthfulness of its scientific knowledge and the dangers to freedom posed by its self-understanding as the moment when man finally becomes truly free. Because we can no longer see modern science and modern freedom as unquestionably true and good, because we are aware of the crisis of modernity, we know that we need liberal education. Klein's defense shows that it is not due to "self-forgetting and pain-loving antiquarianism nor self-forgetting and intoxicating romanticism" that we must seek a liberal education.

Jacob Klein on the Problem of History for Liberal Education

MARY ELIZABETH HALPER

In Plato's *Sophist*, the Eleatic Stranger deploys the metaphor of gigantomachy, a battle between the race of Giants and the Olympian Gods, to describe the dispute between those who "define body and being as the same" and those who "force the simply true being to be some kind of intelligible and bodiless species."[1] The scope of the battle is totalizing, at least from the perspectives of the participants; the proportions of the contest seem to crowd out the possibility of another position or additional player. In this respect, the metaphor is applicable also to the domain of human knowledge, at least since the florescence of modernity and especially as it is found in the research university and its imitators. For this field is occupied exhaustively by the opposing camps of the Sciences and the Humanities.[2] To give a brief caricature: the side of the Sciences claims that human knowledge is found only by rigorous method applied to observable phenomena; to this the defenders of the Humanities emphasize that the *human* part of human knowledge will always limit the rigor of methodology and disrupt the supposed purity of observable phenomena. For their part, the friends of the Humanities claim that human knowledge is most importantly knowledge of the human, that is of the cultures and creations belonging to humanity; against this, the allies of the Sciences cite rhapsodic romanticism as a feeble cover for lazy and ultimately useless thinking. Thus have the battle lines been drawn.

But is this necessary? Must we assent to the terms of this engagement? Jacob Klein's answer is no; indeed, for the partisan of liberal learning, it is necessary to reject these conditions. To reject the battle, and therefore to bring upon oneself the ire of both sides, would require a kind of audacity. As Klein says, invoking another Platonic metaphor, "It takes courage to pursue a rather narrow and steep path hardly visible from the highways of contemporary learning" (138).[3] This call to courage comes at the close of Klein's lecture "History and the Liberal Arts," wherein Klein lays bare how the sides came to be—the Sciences almost entirely from the invention of mathematical physics and the Humanities from the invention of the new history[4]—and thereby undermines their claims to necessity. The call to courage accompanies Klein's recommendation to "ignore history's claims to universality, ignore History itself, if you please, in order to devote our full attention to the development of all the arts of understanding and all imaginative devices man can call his own" (138).

Klein's instruction to "ignore History" is no doubt difficult (as indeed the noble things are). Yet, I contend, the free development of all the arts of understanding demands more; simply ignoring History is insufficient. The purpose of this essay is to inquire after the more complex demands of liberal learning, that is, to go beyond Klein's rhetorical injunction and discern more carefully the footholds of the narrow and steep path of true liberal education. For this task there is hardly a better guide than Klein himself. Consequently, after recapitulating his argument in "History and the Liberal Arts," I will consider other writings from Klein in order to limn a more complete picture of what liberal education demands. Ultimately, I argue that a certain kind of history—what Klein calls "intentional history"—plays a role in liberal education. This kind of history is a genuine history of ideas that unearths the roots of ideas by a process of desedimentation. By deploying desedimentation, the liberal educator is able to meet the problem of history—instead of succumbing to or ignoring it—and therewith bypass the battle that has so much conditioned thinking about education. The liberal educator who is thus educated by Klein is then free to take up the true and pressing task of liberal education.

The Genesis of Historical Consciousness

Klein's lecture "History and the Liberal Arts" is a reflection on the "role and significance of History in a liberal arts curriculum," occasioned by the self-conscious neglect of History in the St. John's College Program (127). In the lecture, Klein argues against the universality and necessity of a historical form of consciousness, or what he sometimes calls a historical *a priori*, by which he means "a form of our thinking that inescapably leads us to see things in an historical perspective" (130). This form of our thinking is supposed to condition all possible meaning, which conditioning makes it possible and advisable to subject any human endeavor to a historical approach. To unseat this approach, Klein investigates different kinds of history in order to discern whether any does or rightfully should make such a claim to universality. Let us recapitulate that investigation here.

Klein considers four kinds of history: pragmatic, genealogical, symbolic, and scientific. Although the paradigmatic instance of each kind falls roughly into a chronological order, Klein's inquiry is not itself a historical inquiry. His task is not to demonstrate how each subsequent form developed from an antecedent form, but rather to determine whether any of the kinds of history presupposes an *a priori* historical sense. For the first three kinds, Klein finds no such sense. It is instructive to parse why the conditions of these kinds of history are not themselves historical, and, therefore, why these kinds of history do not include or demand the historical *a priori*.

Pragmatic history deals with standards of moral virtues and practical maxims. It presents paradigms of virtue or vice "in the unfolding drama of historical successes or catastrophes" (130). But its foundation is not itself historical; instead its source is daily life made brighter and bolder for the sake of practical instruction. As such, Klein points out, it does not even constitute a specific domain of human knowledge. This kind of history is at most ancillary to other disciplines, such as statecraft. In other words, this kind of history arises from a thoroughly practical concern, not an *a priori* form of thought. As such, pragmatic history "is founded on completely 'unhistorical' points of view" and consequently includes no historical *a priori* (130).

The genealogical type of history "comprises notions of origin, source, development, more generally, the notion of temporal order" (130). These notions seem likely candidates for a universal form of thought. For a moment it seems that here we find the historical *a priori*. Klein anticipates this impression and interrupts his presentation of the four types of history to reflect on a difficulty inherent to his present task. The difficulty in giving an account of different kinds of history is to avoid assuming a foundation in History as the conditioning form of human thought and action. Our own temporality, the development of species, the essential role of change in the rise and fall of regimes are easily co-opted by the later "historical sense." But these instances of temporal order and change are not "constitutive categories of historical experience" (130). Instead of being specific to the historical experience, they are prior to that experience, belonging to the realm of nature as much as myth, the political, and the legal. In short, the original realm of these notions is not historical. The genealogical type of history, therefore, also has its foundation in the unhistorical.

With the advent of Christianity, a new type of history begins: symbolic history. Again, at first blush, it seems that we have found the basis of history's universalizing tendency. This history encompasses the whole pageant of human and divine action. Despite the comprehensive and essential quality of this type of history, its condition is not itself historical. This type of history requires an eternal context. Its perspective transcends the temporality it affords, and its patterns do not belong wholly to its unfolding but to a prior and guiding plan. By this form of thinking, we understand our own temporality only as an incomplete existence and therefore only in light of the perfect existence promised us. The playing out of this temporality reflects the timeless purpose of God, "the eternal relations between creation, fall, redemption, and salvation"; consequently, "the history of the world is here a kind of symbolic reduplication of the spiritual history of man" (132). This type of history is still not an example of the historical *a priori*, for behind this form of thinking is the backdrop of eternity.

Pragmatic, genealogical, and symbolic history are similar in that they all presuppose unhistorical conditions. Klein also notes throughout that, in each instance, history as an enterprise of human knowing never makes it into the cohort of the liberal arts. Dante, one of the paradigmatic symbolic historians, marks out ten liberal disciplines (corresponding to the ten heavens of the world), and history is not among them. Even Aristotle, "who investigated, defined, elaborated on every conceivable art and science," likewise does not elevate history (130). The absence of history from lists of liberal arts makes sense: each of these types of history is servile. Pragmatic history serves the formation and instruction of character, especially certain types of characters. Genealogical history, such as Polybius writes, serves a legal or political function. Symbolic history serves salvation.

One type of history, a new type, remains: Vico's New Science. At the foundation of Vico's New Science is the distinction between the true (coordinate with the common, the abstract) and the certain (coordinate with the particular, the individual, the concrete). Vico is in pursuit of the certain and thereby breaks from all previous philosophy, which he identifies as seeking after the true and the common. The category of the common includes what belongs to the world of nature and to the divine which orders that world. The world that man makes belongs to the category of the concrete. The folly of the previous philosophers is their preoccupation with what is impenetrable to the human mind; the innovation and the boon of Vico's science is that it studies what man has made and therefore what man can hope to know. This new enterprise of human knowing, by adhering to the strictures of its own constructions, can attain certainty.

Vico's claims about the unequal intelligibility of the worlds of nature and of man are already historical: the world of nature is mysterious because its origins, its *history*, is known only to God. Thus begins the surreptitious circle of the historical perspective, which eventually encompasses the whole of the Humanities. Vico's science is "historical by definition" (133); that is, it stipulates that the certainties it attains are already and only historical. As Klein notes, this science *is* a history of human ideas, not a philosophical reflection on ideas. Since the aim is a "truthful certainty" and certainty can be had only of the particular, the concrete, and the individual, this aim can be achieved only by the historian (134). With Vico's innovation, all that has to do with the world of man, that is, the Humanities, comes to belongs the realm of History. The historical perspective, or the historical sense, alone can claim universality, since it is the realm in which all human experience plays out.

The new history's claim to universality puts it into competition with the work of mathematical physics. But this tension is superficial and masks a deeper similarity. The tension between history and mathematical physics, or between the Humanities and the Sciences, is posterior to their shared assumption of the distinction between the concrete and the abstract as exhaustive of what is available to the human intellect. History takes up the banner of the concrete, and mathematical physics, with its "screen of mathematical symbols," advances the abstract (135). Even though Vico's pursuit of an "ideal eternal history" has been abandoned, the historical sense behind it has captured and still captivates the Humanities, just as mathematical physics yet grips the Sciences.

The Problem of History and a Simple but Insufficient Strategy

Klein identifies three troubling consequences of developing the historical sense and its absorption of (some of) the liberal arts. When "all the disciplines within the realm of the humanities have become historical to the very core," (1) we inevitably subscribe to value-relativism, (2) we become inordinately preoccupied with trends, and (3) we obscure our own human nature and disinherit ourselves from our traditions (136). All of these consequences alienate us from the aims and ends of an education in the Humanities. The first consequence arises from a stipulation of and subsequent fascination with the past as other. The objects of our education—the books, works of art, architecture, institutions, and customs—become artifacts of "otherness." They are the external signs of an underlying and radically different culture that arose within its own historical context and therefore is impenetrable to us in our historical context. The ensuing relativity of values is unavoidable. The second consequence arises in the practical realm, almost as a perverted application of pragmatic history now in a scientific form. History itself is presumed to teach us where it wishes to go, so we suppose ourselves able to anticipate wheresoever it goes. We are thus swept up in trends generated by the relentless historical flow. Being guided by such trends and submitting to their seemingly undeniable strength puts another barrier between ourselves and what we study: not only are the objects of our study artifacts of a radically *other* culture, they are also woefully outdated. Finally, the third consequence arises from the historical perspective's demand that we understand ourselves as historical beings. By embracing our own historicity, we dissolve, devalue, or ignore our connections to a tradition. By alienating ourselves from these connections, which would allow us to understand ourselves as continuous with the objects of our study, we internalize our own otherness and the Humanities themselves become a kind of farce.

To avoid these consequences, Klein prescribes that we ignore History altogether. But this prescription does more than proscribe; we are to ignore History in order to focus on cultivating "all the arts of understanding and all the imaginative devices man can call his own" (137). Klein calls us to retask our intellectual energies, away from developing our historical sense and toward making sense of ideas, texts, and each other. When we refuses this fealty to History, education turns again into interpretive work in which our own souls are necessarily implicated. In this way, we are able to return to the true work of liberal education: the metastrophic inquiry by which we call ourselves into question along with all we question and which thus "gives [us] the freedom to go to the roots of all [our] questioning."[5]

This strategy is sound, given the nature of the problem of History. The problem of History is that it claims itself to be a necessary form of thinking that informs all attempts at discerning meaning. At stake in the absorption of all attempts of sense-making is the possibility of attaining truth, insight, or understanding. If History succeeds in installing itself as the necessary limit for all inquiry, then we are bound to it and barred from an inquiry that can uncover the roots of our inquiries. Klein articulates the problem thus: "The form of History shapes the material under consideration so as to make anything we look at assume historical clothing, as if the very basis of our looking at things were—we hear it so often—History itself" (131). This totalizing characteristic of the historical approach makes it unsafe to offer it any quarter. Otherwise, History will—and perhaps without our noticing it—conquer the whole territory.

As sound as this strategy is, however, it cannot be the only strategy. Preparation was needed in order to discern this strategy as a strategy. That is, Klein's very lecture allows us to detect the dangerous historical sense in the first place. The primary peril of the historical sense is that it cloaks its own modality: it does not present itself as one form of thinking among others but as the form of thinking already and always presumed—"as if the very basis of our looking at things" (131). Ignoring History is an achievement made possible by the work of Klein's lecture. Klein's lecture thus succeeds because it gives an unhistorical account of History—it presumes the validity of inquiry not captured by History and turns that inquiry onto History itself. In doing so, the lecture is an instance of a tactic that necessarily supplements the exhortation to ignore History.

Klein himself, and others with similar responsibilities and capacities, cannot simply ignore History; they have a different task and must deploy a different tactic. They need to make it possible for those beginning their liberal education to ignore History without falling into the sheer ignorance that so often feeds the historical sense. In other words, the tactic of those at the start of their liberal education should be to ignore History, but the tactic of the ones guiding them should be to make it possible to ignore History. Moreover, since the historical sense, though not universal, is nevertheless invasive, this work must match the historical sense's continual attempt to subjugate. In short, what is required is an approach that promotes the kind of inquiry that belongs to liberal education while preserving that inquiry from the insinuations of History. Again, we take Klein as our guide as we turn to this needful work.

Two Rules of Liberal Education

Klein's lecture itself provides an instance of the kind of work required of liberal educators. But how may we understand this work more generally? To answer this question, it is instructive to turn to another lecture of Klein's entitled "On Liberal Education." There Klein outlines two rules for liberal education whose pertinence has increased as "the background of the educational scene has changed tremendously" (263). In describing the character of this change to the educational scene, Klein rehearses the distinction between Science and the Humanities and concludes:

> All these disciplines [cultivated in our universities] are supposed to be classifiable into two vast domains, that of science proper and that of the humanities. The subject matter of liberal education is thought to belong almost exclusively to the latter domain, the domain of humanities, which includes—we ought to note—history and all kinds of historical disciplines. (264)

It is clear, then, that Klein has the problem of History very much in mind when he describes the two required rules.

"The first rule that liberal education requires—for the learner as well as for the teacher—[is] the practice of philosophical reflection and the awareness of its guiding role" (262). Pursuit of truth is the heart of liberal education, as it is through this pursuit that "the freedom of man was meant to find its integrity" (262). Liberal education cannot be properly liberating if it is bound to a historically conditioned perspective on truth. Accordingly, to adopt the historical sense imperils the possibility of philosophical wisdom, of insight into the whole that provides the intended integrity of man's freedom. Ignoring History is the way the learner abides by the first rule; the teacher's obedience is more complicated.

The second rule addresses the difficulties facing the teacher, who is responsible for preserving the liberal arts through generations of students. The arts that belong to liberal education do not spring fully formed from the head of some god but unfold through sustained investigation, which takes up words in common speech and fixes their originally ambiguous, shaded, connotative meanings to a definite significance. "The passing on of sciences, arts, and skills, especially of intellectual ones, cannot quite avoid the danger of blurring the original understanding on which those disciplines are based" (263). The disciplines preserve technical terms, which become divorced from the original insight behind them. Moreover, as this divorce increases, so also does the obfuscation of their derivative character. "Technical terms begin to form a technical jargon spreading a thick veil over the primordial sources"—sources which thus become sedimented (263). The second rule is therefore that "liberal education has to counteract this process of sedimentation and to find the proper ways of doing this" (263).

Since the process of sedimentation occurs in the perpetuation of the arts, it is primarily the teacher's responsibility to counteract it. The liberal educator must preserve both the sustained investigations that constitute the arts as well as the original insights on the basis of which the arts come into being. In his execution of the second rule, the liberal educator confronts much the same problem as Klein does in the problem of History. The problem of sedimentation is that the technical jargon becomes matter-of-course, simply and unreflectively presumed. The fundamental danger of the problem of History is that the historical form of thinking insinuates itself as a universal form of thinking, which is also unreflectively presumed. As "the form of History shapes the material under consideration so as to make anything we look at assume historical clothing," so also technical terms, by winning acceptance and familiarity, cloak the original insight they were supposed to clarify (131). Both sedimented technical terms and the historical form of thinking conceal their origins by presenting themselves as obvious. Consequently, the way to combat the process of sedimentation is also a way to confront the problem of History.

Desedimentation and Intentional History

Understanding the process of sedimentation is the first step in counteracting it. Klein provides that understanding in an essay on his teacher, Edmund Husserl: "Phenomenology and the History of Science." As the title suggests, history is again under investigation, and again different types of history surface. This time, Klein articulates the problem of History in the context of Husserl's phenomenology. Husserl's phenomenology is "the science of true beginnings, of origins, the ῥιζώματα πάντων [roots of all things]" (64). To establish this science, Husserl must face and overcome the problem of "history"—which, for him, appeared under the guise of "psychologism." History in this sense is a problem for philosophy because it stipulates that the explanation of an idea is necessarily exhausted by its contingent development. Husserl conquers this problem in his *Logical Investigations*, where he shows "irrefutably that logical, mathematical, and scientific propositions could never be fundamentally and necessarily determined by this sort of explanation" (66). Klein describes this demonstration as an act of liberation: Husserl's demonstration begins by freeing the question of origins "from an interpretation of mind that confuses mind with nature" (66).[6]

The relevant confusion of mind with nature is a confusion of the kind of temporality that belongs to each. Nature and natural objects belong to one sort of temporality; although the natural object appears only aspectually, it is given again and again as the same object at distinct, measurable moments. This natural time is time measurable by clocks and calendars. The object of the mind, on the other hand, belongs to an essentially different kind of temporality: "The object of the mind . . . appears as an 'absolute' and at the same time 'as passing in an absolute flow'" (66). It originally shows up for us as immediately present, but this original mode of givenness passes into "the mode of 'just-having-been-experienced'" (73). We then return to and re-examine the mental object through reflection by retaining it in memory. As such, we change its mode of givenness, and by these continuous modifications and successive modes the object "is constituted as persisting, as one and the same (identical 'invariant') object" (73). This succession of modes and continual modifications does not occur within natural time, but within an internal temporality: "The object of the mind is immersed in 'eternal' time, 'a time which cannot be measured by any chronometer' " (66).

The mistake psychologism makes is to collapse this distinction: "As a result, mind itself and all its objects become natural objects, and all problems of origin become problems of origin within natural time" (66). This mistake is parallel to the one modern scientific history makes; indeed, Klein claims that for Husserl, historicism is "an extension and amplification of [psychologism]" (68). The historical sense engendered by modern scientific history situates all human achievements, all objects of valid investigation, in the flow of natural time without remainder. History claims all time under its dominion, and time is indexed only to the measurements of History. History thus becomes the measure of all things, of what is and what is not. Whatever it cannot conscript, such as the eternal time proper to mental objects, is effectively designated as what is not.[7]

The distinction between natural time and internal temporality is difficult to maintain because the descriptions that arise from the psychologized or historicized approach may not look any different from those produced by a phenomenological, liberated approach: "the psychological and phenomenological description of logical operations may be identical, although their real significance differs profoundly" (69). The two approaches may yield superficially indiscernible results, but the difference between them must be maintained. Otherwise the accounts of meaning that are supposed to be governed by internal temporality will slip into the historical sense we are trying to avoid. The distinction between historicized and liberal inquiry lies chiefly "in the fundamentally different attitude of the thinker toward his objects" (69).

Husserl succeeds in liberating the problem of origins from the tyranny of naturalistic psychologism (and historicism) by maintaining a fundamentally different attitude towards the objects of his inquiry. The achievement of this attitude and the freedom it yields opens a new field of inquiry, a new kind of history—"intentional history"—and with it a new problem of history (70). This new problem of history concerns the connection of intentional history to actual history, or, the conjunction of internal temporality and natural time.[8] This problem of history is not a problem that History or historical consciousness poses to the investigation, but a problem within the investigation itself, and so is not itself historical.

Intentional history is the account of the genesis of a significant or intentional unit. Insofar as it is a description of the constitution of these significant units, it is a description of intentionality at work. Intentionality is, for Husserl, a technical term that picks out the directedness of our consciousness. Psychic states are always about something, they always intend something: "In perception something is perceived, in imagination, something imagined, in a statement, something is stated, in love something loved, in hate hated, in desire desired etc."[9] Intentionality is at work when it constitutes any possible object as a unit of significance. The task of Husserl's transcendental phenomenology (and, according to Klein, of intentional history) is "to reveal this working life [of intentionality at work] in its totality, to make everything that 'is' intelligible, ultimately out of its constitutive origins" (68). This task, however, also implicates the definite moment of an original foundation—a moment that belongs to "actual history" and thus is found in natural time. In other words, the subjective intentional product has an essential connection to a definite moment in actual history. As Klein emphasizes, the supertemporal constitution of these subjective intentional products "presupposes, of necessity, the whole complex of experiences leading to the situation in which [these intentional units are] capable of being 'anticipated' *and* 'intended' " (76).

Here sedimentation and reactivation, or desedimentation, enter. The "whole complex of experiences" belongs to a definite moment within the course of actual history, but in order for the science that arises from it to achieve ideal objectivity, that whole complex of experiences necessarily recedes. The path to a lasting existence of ideal objects includes several intervening steps. First the original evidence passes into retentional consciousness, then the experience of that evidence becomes embodied in speech, and finally that spoken word is translated into the written word. Each stage involves a deeper—though never radical—forgetfulness, which Husserl calls "sedimentation." But reactivating the original evidence and therefore restoring the significance of all the previous steps is possible. For Husserl, this kind of reactivation became imperative vis-à-vis the sciences of nature because their sedimentation of significance threatened to deprive them of significance altogether. This reactivation also can serve liberal education more broadly insofar as it grants access to the only form of history that is pertinent to liberal inquiry. Klein goes so far as to say:

> The interlacement of original production and 'sedimentation' of significance constitute the true character of history. From that point of view there is only *one* legitimate form of history: the history of human thought. . . . History, in this understanding, cannot be separated from philosophy. (78)

Deploying Desedimentation in Liberal Education

Desedimentation is the work of uncovering "the strata of occulted meanings" in order to reactivate the original and originating experience that produced those meanings.[10] Both Klein and Husserl deploy desedimentation in the context of the idealization of meaning-structures perpetrated by modern mathematics and natural science. In doing so they recover insights at the roots of modernity. This approach is appropriate to (and required for) unmasking the peculiar self-masking of modernity. The task of desedimentation as the task belonging to the true historian, and therewith the philosopher, also has a broader—though no less nuanced—application. If we recall the first rule of liberal education, that philosophical reflection must play a guiding role, then we find that the task of desedimentation belongs also to liberal education.

Because the task of desedimentation involves an attentive intimacy with the history of ideas, this task belongs to the liberal educator. How then does this task fit with the work of the liberal educator? In his lecture "On Liberal Education," Klein outlines "two ways of describing teaching and learning in an appropriate manner" (267). One way is generative, the way of "begetting and conceiving" (the "Aristotelian view"); the other is recollective, the way of "eliciting answers and gaining insight from within" (the "Socratic and Platonic view") (267). In the first way, "the word of the teacher acts as the form which in-forms the material of the learner's soul" (267). In the second way, the teacher's questioning "compels the learner to pull out of himself, as it were, something slumbering in him at all times" (267). Desedimentation functions differently in each view.

In the generative view, the work of desedimentation requires that the teacher not rely on inert, technical jargon, but that his in-forming word be fresh and living. Indeed, if the teacher is supposed to beget in the learner a knowing soul, only living words will do. Instead of passing along terms of art as already achieved, the teacher guides the student through the original achievement of the insights that yield those terms of art. The student, under the guidance of the teacher, performs the very activities whereby those insights are first achieved. In teaching a language, the teacher demands that the student translate or compose; in teaching mathematics, he demands that the student demonstrate or construct; in teaching music, he demands that the student sing. The teacher's demands take the form of speeches that call forth. In this way, the teacher's in-forming word also trans-forms the capability of the learner's soul so that it becomes of itself a knowing soul. The achievements of the arts of language, mathematics, or music (to name a few) are at work in the learner's soul as he himself works at them. This vitalization is due, certainly in part, to the unceasing spring of life that belongs to these arts themselves (or to the human interest in them), but the teacher's causal role lies in uncovering or recovering that liveliness. This vitalization is therefore a revitalization and thus is a task of desedimenting.[11]

In the recollective view, the work of desedimentation requires that the teacher articulate and pose questions that stir up the silt of sedimented significance. These are questions that touch both that of which the students are presently aware and that which waits already within them unnoticed. They are questions that are accessible at the surface of the students' opinions and that intimate the roots of the truth being sought. The duality of these questions unearths a depth in the learner's soul, one coordinate with the depth uncovered by the work of desedimenting. This depth of meaning guides the teacher in forming questions that may in turn deepen his students' souls. That the teacher already has a sense of this depth of meaning does not mean—indeed cannot mean—that the teacher makes the meaning into an artifact or that he treats his uncovering of the meaning as his accomplishment. In other words, it is *not* the case that the student is to inquire after the teacher's meaning. Even if the teacher has achieved much familiarity with the sought-after significance, the task of desedimentation demands that this familiarity not be allowed to breed contempt, nor be left to go stale. To this end, the teacher's work with the student also works on himself, for in rousing the student's soul to latent significance, he nourishes the vitality of that significance for himself as well. In this way, the teacher deploys desedimentation in his recollective work.

On this last point, we can see that desedimentation serves the end of liberal education both with respect to the content of that education and with respect to its execution. Desedimentation liberates the object of learning from the layers of occluding meaning and therewith liberates the souls of those who would behold that object, but it also demands a certain kind of responsibility from those who deploy it. In this latter way, it functions within and, in turn, supports a form of teacher–student relationship that befits liberal education specifically. The freedom promised by liberal education cannot be presupposed or achieved once and for all; it must be continually practiced and renewed. Consequently, liberal education is necessarily an ongoing undertaking. This ongoing character matches not only the ever-arising need to educate the next generation but also and more fundamentally the demands of the activity itself. Desedimentation supports this character of liberal education by demanding that its deployer again and again reactivate the significance of the object. The teacher's work of uncovering, reactivating, and subsequently interpreting is essentially the same work he demands of his students. Every calling forth from a student's slumbering soul is at the same time an excitation of the teacher's. In short, the teacher is also always a learner.

Desedimentation as a way of conducting liberal education draws from and keeps alive a reservoir of eminently shareable meaning.[12] Yet the work of desedimentation is not to be shared; it properly belongs to the teacher. This division of labor abides by Klein's initial exhortation to ignore History. For, in order that the true history succeed, it must be kept separate from the insidious historical sense that already occupies the souls of so many students. The teachers take up this true history, but it ought not be announced as history to the students. To so announce is to invoke History when it ought to be allowed to recede. The teacher must trust that the historical sense will eventually yield—even without his explicit effort—to the beauty and force of the ideas he helps uncover for his students.

Klein as Educator of Educators

To recapitulate the argument: the long-standing division of the enterprise of human knowing into the Sciences and the Humanities is grounded in the genesis of the correlative projects of mathematical physics and history. An inquiry into the genesis of the historical perspective reveals that it cannot support its claim to apriority or universality, that it is neither necessary nor just for historical consciousness to absorb all attempts to understand the human things, but that it nevertheless succeeds in this absorption. It is therefore necessary to combat History in order to recover and preserve the integrity and radicality of liberal education. The tactics required to resist History differ for students and teachers. Students should ignore History and dedicate their intellectual energies to cultivating all the arts of understanding and imaginative devices as they encounter and dwell with the greatest works of human intelligence. Teachers, on the other hand, must counteract the insinuation of History by disentangling the occluding layers which overlay the original meaning-formations. This task of desedimentation frees the roots of inquiry from the conscriptions of the historical sense. In executing this intentional history, the teacher liberates meaning from the parochialization of History and uncovers a commonly accessible sense that belongs to human beings as such.

To assent to the terms of the gigantomachy between the Sciences and the Humanities is to abdicate essential elements of liberal education. In the first place, such a concession forsakes the integrity of liberal education—two exclusive camps replace the varied but ultimately unified tapestry of liberal arts. In the second place, it surrenders each part to edifices—mathematical physics and history—that forswear their own status as traditions, thereby stunting the essential depth of liberal education. Both of these edifices cut off human knowing from its ground in human experience, impeding access to that ground precisely while presenting themselves as the only paths to knowledge. For liberal education to be liberating, it must be delivered from the division of the Sciences and the Humanities and from the totalizing forms of thought that belong to mathematical physics and to history. Desedimentation is a mode of such a delivery and, as we have seen, a preferred strategy of Jacob Klein.

Desedimentation is a kind of hinge between the two halves of Klein's life, halves described by Eva Brann as the European Scholar and the American Teacher.[13] Desedimentation is clearly a crucial tool for Klein's scholarly work on the conceptual generation of symbolic number. But, as has been suggested here, desedimentation can enjoy a broader application. Klein uses it to expose the conceptual generation of History, which, in turn, serves the enterprise of liberal education to which he devoted the latter half of his life. In the preface to Burt Hopkins's *The Origin of the Logic of Symbolic Mathematics*, Brann says:

> It is not entirely implausible that Klein's *Origin of Algebra* might, for all its scholarship, eventually play a role in the ever-current effort to revivify the liberal arts in American higher education. It is, after all, itself an example of the kind of inquiry that can be carried out only on the basis of broad liberal learning that unites language studies, ancient and modern, as well as mathematics and science with the discipline of letting the textual sources speak for themselves. Moreover, it is a model of the value of such learning to us, now, in achieving self-knowledge and self-orientation in our own speech.[14]

The present essay has attempted to support the plausibility of Brann's claim by demonstrating that the kind of work Klein undertakes in *Greek Mathematical Thought and the Origin of Algebra*, the work of desedimentation, is an appropriate and effective strategy for the revivification of liberal arts education.

Klein is thus an educator of educators. As he was for scores of colleagues and students during his time at St. John's College, so he is for the many more who find his writings: an indispensable guide for those lovers of liberal learning who are compelled to share their love.

The Role of "Intentionality" in Jacob Klein's Account of the Historicity of the Concept of Number

BURT C. HOPKINS

Introduction

Readers of the English translation of Jacob Klein's *Greek Mathematical Thought and the Origin of Algebra*[1] understandably come away with the impression that the concept of "intentionality" plays a crucial role in that book's analysis of its central subject matter, the concept of number. On the one hand, Klein's major thesis behind that analysis apparently appeals to the fundamental difference between the intentionality belonging to the Greek concept of number, as *Anzahl* (a determinate amount of items), and the intentionality belonging to the modern symbolic concept of number, as *Zahl* (a conventional sign that represents number without referring to anything other than itself). On the other hand, Klein apparently articulates the transformation that the concept of number undergoes from its Greek to its modern intentionality by appealing to the scholastic Eustachius's account of the medieval distinction between first and second intentions. Moreover, chapter 9, "On the Difference between Ancient and Modern Conceptualization," in which Klein anticipates the contrast between the ancient and modern "intentionality" to be established in the second part of the book, contains a definition of intentionality added by the translator together with a reference to an article written by Klein, titled "Phenomenology and the History of Science."[2] The definition of intentionality reads: "By intentionality is meant the mode in which our thought, and also our words, signify or intend their objects" (118). The referenced article, written and published after the two long articles that compose the German basis of the English translation of *GMTOA*, contains a detailed discussion of Edmund Husserl's account of what Klein calls "intentional history,"[3] which Husserl developed in his last writings and which were posthumously published in the late 1930s by his associate Eugen Fink.[4]

Klein's article presents Husserl's account of the intentional history at work in the Galilean impulse to mathematize nature. Klein argues that Husserl's account of the modern project of mathematizing nature needs to be supplemented by an account of the intentional history at work in François Viète's invention of symbolic algebra. Given the reference to this article following the translator's insertion of a definition of intentionality in Klein's book, the assumption that there is a close connection between Husserl's concept of intentionality and the concept of intentionality operative in that book would seem reasonable. In fact, just this assumption was made by Hiram Caton in his seminal review of *GMTOA*, where he argued that precedence for the account of symbolic thinking found in that book "should go to Husserl, who formulated a similar theory in the *Logische Untersuchungen* (Vol. II/I, par. 20)." Caton considers Klein's "failure to cite Husserl as the source of his Husserlian terminology" to be significant because of its bearing on "Klein's interpretation of his historical method." Caton maintains that, "by citing the scholastic Eustachias as illustrating the sources of the thinking of Vieta and Descartes . . . , Klein ingeniously" capitalized on the genealogy of Husserl's concept of intentionality, since Husserl took it "from [Franz] Brentano, who in turn took it from medieval logic." According to Caton, "In this way, Klein lends plausibility to his claim to interpret these Renaissance figures in accordance with the conceptuality of their *milieu*, while in my opinion Klein projects Husserl back upon Vieta and Descartes via Eustachias."[5]

Despite both the prevalence of the word *intentionality* in the English translation of Klein's book and the reference to it in Klein's article on the notion of intentional history in Husserl's last writings, the truth is that Husserl's concept of intentionality does not figure at all in *GMTOA*. To begin with, the word *Intentionalität* does not appear even once in Klein's German text. The German word that is consistently translated into English as *intentionality* is rather *Begrifflichkeit*, whose literal translation in English as *conceptuality* captures quite adequately the meaning of the German word. On purely philological grounds, then, the technical meaning of *Begrifflichkeit* must be kept apart from Husserl's conception of intentionality. But there are substantive reasons to keep Husserl's *intentionality* separate from Klein's *Begrifflichkeit* (hereafter *conceptuality*). Klein uses *conceptuality* to refer to the *formation* of concepts. Hence, his *GMTOA* argues that concept formation in ancient Greek mathematics, as evidenced paradigmatically in the concept *number*, differs radically from the symbolic mode of concept-formation in modern mathematics. Therefore, Klein posits a general opposition between Greek and modern *conceptuality* and not, as the English translation has it, between Greek and modern intentionality.

When Klein wrote *GMTOA* in the early 1930s (it was finished in 1934 and published in 1936), Husserl hadn't yet developed his account of intentionality in the direction of history, that is, in terms of the historicity of intentional meaning. Moreover, not only was Husserl's account of intentionality a-historical prior to the last phase of his thought, but he conceived it from the level of concept-formation whose origin Klein was endeavoring to provide a philosophical account of in his *GMTOA*. As Klein put it in his 1940 article mentioned above, "Husserl's logical researches amount in fact to a reproduction and precise understanding of the 'formalization' which took place in mathematics (and philosophy) ever since Vieta and Descartes paved the way for modern science" (*PHS* 70). The theory of intentionality Husserl developed to understand this formalization both presupposes and operates at the level of symbolic thinking. Klein, of course, would have been acutely aware of this, which explains why he didn't invoke Husserl's theory of intentionality or use that term in his characterization of the difference between the ancient and modern modes of concept-formation.

A brief look at the development of Husserl's theory of intentionality will highlight the state of affairs involved here. Contrary to Caton's claim, Husserl didn't get the theory of intentionality from Brentano. It's much closer to the truth to say that Husserl's theory of intentionality developed in response to his recognition that Brentano's concept of intentional object didn't have the resources to account for the formalized symbolic reasoning operative in general arithmetic. The problem according to Husserl was that Brentano understood a symbolic representation to be a surrogate for the intuitive presentation of cognitive contents. Husserl's research into the logic of arithmetic in his first book, *Philosophy of Arithmetic*, arrived at the discovery that the symbolic presentation of "imaginary"[6] numbers presupposed by general arithmetic—for example, negative numbers and irrational numbers—can in no way be conceived as the surrogate for their intuitive presentation. In that book Husserl was trying to demonstrate, following his teacher Karl Weierstrass, that all the higher operations of general arithmetic (*universal analysis*, as it was then called) can be derived from operations on numbers conceived as whole positive integers. But he came to realize that symbolic representations of imaginary numbers do not have an intuitive correlate in the operations on number so conceived. Because Husserl's theory of intentionality was developed in response to this very specific problem, its conceptuality presupposes the symbolic cognition characteristic of symbolic mathematics. That is, it presupposes a distinction, which we find in Descartes, between symbolic cognition, which is purely conceptual and non-intuitive, and an intuitive, non-conceptual mode of cognition. Because Husserl's theory presupposes this distinction within mathematical thinking, his theory cannot be useful for Klein in accounting for the difference between the ancient and modern modes of conceptuality.

Klein locates the origin of the distinction between the intuitive and the conceptual in Descartes, whose account of the abstraction responsible for the concepts operative in symbolic mathematics "first gives rise to the possibility of contrasting 'intuition' and 'conception,' and of positing 'intuition' as a *separate* source of cognition alongside of reason" (212/202). Husserl formulated his theory of intentionality on the basis of the primitive distinction between non-intuitive and in precisely this sense "empty" intentions and intentions that intuitively present ("fulfill" in Husserl's language) the non-conceptual content pre-delineated by the conceptual meaning that composes these empty intentions. To consider a simple example, we intend the factors of the number 378 emptily when we simply designate them by that phrase; we fulfill that intention when we determine what those factors are. Husserl uses this distinction to address symbolic mathematical intentions that cannot be filled in intuition, but he takes for granted the existence of those intentions. This, I submit, explains why Klein used *conceptuality* instead of *intentionality* to address the specific differences between ancient and modern modes of concept-formation. Moreover, it also explains why he employed the scholastic distinction between first and second intentions and their objects (182/174–75, 200/192, 221/207, 222/306n324). A first intention is directed to a thing in *rerum natura*, while the latter, its object, is understood as "a 'being' that is directly apprehensible" (192/175). A second intention—in the words of Eustachius a Sancto Paulo quoted by Klein—is "'the very operation of the mind by which it secondarily . . . intends a thing already conceived before, insofar as it has been conceived" (222/306n324). The object of a second intention is understood as a "concept which itself directly means (*gemeinen*) a concept and not a being" (182/174). Klein says Eustachius, who is "appealing to established usage," defines the second-intentional object "more narrowly as an *ens rationis* 'which is conceived as belonging to a thing known by virtue of its being known, and which cannot exist except *as something present in the intellect*, since it is conceived . . . *secondarily and by a reflexive operation of the mind*'" (221/207; internal quotation is from Eustachius).

On Klein's view, ancient Greek and modern conceptuality employ concepts differently in relation to beings that are directly accessible in apprehension. We apprehend sensible beings, like trees and rocks, directly in perception, and we apprehend intelligible beings, like monads and geometrical points, through images in thought. Accordingly, Klein shows that the sciences of the ancient Greeks conceptualize beings apprehended directly in perception and thought. The direct accessibility of beings, for Klein, takes place in the above-mentioned first intentions.[7] In contrast, modern science conceptualizes not *beings* accessible in direct apprehension but *concepts* whose meaning is at most indirectly related to beings. The concepts in question, according to Klein, are apprehended in the above-mentioned second intentions. Moreover, Klein maintains that the concepts employed in this way—as immediately meaning concepts and only indirectly (if at all) relating to beings—are nevertheless themselves made accessible in a manner akin to the beings that are accessible in a direct, first-intentional apprehension, by the close association of letter signs with these concepts. That is, even though the meaning of the letter signs is stipulated to be conceptually determined and therefore not directly related to a being accessible in direct apprehension, the letters that symbolize the conceptual meaning are themselves accessible in direct apprehension. Hence, the mathematical symbol expresses the general shift that the meaning of the concept undergoes in the transition from ancient to modern science, from (1) its role in the apprehension of the beings in the *intentio prima* to (2) its immediate conceptual apprehension itself as an *intentio secunda*, together with the *simultaneous* identification of the apprehended first-intentional being of the letter sign with the second-intentional concept designated by it. Precisely this identification composes, for Klein, the conceptual structure of the symbol's novel mode of being.

Klein locates the shift from ancient conceptuality to modern conceptuality in the invention of modern algebra by Viète and analytic geometry by Descartes. Where ancient science employed first intentions, modern science employs second intentions symbolized by letter signs that themselves may be grasped by first intentions. Klein uses the medieval distinction between first and second intentions to clarify *philosophically* this shift in conceptuality. Thus, Klein's appeal to these medieval distinctions does not mean that the innovators of modern algebra themselves understood their innovations in these terms. There's absolutely no evidence in Klein's text to support such a claim and in fact ample evidence against it, since Klein shows these innovators understood themselves to be restoring ancient mathematics and thus to be, in some sense, in continuity with it. Indeed, it is precisely this attenuation of the originality of their new mathematics that, for Klein, made it possible for Viète and Descartes to interpret their mathematics as dealing with the same objects as ancient mathematics.

Klein illustrates the shift in conceptuality that marks the emergence of modern science by using the distinction between first and second intentions to explain the radical transformation of the basic concept of mathematics—number—taking place with the invention of symbolic mathematics in the sixteenth and seventeenth centuries. Understanding Klein's argument, then, requires us to understand his use of this distinction. Among the many historians of mathematics who have discussed Klein's thesis,[8] Reviel Netz is the only one I know of who attempts to take into account Klein's employment of the scholastic distinction. Unfortunately, Netz's discussion is considerably off the mark. Nevertheless, a brief consideration of its shortcomings brings into relief the general outline of Klein's argument, in advance of my detailed discussion to follow.

Netz presents Klein as claiming that modern mathematics, unlike ancient mathematics, is based on "second-order intentionality"[9] or "second-order ontology" that employs "symbols that only then, indirectly, refer to objects."[10] Ancient mathematics, on the other hand, "referred to objects, directly." Netz also characterized Klein's thesis in terms of "the basic distinction . . . between first-order and second-order concepts."[11] By contrast, Klein speaks simply of first and second intentions and the objects of those intentions. Netz invents the terms "second-order intentionality," "second-order ontology," and so on. Perhaps because he has not carefully followed Klein's terminology, Netz has missed Klein's argument that the symbolic character of modern mathematics cannot be characterized simply as a shift to second intentions. Instead, Klein's crucial claim is that in modern mathematics the letter signs that mark the objects of second intentions are themselves apprehended as the objects of first intentions. The close consideration of Klein's argument to follow will show that he employs the scholastic distinction between first and second intentions in a non-scholastic way in order to capture what he maintains is distinctive about the mathematical symbol's specific mode of being. Thus, Klein argues that the cipher or letter functioning as a mathematical symbol is not a sign that signifies, which is to say, points to, a concept other than the cipher or letter itself. On the contrary, its mode of being is symbolic in the precise sense that the sense-perceptible mark in either case is apprehended straightforwardly as the concept in question. The symbolic being of the cipher *3*, for instance, presents itself as an object—*the* number three—and not as a sign that refers to the exact amount—three—of a multitude of any arbitrary items whatever.[12] Likewise, the symbolic being of the letter *a* does not present itself as a sign referring to any arbitrary multitude whatever, but, rather, presents simply a mathematical object: the variable *a*. Or so I will maintain in my presentation to follow of Klein's philosophical argument and the account of Viète's and Descartes's mathematics upon which his argument rests.

Klein's Account of the Conceptual Presuppositions Belonging to Viète's Interpretation of Diophantine Logistic

Klein begins by investigating the conceptual presuppositions of Viète's interpretation of the Diophantine logistic. Klein focuses on the following questions: "*What* does Viète understand by the species which form the object of the 'general analytic' and *in which way* does he understand them?" (*GMTOA*, 178/171). Klein says Viète subjects Diophantus's concept of εἶδος to a "universal extension [*universale Erweiterung*]" such that "the species become the objects of a 'generalized' [*allgemeinen*] mathematical discipline that is identifiable *neither* with geometry *nor* with arithmetic" (179/172). As to the way in which Viète understands these generalized quantitative species, Klein says Viète understands them to retain a "direct connection with the 'logistice numerosa', i.e., with 'calculation'," and, with this, a direct connection to "a homogeneous field of monads presupposed by its original meaning." Because calculation (*logistice numerosa*) "is dependent upon 'definite amounts of definite objects' [*Anzahlen*][13] and their relations," Viète's generalized species are understood as open to arithmetical operations. Viète's "fundamental rules" for calculating with species, what he calls "'*the canonical rules of species calculation*,'" "correspond to the rules for addition, subtraction, and multiplication used for instruction in ordinary calculation" (180/172).

Klein illustrates the nature of Viète's calculations with this example[14]:

$$\frac{A \text{ cubus} - B \text{ solido } 3}{C \text{ in } E \text{ quadratum}}$$

in modern notation:

$$\frac{x^3 - 3b}{cy^2}$$

We read Viète's calculation as "*A* cubed minus three times *B* solid, divided by *C* times *E* squared." He represents each species "by a *letter* (the vowels being assigned to the unknown, the consonants to the known magnitudes . . .), to which are joined the designation of the degree or genus, beginning with the second degree" (180/172–73). The degrees or *genera* of the species (indicated by words like *solidum*, *cubus*, and so on) are necessary to designate which species may and may not be immediately subject to addition and subtraction. Viète uses one set of terms to designate the rankings (or "rungs") of the unknown magnitudes (e.g., *quadratus*, *cubus*, and so on) and a second set to designate the rungs of known magnitudes (e.g., *planum*, *solidum*, and so on); they ascend with no definite limit.

In addition to the "*canonical rules of species calculation*," Klein stresses that we must always keep in mind Viète's " 'first and eternal law of equations and proportions,' " the "*law of homogeneity*," according to which "only such magnitudes can be related by way of addition or subtraction as belong to the same or the corresponding 'rung', although this does not hold for multiplication and division" (180–81/173).[15] On Klein's view, Viète's "law of homogeneity" is not connected with the ancient Greek definition of a *ratio* as something that "can only exist between 'homogeneous' magnitudes," since it "certainly is not unusual for ancient mathematicians to 'compare', for instance, a ratio of *lengths* with a ratio of *planes*, and to bring both into one '*proportion*'." Rather, as mentioned above, Viète's calculation with *species* reflects that every calculation depends "on 'counting off' the basic units" and thus "presupposes a field of *homogeneous monads*" (181/173–74). In

"Diophantine 'logistic'" the law of homogeneity is "fulfilled as a matter of course, because it already operates within such a field of 'pure' monads." Because Viète's "logistice speciosa" deals with several diverse genera, "Viète, in contrast to the 'ancient analysts' (veteres Analystae), expounds the 'lex homogeneorum' as the foundation of the 'analytical art'" (181–82/174).

Klein thus acknowledges that Viète's species is a general concept, and yet, "*The character of* 'ἀριθμός' *as a 'definite amount of . . .' is preserved in it in a peculiarly transformed way*" (182/174). In order to articulate this preservation and transformation, Klein unfolds the non-Aristotelian abstractness proper to Viète's symbolic number concept as follows:

> While every ἀριθμός means *immediately the things or the units themselves* whose "definite amount" it exhibits exactly, Viète's letter signs first of all mean precisely this *concept* of an amount [*Anzahl*] as a determination insolubly related to things or units,[16] and thus it *immediately means the general character of being an amount* that belongs to every possible definite amount—i.e., "amount overall"—and only *mediately* the things or units that may be present in any particular definite amount. (182/174)[17]

When Viète's letter signs, together with the *genera* of the unknown and known magnitudes (e.g., "*A* cubus," "*B* solido," and so on) become the focal point of calculational operations, we see what Klein regards as the "decisive turn":

> The 'rung' designation, which taken independently corresponds to the Diophantine εἶδος, *thus transforms the object of the* intentio secunda, namely the 'general amount' meant by the letter sign, *into the object of an intentio prima*, of a '*first intention*', namely into a 'being' which is accessible in a direct apprehension and whose counterpart in the realm

> of ordinary calculation is, for instance, 'two monads', 'three monads', etc." (182/174–75).[18]

When the letter sign itself is perceived as something that exists independently of what it designates, the "*merely possible objectivity*" of the εἶδος or species is understood as an "actual [*faktische*] objectivity" (183/175). Klein adds, "the possibility of being able to see a 'number' [*Zahl*] in the isolated letter signs 'A' or 'B' is, however, obviously possible only through the syntactical rules which Vieta gives, in the fourth chapter of the *Isagoge*, in derivation from the operating rules of the 'logistice numerosa'" (183–84/176). In Klein's judgment, the symbolic nature of Viète's concept of species is most readily apparent "in the species of the first degree, where the designation of the 'rung' is not appended to the letter sign and is thus, so to speak, collapsed into it" (183/176).[19] Thus, instead of designating the "rung" *latus seu radix* (side or root), which for Viète represents the first rung or degree of the *genera* of unknown magnitude, as *A latus* or *A radix*, Viète's notation simply designates it as *A*.

These considerations lead Klein to conclude that Viète's syntactical rules "therefore represent the first modern *axiom* system; their systematic connection is what initially 'defines' the object to which they refer" (184/176).[20] He continues:

> [T]hese rules are directly read off the "calculation" with determinate amounts of monads. This means that, ultimately, it is only possible for the transformed mode of the species to retain an amount or quantitative character [*Anzahl Charakter*] and therewith to become a 'number' [*Zahl*], namely to become an object of 'calculational' operations, *because the ancient 'determinate amounts of monads' are themselves also interpreted as 'numbers'* [*Zahlen*], which means that they are conceived from the point of view of their symbolic representation. (184/176)

Two factors enable Viète's species to retain the general character of number in the Greek sense: (1) the *reinterpretation* of the Greek ἀριθμός as a number in the modern sense (*Zahl*), that is, as a sign the numerical status of which is *not* characterized by its reference to a definite amount of things (or monads) but by its representation of the general character of being just this one number (for example, the sign *2* would represent "twoness"); (2) the *interpretation* of the determinate amounts of monads (ἀριθμοί) as being "at the same time" numbers (*Zahlen*) in the symbolic sense.[21] Klein's 1932 lecture "The World of Physics and the 'Natural' World" clarifies the issues here by showing how "the concept of 'two' no longer refers, as it did for Diophantus, directly to an object, viz., to two pure monads." Rather, it "already has a 'more general' character," insofar as "'Two' no longer means in Viète 'two definite things', but the general *concept* of twoness in general." With this, the numerical sign "2" "no longer means or intends a determinate number of things, but the general number-character of this one number." Similarly, the algebraic symbol *a* "represents the general numerical character of each and every number" and therefore "represents 'more' than the sign '2'." To return to what Klein emphasizes as "the decisive thing," just as Viète identifies his species symbols with Diophantus's signs for the unknown, Viète likewise identifies the symbol *2* "with the sign employed by Diophantus" for two, which means, "The concept of twoness is at the same time understood as referring to two entities."[22] Klein stresses the lasting significance of Viète's innovation: "This reinterpretation has to this day remained the foundation of our understanding of ancient 'arithmetic' and 'logistic'" (184/176).

On the basis of Viète's concept of species, Klein argues that the "numerically" indeterminate status proper to this concept[23] prepares the way for numbers as "'definite amounts' ['*Anzahlen*']" to be "conceived as 'ordinary numbers' ['*gewöhnliche Zahlen*']" (185–86/177–78). This conception, moreover, means that "for the everyday understanding, which in effect determines the actual [*faktische*] formation of concepts, these definite amounts coincide with the 'numeral' *sign* ['*Zahl-Zeichen*'] as such, especially in the course of specific calculational operations" (186/178). Klein also maintains that this reinterpretation of the traditional ἀριθμός concept "was supported by the 'Arabic' positional system of ciphers, which had been spreading in the West since the twelfth century and whose 'sign' character is much more pronounced than that of the Greek or Roman notation." However, he maintains, "it would be a mistake to attempt to understand the origin of the language of symbolic formalism as the final consequence of the introduction of the Arabic sign language." Rather, "The acceptance of this sign language in the West *itself presupposes a gradual change in the understanding of number as a definite amount of definite objects* [*Anzahl*]" (184n130/277n259).

For Klein, then, even though the new concept of species introduced by Viète "actually realizes the fundamental transformation of the conceptual foundations" of the Greek ἀριθμός, the "new '*number*' *concept* ['*Zahl*'-*Begriff*] *as such*, the basis of the 'symbolic' procedure" that is invented by Viète with this new species concept is not made "completely explicit" by him, but by Simon Stevin (152/148–49). Nevertheless, because Viète's species are "comprehensible only within the language *of symbolic formalism*," within, that is, what Viète calls "the '*finding of finding*,' namely, zetetic" analysis, Klein credits him with making possible "the most important tool of mathematical natural science, the *formula* . . . which, above all, opens up a new way of 'understanding' that was inaccessible to ancient ἐπιστήμη" (183/175).

Klein's Use of the Scholastic Distinction Between First and Second Intentions to Fix the Status of Descartes's Symbolic Concepts

Klein maintains, "Descartes' '*mathesis universalis*' corresponds completely to Viète's 'zetetic' [analysis—BH], by means of which is realized, with the aid of 'logistice speciosa', the 'new' and 'pure' algebra, interpreted as a general 'analytical art'" (217/206). They differ in the how they relate to traditional arithmetic and geometry. On Klein's view, "Viète sees the most important part of analytic in 'rhetic' or 'exegetic' . . . , in which *numerical* [*numerischen*] computations and the geometric constructions represent two different possibilities of application (so that the traditional conception of geometry as such is here preserved)." In Descartes, however, the traditional conception of geometry is not preserved, as he "*begins* by understanding geometric 'figures' as formations whose 'being' ['*Sein*'] is determined *solely* by their 'symbolic' character." Indeed, Klein reports, "Descartes, incidentally, from the very beginning distinguishes 'two kinds of figures' (duo genera figurarum), namely those which represent a 'multitudo', e.g., ∴, i.e., a numerus triangularis . . . and on the other hand, those which represent a 'magnitudo', e.g., Δ, etc. (Rule XIV, 450 f.)." However, "The symbolic 'figure' which forms the object of the *mathesis universalis*" is *not* to be found among these "completely traditional *nonsymbolic* formations," as it is rather precisely "what is 'common to' such figures, that is, 'figurality' itself" (215–16n189/299n319).

Klein again uses the scholastic distinction between first and second intentions to elucidate Descartes's account of the activity of intellect in relation to imagination. He begins by establishing a connection between Descartes's designation of "the 'sola multitudo' which the intellect 'separates' from the 'idea' of number [*numerus*] it finds available in the imagination as an 'abstract being' (ens abstractum)" and what is "called an *ens rationis* in the language of the schools" (220/206). Following Étienne Gilson,[24] Klein reports, "the *Summa* of Eustachius a Sancto Paulo, IV" characterizes "'*second intentions*'"—or, more precisely, the objects of second intentions—as a kind of "'entia rationis'" ('beings of reason') that "owes its 'being' ['*Sein*'] to the operation of the intellect alone" (220–21/206–7). Thus second-intentional objects, in Eustachius's words quoted by Klein, "'do not belong to things *unless a certain operation of the intellect is presupposed*, wherefore these beings of reason are said to depend on the intellect for their existence and connection.'" For Klein, then, Descartes's "'mere multitude' (sola multitudo), 'quantity' [*Mengenhaftigkeit*] as such, which has its 'being' by grace of the 'pure intellect', is truly an *ens abstractum* or *ens rationis* in the sense of a '*second intention*'" (221/207).

Moreover, the "process of 'separating'" that Descartes says the intellect performs in relation to the imagination "must [*muß*]," according to Klein, "be more precisely described" in a manner that takes its cues from Eustachius's "more exact" determination of the second intention. In this determination Eustachius,

> appealing to prevailing terminology, defines 'second intention' as an *ens rationis* 'that is conceived as belonging to a thing known by virtue of its being known, and which cannot exist except *as something present in the intellect*, since it is conceived [not originally but—JK] *secondarily and through a self-relating action of the mind*.' (221/207)

Klein describes, as follows, Descartes's "process of separating": "The intellect, when directed to the 'idea' ['*Idee*'] of a number [*numerus*] as a 'multitude of units' (*multitudo unitatum*—πλῆθος μονάδων) offered to it by the imagination . . . turns, as its nature requires, toward its own 'directedness', its own knowing" (221/207–8). In so doing, "it sees the multitude of units no longer 'directly', no longer in the 'performed act' (*actus exercitus* . . .), but 'indirectly', 'secondarily' (*secundario*), or, in the terms of another scholastic expression, in the 'signified act' (*actus signatus*[25])" (221/208). With this turn, then, what "is now immediately 'objective' ['*gegenständlich*']" for the intellect "is its own conceiving of that 'multitude of units'," a conceiving that having become "objective" is equivalent to "the 'concept' (*conceptus*) of number [*numerus*] as such." Despite the fact that the intellect is conceiving a *multitude* of units, "this *multitude itself* nevertheless appears to it as 'something', namely as *one* and therefore an 'ens', a '*being*'." For Klein, "[t]his is precisely what the 'abstraction' ['*abstractio*'] which the intellect undertakes consists in: It transforms the multitude of the number [*numerus*] into a seemingly 'independent' being, into an '*ens*', if only an '*ens rationis*'." In order for this abstraction to generate a symbol, "the '*ens rationis*' as a 'second intention'" (221–22/208) or, more precisely, "as the intended [*intendierte*] object of a second intention" (222n194/306n324) must become "graspable [*faßbar*]—with the help of the imagination—in the mode that the intellect, in turn, is able to take it up as a 'first intention.'" This is to say, the imagination assists the intellect in making into *the object of a first intention* something that, in the language and conceptuality of the schools, *is properly the object of a second intention.* When this happens, "we are dealing with a *symbol*, either with an 'algebraic' letter-sign or with a 'geometric' figure as understood by Descartes" (222/208).

Klein's Account of "Abstraction" in Descartes as "Symbolic Abstraction"

Klein maintains, "the 'abstraction' being spoken about here must accordingly be called '*symbolic abstraction*'" (211–12/202).[26] He highlights both the novelty of this "symbolic abstraction" and its distinction from the "ancient mode of separation or 'abstraction' (ἀφαίρησις)." From "here on" the ancient mode of abstraction "appears . . . as a 'direct' or 'imaginative' abstraction: The insights of the ancient mathematicians 'pertain more to the eyes and the imagination than to the intellect' (. . . —Rule IV, 375, 18 f.)." Indeed, on Klein's view, precisely the presupposition of the Cartesian "symbolic abstraction" explains "why the ancient 'number' concept ['*Zahl*'-*Begriff*] can at present[27] be characterized as having its 'intuitability' ['*Anschaulichkeit*']." Additionally, Klein shows the foundational significance of symbolic abstraction for what will become the opposition between "'intuition' ['*Anschauung*'] and 'conception' ['*Begriff*']" in post-Cartesian thought. Cartesian symbolic abstraction makes it possible "to posit 'intuition' as a *separate* source of cognition *alongside* of that belonging to the understanding [*Verstandes*]" (212/202).[28]

In clarifying the imagination's role in making symbolic representations of the intellect's pure concepts Klein begins with the "*figural* representation" characteristic of Descartes's geometry. Klein stresses, "Everything depends on understanding that the 'figures' with which the '*mathesis universalis*' deals, namely 'rectilinear and rectangular planes' as well as 'straight lines' . . . have, as far as their mode of being is concerned, no longer anything to do with the 'figures' of what had up till then been the ordinary 'geometry'" (214/203). He quotes Descartes at length to support this:

> 'We easily conclude: here propositions must be just as much *abstracted from those very figures with which geometers deal*, if the inquiry involves these, as from any other subject matter; and for this purpose none need be retained besides rectilinear and rectangular plane surfaces, or straight lines, which we also call figures because by means of them we can imagine a subject which is in truth extended [namely in three "dimensions"—JK] just as well as by means of a plane surface.' (. . . —Rule XIV, 452, 14 ff.) (214/203–4)

Klein also points out that for Descartes the proportions and therefore equations with which geometry deals can, if a certain condition is met, "be understood as 'numbers' [*Zahlen*]." That is, proportions and equations can be understood as "multitude," in the sense belonging to "one of those numbers with which 'algebra' deals in setting up proportions among 'A', 'B', and 'C'." The condition is that the "'common measure' (communis mensura)," specifically, the "particular '*unit*' (unitas)," must be "known for each case" in the instance of the comparison of "'*continuous* and undivided magnitudes' (magnitudines continuae et indivisae), 'lines' and 'planes'", which then permits "us to set up proportions (and thus equations)." Thus, "if that condition is met, these continuous magnitudes can immediately be understood as [such—BH] 'numbers' [*Zahlen*]," which "need no longer be referred to the 'common measure' because measuring (mensura) as such is here no longer the concern, but only 'arrangement' (ordo)" (214–15/204). Klein quotes Descartes to this effect:

> 'We are able afterwards to *arrange the multitude of units in such an order* that the difficulty which before was one of solving a problem of measurement now depends only on observing an order, and that the aid which our art gives us in this process is very great.' (... Rule XIV, 452, 2–6). (215/204)

On Klein's view, a major consequence of Descartes's understanding proportion in terms of "*ordo*" and not "*mensura*" is that "a plane or linear 'figure' represents no less and *no differently* a 'multitude or number' (multitudinem sive numerum) than a 'continuous magnitude'" (215/204). Accordingly, "Each 'figure' is therefore not a representation of a *determinate amount* [*bestimmten Anzahl*] of units of measurement (as are the straight lines of Euclid's arithmetical books)" (215/205). Rather, "it is the primary task and the *truly proper function* of such 'figures' 'to image' ['*abzubilden*'] the 'true idea' (vera idea) of number [*numerus*]" (215/204–5). When we are "[c]onfronted with an indeterminate multitude, i.e., with any algebraic quantity," we are therefore in a position to be "misled by the pure intellect" and to "want to understand" such a quantity "as a 'mere multitude' (*sola multiduto*), that is, as a formation [*Gebilde*] separated from all 'enumerated things' (*res numeratae*)." In order, then, to "not fall into error, we must indeed—as we have seen—'represent' to ourselves 'some subject measurable by many units' (*subjectum aliquod per multas unitates mensurabile*)," which, according to Klein, we do with Descartes's "figures." Like the letters in algebra they are visible and thus "measurable by many units," but they are not the same as the figures belonging to ordinary geometry. In other words, Descartes's "figures" represent an "indeterminate multitude" which, although it is not separated from enumerated and extended things, is nevertheless *not* conceptually equivalent to them either. This is to say, Descartes's "figure" is "a 'symbol'—obtained through 'symbolic abstraction'—of an *indeterminate multitude*." Moreover, Klein holds that this symbol "is exactly the same as the letter sign [*Buchstabenzeichen*] (together with its 'degree' designation) that occurs in 'algebra', especially in Vieta's analytic" (215/205).

Klein adds, "This 'symbolic' character of Cartesian 'figures' first makes possible that mutual correspondence of 'lines' with 'letter signs' or 'ciphers' which obtains in Cartesian mathematics" (215–16/205). Klein asserts, "Descartes himself says [this—BH] explicitly: 'It should be noted . . . that we . . . here *abstract no less from numbers themselves than* we did just before . . . *from geometric figures* or from anything else you like' (. . . Rule XVI, 455 f.)" (216/205). Thus, Klein concludes, "Precisely the same reinterpretation which the traditional concept of ἀριθμός undergoes at the hands of Vieta, Stevin, and the other contemporary algebraists, is effected by Descartes—and this is his original achievement—in the realm of traditional γεωμετρία" (217/206). Hence, on Klein's view, "The symbolic abstraction which leads from the ordinary numbers [*numeri*] to letter signs . . . , needs the imagination in exactly the same way as when it leads to 'figures'" (216/205). In connection with this, Klein stresses: "The mode of being of these 'figures' is, therefore, to repeat, none other than that of algebraic 'numbers' [*Zahlen*]—of Vieta's 'species'" (216–17/206).

Summary and Conclusion

Klein's seminal account of the transformation of the concept of number as it appears in Viète's invention of symbolic mathematics employs the medieval distinction between first and second intentions and between their respective intentional objects to articulate both the conceptual shift embedded in this innovation and the novel mode of concept-formation behind it. Klein likewise employs these medieval distinctions to characterize the conceptual shift initiated by Descartes's analytical geometry and Descartes's own account of the role played by the power of the imagination in the abstraction of generalized mathematical objects. Klein's use of these medieval terms outside of their proper historical milieu permits him to make evident the radical shift in the conceptuality of number brought about by the origin of symbolic algebra in comparison with the non-symbolic conceptuality of number in pre-modern mathematics. The most salient characteristics of this shift concern (1) the ontological status of modernity's generalized mathematical objects as second-intentional beings of reason, in contrast to the first-intentional status of the mathematical objects in pre-modern mathematics and (2) the first-intentional mode of presentation of the letter signs or figures that express the generalized mathematical objects and into which they collapse, giving birth to the mathematical symbol.

Klein later referred to the "symbolic unreality"[29] of the concepts generated by symbolic abstraction. This expression captures precisely the structural ambiguity of the mathematical symbol as a unit of meaning. For, on the one hand, lack of direct reference to real things characterizes the objective indeterminacy of the generalized mathematical objects. On the other hand, these concepts are presented in real things, namely, in sense-perceptible letter signs. This structural ambiguity gives rise to the paradox that to this day casts its shadow on the attempt to grasp the nature of the being of symbolic mathematical objects. The paradox is that despite their worldly, sense-perceptible appearance, they nevertheless are only intelligible in terms of the otherworldly, generalized concepts that somehow coalesce with these signs in the language of symbolic mathematics. Thus, to this day, the dispute announced by Aristotle in his disagreement with Plato regarding the mode of being of mathematical objects remains unresolved. Do terms like *triangle* and *three* signify beings that exist somehow, or do they signify concepts of the mind? Careful attention to the implications of Klein's account of the origin of this language may disclose that the answer to this question is undecidable within the conceptuality of symbolic mathematics.

Viètian Magnitudes

Is Viète's *Isagoge* an Attempt to Overcome the Euclidean Distinction between Magnitude and Multitude?[1]

MICHAEL DINK

In Euclid's *Elements*, a sharp distinction is made between magnitudes and numbers, as reflected in the separation of proofs concerning ratios and proportions involving each of these into different books, Book V for magnitudes and Books VII–IX for numbers. Yet in two pairs of propositions, Euclid shows certain analogies between ways of manipulating the two that later authors will seek to turn into bridges allowing us to overcome the distinction. I will be examining Viète's efforts to do this in his *Isagoge in Artem Analyticem* (or *Introduction to the Analytic Art*) both because it is interesting in itself and because it might shed light on Klein's treatment of Viète's role in the creation of modern symbolic mathematics.

I. Magnitude and Multitude in Euclid: Distinction and Analogy[2]

In Book VII of Euclid's *Elements*, a number is defined as "a multitude composed of units" (Def. 2).[3] Relations among numbers are described starting with the notion of one number measuring another. Although Euclid does not define this notion, it appears to mean that a number measures a number when the measuring number is contained a certain number of times in the measured number, with no units left over in the measured number. For example, three measures six, but not seven. A number that measures another is said to be a part of it; if not, it is said to be parts of it. This inference—if not a part, then parts—is based on the definition of number as a multitude of units, since any two numbers will have at least the unit as a common measure, and hence a common part. A greater number is a multiple of the lesser when it is measured by it. These relationships allow Euclid to define a proportion among numbers as follows: "Numbers are proportional when the first is the same multiple, or the same part, or the same parts, of the second that the third is of the fourth" (Def. 20). Examples: 10:5::12:6, ten is the same multiple of five that twelve is of six, namely, twice; 2:6::8:24, two is the same part of six that eight is of twenty-four, namely, one third; 3:5::6:10, three is the same parts of five that six is of ten, namely three fifths; 5:3::10:6, five is the same number of parts of three that ten is of six, namely, five thirds.

In Book V, magnitude is not defined. The first two definitions define *part* and *multiple* in the same way they are defined for numbers in Book VII. The third definition, however, defines a term that does not occur in the definitions of Book VII (although it occurs in many of the propositions of Books VII, VIII, and IX): "A *ratio* is a sort of relation in respect of size between two magnitudes of the same kind." The reference to size seems to suggest that a magnitude is anything that has size, or, in other words, anything that can have the relations of greater than, less than, or equal to other things in some respect. As the bulk of Euclid's *Elements* is concerned with plane geometry, the mathematical entities with which he deals are mostly lines, rectilinear plane figures (triangles, rectangles, parallelograms, etc.), circles and their parts, rectilinear solids, and spheres. In the case of all these geometrical entities, Euclid applies the terms *equal*, *greater*, and *less* to the geometrical entity itself, and he does not give a separate name to the magnitude of the entity. Examples of this include: lines, not lengths; rectangles, not areas; cubes, not volumes.[4]

In Definition 4, Euclid indicates what he might mean by "magnitudes of the same kind": "Magnitudes are said to have a ratio to one another which are capable, when multiplied, of exceeding one another." This rules out ratios between some of the entities with which he deals, for example, between a line and a rectangle. Since it is not possible, by taking a line some number of times, to make it exceed a rectangle, it is not possible to specify a relation of size between a line and a rectangle. Some cases are ambiguous: are a straight line and an arc of a circle of the same kind? A rectangle and a circle?

Definition 4 suggests that the number of times one magnitude must be multiplied to exceed another might be some indication of its ratio to that other. This suggestion is given precision in Definition 5, Euclid's famous definition of *same ratio*. This definition is justly famous because it confronts the problem of incommensurability, which means that there exist pairs of magnitudes, such as the side and the diagonal of a square, which do not have to one another the same ratio as any number has to any other number. This fact of incommensurability precludes the use of the definition of proportion given for numbers in Book VII as universally applicable to magnitudes. In other words, there is no magnitude of the same kind that is a common measure of the two given magnitudes.

The discovery of incommensurability was supposed to have been a great shock to the followers of Pythagoras, who had wanted to believe that numbers were the being of all things. It seemed to establish, on a demonstrative foundation, the intuitive distinction between the discrete, which is naturally numerable, and the continuous, now revealed as intrinsically and intractably resistant to complete enumeration by a common unit.

Euclid's definition of *same ratio* is notoriously difficult to grasp, so I won't try to explain it here. Its accomplishment was to give a precise sense to sameness of ratio in cases where the magnitudes in the ratio are incommensurable, which allows it to serve as the basis for proofs about sameness of ratio among any magnitudes, as in the first proof of Book VI of the *Elements*, that triangles under the same height have the same ratio as their bases.

There is, however, one detail of Euclid's definition that I cannot pass over. It involves taking equimultiples of certain pairs of the magnitudes involved in the two ratios. That is, it involves using numbers and multiplication in relation to magnitudes. Here, 'multiplication' means taking a given magnitude a certain number of times, thus producing a larger magnitude of the same kind. In this kind of multiplication, the multiplier is a number, the multiplicand is a magnitude, and the product is a magnitude of the same kind as the multiplicand, only larger.

It is also possible, of course, to multiply a number by a number. In such a case, in contrast to the one just given, it might seem that there is no distinction between the multiplier and multiplicand, since both are numbers. For Euclid, however, this is not quite true. The multiplicand number is analogous to the multiplicand magnitude; it has a certain size, a certain multitude of units. The multiplier number, however, has as its units the repeated "takings" of the multiplicand number. In other words, it is the number of times that the multiplicand is "taken" or "laid down." The product, however, is of the same kind as the multiplicand, a multitude of whatever kind of units it consists of. For example, if we see five apples at the grocery and ask for three times that many, the three is not three apples, but the number of times we want the multitude of five apples put into our shopping bag, and the result is fifteen apples in our shopping bag. But the important point is that the multiplier is not a number of apples and hence is different in kind from both the multiplicand and the product.

What is not possible, indeed not intelligible, for Euclid is to multiply a magnitude by a magnitude, as for example, we are encouraged to think we are doing by the high school formula for the area of a rectangle: area = width × length. As we have seen, the multiplication of a magnitude means taking that magnitude some number of times, so that the multiplier must be the number of times the magnitude is to be taken. To try to make another magnitude the multiplier is just nonsense.

Yet Euclid is not uninterested in the question of how the magnitudes of rectangles are related to the magnitudes of their sides. He investigates this in terms of how the relationship in size (that is, the ratio) of two rectangles is related to the relationships in size (that is, the ratios) of the sides of one rectangle to the sides of the other. The two most important propositions in which he deals with this are VI.16 and VI.23. As it turns out, there is an analogue to each of these in the number books, VII.19 for VI.16 and VIII.5 for VI.23.

The enunciation of VI.16 is as follows: "If four straight lines be proportional, the rectangle contained by the extremes is equal to the rectangle contained by the means; and, if the rectangle contained by the extremes be equal to the rectangle contained by the means, the four straight lines will be proportional." It follows from this proposition that a proportion of four lines is equivalent to an equation of two rectangles, and vice versa. Euclid presents this as a knowable truth involving four lines and two rectangles, not as a truth about the relation of the sides of a rectangle to that rectangle, much less as an operation relating the sides of one rectangle to that rectangle, or the length of those sides to the area of that rectangle, or finally and least of all, as an operation on lengths which yields an area.

There is, however, a proposition about numbers analogous to VI.16, namely, VII.19. Its enunciation reads as follows: "If four numbers be proportional, the number produced from the first and fourth will be equal to the number produced from the second and the third; and, if the number produced from the first and fourth be equal to that produced from the second and the third, the four numbers will be proportional."

Let us explore the analogy between this proposition and VI.16. Here the four proportional numbers are analogous to the four lines of VI.16. The analogues to the rectangles of VI.16, that is, the entities that are said to be equal to one another, are here also numbers, and thus of the same kind as the four proportional numbers, whereas in VI.16, the equal rectangles were magnitudes different in kind from the four lines. While the rectangles are magnitudes different in kind from the lines, they are not unrelated to them. Rather, each of the rectangles is said to be "contained by" two of the lines. This relationship might also be expressed by saying that the lines are the sides of the rectangle. In the case of VII.19, the numbers whose equality is inferred are each identified only as a number "produced by" two of the numbers in the proportion. In order to understand this phrase, we must refer to Definition 16 of Book VII: "And, when two numbers having multiplied one another make some number, the number so produced is called plane, and its sides are the numbers which have multiplied one another." Thus, a number is said to be "produced" when two numbers "multiply one another." This number resulting from the multiplication of two other numbers is called a "product" in modern terminology. Hence the analogue in this proposition of a rectangle in VI.16 is a number resulting from the multiplication of two numbers, which are the analogues of the lines by which the rectangle in VI.16 is said to be contained. The upshot is that the analogy between these two propositions is the planting of the seed of the idea that the sides of a rectangle have to the rectangle a relation similar to that which numbers multiplying one another have to the number that is their product.

The second pair of analogous propositions presents a somewhat more complicated relationship, but one that further fosters, without yielding to, the temptation to think of sides of rectangles as bearing to rectangles a relationship like that of numbers to the product that results from their multiplication.

The enunciation of VI.23 reads as follows: "Equiangular parallelograms have to one another the ratio compounded of the ratios of their sides." This proposition generalizes VI.16 in two ways. First, it generalizes from pairs of rectangles, which are parallelograms in which all the angles are right angles, to pairs of any equiangular parallelograms. Second, it generalizes from the case in which the rectangles are equal, that is, have a ratio of equality to one another, to a case in which they can have any ratio whatever to one another.

In order to accomplish this generalization, the proposition must introduce and illustrate, albeit without explicitly defining or explaining, a new procedure or operation, the compounding of two ratios to produce a new ratio. In the simplest case, where the consequent of the first ratio is the same as the antecedent of the second ratio, the ratio compounded of the two ratios is implicitly defined as the same as the ratio of the antecedent of the first to the consequent of the second. For example, if the two ratios are A:B and B:C, then the ratio compounded of the two ratios is A:C. If the ratios do not share a common term in this way, then the procedure is to find two new ratios, one of which is the same as the first given ratio and the other the same as the second given ratio, but with the specification that the consequent of the first new ratio be the same as the antecedent of the second new ratio. For example, if the two given ratios are A:B and C:D, then we take an arbitrary magnitude of the same kind as A and B, let it be K. We then find a new magnitude L as the fourth proportional to A, B, and K. Euclid has shown how to do this, *when the given magnitudes are lines*, in Proposition 12 of Book VI. So, when A, B, and K are lines, we can find line L such that A:B::K:L. Now we take lines C, D, and L, and find line M as the fourth proportional, so that C:D::L:M. Now, by the implicit definition of compound ratio in the simple case, K:M is the ratio compounded of K:L and L:M. But K:L is the same ratio as A:B and L:M is the same ratio as C:D. Therefore, K:M is also the ratio compounded of A:B and C:D. Since Euclid has only shown how to find a fourth proportional in the case where the three given magnitudes are lines, we are strictly speaking only able to carry out the operation of compounding ratios when the given magnitudes are lines. It seems, however, that the procedure could be extended to other kinds of magnitudes, provided that we have a way of showing that the ratio of two such magnitudes is the same as that of two lines. At this point in the *Elements*, Euclid has shown how to do this only for rectilinear figures.

Although VI.23 generalizes VI.16, it nonetheless respects the same limits. It states a truth about the relationship of a proportion of four lines to the ratio of two parallelograms, not about the relation of the sides of a parallelogram to that parallelogram, or about the length of those sides to the area of that parallelogram, and least of all about an operation on lengths of sides which yields the area of a parallelogram. Insofar as the proposition involves something that could be called an operation, it is an operation on two ratios of lines, called compounding, which results in a new ratio between lines. Nevertheless, the proposition does show that when the ratios of lines are those between corresponding sides of two equiangular parallelograms, the ratio that results from the operation of compounding them is *the same as* the ratio of the parallelograms.

Proposition VIII.5 treats the analogous case of numbers. Its enunciation reads as follows: "Plane numbers have to one another the ratio compounded of the ratios of their sides." In order to understand this enunciation, we have to return to Definition 16 of Book VII: "And, when two numbers having multiplied one another make some number, the number so produced is called plane, and its sides are the numbers which have multiplied one another." In modern terminology, a plane number is simply the product of two other numbers, that is, of its factors. So the proposition could be restated as saying that two products have to one another the ratio compounded of the ratios of their factors.

Clearly, the plane numbers, or products, are analogous to the equiangular parallelograms of VI.23, and the sides, or factors, are analogous to the lines that are the sides of the parallelograms. In the case of the numbers in VIII.5, we already have a way of determining the ratio of the plane numbers or products on the basis of their factors or sides, independently of the way to be proved in the proposition. Since the plane numbers are defined as the result of multiplying their sides by one another, if the pair of sides or factors are given for each plane number, we multiply each pair together and take the ratio of the results in order to get the ratio of the plane numbers or products.

What then does this proposition add to our knowledge? It simply shows that the method of compounding ratios, implicitly defined in VI.23 for lines, when applied to numbers yields the same result as that which is found by multiplying the sides or factors of a plane number.

Let's consider an example. Take the plane numbers 21 and 20. The sides or factors of 21 are 3 and 7, and the sides or factors of 20 are 4 and 5. Hence the ratios of the "corresponding sides" are 3:4 and 7:5. We wish to find the ratio compounded of these two ratios. Let us choose the number 21 and find the fourth proportional to 3, 4, and 21. Euclid has shown how to do this for numbers in VIII.4. As 3 is the seventh part of 21, we want the number of which 4 is the seventh part, namely, 28. Therefore, 3:4::21:28. Now we take the three numbers 7, 5, and 28 and find the fourth proportional. Since 7 is the fourth part of 28, we want the number of which 5 is the fourth part, namely, 20. Hence, 7:5::28:20. Therefore, the ratio compounded of 3:4 and 7:5 is 21:20, which is the same as that of the given plane numbers.

The upshot of VIII.5 is that, in the case of numbers, the ratio compounded of two ratios is the same as the ratio of the product of the antecedents of the given ratios to the product of the consequents of the given ratio. In our example, the ratio compounded of 3:4 and 7:5, which we showed to be 21:20, is the same as the ratio of 3 × 7 (= 21) to 4 × 5 (= 20). Considering the analogy between VI.23 and VIII.5, we are tempted to say that, if it made sense to multiply a line by a line, then the ratio of two equiangular parallelograms would be the ratio of the product of two adjacent sides of one parallelogram to the product of two adjacent sides of the other parallelogram. This in turn might tempt us to say that somehow the product of the adjacent sides is equal to the parallelogram in each case. But precisely because it does not make sense to speak of multiplying a line by a line, Euclid is not in danger of yielding to this temptation.

II. Diophantus: Multitude Only, but Equations with Unknowns

In Diophantus's *Arithmetic*, no issue concerning magnitude and multitude arises, because the only objects of the treatise are numbers. There are nonetheless at least three innovations in comparison to Euclidean practice: first, the very enterprise of setting and solving problems with numbers by means of writing and solving equations; second, the use of a sign for an unknown number which is sought as the solution of the problem, in such a way that this sign undergoes the same manipulations and operations as the numbers in the course of solving the equation; third, the willingness to use fractional parts of the unit in expressing parts of the original unit as numbers of the new fractional part taken as a unit.

Because Klein wants to argue that it is Viète's transforming appropriation of Diophantus's *Arithmetic* that first introduces symbol-generating abstraction into modern mathematics, he is at pains to establish that Diophantus's use of the unknown is not itself symbolic, but rather remains fundamentally within the Greek understanding of number as a definite number of definite things (130–31, 137).[5]

While he admits that the use of a sign for the unknown number being sought as the solution of an equation involves some indeterminacy, he wants to insist that this is not genuine indeterminacy, but merely a provisional indeterminacy: the number being sought is in fact determinate *in itself*, but is indeterminate only *for us* (140). Moreover, Klein lays stress on the fact that Diophantus's sign for the unknown, a final sigma, is more properly regarded as an abbreviation for the word *arithmos* (146).

Klein also acknowledges that in some of Diophantus's problems there is a stage that can be called an "indeterminate solution," in which the unknown number is expressed in terms of the known numbers, without the calculation being completed to make the unknown number determinate. But he insists that this "indeterminate solution" is for Diophantus always instrumental, always a stage on the way to the real solution, which is a determinate number (134).

III. Klein on Viète

Klein's account of Viète begins with an explanation of how he conceives of his "analytic art" as the rediscovery of the unified art that lay behind both Diophantus's art of solving numerical problems in the *Arithmetic* and the procedure of geometrical analysis employed by Euclid, Apollonius, and Pappus, and discussed by Pappus and in scholia to Euclid's *Elements* (154–58). Viète saw the writing of an equation using a sign for the unknown number being sought in Diophantus as analogous to the taking as given the thing sought to be proved in geometrical analysis (163). He then took the stage of the indeterminate solution, which was always auxiliary in Diophantus, as the true result of the analysis, and the calculation of the determinate numerical value of the unknown as the beginning of the synthesis (162–63). The part of analysis that carries out this process, Viète calls *zetetic* (sometimes adding *poristic*, without ever precisely defining it in distinction from *zetetic*), while the part that produces the determinate thing sought, he calls *rhetic* in the case of numbers and *exegetic* in the case of magnitude (166–68).

The fact that the results of zetetic analysis need to be interpreted in one of two ways in order to produce a determinate result seems to Klein to indicate that the things represented and manipulated in the equations of zetetic have an indeterminacy of a more radical kind than the provisional indeterminacy of Diophantus's sign for the unknown number (167). Furthermore, at least one aspect of this indeterminacy seems to be that between magnitude and multitude (172).

On Klein's account, the things manipulated in the equations of Viète's zetetic art are species, and these species are symbolic, the results of symbol-generating abstraction (171–75). There are, however, in my opinion, ambiguities in Klein's account of what the objects of the analytic art are, and what their relationships are to species on the one hand, and to Euclidean magnitudes and numbers on the other hand.

In giving his account, moreover, Klein does not walk us through the sequence that Viète himself goes through in the *Isagoge*, nor does he focus very explicitly on the role that overcoming the distinction between magnitude and multitude plays in the development of the analytic art and in the reckoning with species, and hence in the emergence of and sense of the symbolic nature of Viète's analytic art. In the next section, I undertake this very task in order to see if it confirms, calls into question, or complicates Klein's claims.

IV. Magnitude and Multitude in the *Isagoge*

In chapter 1, Viète divides his analytic art into three parts and makes some claims about the objects with which it deals. He claims that his art derives from the procedure of analysis found in ancient mathematics. He both reports the claim that this procedure was discovered by Plato and quotes a description of it, which he attributes to Theon, found as a scholium to Book XIII of Euclid's *Elements*: "taking the thing sought as granted and proceeding by means of what follows to a truth that is uncontested" (320).[6] He takes over from the ancients the names for two parts of the analytic art, zetetic and poristic, and proposes adding a third part, with a double name, rhetic or exegetic.

In explaining these three parts, he begins to make claims about the objects with which they are concerned. First, "there is a zetetic art by which is found the equation or proportion between the magnitude which is being sought and those that are given" (321). This seems to clearly indicate that the objects intended by the signs used in the equations and proportions of the zetetic art are to be called *magnitudes*, although it is not yet clear what Viète may mean by this term. Second, there is "a poristic art by which from the equation or proportion the truth of the theorem set up is investigated" (321).[7] This characterization of poristic avoids any mention of the objects intended, referring only to equations and proportions. Third, there is "an exegetic art by which from the equation set up or the proportion there is produced the magnitude itself which is being sought" (321). This formulation seems to confirm that the objects of the whole analytic art are "magnitudes."

This conclusion is, however, slightly complicated by Viète's later explication of what he leaves unexplicated here, namely, the distinction between the rhetic and exegetic versions of the third part of the analytic art. This explication does not come until chapter 7, "Concerning the Function of the Rhetic Art": "the rhetic or exegetic art . . . performs its function both in regard to numbers if the problem concerns a magnitude *that is to be expressed by number*, and in regard to lengths, surfaces, and solids if it is necessary to show *the magnitude itself*" (346, my emphasis). Viète goes on to say that in the latter case the analyst appears *as a geometer* and in the former *as a logistician*, operating in the realm of arithmetic. While the parallelism of the two options, which seem intended to correspond to the two names, rhetic and exegetic, might seem to suggest, as Klein maintains, that the object of zetetic is distinct from and more general than either the magnitudes found in geometry or the numbers found in arithmetic, Viète's language casts some doubt on this interpretation. He makes the contrast between "the magnitude *itself*" and "the magnitude *expressed by* number." This seems to suggest that he regards the object of zetetic as "the magnitude itself," while number is merely an optional way of expressing this magnitude.[8] This passage thus confirms, rather than calls into question, our initial impression that magnitudes are the intended object of the analytic art, while perhaps leaving the impression that these are the same as the magnitudes treated in geometry, an impression that subsequent parts of the text will call into question.

Let us return to chapter 1, where Viète, having explained the threefold division of the analytic art, now appears to say something about the rules that govern it, although he states the subject more vaguely, as "what truly pertains to the zetetic art" (321). If we arrange the items he mentions in their logical order, from premises to conclusions, we get the following list: (1) common notions, as well as theorems demonstrated by the power of analysis; (2) stipulations by which equations and proportions are arrived at; (3) syllogisms and enthymemes based on the stipulations. Here the objects are not specified, but are only indicated as involved in equations and proportions. The stipulations here referred to will be spelled out in chapter 2.

Before considering those stipulations, we should note that Viète ends chapter 1 with a qualification, introduced by a "however," suggesting that the qualification might be contrary to our expectations. There is a "form of proceeding" peculiar to the zetetic art, namely, that it does not employ its logic on numbers, "which was the tediousness of the ancient analysts" (presumably including Diophantus), "but uses its logic through a logistic which in a new way has to do with species" (321). This newly introduced notion of species is here contrasted with numbers, not, however, as a new *object* of the zetetic art, but rather, it seems, as something it uses, perhaps like a tool. When he now contrasts his new "logistic of species" with the old "numerical logistic," he claims that the former is much more powerful than the latter "for comparing magnitudes with one another in equations" (322). Here at least, it seems that Viète is not introducing the species as a new object of higher generality than either number or magnitude, but rather as an alternative to number as a way of expressing and representing the true object of analysis, that is, magnitudes.

Finally, Viète tells us that there is a condition that must first be fulfilled before species can be used to compare magnitudes with one another in equations. Specifically, something he calls the "law of homogeneity" must be established, and with it there must be set up "a series or ladder, hallowed by custom, of magnitudes ascending or descending by their own nature from genus to genus" (322). In order to determine what Viète means by *magnitude* as the object of the analytic art, we will have to investigate what he says in chapter 2 about the stipulations governing equations and proportions and in chapter 3 about the law of homogeneity.

Chapter 2 simply consists of a list of sixteen "stipulations governing equations and proportions" (322–24). Most of them are stated in a way that avoids specifying what kind of objects are being related in the equations or proportions. But in 7, 14, 15, and 16 these objects are specified as magnitudes. Of the 16 stipulations, however, only the first 9 are based on Euclidean statements that are unambiguously applicable to magnitudes (1–4 from Common Notions, 5 and 6 from spurious Common Notions, 7, 8 and 9 from Book V). Stipulations 10 through 16 all involve multiplication and division and therefore would be legitimate in Euclidean terms only in cases where at least the multipliers and divisors are numbers, not magnitudes. Viète makes no such restriction. The statement of stipulation 14 suggests and those of 15 and 16 make fully explicit that Viète does indeed intend to speak of the multiplication and division of magnitudes by magnitudes, contrary to Euclidean theory and practice. Indeed, stipulations 15 and 16 are nothing but the conflation of the first of the two pairs of analogous propositions we have examined in Euclid, namely VI.16 and VII.19. The conflation is achieved either by substituting magnitudes for numbers in VII.19 or by substituting the product of the multiplication of two magnitudes for the rectangles contained by two sides in VI.16.

An attempt at justifying this conflation is made in two additions to Viète's text, placed after stipulations 10 and 11, which speak of the multiplication and division of proportionals by proportionals. According to J. Winfree Smith, author of the *Isagoge* translation in Klein's book, these were annotations made by the editor, F. van Schooten, printed in the 1646 Leyden edition of the *Isagoge* (315n1). Here is the alleged justification: "For when proportionals are multiplied by proportionals, the same ratios are being compounded. . . . But the compounding of ratios is effected by the multiplication of the antecedents and the consequents respectively, as is clear from those things that Euclid shows in the twenty-third proposition of the sixth book and the fifth proposition of the eighth book of the *Elements*" (323). Van Schooten's purported justification is in effect an appeal to the conflation of VI.23 and VIII.5, which is indeed a more general form of the conflation of VI.16 and VII.19 (as explained above). But since multiplication only applies to the numbers in VIII.5 and not to the lines in VI.23, the purported justification is just an assertion at a more general level of the conflation which needs to be justified—a classic case of begging the question in the classic sense of that phrase!

The stipulations thus show that Viète wants to mean by magnitudes something capable of being both multiplier and multiplicand in the operation of multiplication and both divisor and dividend in the operation of division. Since Euclid does not regard the attempt to apply these operations to magnitudes as meaningful, it would seem that Viète must do at least one of two things: (1) redefine magnitudes or (2) redefine the operations of multiplication and division.

My colleague, Henry Higuera, has suggested that the van Schooten additions can be taken as implicitly doing the second, that is, redefining multiplication and division.[9] He offers the following formulation of this redefinition. Magnitude P1 is the product of magnitudes a1 and b1 and magnitude P2 is the product of magnitudes a2 and b2 only if the ratio of P1:P2 is the same as the ratio compounded of a1:a2 and b1:b2. This proposed definition of multiplication of a magnitude by a magnitude is a precise way of codifying the conflation of VI.23 and VIII.5. It is not yet, however, quite sufficient to justify statements of the form a1 × b1 = P1. This is because P1 and P2 are by no means a unique pair of magnitudes satisfying the requirement that they have the same ratio as the ratio compounded of a1:a2 and b1:b2; indeed, we can find as many such pairs as we please. What would be required is some way of specifying a common unit to which all of the magnitudes involved could be referred, that is, to which each of them can have a determinate ratio, even if the "unit" does not measure them in a Euclidean sense.[10]

The specification of such a common unit, however, runs up against another aspect of Viète's understanding of the multiplication and division of magnitudes, as stated in chapter 3 as a part or consequence of the law of homogeneity: "If a magnitude is multiplied by a magnitude, the magnitude that is produced is heterogeneous in relation to both" (325). Thus there cannot be a common unit for *all* magnitudes, but only for magnitudes of the same kind, and in every instance of multiplication, the "product magnitudes" are of a different kind than each of the "factor magnitudes," which may also be of a different kind from one another.

The source of Viète's treatment of homogeneity and heterogeneity in magnitudes is pretty obvious. It is precisely the geometrical side of the analogous pairs of Euclidean propositions that he has been exploiting. In VI.16, the pair of lines that form the extreme terms of the proportion and those that form the mean terms enter into an equation only as the sides of two equal rectangles. When Viète interprets VI.16 as involving the multiplication of these lines by one another, he is also drawn to interpret the resulting equal rectangles as the products of these multiplications. Likewise, in VI.23, just as the compounding of the ratios of lines is interpreted as yielding a ratio of the products of pairs of lines, so these products are interpreted as the parallelograms whose ratio has been shown to be the same as the ratio compounded of the ratios of the sides. So in both cases, the "multiplication" of one magnitude with another of like kind (namely, two lines) yields as a product another kind of magnitude (namely, a rectangle or parallelogram). A line and a rectangle are not magnitudes of the same kind because they cannot have a ratio to one another or because one cannot be made to exceed the other by being multiplied (in the old Euclidean sense) a finite number of times. Although Euclid himself does not give us propositions analogous to VI.16 and VI.23 to show when two parallelipipedal solids are equal or to show how to get their ratio by compounding the ratios of their sides, such propositions seem possible on Euclidean grounds, and he does demonstrate a special case, namely, that similar parallelipipedal solids have to one another the triplicate ratio of their corresponding sides (XI.33).

Strictly speaking, however, Viète does not simply take Euclidean lines as factors and Euclidean rectangles and rectilinear solids as products. This becomes evident from the fact that Viète's series of ladder magnitudes does not end with the geometrically available magnitudes, at the third dimension, but continues indefinitely into higher dimensions. Although Viète names these higher dimensional magnitudes with expressions analogous to those of geometry (for example, *plane-plane* for the fourth "rung" and *plane-solid* for the fifth rung), it is clear that these magnitudes are no longer geometrical, and hence neither are those on the first three rungs.[11]

Thus the law of homogeneity as well as the series of ladder magnitudes that results from the heterogeneity of factors and products in multiplication reveals that Viète has chosen *both* of the alternatives mentioned above as his means of rationalizing his conflation of Euclidean magnitude and multitude. That is, he has *both* redefined the operations of multiplication and division *and* redefined the meaning of magnitude.[12]

The motive for these redefinitions is clearly stated in the last line of the *Isagoge*: "*Nullum non problema solvere*," or "There is no problem which cannot be solved." Viète's method for solving problems is to write an equation with a sign for an unknown and other signs for knowns and to solve the equation, that is, to isolate the first power of the unknown on one side of the equation and all the signs for the knowns on the other side. If the signs stood for Euclidean numbers, then in many cases the expression resulting on the other side of the equation than the sign for the unknown (as well as many other expressions encountered in the course of the solution) would not be able to stand for a Euclidean number, that is, a multitude of units. This is because many operations performed on Euclidean numbers do not yield Euclidean numbers as results: for example, dividing an odd by an even, subtracting a greater from a lesser, and finding the mean proportional between two non-square numbers. On the other hand, if the signs stood for geometrical magnitudes, the sign for the result of any operation ascending above the third power or below the first would not have an object.[13] Thus Viète's redefinition of the objects and operations of zetetic are intended to ensure that any "well-formed expression," that is, an expression formed following the operations and rules of zetetic, will have an object.

Viète's chapter 4 is entitled "On the Precepts of Reckoning by Species." Klein says, "it is obviously impossible to see 'numbers' in the isolated letter signs 'A' and 'B,' except through the syntactical rules which Viète states in the fourth chapter of the *Isagoge*" and "These rules therefore represent the first modern axiom system" (176). It seems to me, however, that the heavy lifting has already been done by the stipulations in chapter 2 and the law of homogeneity in chapter 3, which have already determined the character of the objects intended by these letter signs, which objects I call "Viètian magnitudes" to mark their difference from Euclidean magnitudes.[14] What is remarkable about the precepts in chapter 4 is how empty they are. They do little more than show how to express in the letter symbolism the "magnitudes" whose character has already been determined by the previously laid down stipulations and laws. Particularly conspicuous by its absence is any actual procedure for carrying out the operations of multiplication and division of magnitudes.

At this point, I am going to abandon the project of going through the *Isagoge* step by step. It seems to me that we have seen enough of Viète's articulation of his project to take stock of it as well as of Klein's account of it.

Let me first state the conclusions I think have emerged. First, it is clear that Viète wants to call the objects of his analytic art *magnitudes*. The species are for him not its objects, but either are tools by means of which calculations are performed on the objects or are signs that represent those objects. The additions, subtractions, multiplications, and divisions that the reckoning by species keeps track of are in fact operations to be performed on magnitudes, although the magnitudes on which they are to be performed are not yet specified or determined.[15] Second, the magnitudes that are the objects of the analytic art are neither Euclidean magnitudes nor Euclidean numbers, although they are such that inferences about one or the other of these can be drawn from them by means of the rhetic and exegetic arts.[16] Third, these new Viètian magnitudes are determined in their character by the rules that govern them, that is, the stipulations of chapter 2 and the law of homogeneity. These rules have as their salient character the conflation of the continuity of Euclidean magnitudes with the calculability, primarily the ability to be multiplied and divided, of Euclidean number.[17] In addition, they preserve the dimensionality of Euclidean magnitudes, but remove its restriction to three dimensions.

These conclusions have somewhat complicated relations to Klein's own conclusions, in part, I think, because of certain ambiguities in Klein's own treatment, which seems to waver among three alternatives: (1) the object of Viète's analytic art is "general magnitude," understood as a concept itself intending particular numbers or magnitudes, represented by the species—on this view, the species signs are second intentions in that they designate a general concept that in turn refers to determinate objects (165–66, 174); (2) the object is the species itself, an object whose character is defined by the rules (or axiom system) which govern its manipulation—in this version, the species, in so far as they are wholly dependent for their being on the laws that govern their behavior, are themselves *objects* of a second intention, but do not themselves have a determinate object (176, 178–79); (3) the object is the very letter sign itself which purports to intend the species, now identified with that which it intends, namely, the concept of "general magnitude."[18]

Here is how my reading modifies these three claims and seeks to fit them together into a consistent account. The object of Viète's analytic art is best described as "Viètian magnitude," which is indeed both conceptual and general, but in senses that can be more precisely specified. It is general not merely in the sense of being indeterminate in its reference to definite numbers or definite magnitudes. Rather, it is general in the sense of being a new kind of mathematical object, which combines some desirable features of Euclidean magnitudes with some desirable features of Euclidean numbers, while also rejecting some limiting features of each. It is conceptual not by virtue of having its first-intentional intending of determinate magnitudes or multitudes made into the object of a second intention (as in alternative (1) above). Rather, it is conceptual precisely in the sense of another version of Klein's characterization of modern conceptuality, namely, that in which the rules or axioms determine the character of the objects they govern (as in alternative (2) above—see

121, 142, 176). Such rule-determined objects are emphatically and radically "entities of reason," but this does not mean that they are concepts having a first-intentional object. Whether or not they are distinct from the signs that claim to represent them seems to me an open and debatable question. As a matter of interpreting Viète's text, it seems clear to me that he intends to maintain the distinction between the species signs and the 'Viètian magnitudes' which they represent. If Klein wants to claim either that there is something in Viète's practice that undermines his ability to do so or something intrinsic to this kind of rule-determined object that makes it impossible to do so, I think further argument is needed beyond what I find in his book. Finally, it seems to me that the species signs do not "indirectly intend" Euclidean magnitudes or Euclidean numbers. Rather, the task of the rhetic and exegetic arts is not to specify general magnitudes as determinate Euclidean numbers or geometric magnitudes, but rather to *translate* the Viètian magnitudes of the zetetic art into corresponding Euclidean numbers or magnitudes. In the case of Euclidean numbers, what is required for the translation is to specify a numerical interpretation for each known Viètian magnitude. In chapter 7, Viète speaks of a [Viètian] "magnitude that is to be expressed by a number" (346). In the case of geometric magnitudes, one can only translate equations of three dimensions or less, by choosing a determinate magnitude and situation corresponding to the known "lengths" in the equation, in a way consistent with the relations specified by the equation.[19]

Conclusions and Further Questions

Looking at Viète's project as an attempt to overcome the Euclidean distinction between magnitude and multitude makes possible the clarification of some ambiguities in Klein's account. The object of Viète's analytic art is Viètian magnitude. This is a new mathematical object, not one immediately given to first-intentional thought, but rather one created as a being of reason by virtue of a set of rules that seek to determine the character of this object. It is nevertheless in some way dependent not just on the Euclidean concept of number but also on the Euclidean concept of magnitude, insofar as the rules that determine it are chosen precisely in order to attempt to capture the desirable features and to dispose of the undesirable features of each of its Euclidean forebears. Insofar as we take Viète's rules as an axiom system determining Viètian magnitude as its object, it is not yet clear whether they constitute a *coherent* axiom system and thus determine Viètian magnitude as a *viable* mathematical object. Descartes will have another go at this project. Dedekind will argue that no one before him succeeded in putting numbers and continuity together in a rigorous and coherent way. The question on which Klein seems to me to vacillate—whether the object of Viète's analytic art is something intended by the species, either a "general object" (124) or "general magnitudes" (166) or "the general character of being a number" (174) or "general number" (174), or whether it is finally just the species themselves—seems to me to remain a general and unresolved question about mathematics understood as axiomatic systems. Do such systems consist simply of symbols and the rules for manipulating them, or do these taken together determine or create or give access to an object separate from them? It seems to me a further unresolved question whether the modern axiomatizations of the "real number system" succeed in freeing themselves from any problematic dependency on first-intentional Euclidean multitudes and magnitudes.

Addendum in Response to Oaks

The crucial issue raised by Oaks's article concerns the objects intended by the species in the *logistice speciosa* of Viète's analytic art. Klein claimed that these objects are symbolic in character, while Oaks claims to have shown that they are simply geometric magnitudes, and hence not symbolic. In Klein's account, at least as Oaks understands it, the argument for the symbolic character of the objects of the species depends on the claim that the species intend neither numbers nor geometric magnitudes, but something else, which can then be interpreted in the rhetic part of the analytic art as numbers or in the exegetic part as magnitudes.[20]

In my own view, Oaks has indeed convincingly shown that Viète understood the intended object of the species to be magnitudes, and not something more general, which can be interpreted either as number or as magnitude. I am not, however, completely certain that this settles the question of whether the intended objects of the species are symbolic in character or not. I continue to have doubts about this because Viète's assertion that operations on magnitudes are governed by the stipulations of chapter 2 and the law of homogeneity of chapter 3 of the *Isagoge* entails a radical change from the Euclidean understanding of magnitudes and the kind of operations they are subject to, as my paper tried to show.[21] This change might well be understood to constitute a change in the very meaning of *magnitude*, so that the objects of Viète's analytic art, as I have argued, can by no means be identified as *Euclidean* magnitudes, but instead merit the new name *Viètian magnitudes*, which I have given them here. The stipulations and the law of homogeneity might after all amount to an axiom system, at least an embryonic one, which determines the character of its new objects, Viètian magnitudes, and hence arguably renders them symbolic in character.[22]

Oaks's paper also contains at least an implicit argument against the interpretation I have just sketched. In his view, the stipulations at least, if not also the law of homogeneity, merely codify a long-established practice among Viète's mathematical predecessors of at least blurring (1) the firm Euclidean distinction between (a) resolving a proportion of four lines into an equality of two rectangles and (b) multiplying the lines by one another to produce two equal rectangles or (2) that between (a) forming a rectangle with two lines specifying the magnitude of its sides and (b) multiplying the sides to produce a rectangle as the product of the multiplication.[23]

Against this implicit argument, I would urge that there is a significant difference between blurring an inherited distinction in practice, while not even thematizing this blurring, much less attempting to justify it, and openly and explicitly proclaiming the novel interpretation of the practice as a central piece of a new analytic art and devoting two chapters to the justification of the practice.[24]

It is admittedly difficult for us, four centuries later, to be confident in assessing Viète's own self-understanding of his project. After studying Oaks's article and the evidence it compiles, I believe that my paper most likely overstates the self-conscious radicality of Viète's project, to the extent that it attributes to him a self-conscious intention to overcome the distinction between magnitude and multitude by devising a new mathematical object by means of his stipulations and law of homogeneity, understood as an axiom system.

On the other hand, the bold rhetoric of the *Isagoge* seems to suggest that Viète understood himself as making some kind of fairly substantial innovation, and one that allowed operations previously understood as arithmetical to be applied to "magnitudes." He does not, however, tell us if he thinks his stipulations are already widely accepted or if they are a crucial part of his innovation. At any rate, it may well be anachronistic to attribute to him an intention to propose an axiom system to determine a new kind of mathematical object. But it is not clear that the character of what he in fact did is simply determined by his intention. Perhaps the notion of an axiom system determining its objects is in some sense implicit in Viète's project, present in embryo or germ in a way that makes its further development along these lines necessary or likely or more readily possible. If so, one could say that there is a sense in which "Viètian magnitudes" are at least implicitly symbolic and that if he himself understands them simply as "Euclidean magnitudes," this is possible only by a kind of equivocation.

Simon Stevin and the Matter of Number

DANIEL P. MAHER

Introduction

Simon Stevin of Bruges (1548–1620) was an intellectually and politically influential polymath, with notable achievements in mathematics and engineering. Close to Prince Maurice of Nassau in the emerging Dutch Republic, he served as quartermaster of the States Army and professor of engineering at Leiden University. A theoretician who prioritized practical applications, Stevin deserves to be remembered for developing and popularizing techniques for artisans and merchants to calculate fractional parts of their various units by deploying Arabic numerals in positional, decimal form. He published a collection of mathematical works in 1585, including a short work in both Dutch and French versions explaining his method. That work, called *De Thiende* (Dutch) or *La Disme* (French), was translated into English as *The Tenth* or *The Dime* as early as 1608 and again in 1619. According to D. J. Struik, this text is

> by far the best known of Stevin's publications; it earned him the title of inventor of the decimal fractions. The title, if taken with a grain of salt, is deserved. It is true that decimal fractions appeared long before Stevin, but it was largely through his efforts that they eventually became common computational practice. It was also Stevin who

> first showed the advantage of systematic decimal division of weights and measures.[1]

His works on arithmetic exhibit a conception of numbers and their relation to the natural world that earned him a place in Jacob Klein's account of the emergence of modern mathematics.

In this paper, I examine Stevin's innovations in relation to Klein's thesis about the conceptual interdependence of Greek ontology and mathematics:

> [A]ny attempt to understand Greek mathematics as a self-sufficient science must fail. It is impossible to disregard the ontological difficulties which fundamentally determine its problems, its presentation, and its development, especially in its beginnings. It is just as impossible, on the other hand, to understand Greek ontology without reference to its specifically 'mathematical' orientation.[2] (*GMTOA* 61)

Herein Aristotle represents the Greek tradition and serves as a foil to clarify Stevin's innovative understanding of the relation between mathematics and nature. Where Aristotle emphasizes the role of form in relation to number, Stevin emphasizes matter, and the contrast illuminates Klein's emphasis on mathematical physics in modernity: "The problem of the origin of mathematical physics is the crucial problem of modern history and modern thought. . . . The establishment of modern physics is founded upon a radical reinterpretation of ancient mathematics."[3]

It helps to begin with a summary of Aristotle's account of the relation between number and being.[4] Aristotle's famous formula, "being is said in many ways," denies the Parmenidean notion that being is one only. *Many* means *many ones*, and so, in Aristotle's view, being is not continuous and undifferentiated but discretely divided into various ones or units. Each of the several units that constitute being as multiple is essentially indivisible as a sense of being. Aristotle distinguishes the many senses of being by identifying the several ways beings are indivisible. Against a Parmenidean view (and in contrast to a postmodern view), according to which human thinking constructs the divisions in being, Aristotle argues that at least some divisions arise due to formal units dividing one sense of being from another. Whereas for Democritus indivisibility arises due to the hardness of atoms, Aristotle traces indivisibility to form (*eidos*), which causes each being as being to be one. A multitude is not a being but a number of beings. The first number is *two*, and *one* is not a number. One is the principle of number because whatever is one (say, a dog or a book) causes any given plurality of such beings to be just so many in number. On this view, neither *one* nor *zero* nor any fraction is a number. Rather, a number is always a definite multitude of items determinate in kind.

In open opposition to this tradition, Stevin denies that one not is a number and emphasizes matter rather than form. When his view is incorporated into mathematical physics, no place remains for form and, thus, for natural kinds in our science of nature. Both Bacon and Descartes depreciate form in nature, paving the way for a science aimed at expanding human power to transform nature. Because Stevin argues explicitly for the superiority of his approach to that of the ancients, his thinking helps us understand the then-emerging science of nature.

The phrase *matter of number* in my title refers not only to a subject matter, but also to Stevin's peculiar appeal to matter in his reinterpretation. I examine this in the first and longest part of the paper below, focusing on Stevin's justification for taking one as a number and not the principle of number. For Stevin, number is not essentially discrete, but "to a continuous magnitude there corresponds the continuous number that one attributes to it."[5] In making this "new '*number*' *concept* . . . completely explicit" (*GMTOA* 148), he does not offer merely an alternative view that affords new mathematical possibilities. No, he enthusiastically rejects the traditional view as mistaken, harmful, and unnatural.[6]

By confronting the tradition he rejects, Stevin resembles Bacon more than he does Descartes, who "is notorious for his failure to discuss the views of Aristotle and his other predecessors."[7] In the second part, I review other aspects of Stevin's thought that suggest he is not merely a mathematician dabbling in ontological matters over his head but someone of greater significance for early modern philosophy.

To conclude this introduction, I note that Klein sometimes minimizes Stevin's stature. He says, "Descartes' conception of 'numbers' is far more tradition-bound than Stevin's, although, on the other hand, he sees through their conceptual structure with much more clarity" (*GMTOA* 197). Yet in an essay devoted to Stevin as one of two men who laid the foundations of modern mathematics (the other is Viète), Klein credits Stevin as contributing "more than anybody else to Descartes' discovery of Analytical Geometry. Descartes—and this applies more or less also to Fermat—interpreted Apollonius, as it were, through the eyes of Stevin."[8] And with respect to Stevin's "perfect correspondence" between number and magnitude, "his influence on Descartes cannot be overstated."[9] Nevertheless, *GMTOA* subordinates Stevin to Viète.

> Diophantus is put in modern 'symbolic' form in 1585 by Stevin and in 1591 by Vieta. Although Stevin . . . already makes the new '*number*' *concept* which is the basis of the 'symbolic' procedure completely explicit, it is Vieta who . . . actually realizes the fundamental transformation of the conceptual foundations. (*GMTOA* 148–49)

Accordingly, Klein prioritizes Viète in chapters 10 and 11 of his book, and then he turns to Stevin's earlier work in the first part of chapter 12. Perhaps Klein regards Stevin correctly as important but not philosophical, but Stevin deserves a closer look before we adopt this verdict.

Part One: The Matter of Number

A. STEVIN'S *L'ARITHMÉTIQUE*

In 1585, Stevin published his *L'Arithmétique* in French (there was no Dutch version). It consists of one book of definitions and a longer book on operations. He included a paraphrase translation of four books of Diophantus's *Arithmetica* and published this together with his *Practique d'Arithmétique*, which is itself a collection of shorter texts, including *Tables of Interest*, a treatise on incommensurable magnitudes, and the French edition of *De Thiende*, entitled *La Disme*. The first book of *L'Arithmétique* contains forty-four definitions, along with several explanations, notes, and diagrams in about sixty pages of text. He devotes eight pages to explaining his definition of number: "Number is that by which the quantity of each thing is explicated."[10] Each thing has quantity; number expresses it. The quantity of a thing could be its weight or its size as well as its being, say, one horse or one dog. In an appendix to *La Disme*, in the fourth article, Stevin describes a rectangular column's length, breadth, and height, and then says, "The question is how much the matter [of that pillar] is."[11] A number makes known the quantity of the pillar. Stevin does not define number originally as multitude and then adapt it to continuous quantities; he defines it to express either quantity. The question "What is the number of books in the room?" has no unique true answer. The quantity of books could express the number of volumes, the number of pages, the size of the space they occupy, their weight, their cost, their resale value, or what have you. No special priority belongs to their being a determinate number of beings determinate in kind. Accordingly, no unit enjoys priority in measuring the quantity of the books.

To clarify the stakes in Stevin's departure from tradition, I turn to a distinction Aristotle draws in the tenth book of his *Metaphysics* (see chapters 1 and 5). He distinguishes between what is one in itself and what is one in the sense of a measure.

One in the sense of measure is opposed to what is two or more. To call something *one* in this sense denies plurality, and for that reason it serves as the principle of number. The other sense of *one*, namely one in itself (*hen kath'auto*), is ontologically prior to one in the sense of the measure of a multitude. To say something is one in itself denies internal division: that is one in itself which is not a heap or a pile. A horse is one being in itself, essentially a whole rather than a plurality of cells or molecules, but a pile of gravel is not one in itself. A heap (*sôros*) is essentially plural even though it can be named by a collective noun. Naturally unified wholes, Aristotle argues elsewhere in *Metaphysics*, have their diverse material parts unified by non-material form. Form causes the horse to be determinate in kind and to be an integral whole. An artifact can be one in a similar albeit artificial sense. However the form *book* should be defined, as a formal cause it overcomes the multiplicity of words expressed on many pages and brings them to intelligible cohesion and completeness. According to Aristotle, for a book or a horse to be one is an ontological achievement as distinct from simply being few in quantity.

For Stevin, one is a particular quantity, but it is not the indivisible principle of number. His one is closer to Aristotle's one in the sense of measure because it is related to quantity, but to speak of *one book* does not identify a determinate kind of being constituted as a whole; it is to speak rather of a quantity coupled with a nominal identification of what sort of thing is being quantified. The text immediately following his definition of number, which is labeled *explication*, helps to make this clear:

> Comme l'unité est nombre par lequel la quantité d'une chose expliquée se dict un: Et deux par lequel on la nomme deux : Et demi par lequel on l'appelle demi : Et racine de trois par lequel on la nomme racine de trois, &c. (*Arithmétique*, *PW* II 495)

> (As the unit is number by which the explicated quantity of a thing is *said* [to be] one; and two by which one *names* it two; and half by which one *calls* it half; and root of three [√3] by which one *names* it root of three, and so on.)

My translation emphasizes the verbs, all of which involve labeling things according to certain numbers. Stevin avoids speaking of what the quantity of something *is*. We *call* a thing one or two or half. His language suggests a non-metaphysical view of number, and additional evidence supports that reading. For example, Stevin describes the origin of the use of numbers:

> It is necessary then to know that men, a long time ago, seeing that it was their business to talk about and understand the quantity of things, would *name* each simple thing *one*, and when to the same would be added yet another, they would *call* them together *two*, and when the proposed simple thing would be divided in two equal parts, they would *name* each part *half*, and so on.[12]

Each quantitative term is a name we apply to things; the thing called *half* would presumably also qualify as something simple, so that it too could be called *one*.

In the remainder of the explication, Stevin asserts and defends two theses: (1) That the unit is number and (2) That number is not discontinuous quantity. He spends the most time and energy on the first because the conception of number operative in the supporting argument entails the denial of a principled difference between discrete and continuous quantity. Stevin introduces the first thesis by claiming to have examined at length "all philosophers ancient and modern" and to have discussed the matter with learned men who disagree with him, but he is confident "as if nature herself had told me from her own mouth" that all who disagree with him are in error. Mistaken, vulgar opinion holds that unity is not number but only its principle or origin (*commencement*). Against this mistake, Stevin argues as follows, italicizing his words and setting them off from the body of the text, devoting one line to each assertion:

> *La partie est de mesme matiere qu'est son entier,*
> *Unité est partie de multitude d'unitez,*
> *Ergo l'unité est de mesme matiere qu'est la multitude d'unitez;*
> *Mais la matiere de multitude d'unitez est nombre,*
> *Doncques la matiere d'unité est nombre.*
> (*Arithmétique*, PW II 495)

> (The part is of the same matter as its whole,
> A unit is part of a multitude of units,
> Therefore, the unit is of the same matter as the multitude of units;
> But the matter of the multitude of units is number,
> Then the matter of a unit is number.)

Concentrating on the first and the fourth assertions, Klein says that in order to avoid an invalid argument Stevin "understands this conceptual determination [i.e., being a number] as the 'material' of the thing to be defined" (*GMTOA*, 191–92). Stevin advances a new understanding of number, as distinct from merely extending the traditional conception to something previously excluded from the class of numbers. Note that Stevin says the *matter* of a unit is number, which he reinforces by adding, "And he who denies it does the same as the one who denies that a piece of bread is bread."[13] *Any* piece of bread is bread, and so the unit is the same as any other piece of a number. This view both removes the privileged character of the unit as the indivisible element in a number and conceives number as indefinitely divisible into number, that is, *not* into determinately several ones, but into whatever amounts may be convenient. Nothing in the matter resists division, which shows that he conceives matter without the determining influence of form.

Antoine Arnauld (1612–1694) may have been the first to object to Stevin's first premise. He gave several counter-examples, including a soldier in relation to an army and a semicircle in relation to a circle.[14] Primarily, Arnauld wants to reserve the name *number* for a multitude, even though he grants that the unit "has something in common with the whole multitude of units, according to which we could say that they have the same nature."[15]

Although Arnauld's form of the objection is not meaningless, it misses Stevin's point. Arnauld's objection conceives the number as analogous to a whole circle, whose nature is not preserved in its fractional parts. By contrast, the tradition prioritizes the unit's indivisibility, while the wholeness of numbers is, at least for Aristotle, more problematic.[16] If numbers are multitudes of indivisible monads, then the monad or unit enjoys ontological priority to the number, which is essentially determinately plural. Stevin denies any indivisible unity at the level of the whole quantity or of its parts. There is no natural unit of bread (the slice, the loaf, the dinner roll) and no limit on our ability to add bread to bread and arrive at anything other than bread. Matter is extension, understood as quantified.

B. DIGRESSION: CLARIFICATIONS FROM STEVIN'S OTHER WRITINGS

Stevin's other works develop this understanding. In *Practique d'Arithmétique*, he justifies proceeding from the general theory of arithmetic to its applications in particular areas, such as commerce and land measurement: "It is convenient to follow nature as a sure guide, learning first the general foundations, which are about pure numbers, abstract from all matter [*de nombres purs, abstraicts de toutes matieres*]."[17] If *L'Arithmétique* treats pure numbers as distinct from those particularized materially in dollars, gallons, tons, octaves, and so on, Stevin's appeal to "the matter of number" in that text is puzzling. The tension between the two texts regarding the inclusion of or abstraction from matter provides, I think, some evidence in support of Klein's claim that Stevin may be blending two ways of conceiving number into a symbolic conception. According to its characterization as "pure" and separate from all matter, number is somehow a general object, and yet, in the argument concerning the unit, that same number is conceived as having material parts or as being divisible into parts as matter.[18]

We find additional clarification in *De Thiende*, where Stevin's first definition asserts, "Dime is a kind of arithmetic."[19] His dime is not the only way to calculate but the most efficient technique because it deals exclusively with whole numbers in all cases. In a striking parallel to Viète's formula "the art of arts," Stevin says his "dime could be called, by another name, the practice of practices."[20] As a species or technique of arithmetic, the "matter" on which it operates is number (*Thiende*, *PW* II 393). The dime presupposes something given as one, that is, as "the unity of commencement," and then "Each tenth part of the unity of commencement we call the prime, . . . and each tenth part of the unity of prime we call the second, . . . and so of each other tenth part of its preceding sign" (*Thiende*, *PW* II 405). He presupposes the ready divisibility of each unit into tenths and of each part of each unit as far as is convenient.[21] Furthermore, we may choose our principles of division. Whereas astronomers use the sexagesimal system, surveyors use rods, feet, and inches. Money-masters, merchants, measurers of tapestries, and wine-gaugers have various units of measure, most of which make calculations difficult and prone to error. The dime is discovered or "invented"[22] for "the easy performance of all reckonings, computations, and accounts, without broken numbers" (*Thiende*, *PW* II 397).

His "broken numbers," that is, fractions, offer another confirmation that Stevin conceives number symbolically. Dividing with "dime numbers" leads him to the difference between the fractional expression 1/3 and its decimal expression as infinitely repeating .333.

> It happens also sometimes that the quotient cannot be expressed by whole numbers, as 4(1) divided by 3(2) [.4 divided by .03], in this sort, whereby appears that there will infinitely come 3s, and in such a case you may come so near as the thing requires, omitting the remainder. It is true, that 13(0)3(1)3⅓(2) or 13(0)3(1)3(2)3⅓(3) etc. shall be the perfect quotient required. But our intention[23] in this Dime is to work all by whole numbers.[24] (*Thiende*, *PW* II 421, 423)

Although everything to the right of the "commencement sign" (corresponding to our decimal point) signifies a number of fractional parts of the unit, Stevin speaks of working "all by whole numbers." Each positional, numeric sign signifies a whole number. George Sarton says, "As soon as our fractions are put in the decimal form . . . they disappear."[25] Stevin's notation obscures this somewhat, but Klein's charge appears justified: "As 'arithmetician' Stevin no longer deals with numbers of units which are determinate in each case but with the unlimited possibility of combining ciphers according to definite 'rules of calculation'" (*GMTOA* 193).

C. RETURN TO *L'ARITHMÉTIQUE*

We return now to *L'Arithmétique* and its semi-material numbers. A long time ago, Stevin says, men "would name each simple thing *one*," and if another were added to it, "they would call them together *two*." If the simple thing were divided equally, they named each part *half*.

> Then, considering that *one*, *two*, *three*, *half*, *third*, and so on were proper names and suitable for making that quantity known, they saw that it would be necessary to include all these species under one genus (for it is their manner of doing this in all similar cases, as wheat, barley, oats, they named

> under the genus *Grain*; eagle, turtledove, nightingale, in the genus *Bird*), which genus they would call number.[26]

On this view, number is a genus, while *one*, *two*, *three*, *half*, and so on are its species. These species are themselves classes abstracted from particular or material ones, twos, threes, and halves, just as the species eagle is immaterially separate from each particular eagle.

This resembles a passage in Aristotle's *Physics* (4.14.224a2–15) where he draws an analogy between geometrical figure, understood as a genus with respect to its species (circle, triangle, square, and so on) and number, understood as a genus with respect to its species, which are said to be the decad or the ten, and presumably the ennead or the nine, and so on. Just as triangle could be subdivided into isosceles and scalene, so decad could be divided into ten horses and ten dogs, and then we could still speak of particular isosceles triangles and particular groups of dogs. Whatever the merits of this analogy, Aristotle invites us to see a fundamental difference. Figure and triangle enter into the essential being of particular triangles, but number forms no part of the nature of dog or horse. Ten is not common to ten horses and ten dogs in the way that triangle is common to its species or in the way that animal is common to horse and to dog. We can understand *dog* without understanding *ten*, but we cannot understand dog without understanding animal. Triangle is part of what the equilateral triangle is, but ten is not ingredient to the being of dogs or horses. On my reading, Aristotle expects us to see the disanalogy between number and a true genus that partially constitutes the being of its species.

Stevin, by contrast, exploits the independence of number from the determinate character of beings. Because *one*, *two*, *three*, *half*, and so on—understood as species of number—have no intrinsic connection to any determinate kind of being, "Number is that by which the quantity of each thing is explicated." That Stevin's species, including the unit, are purely conventional becomes obvious in the final portion of the explication, where he argues that number is not discontinuous quantity. The number sixty, to use Stevin's example, does not have sixty parts more properly than it has thirty, twenty, or however many parts it may please you to find. Indeed, sixty may be divided into the square root of sixty and sixty minus its square root. Each of these two parts is number. Neither a magnitude nor a number is discrete quantity. Each admits the same indefinite divisibility: "to a continuous magnitude there corresponds the continuous number that one attributes to it, and such discontinuity that the magnitude receives thereafter by some division, also its number receives a similar discontinuity."[27]

Most of the defense of this interpretation depends on his showing that one is a number (and hence divisible) and that zero is the principle of number. An ancient error led to the denial that one is a number, but he says all philosophers agree that nature testifies we must examine any quantity beginning from its principle. For magnitudes the manifest principle is the point. While some have said the point corresponds to the unit, Stevin systematically contrasts the point and the unit. First, the unit is divisible, but the point is not. He admits that the ancients deny this divisibility, but nothing they can say suffices to stifle its nature as number; nothing keeps it from manifesting its essence by force. He appeals to Diophantus, "the prince of arithmeticians," and others who divide the unit in calculation. Second, two units are number, but a thousand points do not make a line. Third, the unit is a part of number, but the point is not a part of the line; the unit is not in the number as the point is in the line (*Arithmétique PW* II 497–98).

The sense in which this last claim is true for Stevin provides an illuminating contrast with Aristotle. Stevin means that the point does not constitute a material element making up the line, whereas the unit does so make up the quantity of the number. On the other hand, as Stevin has already suggested and is about to make completely explicit, the units are not rigidly present in the number; each part of a number is, for Stevin, potential not actual, in Aristotle's language. For his part, Aristotle would also say that the point is not in the line in the way that the unit is in the number, but he would mean that the unit is present actually and the point only potentially.[28]

Perhaps the simplest way to grasp Stevin's notion that zero constitutes the principle of number is to consider time. A child has already lived some quantity of time before reaching the age of one. Therefore, one is not the beginning of number. Stevin makes a similar point through a much more complicated calculation with the circumference of the circle, but he subordinates that argument to simpler ones, such as the "bread argument," considered above. A second analogy may be called the "water argument," which he uses to argue that number is not discontinuous quantity. The two are mutually reinforcing or interdependent.

> And finally, to speak by example, number is some such thing in magnitude as wetness in water, for as this is extended through all and in each part of the water, so the number allotted to some magnitude is extended through all and in each part of its magnitude; again just as to one continuous water corresponds one continuous wetness, so to one continuous magnitude corresponds one continuous number; again just as the continuous wetness of the whole water suffers the same division and disjunction as its water, so the continuous number suffers the same division and disjunction as its magnitude; such that its two quantities could not be distinguished by continuous and discontinuous.[29]

The reference to "two quantities" indicates that number and magnitude are still two quantities for Stevin, but they "correspond." Magnitude has not yet become "length," but that is in the offing.[30] Antoni Malet comments on the significance of the water argument for Stevin:

> In Stevin's intellectual milieu . . . "wetness" was one of the defining traits of the Aristotelian element "water" (water was wet and cold, earth was dry and cold, and so on). Through such a philosophical reference Stevin effectively suggests that number *essentially* belongs in the nature of magnitude.[31]

However true this may be, it overlooks the more fundamental point that Stevin's number is essentially indifferent to what it quantifies. That can be made clearer by contrast with Aristotle:

> A man is one and indivisible as a man, and the arithmetician posits one indivisible, then studies what is incidental to man as indivisible; the geometer, on the other hand, studies him neither as man nor as indivisible, but as a solid object. For clearly properties he would have had even if he had not been indivisible can belong to him without them.[32]

For Aristotle, discrete and continuous quantity are founded in the same natural being, but he preserves the difference between them. Stevin, by contrast, finds no principle of unity in magnitude. As Jurgen Naets puts it, "The original character of Stevin's conception of number lies . . . in his position towards the ontological interpretation of the unit contained in the classical view that underlies the formula, namely the notion that units were abstracted, individualized things."[33] The ease with which Stevin accepts the divisibility of the unit reveals his distance from the ontological basis of discrete number in Aristotle.

D. STEVIN AND THE ART OF DEMONSTRATION

Beyond these ontological differences between Aristotle and Stevin, Klein identifies features of modern conceptualization that surface elsewhere in Stevin's thinking. Klein emphasizes that modern concepts are primarily defined in relation to one another rather than by their immediate connection with the beings we conceive through them. According to Klein,

> No longer is the thing intended by the concept an object of *immediate* insight. Nothing but the internal connection of all the concepts, their mutual relatedness, their subordination to the total edifice of science, determines for each of them a *univocal* sense and makes accessible to the understanding their only relevant, specifically scientific, content. . . . Thus every one of the newly obtained concepts is determined by *reflection on the total context of that concept.* (*GMTOA* 121)

Naets appeals to Stevin's writings on rhetoric and demonstration, available at present only in Stevin's Dutch,[34] to show that Stevin deliberately embraced a version of this understanding of scientific reasoning under the influence of Peter Ramus and that he rejected the Aristotelian claim that we can know natural kinds. According to Naets,

> Stevin challenges the opinion that the artificial Aristotelian method of definition, which produces categories such as genus and species, could somehow illuminate the inner nature of things.[35] Since we are not naturally endowed with an innate awareness of the causes of natural phenomena, Stevin argues that a thing cannot be defined in quo, and for that reason, a quidditative or real definition is impossible.[36]

Naets says Stevin regards Aristotle's intelligible forms and sensible species as necessarily uncertain.

> We must abandon the belief that definitions convey the nature of things. Instead, definitions derive signification from the way their objects are conceptualized by a discur-

> sive community. Hence, definitions are not timeless, idealized truths, but artificial compounds constructed in a discursive practice, which are judged true or false depending solely upon whether they meet some criteria set forth in a prior praxis.[37]

Naets holds that Stevin, like Ramus and Agricola, doubts that visual appearances can convey intelligible species. Ramist logic turns away from intelligible *eidê* and "deals with relations rather than objects, which means that the distinction between things, ideas or words, is unintelligible apart from the system of semiotic relations in which such terms are embedded." Naets also writes: "For Ramus and Stevin . . . the meaning of each thing is defined by its function or place (topoi [*sic*]) in a structure of relations. Concepts and definitions owe their intelligibility to the artifices of comparison and division."[38]

In light of this we see that in the wetness argument quantity is conceived according to the practice of measurement: "to one continuous magnitude corresponds one continuous number."[39] The arbitrariness of whatever constitutes the unit at any level is presupposed in accord with Stevin's skepticism regarding our ability to know what things are. Stevin appears to be already where Descartes arrives at the end of the *Meditations*: the material world is knowable with certainty only as quantifiable extension. The proto-Cartesian character of his thinking and its fitness for a practicing engineer are unmistakable. Moreover, Naets's characterization of Ramist logic coheres very well with Klein's analysis of early modern scientific thinking generally.[40] According to Klein, Descartes disengaged this mode of thinking from its subordinate place within mathematics and assigned it the central and most authoritative role in human knowledge.

> From now on the fundamental *ontological* science of the ancients is replaced by a *symbolic* discipline whose ontolog-

> ical presuppositions are left unclarified. This science, which aims from the first at a comprehension of the totality of the world, slowly broadens into the system of modern mathematical physics. Within this discipline the things in this world are no longer understood as countable beings, nor the world itself as a *taxis* determined by the order of numbers; it is rather the structure of the world which is grasped by means of a symbolic calculus and understood as a *'lawfully' ordered course of 'events.'* (*GMTOA* 184–85)

Part Two: Does Stevin Matter?

In the second part, I turn to other aspects of Stevin's thought illustrating his embrace of features characteristic of modernity. Together they show that Stevin is not simply an engineer or mathematician who has drifted into our path due to oddities in his conception of arithmetic.

First, as Klein explains at some length, Stevin writes in several texts of a lost Wise Age or Age of Sages. Even though no one knows where or when or who these people were, we can be sure this age existed, he says, and that they spoke Dutch.[41] In a discourse on the worth of the Dutch language, he insists that this age antedates all public records,[42] notably the Bible. Indeed, the wise age was wise not by divine gift, but because they "reached this condition after a long time and through much experience" (*Art of Weighing*, *PW* I 91). As Klein indicates, Stevin uses the "wise age" simultaneously to appeal to ancient authority and to bypass all known authority as he outlines his projected restoration of the sciences (*GMTOA* 186–90). The very description of the wise age by extant "signs" also details what "we can set out to attain . . . again" (*Geography*, *PW* III 607), which is the reason Stevin writes.[43] Klein lists the five signs presented in the French edition of Stevin's works prepared by his student Albert Girard. Klein acknowledges "Girard permits himself some abridgements"

(*GMTOA* 286n283), but Klein does not mention that Stevin's Dutch text includes a sixth sign of the wise age.

> The sixth sign is magic, which is said to have been diligently practiced a very long time ago by certain nations with knowledge of the causes, for though this is frightening, it is yet perceived what great learning has resulted from mathematics, which is regarded as the cause of such thorough knowledge, and what extraordinary wisdom existed among men in former ages, which time we call the Age of Sages. (*Geography*, *PW* III 607)

Francis Bacon, who endorsed some form of a wise age, also spoke of the need to "revive and reintegrate the misapplied and abused name of *natural magic*; which in the true sense, is but *natural wisdom*, or *natural prudence*; taken according to the ancient acception, purged from vanity and superstition."[44] "The true Natural Magic . . . is that great liberty and latitude of operation which dependeth upon the knowledge of Forms."[45] There is great affinity between the interests of Bacon and Stevin in magic and transformative alchemy or chemistry, as an inquiry into the "essence of matter" and the true causes operative therein (*Wysentyt*, *PW* III 605–7).

Second, Stevin exhibits in several of his writings the characteristically modern view that theory is prior to practice.[46] Indeed, he claims theoretical inquiry exists for the sake of practical application and the benefit of mankind. This appears in particular contexts, such as an appendix to *Art of Weighing*, where he and Prince Maurice begin with mathematics in order to build better bridles for horses. They dismiss the structures used by practicing horsemen on the strength of the certain knowledge they have gained through mathematics.[47] He formulates the relationship more generally in the *Geography* in a short passage called "On Theory Mixed with Practice."

> The property and the end of theory is that it furnishes a sure foundation for the method of practical operation, in which by closer and more painstaking care one may get as near to the perfection of the theory as the purpose of the matter requires for the benefit of man. (*Geography*, *PW* III 619)

In another text, he suggests the vanity of knowledge sought for its own sake.

> Just as it would be useless expense to lay large and strong foundations which can support a heavy edifice without ultimately wishing to erect any building thereon, thus in the elements of the arts theory is labour lost when the end does not tend to practice. Just as, in the natural order of things, the foundation precedes the building, thus theory precedes practice. (*The Practice of Weighing*, *PW* I 293)

Theoreticians furnish practitioners with "material," thereby contributing to general utility. A theoretician is like a lumberjack, "But if he were to cut down those trees to let them rot, without expecting any benefit of them, that would be acting foolishly;" the goal of science is practical benefit for all mankind (*Geography*, *PW* III 621). At both the beginning and end of the preface "To the Reader" of *L'Arithmétique*, Stevin appeals to the utility of this theoretical science for individuals and for the whole republic (*PW* II 489–90).

Third, Stevin's motto was *Wonder en is Gheen Wonder*, usually translated as "Wonder Is No Wonder" or as "Magic Is No Magic." Stevin helps us understand his motto with these words:

> It is true indeed that in Nature there is nothing mysterious (*wonderlick*); nevertheless, in order to differentiate between the things we understand through their causes and those

> whose causes are unknown to us, we rightly call the latter miraculous (*de name van wonder*), not because they are really so, but because they appear so to us. (*Art of Weighing*, *PW* I 59)

In spirit this resembles Aristotle's remarks about recognizing the incommensurability of the diagonal with the side of a square.[48] Crucially, Stevin's discovery of true causes does not end in contemplation but in practical application. His trademark, known as the clootcrans or "wreath of spheres," illustrates the point. The image of four spheres balanced by two spheres in proportion to the length of two sides of a triangle appears in Theorem XI, proposition XIX, in book I of his *Art of Weighing*. According to George Sarton, Stevin here demonstrates the law of equilibrium on an inclined plane

> based upon the postulate of the impossibility of perpetual motion (1586). Hence are implicitly deduced: the general law of composition of forces (parallelogram of forces), the decomposition of a single force (e.g., the weight of a body) into two normal components (see also *Spartostatica*, 1605).[49]

Sarton's statement suggests that the trademark emblematically expresses the reductive resolution of natural forces into separately acting components. According to Richard Hassing, the universal reductionism famously described by Laplace is prepared by Newton's account of the parallelogram rule for the resolution and composition of forces. A planet's elliptical motion, for example, is understood as composed of separately acting rectilinear forces. The key assumption is that forces acting simultaneously operate independently, that is, as if the other did not exist. In this way, wholes are conceived as the combined effect of their several parts and not as in any way causing or shaping their parts.[50] Stevin's thinking appears consistent with if not structured by this reductionism. Even Stevin's preference for Dutch should be understood not as chauvinism but as opting for a language that mirrors a reductive grasp of nature. Dutch, he argues, abounds in monosyllabic words, which leads to the ready formation of compound words, and such a language is uniquely fitted for describing nature with clarity and accuracy.[51]

Fourth, and finally, Stevin's short treatise entitled *Vita Politica* is unmistakably modern.[52] He compares the political community to a boarding house, where being a good citizen means obeying the rules, whatever they happen to be, or going elsewhere. He distinguishes four types of political order, but he shows no concern for the justice of claims to rule. His advice for adapting one's actions and concealing one's thoughts in the face of religious authority with which one disagrees reads like an intriguing draft of Descartes's first maxim of the provisional morality in the third part of *Discourse on Method.* The goal of political life seems to be civic peace and order, whereas making philosophical arguments encouraging virtue for its own sake amounts to "knocking at the door of a deaf man."[53] He suggests a separation of the concerns of divine rules and civil rules, and he nakedly subordinates religion to public order. Here, God serves as Leviathan, the source of overarching fear. Stevin, who was familiar with Machiavelli,[54] also reveals significant affinities with the political views of Hobbes and Descartes, all expressed as practical advice to the individual, whether citizen or not, for governing his own conduct in any political community he chances to inhabit. With this text Stevin shows himself to be not merely a mathematician or an engineer, but someone who incorporates his understanding of science and nature with his understanding of the human being, which makes him a philosophical rather than simply a technical or, in the modern sense, a scientific thinker.

Conclusion

Even if he does not amount to a thinker of the first rank, the preceding summary of features indicating Stevin's modernity helps demonstrate considerable integrity to his thought and its coherence with more famous founders of modernity. Klein grants Stevin greater prominence than he enjoys in most accounts of the emergence of modern science and modern politics. Accordingly, his proper place remains somewhat difficult to determine, but it would be most interesting if one could establish more substantial connections with people like Bacon, Descartes, and Hobbes. Like Bacon, Stevin engaged with the tradition he rejected, and like Descartes he grasped the importance of a new form of mathematics for thinking about nature. Klein's emphasis on the centrality of mathematical physics for all of modern thinking has guaranteed a role for Stevin in the drama of the modern project, even if it remains somewhat unclear how large Stevin's role should be. The fact that Stevin has a share in both poles of what is especially new and extraordinarily successful in modernity—the new science and the new politics—suggests that we should suspend any final verdict on his significance at present.

Two Reflexivities

Scholastic and Cartesian Second Intentions in Klein's *Greek Mathematical Thought and the Origin of Algebra*

RICHARD F. HASSING[1]

"I don't think the Greeks had concepts.
Concepts have cogito-like reflexivity."
Ed Halper[2]

Introduction

Jacob Klein has several characterizations of the distinctive manner in which algebraic symbols exist. I have found eight:

1. The objects represented by, for example, numerical variables and constants, are identified with the means of their representation, for example, *x*, *y*, *a*, *b*, =, and signs for operations (123, 178, 224). Accordingly, a letter sign (or Cartesian line segment) has meaning only within the sign system as a whole with its constitutive rules of calculation; it is "comprehensible only within the language *of symbolic formalism*" (174–76 [here 175], see also 193).
2. Potential determinacy is taken as actual determinacy in calculation, that is, we calculate (add, multiply, subtract, divide) with indeterminate *x* and *y* as if they were determinate numbers (123, 175).

3. The mode of being of the object, for example, a multitude of units, is identified with the mode of being of the general concept related to the object, for example, "multitudinousness as such," "mere multiplicity in general" (192, 200–2, 208; *WPNW* 26).
4. The object of a second intention is represented by and as the object of a first intention, namely, a particular letter sign or Cartesian line segment (174–75, 192, 207–8; *WPNW* 26; *MR* 60–63).
5. Continuous variability of ratio-numerical magnitudes (letter sign or line segment): a second intention is taken as first intention via Kantian schematic imageability (*WPNW* 20–21, 26).
6. Dimensionlessness: numbers are conceived as pure (dimensionless) ratios with the unit as the consequent (218–23).

Overarching and emblematic of all of the modern conceptions (Viète, Stevin, Descartes, Wallis):

7. Rejection of the distinction between discrete number (*arithmos*) and continuous magnitude (*megethos*) (178, 219–21).
8. Rejection of the tenet, one is not a number but the principle of number (191, 212).

I focus here on the fourth: Klein's use of the scholastic doctrine of first and second intentions to clarify the symbolic concept of number in Part II of *GMTOA*. Note, however, the importance of *calculation* in the first two descriptions, and thus of the syntactical rules (the axioms) of calculational operations ("These rules . . . create the systematic context which originally 'defines' the object to which they apply . . . namely an object of 'calculational' operations"—176; *GL*-II 184).[3] We shall see that the fourth description would be impossible without calculational syntax (the axioms). We shall also see that the fourth description would be impossible without a distinctively Cartesian difference from the scholastic account of second intentions. The difference concerns *reflexivity*—scholastic versus Cartesian—and is presented by Klein on page 208 of *GMTOA*. The purpose of this paper is to clarify that account.

Klein's most complete presentation of the scholastic doctrine of second intentions as a means to understanding the conceptual structure of symbols is in Chapter 12B of *GMTOA*, on Descartes.[4] Klein there uses Eustachius of Sancto Paulo (1573–1640) as a source for the scholastic doctrine. In the present paper I supplement Klein with Joseph Owens's account of intentional beings, first and second, in his *Elementary Christian Metaphysics*. Owens is useful for enabling us to see the difference between scholastic second intentions and Cartesian second intentions because Klein is not completely clear at *GMTOA* 208 as to where the scholastic account ends and the Cartesian account (as interpreted by Klein) begins. It is the latter (Cartesian) that leads to symbols and symbolic mathematics, not the former (scholastic).[5] As noted, the difference involves reflexivity, and, ultimately, the relation between mind and world as understood by scholastic-Aristotelianism (shown below to be a form-receptive realism[6]) and as conceived by Descartes (as explicated in the following).

Among the modern founders examined by Klein, Descartes is unique in being the most philosophical, thus most aware of the need to give an account of his own doings. In the *Rules for the Direction of the Mind*, Descartes endeavors, "with an explicitness perhaps novel in the history of science," to explain the "new mode of 'abstraction' and a new possibility of 'understanding'," namely, through the language of algebraic equations and their graphs (200). The basis of Descartes's epistemology of symbolic abstraction (Klein: *symbolische Abstraktion*)[7] is his model of pure intellect and corporeal imagination, the latter being "a true part of the body," "nothing but a real body with real extension and shape,"[8] in Rules 12 through 14. There, intellect, pure of all images, "applies itself"[9] in a twofold way to the corporeal imagination: first, by *passively* receiving figures or traces imprinted on the imagination (via nerves and animal spirits from sense organs and the external objects that stimulate them), then, second, by *actively* using the imagination to form new figures. But new figures of what?

Between the passive and active uses of imagination, pure intellect exercises a power proper to it alone, namely, that of "separating abstract entities,"[10] such as "mere multitude" (*solam multitudinem*)[11] or (as Klein calls it) "multitudinousness as such" (200, 201; *Mengenhaftigkeit als solche—GL*-II 209, 211),[12] that is, generic manyness, which, like anything generic (say, generic animal or generic triangle), is unimaginable (it lacks individuality and specificity) and exists only in the intellect. But this—generic manyness—is what is *symbolized* by figure-forming, intellect-active imagination: "*Thus the imaginative power makes possible a symbolic representation of the indeterminate content which has been 'separated' by the 'naked' intellect*" (202, emphasis Klein's).[13]

It will be argued in the following that, whatever its precise meaning, "multitudinousness as such" (*sola multitudo*) does not refer to discrete number (*arithmos*) in contradistinction to continuous magnitude (*megethos*). Rather, in accordance with description 7, above, it supersedes that long-standing distinction. In accordance with description 8, it rejects the long-standing tenet that *one is not a number but the principle of number* (the arithmetical unit or monad is not a principle of multitudinousness as such).

The algebraic symbol, *x*, intends generic manyness, like a concept, yet is a sense-perceptible individual that is subject to calculational operations (see note 3). *Calculability* seems to be the determinate sense of the indeterminate *x*. This is striking, even paradoxical. It is as if there were "generic animal," which can exist only in the intellect, that we could nevertheless feed and pet.[14] As Hopkins aptly puts it:

> The indeterminate [it means neither multitudes of units nor geometrical magnitudes; *OLSM* 518] general object yielded in "symbolic abstraction" is neither purely a concept nor

> purely a "sign," but precisely the unimaginable and unintelligible identification of the object of a second intention with the object of a first. This identification is "unimaginable" because "images" properly . . . refer either to particular objects of first intentions or to their particular "common qualities." The identification of second and first intentional objects is "unintelligible" because, for "natural" predication, to say that a concept is both general and particular "at the same time" is nonsensical. (*OLSM* 509–10)

The distinction within ordinary predication between first and second intentions is elaborated by means of Owens in Part II–IV, following. To introduce and motivate that account, consider the two sentences, "Socrates is a man" and "man is a species." The term *man* cannot mean the same thing in these two sentences lest it follow that Socrates is a species. There are two different concepts of man here, or, more generally, two types of concepts differing in how they are formed and how they refer to their objects. 'Man' as understood in the first sentence is called a first intention. 'Man' as known in the second sentence is called a second intention.

The once-novel products of intellect and imagination pioneered by Descartes (as well as Viète, Stevin, and Wallis) became over three centuries the symbols—letter signs and numerals, equations, coordinates and graphs—of our now taken-for-granted algebra, analytic geometry, and advanced mathematics.[15]

Klein's account of Descartes addresses two interconnected questions: (1) How does Descartes's model of pure intellect and corporeal imagination work? (2) What is the distinctive conceptual structure of the resulting algebraic symbols and symbolic geometrical figures? In addressing these questions, it is essential to keep the following remark in mind:

> Here the constant presupposition is that *the "pure" intellect in itself has no relation at all to the being of the world*

> *and the things in the world.* What characterizes it is not so much its "incorporeality" as just this unrelatedness. (202; see also *MR* 63)

Descartes conceives mind and world as radically separate.[16] This is the key difference between Cartesian and scholastic intentionality. It means that in the Cartesian theory of knowledge there is nothing like the scholastic first intention. This is at present not obvious; Owens's account of scholastic intentionality, below, will enable us to see it.

For Cartesian mind to come into contact with the world, the passive and active (figure-forming) functions of the Cartesian imagination are required, especially the latter. Let us proceed with Klein's account in *GMTOA*, Chapter 12B. (The other approach would be to analyze Descartes's algebra of line segments set out in the opening pages of his *Geometry*, for which see Romiti, *CM*, Chapter 3 or "The Symbolic Space of Descartes's *Geometry* and its Symbolic Mathematical Underpinnings," contained in the present volume.)

I. Klein's Use of the Scholastic Intentionality Doctrine—Part I: Eustachius

It is worth quoting Klein's introduction of the scholastic doctrine at length. In the following, brackets enclose supplementary references and an explanatory phrase. Klein's original German of the most important clause is inserted in parentheses:

> We are now able, by using Descartes' assertions as a basis and taking into account the contemporary literature of the schools, to fix yet more exactly that conceptual character of algebraic symbols which has already been variously outlined [174, 184]. We saw that Descartes designates the "sola multitudo" which the intellect "separates" from the "idea"

of number [for example, an array of points, 201 (see also *MR* 62)] it finds available in the imagination as an "abstract being" (ens abstractum), also called an *ens rationis* in the language of the schools. In the *Summa* of Eustachius a Sancto Paulo, IV, 17–19 (quoted after Gilson, *Index*, p. 107) three kinds of "entia rationis" are enumerated: "Beings of reason are either negations, or privations, or *second intentions*. . . . The two first kinds appertain to things in their own mode before any operations of the intellect." . . . [O]nly the third kind owes its "being" to the operation of the intellect alone: "But the last kind does not belong to things *unless a certain operation of the intellect is presupposed*, wherefore these beings of reason are said to depend on the intellect for their existence and connection; . . . this is why a 'being of reason' in its proper and strict sense is agreed to be only the last kind." . . . Thus "mere manyness" (sola multitudo), multitudinousness as such, which has its "being" by grace of the "pure intellect," is truly an *ens abstractum* or *ens rationis* in the sense of a "second intention." . . . Now Eustachius, appealing to established usage, defines "second intention" more narrowly as an *ens rationis* "which is conceived as belonging to a thing known by virtue of its being known, and which cannot exist except *objectively in the intellect*, since it is conceived [not originally but] *secondarily and by a reflexive operation of the mind*" (*und das in keinem anderen Sinne 'sein' kann, als* für den Verstand gegenständlich ist: *denn es wird ja [nicht ursprünglich, sondern] nachträglich und durch ein* auf sich selbst bezogenes Tun des Verstandes *erfasst*) (quodque non aliter potest existere quam objective in intellectu, cum secondario et per reflexam mentis operationem concipitur). (206–7; *GL*-II 221)[17]

Here we are given Eustachius on second intentions and *reflexivity*, after Descartes on multitudinousness as such, and a particular multitude, say, five points, on the corporeal imagination. Reflexivity is the ability of the mind to "look" in different directions and to turn from looking wholly "outward" at extra-mental beings (not at all at itself) to looking, partly or wholly, at itself in its own activity and products (it is "a self-related operation of the mind"—see *GL*-II 221). Klein quotes Descartes, *Meditations*: "'the mind, when it thinks [reflexively], in a way turns *itself toward itself*' (. . . mens, dum intelligit, se ad seipsam quodammodo convertat; cf. *Meditations* VI, [AT VII 73:15 ff.])" (200). Similarly, Hopkins speaks of "Vieta's redirection of his cognitive regard" (*OLSM* 521). Owens, as discussed below, speaks of "the intellect in its reflexive [not direct] gaze" (*ECM* 239).

Note that Klein, using Eustachius, has proceeded to second intentions, not by prior contrast with first intentions,[18] but from within the category of beings of reason. The alternative order of presentation would be, within the scholastic doctrine of intentional beings, to set out first intentions, then second intentions.[19] Owens is useful because he gives an account of first intentions, then second intentions, in terms of the turning "gaze" (an activity) of the intellect, or reflexivity. From Owens, below, we shall learn that man and animal are first intentions; species and genus are second intentions. We thus have at this point a fruitful question: why is mere manyness necessarily a *second* intention? Why could it not be a first intention related to a particular multitude, say, five units, as man and animal are related to a particular human being, say Socrates? Granted, a substance is precisely one and not many.[20] But could we not make an analogy—despite disanalogies—between one substance (Socrates) and one multitude (five units), predicating man and animal of the former and fiveness (like man) and mere manyness (like animal) of the latter? This question gets to the heart of the matter. I have asserted above that mere manyness (*sola multitudo*) does not refer to discrete multitude in contradistinction to continuous magnitude, that it falls under descriptions 7 and 8 of modern symbolic number. Does the proposed analogy (between a substance and a number of units) likewise overcome the discrete-continuous distinction, or rather does it leave it intact? If the latter, it would not get us to Descartes's *sola multitudo*. I attempt to resolve this in Part V, below. For now let us turn to Owens's account. I should note that I find Klein, Eustachius as reported by Klein, and Owens all in accord on the scholastic doctrine.

II. Owens: First Intentions

A preliminary caution: Although useful, Owens's description is potentially confusing for us because he employs the scholastic and pre-Cartesian meaning of *subject* and *object*. For example, "[t] he one real thing becomes a number of different objects" (*ECM*, 238). In this now-forgotten understanding, it is the subject that is outside the intellect; the object is in the intellect. For example, Eustachius, quoted above: "*[quod] non aliter potest existere quam objective in intellectu*" ("which cannot exist except objectively in the intellect"), rendered by Klein (*GL*-II 221) as "*in keinem anderen Sinne 'sein' kann, als für den Verstand gegenständlich ist*" ("can exist in no other sense but objectively for the intellect"). So the fire in the fireplace—by which I can warm or burn myself—is the subject; the fire in my knowledge is the object (literally "thrown against" my intellect by the subject). I cannot warm or burn myself by the objective fire. In modern, post-Cartesian language, I am the subject, the fire in my mind is the concept, the fire in the fireplace is the object. This suggests, however, that the Cartesian object could be identified with the scholastic subject. Anyone familiar with Descartes's science knows how mistaken this identification would be. To continue with the example above, for scholastic-Aristotelian realism, the fire is in itself hot and luminous; for Cartesian science, heat and light are intramental re-presentations of purely corpuscular interactions—thus, a concept-construction or model replaces a form-matter substance for a mind that is conceived to have no direct access to the world.[21] The question of the distinction between what first exists outside the intellect—the things to be known—and their subsequent existence as known by the intellect is removed (this is implied by description 3, above). For Klein, "[t]his means that the one immense difficulty within ancient ontology, namely, to determine the relation between the 'being' of the [extramental] object itself and the 'being' of the object in thought [intentional being], is . . . accorded a 'matter-of-course' solution whose presuppositions and the extent of whose significance are simply bypassed in the discussion" (192).[22] Symbolic concept-formation, and thus modern algebra, is a necessary condition of this historic transformation in mind-world relation, and thus in our understanding of what things are (see *OLSM* 4).[23]

Back to the task at hand: In the following scholastic account by Owens, the object always exists in the intellect. Intentional being, whether first or second, is always cognitional or *objective* being, being as known. Outside of the intellect are *real* beings—determinate and sensible individuals possessing *per se* natures or quiddities in function of their form-matter composition.[24] Accordingly, for the reading of Owens, I designate *object* in this sense either as "[scholastic] object," in quoting Owens, or as objects with subscript *s*. My intention is to bring into clear relief the transition to Cartesian (wholly self-relating) second intentions, and thus finally to symbols on *GMTOA* 208.

Owens:

> Socrates is known as Socrates, as a man, as an animal, as a living thing . . . in a process by which he is seen respectively in comparison with other men, other animals, other living things. . . . All these aspects [he's a man, an animal, alive] . . . are present in the sensible individual as first known [that is, the contents known—humanity, animality, life—are not constituted by the operations of the intellect, are not beings of reason]. . . . The wider aspects are

> isolated through the process of [Thomistic] abstraction, by successively leaving the differentiae out of consideration. In all these abstractions the sensible thing is what is *directly* known, as Socrates, a man, an animal, and so on. The gaze of the intellect is still focused upon the sensible thing itself. The *direct* gaze of the intellect upon the thing itself throughout these various abstractions is called technically the first intention. (*ECM* 237–38; italics and bracketed explications mine)[25]

I have italicized *direct* because it is about to be contrasted with *reflexive* in the transition from first to second intentions. Let us prepare that by the following considerations: "All these aspects . . . are present in the sensible individual as first known." There is in Socrates the quiddity or nature *man*, the quiddity or aspect *animal.*[26] The universal *man* is a first-intentional objects or objects of a first intention. Similarly, the universal *animal* is a first-intentional objects. In contrast, the real being, the sensible individual existing independently of the intellect of the knower (the scholastic subject), is Socrates.

Note the sharp contrast with Cartesian mind-world separation (discussed above): Owens's judgment that man and animal "are present *in* the sensible individual" (after *Physics* 192b22; my emphasis) as real, Aristotelian and Thomistic natures that are then received in the soul is, for Descartes, mistaken. Since, for Descartes, no such natures are received, it follows that, in the Cartesian theory of knowledge, there is nothing like the scholastic first intention; see note 21.

Owens speaks here of first intentions in scholastic *natural* philosophy, whose objectss (like "snub"—see *Physics*, 194a7) depend on sensible matter both to be and to be understood. Our interest is not in natural philosophy but in mathematics, whose objectss may or may not first exist in sensible matter (Aristotle says they do, Plato says they do not) but, in any case, do not depend on sensible matter to be understood. What can be said, in preparation for Klein on Descartes, about mathematicals?

Klein shows that the Greek *arithmos* always meant a definite amount of definite things. For Greek thought, an *arithmos* is particular (not general) and determinate (not indeterminate), for example, four monads, represented as :: (four dots) or as M°δ (in Diophantine notation). Therefore, an *arithmos* as known, as existing in the intellect of the mathematician, is a first intention (more precisely, an objects of a first intending).[27] To determine the amount in an *arithmos*, we start the count with *one*, for example, one apple, or one pure arithmetical unit (*monad*), because it is the first of the definite things (apples or pure units) present. The unit, without which the count could not begin, is always, for Greek thought, a positive being, whether sensible (an apple) or intelligible (an arithmetical unit). Therefore, as known, as existing in the intellect, the unit is an objects of a first intention (first intending). What about Greek geometry? The drawn figures visible to us in Euclid and Apollonius are imperfect images of perfect (ideal) forms intelligible to us (somehow). Both the visible figure and, more importantly, the intelligible ideal form (the circle or the ellipse) are, according to Klein, particular—not general like the graph of a circle or ellipse in Cartesian coordinates—and determinate in contradistinction to the variables (x, y) and constants (r, a, b) in the equations of the circle ($x^2 + y^2 = r^2$) and ellipse $(x/a)^2 + (y/b)^2 = 1$ (a difference of possible vs. actual determinacy, as in description 2 above). "Apollonius has in view the *particular* ellipse. . . . The representation in the drawing gives a true '*image*' [*Abbild*] of . . . *this* ellipse" (*WPNW* 16–17). Thus Greek geometry was also first-intentional. Accordingly (as in natural philosophy), the content known in Greek arithmetic and geometry is understood to derive from the intrinsic properties of the things known; it is not constituted by the operations of intellect as is a second intention or being of reason (207–8).

The important case of the general theory of proportions (based in Book V of Euclid's *Elements*), which demonstrates theorems, for example, alternation, for both discrete number (VII.13) and continuous magnitudes (V.16), is discussed briefly in note 37, below. The essential question is, did that general theory posit a correspondingly general (thus univocal) object, like our real number, *x*? I believe the answer is no (for example, alternation of magnitudes is still subject to homogeneity requirements; see note 37).

III. Transition to Owens on Second Intentions

Is there in Socrates the quiddity or nature *species*, the quiddity or common nature *genus*? If so, then we could say, "Socrates is a man, Socrates is a species, Socrates is an animal, Socrates is a genus." But we cannot. The predications, "Socrates is a man," "Socrates is an animal," "man is a species," and "animal is a genus" fall into two different classes with respect to the relation between knower and known: first-intentional and second-intentional. As mentioned above, there are two different concepts of man here or, more generally, two types of concepts differing in how they are formed and how they refer to their objects. In the predications "man is a species" and "animal is a genus" the content known—*species*, *genus*—does not have prior existence in the real individual being. Humanity and animality do (in the scholastic account) have prior existence in the real individual being. Where do the meanings of *species*, *genus*, etc., come from? Answer: from the comparing, separating, grouping operations of intellect, which it performs *after reflecting* on what it has known directly. This means that the meanings of *genus* and *species* here, in the second intention, are partially constituted by the cognitive operations of the intellect, but not wholly, because those meanings are *founded on* the aspects (to paraphrase Owens) known directly, in the first intention. Thus, we could say that the intellect is now looking partly at itself in its own cognitional processes, and partly out at the world of natural kinds (the source of its data—see *De Anima* 3.8, 431b20ff.).

IV. Owens: Second Intentions

Owens, again:

> The intellect is also able to reflect on its own activities and processes. It is able to see that what is one in real being has become multiple in cognitional being, as the one real man is represented separately as Socrates, as man, as animal, as living thing, as body, and as substance. The same thing is seen as several [scholastic] objects, each object having its own separate act of intentional being. These objects of simple apprehension are common natures. Each just in itself has no being, but is able to be either in reality or in cognition. Each is seen by the intellect, first in its real existence, and then, through reflection, in its intentional being. Considered separately as it is in intentional being, each appears as a representation through which the real thing is known.
>
> As the intellect in its reflexive gaze views each of these representations separately, it sees them as ever widening objectivations of the same real thing. It compares them with one another. It sees that the [scholastic] object "man" leaves out of consideration the individual characteristics of Socrates, and so can be found identified equally well in reality with Plato, Caesar, Kennedy, Castro, and innumerable other instances. Understood in this way, the [scholastic] object "man" is technically called a lowest universal or a *species*. The predication "Man is a species" may be made. From the same viewpoint, Socrates, Plato, and the other instances are technically known as *individuals*. You may accordingly make the predication "Socrates is an individual." In a corresponding manner the intellect may leave out of consideration the specific differentia of man and have an object, "animal," that can be seen identified in reality equally well with horses and elephants and hundreds of

other species. So understood, the [scholastic] object is technically called a *genus*, and allows the predication "Animal is a genus." The higher genera are subject to the same process. They are the higher universals.

In all this reflexive activity the intellect is gazing not directly at the thing in its real existence, but at that thing as already objectified in various intentional existences. The view is now of a different kind from the first direct way of looking at the thing in the real world. It is now reflexion, and not direct cognition of a real thing. It is a second gaze at the thing, but now at the thing as found in a new intentional existence. This second or reflexive gaze [an "operation of the mind"—Eustachius (306n324)] at the thing in any of its various representations or objectivations is accordingly called the *second intention*. . . .

Two different types of predicate, therefore, may be applied to a sensible thing. On the one hand, there are the specific [man] and generic [animal] natures that characterize the thing wherever it is found, and the accidents that it has in the real world. These are predicates of the first intention. . . . On the other hand, there are predicates that of their nature apply just to a thing in its intentional being. These are characteristics that arise only when the thing receives cognitional being in the knower ["belonging to a thing known by virtue of its being known" (207) rather than by virtue of its real being]. . . .

Viewed in the first intention, Socrates and man and animal have but one [Thomistic] existential act. Viewed in the second intention, each has its own separate existential act. In real being, they are one. As [scholastic] objects of the second intention, on the other hand, they are diverse in being.

Each [scholastic] object of the second intention is accordingly a distinct "being of reason" (*ens rationis*). (*ECM* 239–41; bracketed explications mine)

The words “reflect,” “reflection” or “reflexion,” “reflexive” appear six times in this passage. It is the same sense of *reflexive* that Klein quotes from Eustachius on page 207. Again (as above), intellect is there looking both at itself and at the world: *at itself,* in its activity of classifying content known from looking *at the world* of real beings in their natural kinds or forms and (Thomistic) common natures. Scholastic reflexivity is restricted because it remains form-receptive.[28] This is the realism of Aristotelian-scholastic philosophy, often called naïve realism to distinguish it from scientific realism in twentieth-century philosophy of science. Greek philosophy generally is based on the premise of a harmony (despite serious distortions) between mind and world.[29] To repeat (it bears repeating), the contrast with Cartesian mind-world separation is salient.

V. Klein’s Explanation of Cartesian Abstraction in Terms of Second Intention

At *GMTOA* 208, Klein extends the scholastic second-intention doctrine to a more radical, Cartesian sense of *cogito*-like reflexivity,[30] in which intellect—“*bare of any immediate reference to the world*” (201:–3)—exercises its unique power of “separating abstract entities” such as “mere multitude” (*solam multitudinem*), “multitudinousness as such,” generic manyness:

> The intellect, when directed to the “idea” of a number as a “multitude of units” [say, points (201:–5)] . . . offered to it by the imagination . . . , turns [in the second intention, but] in conformity to its own [Cartesian] nature (*seiner eigenen Natur gemäss—GL*-II 221), toward its own “directedness,” its own knowing. . . . Consequently it sees the multitude of units no longer “directly,” . . . but “indirectly,” “secondarily”. . . .
>
> Its immediate “object”[31] is now its own conceiving [like

> the *cogito*] of that "multitude of units," that is, the "concept" (conceptus) of the number as such; nevertheless this multitude itself appears (*erscheint*—*GL*-II 221) as a "something," namely as *one* and therefore as an "ens," a "*being*." This is precisely what the abstraction which the intellect undertakes consists in: It transforms the multitude of the number into an apparently "independent" being, into an "*ens*," if only an "*ens rationis*." (208:1–20; the Halper epigraph refers to this text)

The mind's own conceiving is apprehended as something *one*. In the traditional understanding, a number (*arithmos*) is precisely not one, but many, such that the first number is two. Here, in *cogito*-like reflexivity, the Cartesian pure intellect "applies itself," not at all to the world of independently existing species, multitudes and magnitudes,[32] but only to the corporeal imagination. It reflects on its own cognition, something one, of the figure etched on the imagination (a multitude of units, say, a pattern of points). Pure intellect creates by its unique (non-scholastic) power of reflection-*cum*-abstraction the *concept* of the number as such, *sola multitudo*—mere or *just* multitude without regard to determinate amount. This concept is an *ens rationis* but not of scholastic type (based on determinate first intentions); rather it is *self-reflexive* and partly indeterminate. The mode of being of the object (the determinate multitude of units) is thus replaced by the mode of being of this distinctive concept. This concept is related to, but *not a likeness of* the object (a determinate amount of units)[33]; this is description 3 of symbolic conceptuality. To make this clearer, let us briefly review the most essential (*per se*) characteristics of discrete number (*arithmos*) and continuous magnitude (*megethos*) in the pre-modern understanding.

Consider the following: An *arithmos* is finitely divisible into indivisibles without boundaries that can touch. A *megethos* is infinitely divisible into parts having boundaries that can touch.

These statements express the differing *modes of being* of *arithmos* and *megethos*, which are thus like two different species within the genus of the quantified (*to poson*) whose common characteristics are divisibility and being subject to the equal and unequal.[34] Now, is our mentally *conceiving* of number or our *concept* of number (it makes no difference) finitely divisible into indivisible concept-units lacking boundaries that can touch? Is our *concept* of magnitude infinitely divisible into concept-parts having boundaries that can touch? No. However a mental entity may be understood as "stuff," as a material,[35] it is not divisible in the manner of number and magnitude (finitely vs. infinitely, having vs. lacking boundaries that can touch). Therefore, identifying number (*arithmos*)—specifically, identifying its mode of being, which, as just described, differs essentially from that of magnitude (*megethos*)—with the mode of being of the concept related to it, which registers no such difference, removes the distinction between discrete and continuous, leaving something one, intelligible (at least partially), but not imaginable, namely, *sola multitudo*, with which, at this point—having not yet arrived at *symbol*—we can do nothing except think it.

Recall the analogy between substance and number (as man and animal are to Socrates, so fiveness and manyness are to five units). As man and animal remain determinate (we can define them) so fiveness and manyness are determinate as the "form" of five units and as the defining characteristic of "finite divisibility to indivisibles lacking boundaries that can touch." On this account, the substance-number analogy leaves intact the discrete-continuous distinction[36] and, therefore, does not get to Descartes's *sola multitudo*. The Cartesian adjective *sola* ("mere" or, as I suggest, "just") would then be a sign of the shift in intentionality—the gaze of the intellect—from the mode of being of the objects (number and magnitude) to the mode of being of the one, self-reflexive concept related to those objects, *sola multitudo*, multitudinousness as such.[37]

Before taking up Klein on symbol (208:20–28), we have another significant question: pre-symbolic magnitude (*megethos*) is also per se divisible (though differently from number as described above); why is number (*arithmos*) privileged, as it were, in the movement via Cartesian abstraction to generic manyness? Is there not also a corresponding one *ens rationis* from the side of magnitude, namely, *magnitudinousness as such*? Both generic manyness and magnitudinousness are *entia rationis*, Cartesian second intentions. What is the content of generic manyness, *sola multitudo*, that lends it to symbolization in a way that generic magnitudinousness does not? I believe the answer is calculation: How can we calculate (add, multiply, subtract, divide) with continuous magnitudes unless they are conceived as numbers of units of measurement, either actual or potential? (123)[38]

In *GMTOA*, note 319, Klein mentions "figurality" itself ("*Figürlichkeit*" *überhaupt*; *GL*-II 216n189). This important note begins, "[h]ere it is important that the 'figures' appear as 'numbers' only through the '*mediating unit*' . . . and that the *unit* itself is understood as 'unit of measurement'." Klein makes clear (see especially 205) that in fact Descartes begins his explication of the new type of abstraction already from the standpoint of algebra. Indeed, "Descartes' thinking, as he himself points out in the *Regulae*, *presupposes* the fact of symbolic calculation, namely in the form of contemporary 'algebra'" (197). Descartes's objective is to make sense of it in such a way that the new mathematics, specifically, algebraic equations, can be justified as the language of physics. As to how symbolic-algebraic conceptuality historically developed, *GMTOA*, note 259, might pertain: there was "*a gradual change in the understanding of number*, whose ultimate roots lie too deep for discussion in this study" (277).

According to Klein, then, the Cartesian second intention, *sola multitudo*, can be abstracted by pure intellect from either points or lines etched on the corporeal imagination because Descartes preconceives lines as multitudes of units of measurement.

"This 'symbolic' character of Cartesian 'figures' first makes possible that mutual correspondence of 'lines' with [single] letters or 'ciphers' which obtains in Cartesian mathematics" (205). This concludes my account of two reflexivities.

At 208, line 21, Klein turns to description 4: symbols, and the paradoxical identification of a second intention with a first intention (more precisely, a second intend*ed* with a first intend*ed*), namely, the letter sign or line segment of the *Geometry.*

VI. Klein's Use of the Scholastic Intentionality Doctrine—Part II: Symbols

The next step in Klein (208:21) is the intellect-active employment of imagination, that is, the production of symbols, with which we can calculate.

> When now—and this is of crucial importance—the *ens rationis* as a "second intention" is grasped *with the aid of the imagination* in such a way that the intellect can, in turn, take it up as an object in the mode of a "first intention," we are dealing with a *symbol,* either with an "algebraic" letter-sign or with a "geometric" figure as understood by Descartes. This is the sense in which we spoke earlier of "symbolic abstraction."

The earlier passage to which Klein here refers concerns the role of symbolic abstraction in Viète's mathematical procedure:

> The intentional object of an "intentio secunda" is indicated by the letter-sign, namely, a concept that directly means a concept and not a being (*mit dem Buchstaben-Zeichen wird der intentionale Gegenstand einer "intentio secunda" bezeichnet, namlich eines Begriffs, der selbst unmittelbar einen Begriff und nicht ein Seiendes meint*—*GL*-II 182). Furthermore—

> and this is the truly decisive turn—this general character of number or, what amounts to the same thing, this "general number" in all its indeterminateness, that is, in its merely possible determinateness, is accorded a certain independence which permits it to be the subject of "calculational" operations [whereby "intellect can . . . take it up as an object in the mode of a 'first intention'"]. This is achieved by adjoining the "rung" designations [indicating genera or dimensions], whose interconnection according to precise rules indicates the particular homogeneous field underlying each equation which is constructed. . . . *The species* [letter signs and associated genera or dimensions] *are in themselves symbolic formations—namely formations whose merely potential objectivity is understood as an actual objectivity.* They are, therefore, comprehensible only within the language *of symbolic formalism*. . . . Therewith the most important tool of mathematical natural science, the "*formula*," first becomes possible . . . but, above all, a new way of "understanding," inaccessible to ancient *episteme*, is thus opened up.[39] (174–75)

$E = mc^2$ is an emblematic example of a scientific formula.

Hopkins has provided detailed analysis of Klein on Viète, Descartes, and the peculiar first-and-second-intentional structure of algebraic symbols (see *RI* "Klein's Account of the Conceptual Presuppositions Belonging to Viète's Interpretation of Diophantine Logistic", *OLSM* Chapter 22–23 and §§200, 204, and 207). I put forward only the following two supplementary remarks.

First, it should be clear in light of Owens that the first-intentional character of the symbols (ciphers, letter signs, Cartesian line segments), despite their being sensible individuals, is not at all scholastic (realist): The content known in calculating with Viète's species, A, B or our x, v, t (distance, speed, time), and so on is not "present in" extramental beings "as first known" (Owens,

ECM 237), that is, prior to learning the manipulations of algebra and dimensions of physics. In contrast, man and animal *are* first present in Socrates, but we cannot calculate with Socrates, man, animal. Therefore, it is calculability that provides A, B, x, v, t, etc., with first-intentional character as Klein understands it: "[I]t is obviously impossible to see 'numbers' in the isolated letter signs 'A' or 'B', except through the syntactical rules which Vieta states in the fourth chapter of the *Isogoge* [*sic*]" (176). It is in fact impossible to see *any* character in A, B, x, v, t (except the 1st, 2nd, 24th, 22nd, and 20th letters of the English alphabet) in isolation from our ability to "move them around" on the page, back and forth across the equal sign, e.g., x = vt, v = x/t, t = x/v, as we learn in freshman physics. Their calculability makes algebraic symbols first-intentional in Klein's (non-scholastic) sense. This at least is my claim.

Second, the passage from Klein on Viète, above, explicitly mentions *equation* ("each equation which is constructed"). This is a reminder that symbolic concept-formation comes into being historically in the arena of equations (in contrast to sentences or *logos*). An equation is a whole composed of multiple letter signs (variables and constants), signs for the operations (originally addition, subtraction, multiplication, division, taking of roots), and the equal sign between the right- and left-hand sides. In terms of Descartes's account in Rule 14, this means that pure intellect would need to separate from the corporeal imagination not just multitudinousness as an abstract entity, but also the binary operations, and the relation of equality. Equality is easy to accommodate: It falls in the Cartesian category of common simple natures (common to both the corporeal and the intellectual), which "can be known either by the pure intellect or by the intellect as it intuits the images of material things" (Rule 12, AT X 419; CSM I 45). The more challenging question is, how might Rule 14's symbolic abstraction work for the binary operations, and, very specifically, for Descartes's revolutionary "fourth-proportional" definition of multiplication in the opening pages of the *Geometry*? This important question is taken up by Romiti, whose work we are fortunate to have.[40]

Klein and his translator—to whom we in the English-speaking world owe a lot—provide an appropriate conclusion to the present endeavor:

> The whole complex of ontological problems which surrounds the ancient concept of number loses its object in the context of the symbolic conception, since there is no immediate occasion for questioning the mode of being of the "symbol" itself. (213)

"We tend to see and approach our lives and the world through a screen of concepts, techniques, and symbols." —Eva Brann[41]

Acknowledgment

I have benefited from discussions of these abstruse topics over quite a few years with Joseph Cosgrove, Michael Dink, Burt Hopkins, Edward Macierowski, Andrew Romiti, Robert Sokolowski, and Kevin White. Special thanks to Mike Dink, from whose incisive questions I've much benefited despite being unable to answer them all.

The Symbolic Space of Descartes's *Geometry* and Its Symbolic Mathematical Underpinnings

ANDREW ROMITI

> [M]athematical physics is at the foundation of our mental and spiritual life, . . . we see the world and *ourselves* in this world at first quite ingenuously as mathematical physics has taught us to see it, . . . the direction, the very manner of our questioning is fixed in advance by mathematical physics, and . . . even a critical attitude towards mathematical physics does not free us from its dominion. The idea of science intrinsic to mathematical physics determines the basic fact of our contemporary life, namely, our "scientific consciousness."
>
> Jacob Klein, *The World of Physics and the 'Natural' World*[1]

In *Greek Mathematical Thought and the Origin of Algebra*, Jacob Klein sets out to reveal the fundamental difference between the ancient and modern concepts of number in order to clarify the nature of the formal mathematical language that underlies modern mathematical physics. By the end of his analysis, he has shown that the invention of modern symbolic mathematics brings about a difference in the way the concepts of ancient and modern science are formed and used. The identification of this difference, he believes, has widespread implications for the understanding of modern science as a whole and thus also for modern thought at large. In this way, Klein aims to contribute to the goal of investigating the nature and influence of modern science, which he understands to be in need of conceptual clarification. The absence of this conceptual clarity is of great importance to Klein because of the tremendous role modern science plays in shaping the everyday understanding of modern human beings. Klein's work thus initiates an effort to provide the conceptual clarification of which modernity stands in need.

While Klein himself was clearly concerned with the entire chain that begins with the invention of modern symbolic mathematics and runs up to modern thought in its current form, his particular investigations were largely confined to the mathematical realm, leaving to us the task of extending his analysis beyond mathematics to the realm of the mathematical study of nature if we are to move his project closer to modern thought as such. This task entails a long and arduous process of moving step-by-step through the development of modern science and its concepts to see how they've become what they are today; for it is only in this way, according to Klein, that the present state of the sciences and their powerful influence on everyday understanding can be clarified.

It is the goal of the present study to advance a step in this process, thereby furthering Klein's analysis and contributing to the project he began. This will be accomplished by following up on the brief and compact comments Klein makes about the modern concept of space. While these comments are aimed at the modern concept of space in general (that is, as it spans and develops across the modern era), Klein suggests that this concept has its origin in the thought of René Descartes, and it is this facet of his claims that we will explore.

Descartes holds an important place in Klein's analysis because of the multifaceted influence he has on modern mathematics and its role in the sciences: he makes crucial contributions to the development of the modern symbolic concept of number, he singularly provides a philosophical account of its possibility, and he attempts to bring that concept into the domain of physical science, thereby linking the mathematical and physical realms. Central to the connection between these two realms, according to Klein, is Descartes's concept of extension and his closely related concept of space.

In *Greek Mathematical Thought and the Origin of Algebra*, Klein directly ties the concept of space underlying modern science to extension's role of uniting the mathematical and physical realms in the thought of Descartes:

> Extension has . . . a *twofold* character for Descartes: It is "symbolic"—as the object of "general algebra," and it is "real"—as the "substance" of the corporeal world. More exactly, in Descartes' thinking, the dignity of representing the substantial "being" of the corporeal world accrues to extension precisely by reason of its *symbolic* objectivity within the framework of the *mathesis universalis.* Only at this point has the conceptual basis of "classical" physics, which has since been called "Euclidean space," been created. This is the foundation on which Newton will raise the structure of his mathematical science of nature.[2]

Klein gives a slightly more elaborate version of these claims in his essay "The World of Physics and the 'Natural' World" and connects them directly with the modern concept of space in general. There, after a discussion of the peculiar concept-formation that underlies modern symbolic mathematics, he goes on to suggest that this is essential background to understanding that "Descartes' concept of *extensio* identifies the extendedness of extension with extension itself."[3] He then continues:

> Our present-day concept of space can be traced directly back to this [identification]. Present-day Mathematics and Physics designate as "Euclidean Space" the domain of sym-

> bolic exhibition by means of line-segments, a domain which is defined by a coordinate system, a relational system, as we say nowadays. "Euclidean Space" is by no means the domain of the figures and structures studied by Euclid and the rest of Greek mathematics. It is rather only the symbolic illustration of the *general character of the extendedness* of those structures. Once this symbolic domain is identified with corporeal extension itself, it enters into Newtonian physics as "absolute space."

Let us make an initial attempt at unpacking these rather dense quotations in order to anticipate and frame what is to come. Klein claims that Descartes's concept of extension connects symbolic mathematics and the physical world insofar as extension serves as Descartes's symbolic mathematical object while also being taken as the "substance" or essence of body itself. Moreover, this concept of extension conflates "extension itself"—that is, body understood as essentially that which is extended—with "the extendedness of extension" or "the general character of extendedness"—that is, the general property of being extended or what we might call extendedness-as-such.[4] The modern concept of space arises, according to Klein, when this concept of extension is provided a symbolic "exhibition" or depiction by means of line segments (themselves determinate, extended objects), giving rise to a symbolically articulated domain, which is then taken to be the domain in which all extended body exists. In other words, the modern concept of space entails taking a symbolic mathematical domain as the domain of all physical or corporeal existence.[5] Insofar as this symbolically articulated domain can then encompass both the mathematical and the physical, it can serve as a conceptual framework for mathematical physics.[6]

The foregoing serves as merely a sketch of Klein's claims about space. In making these claims, Klein points to Descartes's *Geometry* as the place of origin for the symbolic concept of space, yet he never takes up a direct discussion of that work (not even to spell out its contribution to the invention of the modern symbolic concept of number).[7] The present study aims to substantiate the mathematical aspect of Klein's claims about the symbolic nature of space by providing an analysis of the concept of space at work in Descartes's *Geometry*.[8] It will ultimately be shown that this concept is connected with the symbolic mathematical object contained in the *Geometry* and that the same symbolic concept-formation underlies the two. In order to accomplish this, we must (1) lay out the symbolic nature of the mathematics contained in the *Geometry*; (2) consider Descartes's solution to the Pappus locus problem, highlighting the role played by the "principal lines" in his mathematical procedure; and (3) analyze the concept of space at work in the *Geometry* and establish its relationship to Descartes's symbolic mathematical objects. The following analysis is therefore divided into three sections that correspond to these three tasks.

The Symbolic Mathematics of the *Geometry*

Descartes begins the *Geometry* by declaring that "All the problems of geometry can easily be reduced to such terms that it is only necessary thereafter to know the length of certain straight lines in order to construct them" (369).[9] With this, he initiates his distinctive mathematical program of constructive problem-solving using line lengths. He then goes on, drawing an analogy with arithmetic, to explain that these line lengths can be found by means of the simple operations of addition, subtraction, multiplication, division, and the extraction of roots.

The addition and subtraction of lines to generate other longer or shorter lines calls for no explication, as this is a standard practice. The multiplication and division of lines resulting in another line, on the other hand, is revolutionary, so Descartes must explain how to do this, and in doing so he redefines these operations for his new geometry. In pre-Cartesian geometry, the only way to multiply one line by another is to construct a figure composed of those two lines set at right angles with each other.[10] In this way, the multiplication of two geometric objects of the same kind (namely, two lines) results in a new geometric object of a different kind (namely, a rectangle). Descartes's new understanding of multiplication wipes out this change in kind or dimensionality, which serves as a first indication of the homogenization of mathematical objects that is characteristic of his *Geometry*.

Descartes's new understanding of multiplication amounts to finding a fourth proportional. He describes it thus: "taking one [line], which I shall call unity in order to relate it as closely as possible to numbers, and which can ordinarily be chosen arbitrarily, and then taking two others, find a fourth which is to one of the two as the other is to unity—[this] is the same as multiplication" (369–70). Before considering his example of this procedure, let us first note two other characteristic aspects of Descartes's mathematics that are introduced here, namely, the arbitrary selection of a particular line as the unit and the collapsing of the distinction between multitude and magnitude. Note, too, that Descartes seems to tacitly admit he is redefining multiplication when he says that finding the fourth proportional is "the same" as multiplication, rather than that it *is* multiplication.

Descartes goes on to redefine division as the inverse of this understanding of multiplication and the extraction of roots as the finding of mean proportionals, after which he gives examples to explicate these newly understood operations. His example of multiplication is as follows (see Figure 1): "let AB be unity, and let it be necessary to multiply BD by BC; I have only to join the points A and C, then to draw DE parallel to CA, and BE is the product of this multiplication" (360). (The proof that BE is the fourth proportional—that is, that BA : BD :: BC : BE—lies in the similarity of the triangles ACB and DEB; see Euclid *Elements* Book VI, Proposition 2.)

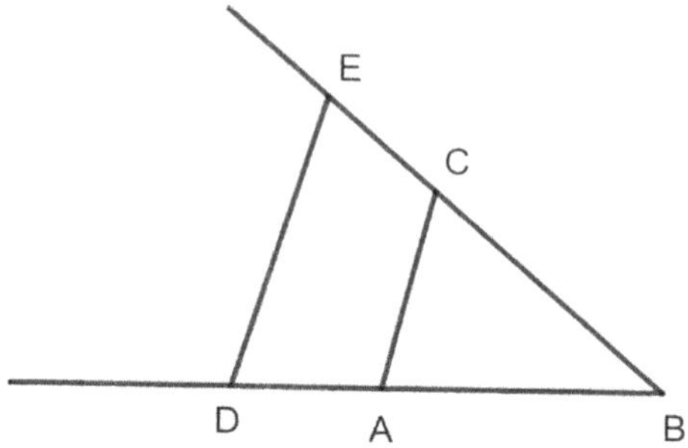

Figure 1

How are we to understand this diagram? Taken in a traditional fashion, this is a perfectly good Euclidean diagram that exhibits two similar triangles with all the attendant properties, including proportionality between the lines that are their sides, but this has nothing to do with multiplication, as there is no indication in the diagram that any calculative operation has taken place. How, then, are we to understand this diagram as exhibiting multiplication, and why does the multiplication of the lines BD and BC result in another line, namely, BE?

Only according to Descartes's new definition of multiplication can we understand this diagram to exhibit multiplication. The diagram itself, however, gives no indication that this is how it is to be understood (as further evidenced by the fact that Descartes goes on to use the same diagram to exhibit the inverse operation of division). The interpretation of the diagram as exhibiting multiplication must therefore be read into the diagram, which is exactly what Descartes asks us to do when he gives a description that allows us to interpret the diagram in a new way that meets his new definition. Even as a Cartesian diagram, then, it does not exhibit multiplication in and of itself, although we can understand it to exhibit that operation insofar as we understand that operation to consist in finding the fourth proportional.

Beyond merely exhibiting this new operation, the diagram also enables us to effect it by actually allowing us to find the fourth proportional of the two lines being multiplied. To do this, however, it is necessary to begin by designating some line as unity, otherwise there would be no way to find a fourth proportional because there would only be two lines under consideration. This shows just how crucial the designation of unity is; without it there would be no way to perform the operation of multiplication. The multiplication of line BD by BC is meaningless without reference to some line designated as unity. Yet that line can be chosen arbitrarily, which indicates that the multiplication of two lines by each other has no determinate result in itself. The multiplication of line BD by line BC only results in a line of length BE when the unit is stipulated as line AB. If some other line had been chosen as the unit, then BE would also be different, while BD and BC—the two lines being multiplied—would stay the same. In fact, the multiplication of these two lines could result in a line of any length; all one has to do is vary the unit line. This provides a striking contrast with the pre-Cartesian understanding of multiplication, where the product of two factors is always of one determinate size.

The specificity of the various lines and lengths involved in this diagram is therefore inter-connected; they are to be considered only in relation to each other, for if a different line were chosen as unity the rest of the diagram would have to be redrawn. The diagram must therefore be understood as a whole in order to represent multiplication. This, coupled with the arbitrariness of the unit and the resulting arbitrariness of the product, reveals that the actual line lengths making up the diagram are not all that is important in Figure 1. While the diagram does allow us to effect the operation of multiplication by finding the determinate length that is sought, it can also be understood as an articulation of the general relationship that holds between the quantities at play in Descartes's understanding of multiplication, namely: as unity is to the first factor, so is the second factor to the product.[11] On this understanding, the lines making up the diagram have no real meaning in terms of their determinate lengths, but rather are used to represent or visually depict the ratio that holds between the various terms that make up Cartesian multiplication.

The diagram can therefore be read in two ways: it can be taken as a Euclidean depiction of triangles made up of determinate lines, which can then be interpreted as and used to effect Cartesian multiplication, and it can be taken as a representation of the general relationship that defines Cartesian multiplication—a representation that is made up of determinate lengths but has no determinate meaning in itself. Given Klein's understanding that a symbol combines an indeterminate object with a determinate representation, we can conclude that this diagram has both a non-symbolic and a symbolic interpretation. In the former, the diagram comprises lines of determinate length that are the objects of a mathematical operation, while in the latter those determinate lines merely represent a general relationship between indeterminate magnitudes.[12]

In the symbolic understanding of the diagram, a general indeterminate abstraction is combined with a determinate, bodily representation: the general relationship that defines multiplication (namely, the proportion between four indeterminate magnitudes—an arbitrary unit-line, two given factors, and a product-line determined by the previous three terms) is provided with a bodily depiction that exhibits that general relationship, presenting it to the eye in Figure 1. While this depiction is made up of lines of determinate lengths, those determinate lengths are completely incidental to the diagram's function as a depiction of the general relationship. In this interpretation of the diagram, then, the individual lines merely serve to represent indeterminate quantities in a general relationship.

This determinate representation of indeterminate quantities allows those quantities to enter into the actual operation of mathematical practice (here, multiplication), thereby completing the process of symbolization as described by Klein; for it is only in the calculative use of such representations that the indeterminate object is actually treated determinately (rather than merely being signaled by some determinate representation). This is exactly what happens as a result of the coexistence of the two interpretations of Figure 1. In Descartes's use of the Euclidean understanding of the diagram (found in concluding BE is the fourth proportional from the similarity of the triangles) the lines are of determinate length and can therefore be considered and manipulated determinately, while in his understanding of the diagram as an exhibition of multiplication those determinate lengths actually stand for indeterminate magnitudes. The lines of this diagram are therefore determinate in themselves while also serving as the representations of indeterminate magnitudes. Their use and manipulation thus put the indeterminate content for which they stand into mathematical operations in a way that would otherwise be impossible because indeterminate magnitudes cannot enter into mathematical calculation on their own, as they have no quantitative value. When, however, indeterminate magnitudes are represented by determinate magnitudes, which do have an inherent quantitative value and therefore can be manipulated, the indeterminate magnitudes can enter into the course of mathematical operation, albeit by proxy. It is significant here, though, that while the two interpretations of Figure 1 function together, they are conceptually separable, which shows that the distinction between the different orders they embody has not been completely collapsed. This is no longer the case, however, in the next step Descartes takes.

Upon completing the explication of how to effect basic arithmetical operations by means of line segments, Descartes introduces algebraic letter signs into his mathematical procedure, thereby taking the symbolic aspect of his mathematics a step further. He does this by saying the following:

> But often one has no need to trace these lines on paper in this way, and it suffices to designate them by certain letters, each [line] by one [letter]. Thus, in order to add the line

> BD to GH, I name the one *a* and the other *b*, and write $a + b$; and $a - b$ in order to subtract *b* from *a*; and *ab* in order to multiply the one by the other; and $\frac{a}{b}$ in order to divide *a* by *b*; and *aa* or a^2 to multiply *a* by itself; and a^3 in order to multiply yet again by *a*, and so on to infinity. (371)

Descartes goes on to clarify the homogenized dimensionality of the referent of his algebraic letter signs, saying that "by a^2 or b^3 or the like, I ordinarily mean only simple lines, although in order to make use of the names used in Algebra, I call them squares, or cubes, etc." (371). He then explains how to operate with letter signs of different degrees in a way that avoids any issues of heterogeneity.

The algebraic letter signs of the *Geometry* thus stand for individual line segments, and they must correspond to the interpretation of Figure 1 in which the line segments themselves stand for indeterminate magnitudes. For these letter signs are not determinate geometrical magnitudes and thus, as drawn marks on the page, cannot be taken in the manner of the Euclidean interpretation of Figure 1. They do, however, enter into the course of calculation, but Descartes must provide instructions for how to operate with them because such letter signs have no quantitative value in themselves and thus there is no intrinsic way to calculate with them. In this way, then, Descartes's letter signs are inherently geared toward capturing indeterminacy and allowing it to enter into mathematical calculation. Furthermore, Descartes explicitly says that the use of these letter signs frequently replaces the need to draw line segments on the page, whereby he shifts the focus even further away from determinate magnitudes, indicating that the algebraic letter signs need not refer to any determinately drawn line-lengths.

The practice of using algebraic letter signs is therefore just another way of producing an external representation of what is considered internally in the mind; for these letter signs serve simply to re-express what was captured in the new Cartesian interpretation of Figure 1. In this way, the transition to algebraic letter signs provides further evidence for a symbolic interpretation of Figure 1 in that it shows that generic letter signs with no determinate geometrical value serve just as well to represent the terms of the multiplicative ratio as do lines of determinate length. We can conclude, then, that the expression by line-lengths and the expression by algebraic letter signs are simply two different ways of articulating the same thing, namely, indeterminate magnitudes and their general relationships.

While both of these depictions are symbolic in that they are determinate representations of indeterminate magnitudes that are used to effect mathematical calculation, they differ from each other in that the symbolic line-segments are geometrical figures that have determinate magnitudinous quantity while standing for an indeterminate quantity, whereas the algebraic letter signs simply have no such determinate value. As marks on a page, these letter signs are determinate bodily figures, but insofar as they are not geometrical figures they do not have any inherent quantitative value that can be used in mathematical calculation. Thus there is no second interpretation of how to read these algebraic letter signs; their use in mathematical operations unavoidably entails the full conflation of general indeterminate content and determinate representation.

While Descartes's algebraic letter signs might therefore be considered more thoroughly symbolic than his depictions by line-lengths, they cannot be used to solve geometrical problems without reference to some geometrical construction. It is thus the duality of Descartes's geometrical figures that is essential in characterizing his new mathematical science as a symbolic geometry; for it is by giving his figural depictions an algebraic character that Descartes brings the symbolism of algebra into the realm of geometry, thereby allowing him to connect his algebraic letter signs with his geometrical constructions.[13]

In fact, the mathematical procedure of the *Geometry* rests on the ability to move back and forth between the algebraic and geometrical expressions of Descartes's symbolic mathematical objects. We begin to see this combination of geometry and algebra in the example of solving a quadratic equation that Descartes offers a little later in Book 1. In order to find the root (that is, the unknown line z) of the equation $z^2 = az + bb$, Descartes says:

> I make the right triangle NLM [see Figure 2], whose side LM is equal to b, the square root of the known quantity bb, and the other LN is $\frac{1}{2}a$, the half of the other known quantity, which was multiplied by z, which I suppose to be the unknown line. Then, extending MN, the [hypotenuse] of the triangle, to O, so that NO is equal to NL, the whole line OM is z, the line sought. And it is expressed in this way: $z = \frac{1}{2}a + \sqrt{\frac{1}{4}aa + bb}$. (375)

To understand what is going on here we must move back and forth between the algebraic expressions and the geometrical diagram. The key feature of the diagram is that as a Euclidean figure $LM^2 = OM \times PM$.[14] The equivalent relationship can be found in the algebraic equation by manipulating it as follows:

$$z^2 = az + bb$$
$$z^2 - az = bb$$
$$z(z - a) = bb$$

The parallelism between this equation and the diagram can be established as follows. Note, first, that PM = OM − OP; then, taking OM as z, and noting that OP = a (because NL is $\frac{1}{2}a$), it becomes clear that PM = $z - a$. Therefore, OM × PM = $z(z - a)$, all of which is equal to LM^2, which by assumption is equal to b^2. In this way, we can see that the diagram has been constructed to capture the relationship expressed in the algebraic equation. Once this par-

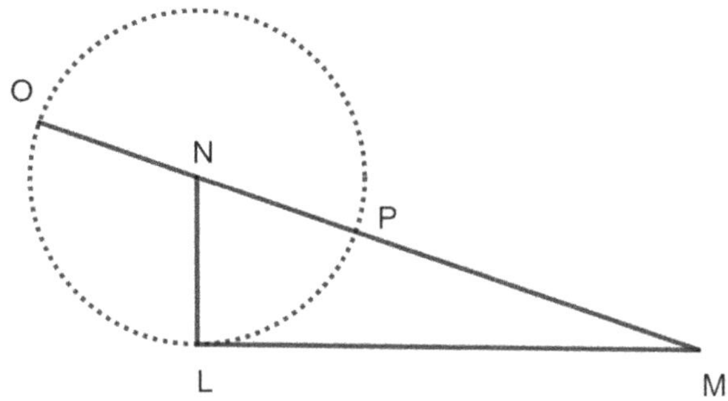

Figure 2

allelism has been established, the value of z can be found by noting that OM = ON + NM, and that according to the Pythagorean theorem NM = $\sqrt{NL^2 + LM^2}$; then, plugging in the algebraic letter signs for the line lengths, OM = ON + NM becomes $z = \frac{1}{2}a + \sqrt{\frac{1}{4}a^2 + b^2}$. Given that a and b were assumed to be known, the value of the unknown z can then be found using this equation.

The foregoing serves as a prime example of the back-and-forth movement between algebraic expression and geometrical construction. Descartes begins with an algebraic equation that captures a general relationship between indeterminate magnitudes (namely, that the square of some unknown magnitude is equal to the sum of its root multiplied by some known magnitude and some other known square magnitude). He then constructs a geometrical figure that depicts that relationship with line-lengths, associating the algebraic letter signs from the equation with various parts of the diagram. In doing so, it is clear that the line-lengths stand for the same indeterminate magnitudes that the algebraic letters stand for. This indicates that the diagram functions symbolically. Yet the line-lengths are also used non-symbolically in the appeal to their geometrical arrangement, both when establishing the parallelism between the geometrical diagram and the algebraic equation and when using the diagram to re-express the value of the unknown in algebraic terms.

At no point in this procedure is any determinate magnitude considered. (Note that Descartes does not even designate a line-length as the unit in this situation since there is no need to do so.) Instead, Descartes is only concerned with a general relationship between indeterminate magnitudes, which have been represented in two different ways on the page, namely, by written letter signs and by drawn figures. It is this combination that allows Descartes to use the geometrical diagram to find an algebraic expression for the unknown line that is sought. In the process, both representations enter into mathematical calculation and are manipulated in a determinate manner—the letter signs when they are moved around in the equation, and the figure when it is considered in a traditional geometrical fashion. There is, therefore, a twofold symbolism at work here, an algebraic one and a geometrical one; in each, indeterminate magnitudes are considered and manipulated determinately in the course of mathematical operations. This is the symbolic mathematics of Descartes's Geometry.

The Pappus Problem, the Principal Lines, and the Admissibility of Curves

We turn now to a consideration of Descartes's solution to the Pappus locus problem, which serves as a further example of the combination of geometry and algebra laid out above. This problem from ancient geometry plays a central role in Descartes's *Geometry*, and his solution is intended as a demonstration of the power and superiority of his mathematical method. In giving his general solution to this problem at the end of Book 1, Descartes introduces his use of "principal lines," which we will see to be intimately connected with his criterion for which curves can be admitted into his mathematics. As this serves as our gateway to the concept of space in the *Geometry*, we must familiarize ourselves with the former as a preparation for our discussion of the latter.

After first stating the problem in its general form, Descartes focuses on a particular version of the Pappus problem in which there are four given lines, but he emphasizes that the solution offered can be applied to more complex versions of the problem with any number of given lines. He lays out the problem as follows [see Figure 3]:

> Let AB, AD, EF, GH, etc., be several lines given in position [but not length], and let it be required to find a point, such as C, from which having drawn other straight lines on the given ones, such as CB, CD, CF, and CH, in such a way that the angles CBA, CDA, CFE, CHG, etc., are given, and such that that which is produced by the multiplication of one part of these lines is equal to that which is produced by the multiplication of the others, or else that they have some other given proportion, for this does not make the question more difficult. (382)

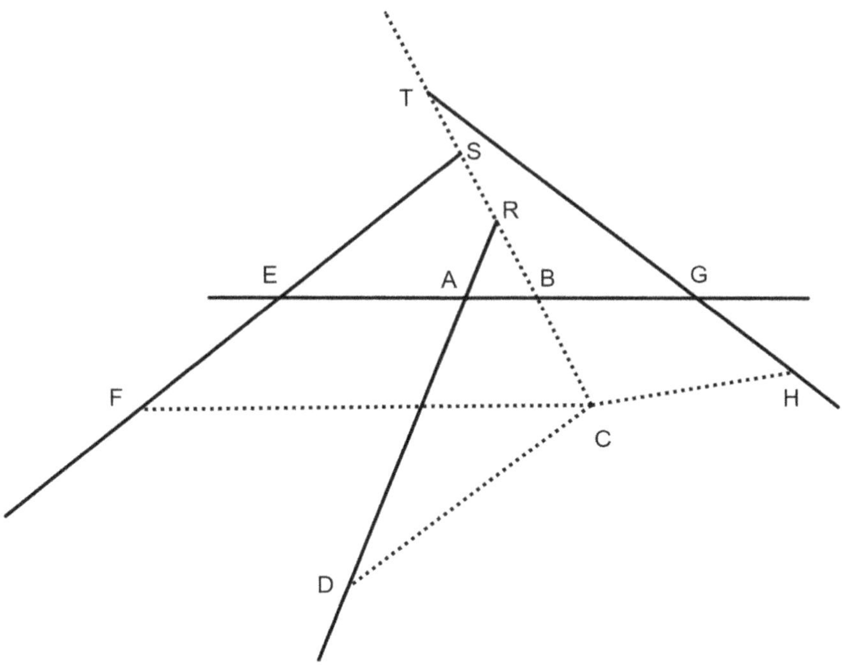

Figure 3

In accordance with the analytic procedure sketched earlier in the *Geometry*, Descartes begins approaching the problem by assuming that it has already been solved. Then, "in order to lessen the confusion" of all the lines, he designates one of the given lines and one of the sought lines as the "principal" lines to which all the others will be related (382–83). In this particular example, Descartes selects the lines AB and BC as his principal lines and names them x and y respectively.[15] He then extends all the given lines so that they intersect these two principal lines at points E, A, and G (on AB) and R, S, and T (on BC). This produces a series of triangles that can then be used to relate the various lines to the principal lines via algebraic expressions. Descartes does this by first noting that all the angles of triangle ARB are given: by supposition the angle ABC is known and the positions of lines AB and AD are given, which together mean that all of the angles of triangle ARB are determined. Accordingly, the ratio between the lines AB and BR is also given, which Descartes "supposes as z to b" (383). Given that AB is x, BR is therefore $\frac{bx}{z}$, as can be seen by rewriting the proportion AB : BR :: $z : b$ as an equation in modern notation: $\frac{\mathrm{AB}}{\mathrm{BR}} = \frac{z}{b}$, and then substituting x for AB and solving for BR. The line CR, composed of CB and BR, is therefore $y + \frac{bx}{z}$. Having established this, Descartes can now apply the same approach to triangle DRC: because all the angles of triangle DRC are given, the ratio between the sides CR and CD is also given, which is supposed as z to c, "so that CR being $y + \frac{bx}{z}$, CD is $\frac{cy}{z} + \frac{bcx}{zz}$" (383). Descartes then follows the same general procedure for triangles ESB, FSC, BGT, and TCH, whereby he finds algebraic expressions—made up exclusively of various knowns and the two unknowns x and y—for all the lines of the diagram, including the four lines that had to be drawn from point C (namely, CB, CD, CF, and CH).

Next, Descartes notes that this procedure can be expanded to apply to any number of initially given lines and that it will always lead to algebraic expressions that are made up of at most three terms with only two unknowns (in modern notation, the expression will always be of the form ax ± by ± c.). Moreover, from this fact it is clear that when any of these lines are multiplied together, the product will contain no higher degree of *x* and *y* then the number of lines multiplied.

Descartes then shows how to find the point C once the algebraic expressions for all the various lines have been found. This is dependent on the stipulation that there is some equality or proportion between the products of two groups of lines drawn from point C. In the particular example under consideration, Descartes has left this stipulation indeterminate, saying simply that there needs to be some such equality or proportion; when he takes this problem up again in Book 2, however, he adds the stipulation that the product of CB and CF is equal to the product of CD and CH (398). By setting up the equation that captures this relationship and plugging in the algebraic expressions for the individual lines, one generates an equation with only two unknowns (namely, *x* and *y*) such that one can arbitrarily assume one of the two unknown quantities and then use the equation to find the other. Descartes points out that when the problem is posed for five lines or less, *x* will not be of a degree higher than two,[16] so that if a known quantity is taken for *y*, then $x^2 = \pm ax \pm b^2$, in which case "one can find the quantity *x* with ruler and compass in the manner explained earlier" (386). Once a correspon°ding pair of *x* and *y* lengths are known, they can be used to determine the location of point C, and one can then go on to find an endless number of such *x* and *y* pairs, whereby they will determine an endless number of different points that satisfy the same requirements as point C. These points can then be used to describe a curved line which is the locus of points that was originally sought.

The most important part of the procedure just outlined for our purposes is Descartes's introduction of the principal lines. These lines are integral to the solution of the problem insofar as their algebraic expression is the basis for the algebraic expression of all the other lines of the problem. In this way, they provide the very frame of reference in relation to which all the other parts of the problem are articulated. It is also important to note that these principal lines are themselves symbolic in that they are instances of Descartes's new mathematical object. This can be seen from the fact that, both as lines in the diagram (namely, AB and BC) and as algebraic letter signs used to designate those lines (namely, *x* and *y*), these principal lines are themselves of an indeterminate quantity that can be given an endless array of determinate values, which is in fact precisely what has to be done in order to solve the problem. In other words, Descartes's solution to this problem consists in first generating, via the principal lines, an articulation of the general relationship between the various lines of the problem—a relationship that is encoded in both the algebraic expressions and the figural diagram—and then, second, specifying determinate instances that fit that general relationship. Insofar as the principal lines are what make that articulation possible at all, they are central to the very possibility of Descartes's symbolic mathematical procedure for solving this problem.

This procedure, initially sketched out for solving the Pappus problem in particular, turns out to be the general method of problem-solving in the *Geometry* as a whole. We can further see the role of the principal lines in this procedure by turning to the beginning of Book 2, where Descartes develops his criterion for which curves can be admitted into his mathematical science. Here, too, the principal lines are of central importance.

Descartes begins laying out his criterion of admissibility by saying the following:

> It is very clear, it seems to me, that if we take Geometry as that which is precise and exact (as one does) and Mechanics as that which is not, and if we consider Geometry as a science which generally teaches how to measure all bodies, one should no more exclude more complex lines than

> the more simple ones, provided that one can imagine them to be described by a continuous movement or by several movements which are successive and of which the latter are entirely regulated by those which precede it; for, by this means, one can always have an exact knowledge of their measure. (389–90)

Here we see that Descartes understands geometry to be concerned with what is "precise and exact" and that any line—regardless of its degree of complexity—meets this criterion if it is described by a completely regular or regulated motion, as this guarantees that its measure is exactly knowable. On the other side of the distinction are those curves that "truly belong only to Mechanics," which are "described by two separate motions which have no relation between them that can be measured exactly" (390).[17] The key issue in this distinction between geometrical and mechanical lines, then, is whether they can be constructed and known exactly.

Descartes then goes on to further specify what makes a curved line geometrical:

> in order to comprehend together all those [curves] that exist in nature and to distinguish them by order into certain classes, I know of nothing better than to say that all the points of those [curves] that can be called Geometrical, that is to say, those which fall under some precise and exact measure, necessarily have some relation to all the points of a straight line, which can be expressed by some single equation for all the points. (392)

Here Descartes reiterates that a geometrical curve must have a "precise and exact" measurement, but this time he specifies that this entails that all the points of such a line have a given relation to the points of some straight line, a relation that is expressible by means of an algebraic equation. From our consideration of the Pappus problem, it is clear that this is a reference to the ability to articulate a curved line in relation to some principal lines, which is what allows for it to be algebraically expressible in equation form. A little later, Descartes repeats the claim that all geometrical curves are expressible by algebraic equations, saying "in whatever way one imagines the description of a curved line, provided that it is among the number of those that I name Geometrical, one will always be able to find an equation to determine all its points" (395). It seems, then, that Descartes has given a second criterion of admissibility, namely, that a line be expressed or determined by an algebraic equation.

These two statements of Descartes's criterion for the admissibility of curves turn out to be integrally connected, in that the complete regulation of the motion generating a curve guarantees that there is an algebraic expression that articulates the relationship between the points of that curve and some straight line (which serves as one of the principal lines).[18] Descartes's criterion for the admissibility of curves thus requires that any geometrically constructible curve must be described by a completely regulated motion, which entails that it is algebraically expressible, which in turn entails that it can be articulated by means of and in relation to the principal lines. Accordingly, all the curves that Descartes admits into his geometry can be articulated in relation to the principal lines, and it is in fact only such curved lines that are admitted. This shows the fundamental importance of the principal lines in that they serve to delimit and articulate the very domain of the geometrical. Moreover, given that that domain is occupied only by the symbolic constructions of Descartes's geometry, and that the principal lines themselves are symbolic, it can be concluded that the principal lines serve to define Descartes's geometrical domain as a purely symbolic one. This, finally, allows us to look at the concept of space at work in the *Geometry*.

The Symbolic Concept of Space in the *Geometry*

The word *space* (*espace*) is mentioned only four times in the *Geometry.* The first two instances appear close together in a passage in which Descartes, referring to Propositions 11–13 of Book 1 of Apollonius's *Conics*, discusses the characteristic properties of conic sections. In relating his analytic procedure to traditionally conceived conics, Descartes speaks of "forming a space" from various parts of the conic (404) and of "subtracting a space" which has a given relationship to various parts of the conic from a given rectangle (405). In both instances, the space to which Descartes refers is the amount or extent of a rectilinear figure which is defined by two lines and understood in the traditional geometrical manner. He thus employs the word *space* here to describe the area contained by a figure. Note that in doing so Descartes uses two lines to articulate and delimit an area contained by those two lines, and it is this region that he calls a space.

In the third instance of *space* in the *Geometry*, Descartes again refers to an area, but this time it is the area contained by a curve. When listing various properties of curves that can be found after their defining relationships have been expressed in an equation, Descartes claims that this includes "almost everything that can be determined regarding the magnitude of the space which they contain" (413). Although he does not expound on this possibility further in the *Geometry*, it is clear that the conception of space that underlies this claim is of a piece with the first two instances of this word. While the space under a curve is different from the space contained by a rectangle in that it can be open-ended, the general understanding of space as a region marked off by boundary lines is the same in all three instances.

In the fourth and final mention of *space* in the *Geometry*, Descartes invokes a broader conception of space. This comes in the concluding paragraph of Book II, where he says that up to that point in the *Geometry* he has only spoken about "curved lines which can be described on a flat surface," but that it is easy to transfer what he has said "to all those [curves] which can be imagined to be formed by the regular movement of points of some body in a space which has three dimensions" (440). Descartes gives only a sketch of how to do this, but the heart of the procedure lies in constructing planes at right angles to each other so that all the points of the three-dimensional curve can be related to a line shared by those planes, which ensures that an equation of the curve can still be attained through the use of principal lines. From this it is clear that in extending his mathematical procedure to three-dimensional objects, Descartes also extends the governing role played by his criterion of admissibility, which we have seen to be intimately connected with his use of the principal lines, to the three-dimensional domain.

As for the understanding of space expressed in this fourth instance, note first that Descartes is contrasting curves described *on* a flat surface with those generated by a body moving *in* a space of three dimensions. This highlights the container-like conception of space at work here in that bodies and curves exist within the region of this space. Note also that Descartes speaks of "a space," implying that there is a plurality of such spaces; this indicates that space is here conceived as a particular region in which some body or curve exists. (Indeed, any set of principal lines establishes *a* space.) Yet there are no lines that mark off the limits of this space—the space is identified by the principal lines within it rather than by any extremities; this indicates that the space itself is unbounded.

The understanding of space invoked in this final instance is thus the very domain in which some particular geometrical bodies exist. This is the broadest conception of space expressed in the *Geometry* and thus seems to govern the other three instances, which retrospectively appear to be more specific or confined versions of this broader conception. Common to all four instances, however, is the idea of an area or domain defined by some line segments, although that defining can occur in different ways: in the broadest conception of space the defining occurs via the principal lines, which are used as the reference in relation to which everything within a space is demarcated, while in the narrower conception the defining is achieved by the particular lines that delimit some specific region within that general domain of space.

We are now in a position to examine the symbolic nature of Descartes's concept of space in the *Geometry*. As we have seen, in its broadest conception this space is the very domain of Descartes's geometrical objects. Given that this domain is governed by the criterion of admissibility discussed above, the range of objects that exist within this space is restricted to those objects that are generated by completely regulated motions, are algebraically expressible, and can be articulated by means of and in relation to the principal lines.

This space can first be characterized as symbolic insofar as the mathematical objects that exist within it are themselves symbolic, for in this way Descartes's geometrical space is a domain made up of nothing but symbolic objects. Given the intimate connection between the principal lines and the criterion of what can be admitted into this space, we can add that the principal lines themselves serve to delimit the domain of symbolic objects existing within this geometrical space in that they establish the parameters within which and in relation to which such objects have their symbolic meaning.

Beyond this, however, we can now explain how the principal lines serve to symbolically represent this geometrical space itself. As lines given in position but indeterminate in length, the principal lines determine the domain and frame of reference within which all the other geometrical objects of a problem exist. In doing so, the principal lines serve to define a geometrical space not only by giving meaning to everything within it, but also by marking it out and visually depicting it on the page. This visual depiction occurs by drawing lines of determinate length that stand for indeterminate quantities capable of taking on an endless range of determinate values. Insofar as it is the very ability of the principal lines to take on this range of values that defines the domain in which all the other geometrical objects under consideration exist, the figural depiction of that domain by means of those lines serves as a visual articulation of that geometrical space. This amounts to a symbolic representation of that space in that the determinate depiction by means of the principal lines is taken to be the indeterminate range for which that depiction stands, whereby that depiction is taken to be the geometrical space itself.

Moreover, we can now see that this symbolic representation of space is a further development of the symbolic concept-formation that underlies the modern symbolic mathematics present in the *Geometry.* This is the case, first, insofar as it stems from a movement from symbolic mathematical objects to the domain in which those objects exist. Second and more fundamentally, however, the concept of space at work here is a product of the same symbolic abstraction that gives rise to the symbolic concept of number, which can be seen as follows. In depicting space on the page by means of the principal lines, the extended character of some particular geometrical objects is used to represent the geometrical domain of extended objects; in this process, the general character of extendedness—an abstraction that exists apart from any particular extended object—is given a figural representation by means of particular and thus determinate lines, and that representation is then taken to be the very space in which the extended objects of geometry exist. In this way, the figural depiction of the principal lines on the page symbolically represents the geometrical domain or space that those lines serve to define.[19]

Conclusion

We have now uncovered the symbolic nature of the mathematical objects found in the *Geometry* as well as the concept of space contained therein, while also establishing the relationship between the two. If we glance back at the claims that prompted this investigation, we can now understand Klein's description of symbolic mathematical space as "the domain of symbolic exhibition by means of line-segments" and "the symbolic illustration of the general character of the extendedness" of geometrical objects.[20] For we have seen that the space of Descartes's *Geometry* is the symbolic domain articulated and displayed by his principal lines. This symbolic concept of space, on Klein's analysis, is the originary form of the modern symbolic concept of space as such. We have therefore taken a first step towards substantiating Klein's broader claims about the symbolic concept of space that underlies modern science and thus shapes modern thought at large.

Klein and Einstein on Cartesian Space

JOSEPH COSGROVE

Jacob Klein begins *Greek Mathematical Thought and the Origin of Algebra* with the observation that "[t]he creation of a formal mathematical language was of decisive significance for the constitution of modern mathematical physics."[1] Thus, before addressing the contemporary problems faced by mathematical physics, Klein maintains, we must "set ourselves the task of inquiring into the origin and the conceptual structure of this formal language" (*GMTOA* 4). This inquiry, preliminary to a discussion of conceptual problems in mathematical physics itself, is the one Klein substantially accomplishes in *Greek Mathematical Thought*. Nevertheless, he stresses that we must never lose sight of the ultimate aim, which is the clarification of conceptual problems arising in mathematical physics:

> Nevertheless, the inquiry will never lose sight of the fundamental question, directly related as it is to the conceptual difficulties arising within mathematical *physics* today. However far afield it may run, its formulation will throughout be determined by this as its ultimate theme. (*GMTOA* 4)

In this essay I shall approach Klein's analysis of symbolic mathematics from the perspective of this ultimate aim, the clarification of problems arising in mathematical physics today.

At the very outset of the section in *Greek Mathematical Thought* devoted to Descartes, Klein characterizes Descartes's singular contribution to the modern symbolic concept of number:

> Descartes' great idea now consists of identifying, by means of "methodological" considerations, the "general" object of *mathesis universalis*—which can be represented and conceived only symbolically—with the "substance" of the world, with corporeality as "extension." (*GMTOA* 197)

This claim—that the symbolic or general object of his universal mathematics is identified by Descartes with the substance of the physical world—I shall call Klein's *identification thesis.* At the conclusion of the same section on Descartes, Klein issues an additional weighty pronouncement on the historical significance of the Cartesian identification of real and symbolic extension:

> Only at this point has the conceptual basis of "classical" physics, which has since been called "Euclidean space," been created. This is the foundation on which Newton will raise the structure of his mathematical science of nature. (*GMTOA* 211)

This second thesis, according to which Cartesian symbolic space, taken as the "substance of the world," furnishes the conceptual grounding for subsequent classical physics, I shall call Klein's *Newtonian thesis.*

For Klein, the identification of symbolic and real extension is the original presupposition of Descartes's universal mathematics and therefore the prime motivation as well for Descartes's increasing preoccupation with method:

> The point of view of "methodical" cognition is therefore secondary for the *original* identification of the "general" mathematical object with extension having figure. But

> since everything depends on the *justification* of this identification, the "method" gradually gains a more and more central significance, *while its rules are borrowed from the "mathesis universalis" itself.* (*GMTOA* 294n310)

However, in *Greek Mathematical Thought*, it is not entirely clear precisely what Klein means by Descartes's having *identified* his symbolic extension with physical extension, something that on its face would seem a rather too obvious confusion. Moreover, Klein adduces no particular evidence in support of his assertion that Cartesian symbolic space grounds Newtonian physics. It would have profound implications for our understanding of modern natural science if a presumptively *empirical* science had, at its very inception, substituted for the experienced physical world as its proper object of study a symbolic object of its own construction.

In connection with these questions, it is of no minor significance that Albert Einstein—on any account a thinker of first rank on the subject of space and time—specifically addressed the historical role of the Cartesian concept of space in two philosophical essays in the 1930s: "The Problem of Space, Ether, and the Field in Physics," published in 1934, and "Physics and Reality" of 1936.[2] Moreover, Einstein's philosophical method is congenial to Klein's in that Einstein traces the meaning of physical concepts historically since, in his words, "we have, so to speak, forgotten what features in the world of experience caused us to frame those concepts, and we have great difficulty in calling to mind the world of experience without the spectacles of the old-established conceptual interpretation" (*PS* 277).[3]

I believe we can profitably avail ourselves of Einstein's reflections on Cartesian space to make better sense of Klein's claims for Cartesian space and its decisive role in the subsequent history of modern physics. In section I, I summarize Klein's account of Cartesian symbolic extension. Then in section II, I bring to bear upon Klein's analysis Einstein's reflections on Cartesian space and its role in modern mathematical physics. Here we shall find that Einstein's account of the "inertia determining" function of Cartesian space in classical physics confirms Klein's Newtonian thesis. Finally, in section III, I shift attention to Einstein's general theory of relativity, analyzing an episode in its development—the "hole argument" and Einstein's eventual resolution thereof—that lends substantial support to both Klein's identification thesis and his Newtonian thesis. For what Einstein discovered is that modern mathematical physics at its inception indeed adopted as its proximate object a symbolic construction—Cartesian coordinate space.

I. Klein on Cartesian Symbolic Extension

In Rule XIV of *Rules for the Direction of the Mind* Descartes observes that in our cognition of the extended world, the pure intellect has the ability of "separating abstract beings" (*abstracta separandi*), as when we say "extension is not body" with "no special idea corresponding to [the term 'extension'] in the imagination."[4] Here one thinks of extension in general or "abstractly," as it were, as if it excluded body, even though it does not. In a non-mathematical context we might similarly say, for instance, "Humanity is not man." But there are other propositions in which the pure intellect likewise separates abstract beings, but this time *without* the abstract terms excluding "anything which is not really distinct from what they denote" (*Rules* 61). For example, we might say that a certain surface is two-dimensional without thereby excluding in thought the fact that such a surface necessarily belongs to a three-dimensional piece of extension. And here the pure intellect, in abstractly conceiving "surface in general," should rely on the imagination, even though the idea of a two-dimensional surface itself remains purely intellectual: for the imagination can direct the pure intellect, which itself bears no direct relation to the corporeal world, to features belonging to the "real idea" of the thing but not conveyed by the specific term in question. Thus, to truly grasp that which has been separated we must reinstate the "real idea" of the thing in the guise of an image—not in the mode of the direct "abstraction" of ancient or scholastic science (the abstract idea of five, for instance, represented by the image of five apples or five points), which would not get hold of the thing separated in its very indeterminateness as such, but rather in the mode of what Klein calls "symbol-generating abstraction."[5]

On Klein's account, the *objectivity* of symbolic extension within the framework of Cartesian *mathesis universalis* is associated essentially with the particular mode of representing the extended corporeal world by means of *real extension* in the corporeal imagination. Extension conceived symbolically is at the same time *real* extension, an actual modification of the part of the brain Descartes calls the "corporeal imagination." The intellect appropriates such modifications or "images," which, according to Descartes in Rule XII, occur literally in the "same way" as the seal in the wax (*Rules* 40), to symbolically represent magnitudes of whatever kind, or better, to symbolically represent indeterminate or general magnitude as such. The key passage on symbolic extension in Descartes's Rule XIV is worth quoting at length:

> The final point to note is this: if we are to imagine something, and are to make use, not of the pure intellect, but of the intellect aided by images depicted in the imagination, then nothing can be ascribed to magnitudes in general which cannot also be ascribed to any species of magnitude. It is easy to conclude from this that it will be very useful if we transfer what we understand to hold for magnitudes in general to that species of magnitude which is most readily and distinctly depicted in our imagination. But it follows from what we said in Rule Twelve that this species is the real extension of a body considered in abstraction from everything else about it save for its having a shape. In that Rule we conceived of the imagination, along with the ideas

> existing in it, as being nothing but a real body with a real extension and shape. (*Rules* 58)

The clear thrust of this passage is that since *any* kind of magnitude can be used to represent "general magnitude," we should use the kind that is easiest for the imagination to handle, namely, a shape or ideally a simple line. We then can trust the objectivity of the operations we perform in universal mathematics because those operations are grounded in a direct and self-evident "seeing" in the imagination that certifies their application to the external physical world insofar as the latter in all its features can be truly conceived in terms of magnitude in general.[6]

Cartesian symbolic extension serves both a heuristic and legitimating function in Cartesian science precisely because *any* kind of magnitude can be used to represent magnitude in general and thus to represent indirectly any other kind of magnitude. Since any kind can be used, it makes sense, in the first place, to use the easiest kind. Moreover, the quantitative relations (ratios and proportions) intuited in symbolic extension hold objectively and indifferently for every kind of quantity. Thus Descartes observes at the end of Rule XIV, "We have as much reason to abstract propositions from geometrical figures, if the problem has to do with these, as we have from any other subject matter" (*Rules* 65).

The exemplary objectivity of extension for representing the corporeal world, however, is not yet the identification of symbolic and physical extension. To get hold of Klein's identification thesis we must bring to bear his analysis of the *numerical* intelligibility of Cartesian symbolic extension. Descartes's challenge, Klein notes, is to reconcile the indeterminacy of his generalized algebraic quantities with the determinateness of "number" in the traditional sense (*GMTOA* 203). This is accomplished, in Klein's preferred formulation, by taking up a "second intention" (in this case, the concept of indeterminate multitude or "multitudinousness as such" separated by the pure intellect) in the mode of a "first intention" (direct cognition of real extension as subject to numerical measure) by subjecting it to arithmetical calculation as if it were a multitude of units (i.e., an *arithmos* or "number" in the traditional sense).[7] Thus symbolic extension is no longer the "representation of a *determinate number* of units of measurement (as are the straight lines of Euclid's arithmetical books) but the '*symbol*' of an *indeterminate multitude*" (*GMTOA* 205). For the same reason, according to Klein, "the 'figures' with which the 'mathesis universalis' deals, namely, 'rectilinear and rectangular planes' as well as 'straight lines' . . . have, as far as their mode of being is concerned, no longer anything to do with the 'figures' of what had up till then been the ordinary 'geometry'" (*GMTOA* 203). The figures of Cartesian geometry, that is, are not geometrical objects in the usual sense but symbolic representations, numerical in their intelligibility, of the general quantitative relations expressed by algebraic equations. These relations are expressible equivalently by line lengths (symbolic extension) or algebraic letter signs.

When the pure intellect turns its gaze upon its own conceiving of indeterminate multitude, the "concept of number as such," it grasps that multitude as "an apparently 'independent' being, an '*ens rationis*'" (*GMTOA* 208). Klein continues:

> When now—and this is of crucial importance—the *ens rationis* as [the object of] a "second intention" is grasped *with the aid of the imagination* in such a way that the intellect can, in turn take it up as an object in the mode of a "first intention," we are dealing with a *symbol*, either with an "algebraic" letter-sign or with a "geometric" figure as understood by Descartes. (*GMTOA* 208)

"Symbolic extension," then, is this very indeterminate multitude taken up in the mode of real extension (the line segments of Cartesian algebra). Indeed, that these line segments are symbolically equivalent to algebraic letter-signs is what allows for the transition to a first-intentional apprehension of the generalized object of Descartes's universal mathematics (*mathesis universalis*). That is, the intentional object of Cartesian symbolic extension is taken up as the object of a first intention, through being subjected to algebraic calculation in the mode of traditional number. As Klein emphasizes, the mode of being of Cartesian symbolic extension is "exactly the same as the *letter* . . . which occurs in 'algebra', especially in Vieta's analytic . . ." (*GMTOA* 205):

> . . . this general character of number or, what amounts to the same thing, this "general number" in all its indeterminateness, that is, in its merely possible determinateness, is accorded a certain independence which permits it to be the subject of "calculational" operations. (*GMTOA* 174)

We see just this numerical calculus of symbolic line segments at the outset of Descartes's *Geometry*, as Descartes employs the ratios and proportions between symbolic line segments to carry out algebraically the numerical operations of addition, subtraction, multiplication, and division. By this means Descartes's symbolic line segments, convertible with algebraic letter-signs, are fused in meaning, as it were, with the general concept of "indeterminate multitude."

Klein next asks, "How can the *mathesis universalis* turn with its [i.e., the imagination's] aid, into 'true physics' as well?" (*GMTOA* 208). According to Descartes in Rule 12, the imagination receives via external impressions (the "seal in the wax") the true extended figure belonging to the corporeal world itself.[8] Moreover, as we saw, the pure intellect must employ the same imagination—itself an extended corporeal organ—to represent to itself in a determinately graspable manner relations between the generalized quantities that serve as the object of universal mathematics. Enlisting for this purpose sensible line segments (replaceable by letter signs), *which are of the same corporeal nature as the imagination itself*, the imagination presents symbolic extension in the mode of the object of a first intention—which is to say, in the mode of real extension—to the pure intellect as the substance of the corporeal world, the object of "true physics."

Thus, extension itself, at once the substance of the corporeal world and the envisaged object of the Cartesian science of geometry, has been fused conceptually in Descartes's account with symbolically conceived extension or "magnitude in general," through taking up the latter in the mode of determinate quantity subject to algebraic calculation. In this sense we can say that Descartes identifies symbolic extension with real extension as the substance of the physical world.[9]

Klein's account in *Greek Mathematical Thought* remains at such a level of generality, though, that it would be helpful to have something more concrete in the way of illustrations from mathematical science itself. Fortunately, Klein furnishes just such a concrete illustration in his analysis of the identification thesis in an earlier essay of 1932, "The World of Physics and the 'Natural' World."[10] Here, in his characterization of the symbolic representation of geometrical figures in Descartes's *Geometry* of 1637, Klein observes that Descartes's drawn figure, an ellipse, for instance, functions as what we today would call a *graph* of the equation for an ellipse, not as an *image* or pictorial representation of the figure of interest such as we would find, for example, in the works of Apollonius.[11] One advantage, for our purposes, of this earlier account of symbolic extension over Klein's analysis in *Greek Mathematical Thought* is that the Cartesian concept of extension was transmitted to Newton and to classical physics via Descartes's *Geometry*, not via the *Rules* (which was published only in 1701). Moreover, even if the *Rules* gives us a better idea of the principal concerns animating the construction of Descartes's universal mathematics, it is his *Geometry* that sets forth this universal mathematics ("general algebra") in its mature form.

Let us consider, then, the graph of an ellipse ($\frac{x^2}{a^2} + \frac{y^2}{b^2} = 1$) in Cartesian coordinates. The algebraic variables (not just x and y but also the "constants" a and b) symbolically represent general magnitudes, and the equation itself expresses general relations between those magnitudes. The equation itself, of course, need not be about a geometrical ellipse, any more than an equation that graphs as a "Bell Curve," for instance, must be about an actual bell as opposed to, say, your students' grades on the last exam. Klein's point is that the Cartesian ellipse symbolically "graphs" the quantitative relations that define "ellipse in general" and is not the direct image of a geometrical figure. Moreover, since Descartes is doing geometry in his book by that name, Klein's identification thesis specifically takes the form of the claim that Descartes *identifies* his drawn figure, a symbolic ellipse or *graph*, with Apollonius's *image* of a geometrical ellipse:

> It is no less essential that these *symbolic* curves [e.g., a graphed ellipse] were *understood* as the images of the curves exhibited by the Ancients. For example, the ellipse inscribed within coordinate-axes was regarded as the very same ellipse treated by Apollonius [whose ellipse was *not* a graph]. Precisely this assumption led Fermat and Descartes to believe that they were not proceeding any differently than Apollonius had. Although, in fact, there has been a shift in conceptual levels, Fermat thinks he has just interpreted many of Apollonius' theorems more generally. . . . What Fermat and Descartes call "generalization" is in reality a complete conceptual process ascending from *intentio prima* to *intentio secunda* while, *at the same time*, identifying these. (*WPNW* 19–20, italics in original, bracketed material added)

Accordingly, whereas for Apollonius and Greek mathematics in general "*generality of procedure* . . . does *not* correspond to generality of object" (*WPNW* 16), for Cartesian analytical geometry, not just the procedure but the object itself is *general*. So even though Descartes is doing geometry, his graph or drawn ellipse is not the visual image of an individual ellipse but rather the visual symbol of the general quantitative relations that define "ellipse in general" (and, we might add, any other potential subject matter characterized by the same general relations expressed in the equation).

With regard to Klein's use of the Apollonian ellipse to illustrate Descartes's identification thesis, however, it bears underlining that Greek geometry itself countenances solid figures, not space per se. Moreover, Greek science had no concept of "mathematical space" in the sense of space itself invested with mathematical properties, although the Greeks certainly had a general and qualitative notion of space in the everyday sense of a "container" or receptacle of bodies. In the Greek context itself, then, it is not clear in what sense the Apollonian ellipse is "in space." But in the Cartesian context it is clear that the ellipse is an extended object, and Descartes identifies extension with real space. Thus, I take it that Descartes's identification of the symbolic ellipse and the Apollonian ellipse is, *ipso facto*, an identification of symbolic space and real space.

Nevertheless, we must remind ourselves that the identification of symbolic space and space itself is possible only under the auspices of Descartes's analytical geometry. That is, the symbolic ellipse can be identified with the non-symbolic ellipse only because the graph of the equation for an ellipse is elliptical in shape. But among the "modes of extension," as Descartes terms them, are those that involve time, for instance, and such temporal modes must also be represented by symbolic extension.[12] Therefore, if we are doing mathematical physics, the identification thesis cannot take the purely geometrical form it does in Klein's example of Descartes's symbolic ellipse. For instance, if we graph the equation for a body falling vertically as a function of time ($s = \frac{at^2}{2}$), the graphed curve takes the shape of a parabola even though a parabola is not the path in space of a vertically falling body. Based on Klein's account of the identification thesis Descartes could not identify the two (although contemporary physicists and philosophers do have a propensity for defining acceleration, for instance, as a "curved line in four-dimensional spacetime").

In light of the considerations above, I would suggest that Klein's identification thesis is best understood in terms of Descartes's ascribing to the corporeal world—time as well as space—the *formal properties* of symbolic extension. In the next section we shall consider a particular example, the appropriation in Newtonian physics of "Cartesian space" as an extended continuum of coordinatized points. This revised formulation has the advantage, I believe, of absolving Descartes of a rather too obvious blunder he most certainly would not have committed (and of which Klein never accuses him)—confusing abstracted "magnitude in general" with corporeal magnitude itself. Descartes is clear enough on that point when he scolds people who, "not realizing that extension taken in this sense [as an abstract entity] cannot be grasped by the imagination, represent it by means of a real idea" (*Rules* 60). Burt Hopkins rightly observes that this kind of "confusion of levels" is not what Klein means, speaking in terms of the scholastic textbooks of Descartes's time, by Descartes's taking up the object of a second intention (abstract "being of reason") in the mode of the object of a first intention.[13] That is, Descartes has not, in Klein's account, confused or "conflated" a second intention with a first intention, but rather taken a second intention (magnitude in general) in the mode of a first intention by employing symbolically the first intention of extended line segments (or corresponding algebraic letter signs) such that general magnitude can be subjected to calculation as if it were the object of a first intention.

We shall now see if Einstein's analysis of Cartesian space can help confirm our revised formulation of Klein's identification thesis and at the same time shed some light on Klein's Newtonian thesis.

II. Einstein on Cartesian Coordinate Space[14]

Summing up his account of Cartesian symbolic extension in 1932, roughly contemporaneous with Einstein's two 1930s essays mentioned in our introduction, Klein drops a tantalizing reference to the theory of relativity:

> Only in this way [taking up the object of a second intention in the mode of the object of a first intention] can we come to understand that Descartes' concept of *extensio* identifies the extendedness of extension with extension itself. Our present-day concept of space can be traced directly back to this. Present-day Mathematics and Physics designate as "Euclidean Space" the domain of symbolic exhibition by means of line-segments, a domain which is defined by a coordinate system, a relational system [*Bezugssystem*], as we say nowadays. "Euclidean Space" is by no means the domain of figures and structures studied by Euclid and the rest of Greek mathematics. It is rather only the symbolic illustration of the *general character of the extendedness* of those structures. Once this symbolic domain is identified with corporeal extension itself, it enters into Newtonian physics as "absolute space." *At the present time it is being criticized by Relativity Theory, which has been steered by the question of "Invariance" into trying to break through these symbolic bounds, while continuing to use this very symbolism.* (*WPNW* 21, italics added to the final sentence)

What is striking about this passage, besides the mention of relativity theory, is its affinity with Einstein's own thinking on Cartesian space, which highlights above all the significance of the assignment of numbers or "coordinates" to points. By this means, according to Einstein, Descartes coins the modern scientific concept of space. I quote from Einstein's 1934 essay "The Problem of Space."

> Space as a continuum does not figure in the conceptual system [of Greek geometry] at all. This concept was first introduced by Descartes, when he described the point-in-space by its coordinates. Here for the first time geometrical figures appear, in a way, as parts of infinite space, which is conceived as a three-dimensional continuum. (*PS* 279)

Similarly in Einstein's 1936 essay, "Physics and Reality":

> In the geometry of the Greeks, space plays only a qualitative role, since the position of bodies in relation to space is considered as given, it is true, but is not described by means of numbers [coordinates]. Descartes was the first to introduce this method. (*PR* 297)

The decisive thing for Einstein is that Descartes's assignment of coordinates to points in space introduces a mathematical concept of space as a whole or *space itself* as a continuum of points. It hardly matters if Descartes's metaphysics of extension excludes empty space, since the very assignment of coordinates posits space itself, as a continuum of points, along with the coordinates. (We shall see below that Descartes's law of inertia presupposes such a concept of space.)

The pre-scientific concept of space, Einstein observes, assumes the concept of the solid body arising directly from experience (*PS* 278). Moreover, two solid bodies that do not touch each other are separated by a directly observable interval, and we find that a third body can fill that interval. We also notice that if two bodies are equivalent as regards filling one particular interval, they will also be equivalent for filling other intervals, and thus is formed the concept of the *interval* as a spatial relation independent of any special body to fill it. Einstein concludes, "In my opinion, this concept of the interval, detached as it is from the selection of any special body to occupy it, is the starting point of the whole concept of space" (*PS* 278). In Einstein's analysis, then, the experiential genesis of the pre-scientific concept of space is: solid body ⟶ spatial relations of solid bodies ⟶ interval ⟶ space. In Greek geometry, however, this concept of space remains pre-scientific and qualitative, since the objects of scientific interest are the solid bodies themselves and their relations, not space per se.

A quantitative concept of space first appears historically, according to Einstein, with Descartes's method of numerical coordinates. For space itself can thenceforth be described quantitatively through relations between coordinates. For example, the distance between two "points in space" is now $x_2 - x_1$ or, more generally in three dimensions, $\sqrt{x^2 + y^2 + z^2}$. Indeed, modern geometry in its most general form—what today we call differential geometry—defines *space* itself in terms of its quadratic distance formula or line element and thus in terms of coordinates. And, as we said, in such a conception of space the points are posited along with the coordinates. Moreover, Descartes's innovation presupposes the symbolic conception of number articulated by Klein in *Greek Mathematical Thought*, since a continuum of points can be coordinatized by numbers only if we implicitly employ the real number line, through which the numerical unit is subject to infinite partition (*GMTOA* 191–92). Klein stresses that the object of Descartes's universal mathematics "acquires its specific characteristics from the *numerical* realm" (*GMTOA* 198). In Einstein's account, this very acquisition is accomplished through the assignment of numerical coordinates to points of space.

The "identification thesis," in our revised formulation above, then, is confirmed by Einstein's interpretation of Cartesian coordinates. The proximate object of Cartesian *mathesis universalis* is, as Klein demonstrates, a symbolic space. But the mere employment of symbolic algebra in geometry does not introduce in itself a symbolic *concept* of space as opposed to merely a symbolic *representation*. Einstein's contribution shows one specific way, not necessarily the only one, by which Descartes invests the physical world itself with a formal property of his symbolic space: its constitution via numerical coordinates as a mathematical continuum of points.

Einstein next observes that Cartesian space, conceived as a continuum of points, serves as a necessary presupposition of Newtonian mechanics:

> In so far as geometry is conceived as the science of laws governing the mutual spatial relations of practically rigid bodies, it is to be regarded as the oldest branch of physics. This science was able, as I have already observed, to get along without the concept of space as such, the ideal corporeal forms—point, straight line, plane, segment—being sufficient for its needs. *On the other hand, space as a whole, as conceived by Descartes, was absolutely necessary to Newtonian physics.* (*PS* 279, italics added)

The indispensability of Cartesian space to Newtonian mechanics lies, for Einstein, in the role of acceleration in Newton's system. If we limit ourselves to the spatial relations *between* bodies, then we can manage in physics without a mathematical concept of space, since, as Einstein notes of Greek geometry, a mathematical account of relations between bodies does not presuppose a mathematical account of space itself. However, in Newtonian mechanics acceleration gives rise to observable effects that cannot be attributed to changes in spatial relations between bodies. Rather, acceleration is attributed to changes in the relations of bodies relative to space itself as a continuum of points absolutely at rest:

> Thus to the geometrical reality of the concept of space a new inertia-determining function of space was added. When Newton described space as absolute, he no doubt meant this real significance of space, which made it neces-

> sary for him to attribute to it a quite definite state of motion [rest], which yet did not appear to be fully determined by the phenomena of mechanics. (*PS* 280)[15]

We may add that this description just as well characterizes time in Newtonian mechanics as it does space, for absolute time, a continuum of uniformly "flowing" point-like moments, equally serves an inertia-determining function in Newtonian mechanics.

The "inertia-determining function of space" to which Einstein refers in the quotation above is implicitly postulated by Descartes himself, some fifty years before Newton's *Principia*, in Part Two of his *Principles of Philosophy*: "*The first law of nature: each and every thing, insofar as it can, always continues in the same state; and thus what is once in motion always continues to move.*"[16] Again, it matters little that in the same work Descartes denies the possibility of void space, for the points of the Cartesian plenum must be assumed at rest if they are to determine the inertial properties of bodies, and it is senseless to ask whether those points themselves are subject to motion, for relative to what frame of rest would they move?[17] And so, with specific reference to Cartesian space in Einstein's analysis, we can say that, in Klein's words, "Only at this point has the conceptual basis of 'classical' physics, which has since been called 'Euclidean space', been created. This is the foundation upon which Newton will raise his mathematical science of nature" (*GMTOA* 211).

III. A Conjecture on Cartesian Space and Einstein's "Hole Argument"

It would be worthwhile to bring our analysis of Cartesian space to bear upon a specific problem in the history of modern mathematical physics. In this final section, I shall make such an attempt with an episode from the history of Einstein's theory of gravity.

The reader familiar with Einstein's theory of gravity knows

that he called it the "general theory of relativity" because he believed that in it he had extended the special principle of relativity, according to which the laws of nature hold for inertial frames of reference (uniformly moving frames of reference), to arbitrarily accelerated frames of reference. Moreover, in Einstein's formulation, a law of nature satisfies a principle of relativity only if the equation expressing the law is "covariant" with respect to a defined group of *coordinate transformations*. This means that while the numerical values of the coordinates (for instance, x, y, and z in three-dimensional Cartesian coordinates) of some physical event vary in a determinate manner in relation to one another (thus, "covariance"), when we transform our coordinates to a new reference system in motion relative to the first, the equation remains valid as an expression of a given law of nature. Einstein was convinced that a generalized principle of relativity, unrestricted to inertial frames of reference, could find mathematical expression solely by a *generally covariant* law of gravitation. That is to say, just as the special principle of relativity finds mathematical expression in equations that are covariant under a restricted group of transformations (called "Lorentz transformations"), the general principle of relativity entails the admissibility of *all* coordinate transformations in general.[18]

At the time Einstein was grappling with gravity in the early twentieth century, Newtonian gravity already had been reformulated in the nineteenth-century as a field theory. That is, instead of being conceived as an attractive force acting on bodies at a distance, Newtonian gravity was recast as a "field of force" propagated by massive bodies, with varying values of intensity at specific points in space and time. By 1912, Einstein had in hand the essential conceptual structure and mathematical building blocks for the theory of gravitation he would publish in 1915. Furthermore, since the Newtonian theory of gravity was known to be highly accurate for gravitational fields such as are found in our own solar system, for example, one of Einstein's heuristic criteria for his new gravitational field equation was that it reduce to the Newtonian equation (or "Newtonian limit") for very weak gravitational fields. But Einstein had run into problems finding a generally covariant field equation that recovered the Newtonian limit for such weak fields. Then, in 1913, he discovered an argument that appeared to prove that no physically tenable gravitational field law could be generally covariant, and, since Einstein had already abandoned general covariance over the problem of the Newtonian limit, this new argument (which Einstein called the "hole argument") evidently came as somewhat of a relief to him.

Newton did not originally publish his theory of gravity as a theory of the gravitational field, we have noted, but rather as a theory of attractive force between masses. Moreover, in his *Principia* of 1687 he presented the theory not in the language of algebraic equations but rather of geometrical ratio and proportion. In Newton's version, the gravitational force between two point masses is jointly proportional to the magnitudes of the masses and inversely proportional to the square of the distance separating those masses. This relation translates into algebra as $Fg = K\frac{m_1 m_2}{r^2}$ (K is Newton's gravitational constant).

Now consider Newtonian gravity recast in the form of a field theory. If we think of the gravitational field of the sun, for instance, we might imagine lines of force emanating from the center of the sun, with the intensity of the force represented by the density of those lines and decreasing as the square of distance as we get farther from the sun. At any point, the value of the gravitational field is defined as the force exerted on a unit mass at that point. Finally, and this is the essential thing, the value of the gravitational field is an algebraic function of the numerical coordinates of the point in question, for, as noted above, in Cartesian space distance is expressed in terms of coordinate differentials.

We are now ready to discuss Einstein's hole argument.[19] We imagine a region of space and time empty of any gravitating matter (thus a "matter-free hole"). Einstein discovered that, because his gravitational field equation is generally covariant, if we solve for the gravitational field at a specific point as a function of the point's numerical coordinates, this very same field is also a solution at any other point.[20] And so, apparently, follows the awkward result of Einstein's hole argument: A generally covariant field equation must fail to uniquely determine the gravitational field at a point, even though the matter sources outside the empty region are the same for any of these solutions. So, for example, at a certain point in the gravitational field of our sun (as long as the point is outside the sun itself), Einstein's gravitational field equation appears to yield an indeterminate value for the gravitational field at that point. But in that case we could not calculate the orbital path of the earth around the sun.

In 1915 Einstein resolved the Newtonian limit problem and once again embraced a generally covariant field equation, but he then had to dispose of the hole argument. The question was whether the distinct fields at the same point represented a genuine physical difference or a merely mathematical difference. Einstein succeeded in resolving the question in favor of the physical equivalence of the different solutions at a point when he realized that the very notion of different solutions to the gravitational field at the "same point" presupposes the preexistence of points in space and time. That is to say, it assumes the concept of Cartesian space as a continuum of coordinatized points. Or more precisely, it assumes that physical space and time are invested with this specific formal property of Cartesian space. For in the absence of matter or at least a physical field the only thing that identifies or individuates the points of Cartesian space is their coordinates. But the coordinate system and along with it the very points of space to which the numerical coordinates attach, Einstein concluded, enjoys a merely mathematical—as we with Klein would say "symbolic"—existence; so there is no question of two different physical fields assignable to the same point: it is the gravitational field itself that physically individuates the points.

In sum, in the construction of the hole argument it is as if we lifted the gravitational field from the region under consideration, without altering it in any way, and simply moved it to a different location in symbolic Cartesian space.[21] Consequently, the indeterminacy at issue—the indeterminacy of the value of the gravitational field at a specific location—is a merely mathematical indeterminacy, an artifact of coordinates and general covariance, and not a physical indeterminacy. Here is how Einstein put it in a letter to his friend Michele Besso in early 1916:

> There is no physical substance to two different solutions $G(x)$ and $G'(x)$ existing with reference to *the same* coordinate system K. Imagining two simultaneous solutions within the same manifold makes no sense, and system K obviously is not a physical reality.[22]

We take this to mean that the coordinate system K is merely a *symbolic space* whose defining formal property, the individuation of points by coordinates, Einstein now realizes was erroneously attributed to *real* space in the Cartesian concept of space handed down via classical Newtonian mechanics.[23] This interpretation accords with one of Einstein's last pronouncements on the matter in the 1952 appendix added to his popular book on the theory of relativity:

> We are now in a position to see how far the transition to the general theory of relativity modifies the concept of space. In accordance with classical mechanics and according to the special theory of relativity, space (space-time) has an existence independent of matter or field. In order to be able to describe at all that which fills up space and is dependent on the coordinates, spacetime or the inertial system with its metrical properties must be thought of as at once existing, for otherwise the description of "that which fills up

> space" would have no meaning. On the basis of the general theory of relativity, on the other hand, space as opposed to "what fills space" . . . has no separate existence. . . . If we imagine the gravitational field, i.e. the functions g_{ik}, to be removed, there [remains] absolutely *nothing*, and also no "topological space."[24]

We may reasonably conjecture, then, that Einstein's reflections on the significance of Cartesian space in the two 1930s essays were likely inspired, at least in part, by his recollection of the difficulties Cartesian coordinate space had caused him in the hole argument.

IV. Conclusion

It is now possible to fully appreciate Klein's assertion, quoted above at the beginning of section II, that the symbolic domain of Cartesian coordinate space is "at the present time being criticized by Relativity Theory, which has been steered by the question of 'Invariance' into trying to break through these symbolic bounds, while continuing to use this very symbolism." The "question of invariance" to which Klein adverts regards the tension between the invariance of the laws of nature in Einstein's special theory of relativity, relative to inertial reference frames, on the one hand, and the privileged reference frame defined by the coordinatized points of Cartesian space (and time) in classical Newtonian mechanics on the other. The theory of relativity must break through the "symbolic bounds" of Cartesian space as a continuum of coordinatized points because such a space is incompatible with the invariance of the laws of nature. That, at least, is my conjecture as to Klein's meaning above. This very symbolic impediment, latent within Newtonian physics from its very inception (in the form of absolute space and time), first explicitly asserts itself in the context of nineteenth century electromagnetic theory in connection with the observed invariability of the velocity of light relative to all coordinate systems (rest frames). That was the initial point of departure for Einstein's special theory of relativity. In his theory of gravity, the general theory of relativity, Einstein by means of the hole argument addresses the very existence of the coordinatized points of Cartesian space. The hole argument thus is a particularly telling illustration of the "symbolic bounds" presented to modern mathematical physics, and relativity theory in particular, by the Cartesian concept of space.

Although I do not think Klein articulated the identification thesis quite adequately (and he never really elaborated the Newtonian thesis), Einstein's reflections on Cartesian space suggest that Klein was essentially right on both the identification thesis and the Newtonian thesis. Moreover, as Einstein's resolution of the hole argument demonstrates, there is significant potential for Klein's kind of analysis to clarify problems in mathematical physics, not just philosophically, but also on the physicist's own terms. When it comes to the ultimate aim identified by Klein in the introduction to *Greek Mathematical Thought*—the "intimate connection of the formal mathematical language with the content of mathematical physics" (*GMTOA* 6)—we have before us a potentially fruitful area for future Klein scholarship.

Notes

Preface by Daniel P. Maher

1. "Jacob Klein: European Scholar and American Teacher," in this volume, 12.

2. https://theimaginativeconservative.org/2019/03/immediacy-ways-of-humanity-eva-brann-90.html.

3. "Two Prescient Discoveries," in this volume, 18.

4. See *Republic* 521c–525a and, for example, *Phaedo* 102b–103c.

5. *Republic* 522c5–7 and 523a2–3. Translation from *The* Republic *of Plato*, 2nd ed., trans. with notes and interpretive essay by Allan Bloom (New York: Basic Books, 1968).

6. See *Sophist* 217a–b. Translation from *Plato's* Sophist*: Part II of the Being of the Beautiful*, trans. with commentary by Seth Benardete (Chicago and London: University of Chicago Press, 1984, 1986), 4.

7. "European Scholar and American Teacher," 6. For the most relevant of David Lachterman's publications, see the bibliography below.

8. "Two Prescient Discoveries," 20.

9. The two articles appeared as "Die Griechische Logistik und die Entstehung der Algebra," in *Quellen und Studien zur Geschichte der Mathematik, Astronomie, und Physik*, Abteilung B: *Studien*, vol. 3, no. 1 (Berlin, 1934), 18–105 (Part I) and ibid., no. 2 (1936), 122–235 (Part II). The English translation appeared as *Greek Mathematical Thought and the Origin of Algebra*, trans. Eva Brann (Cambridge, MA: MIT Press, 1968; reprint, New York: Dover Publications, 1992).

10. "Modern Rationalism," in Jacob Klein, *Lectures and Essays*, edited by Robert B. Williamson and Elliott Zuckerman (Annapolis, MD: St. John's College Press, 1985), 57.

11. Jacob Klein, "On a Sixteenth-Century Algebraist," in *Lectures and Essays*, 35.

12. Jacob Klein, "The World of Physics and the 'Natural' World," in *Lectures and Essays*, 21.

13. Klein, *Greek Mathematical Thought*, 4.

Introduction by Andrew Romiti

1. For a list of Klein's published writings, see the bibliography at the end of this book. For a list of the many lectures he gave at St. John's College (only some of which were recorded or have been published), see *Essays in Honor of Jacob Klein*, ed. Samuel S. Kutler et al. (Annapolis: St. John's College Press, 1976), viii–ix.

2. For some instances of such reports, see "Texts from the Memorial Service for Jacob Klein," *The College* XXX, no. 2 (1979): 20–30.

3. See Jacob Klein to Gerhard Krüger, December 30, 1932: "I believe—so magniloquent this sounds—that I have 'resolved' the *methexis* [participation] problem, I mean—in Plato's sense. . . . The *arithmos eidêtikos* [eidetic number] is nothing other than the Platonic solution of the *methexis* question" ("Selected Letters from Jacob Klein to Gerhard Krüger," trans. Emmanuel Patard, *The New Yearbook for Phenomenology and Phenomenological Philosophy* VI [2006]: 321).

To Flip a Pancake: On "the Human Possibility of a Total Conversion" by Julia Klein

1. Here is a little disclaimer: When I refer to "Klein" throughout this essay, it will be safe to assume that I am not speaking about myself in the third person.

2. Jacob Klein, *A Commentary on Plato's "Meno"* [hereafter *CPM*] (Chicago: The University of Chicago Press, 1989), 186; also see Plato, *Meno*, 76a–b.

3. Jacob Klein, "On the Platonic Meno in Particular and Platonic Dialogues in General," *The New Yearbook for Phenomenology and Phenomenological Philosophy* I (2001): 367.

4. Jacob Klein, "The Idea of Liberal Education" [hereafter *ILE*], in *Lectures and Essays*, ed. Robert B. Williamson and Elliott Zuckerman (Annapolis, MD: St. John's College Press, 1985), 158.

5. All quotations from the *Meno* are taken from: Plato, *Meno*, trans. George Anastaplo and Laurence Berns (Newburyport, MA: Focus Publishing, 2004).

6. Augustine, *Confessions*, trans. John K. Ryan (New York: Image Books, 1960), 1.

7. Jacob Klein, "On Liberal Education" [hereafter *OLE*], in *Lectures and Essays*, 267.

8. Eva Brann, "Depth and Desire," *The St. John's Review* 39, no. 3 (1989–90): 84.

An Introduction to Klein's Response to Heidegger: A Reading of "Aristotle, an Introduction" by Paul T. Wilford

1. "A Giving of Accounts" in *Jewish Philosophy and the Crisis of Modernity: Essays and Lectures in Modern Jewish Thought*, ed. Kenneth Hart Green (Albany: SUNY Press, 1997), 458. *Nota bene*, a public accounting is a justification in both senses of the word—an aspect of the politics of philosophy since Socrates. Klein is here referring to a seminar Heidegger gave in 1924 entitled *Grundbegriffe der aristotelischen Philosophie*. Heidegger's course has been published and translated as Martin Heidegger, *Basic Concepts of Aristotelian Philosophy*, trans. Robert D. Metcalf and Mark B. Tanzer (Indiana University Press, 2009).

2. *Ancients and Moderns: Essays on the Tradition of Political Philosophy in Honor of Leo Strauss*, ed. Joseph Cropsey (New York: Basic Books, 1964), 50–69. Reprinted as "Aristotle, an Introduction" in *Lectures and Essays* [hereafter *LE*], ed. Robert Williamson and Elliott Zuckerman (Annapolis: St. John's College Press, 1985), 171–95. Herein Klein's essay will be identified as *AI*; page numbers given parenthetically within the body of this paper refer to the reprint.

3. Jacob Klein, *Greek Mathematical Thought and the Origin of Algebra* [hereafter *GMTOA*], trans. Eva Brann (Cambridge, MA: MIT Press, 1968; reprint: New York: Dover, 1992), 192. See *AI* 180. Compare Klein's assertion that "the great issue in Greek philosophy" as well as "one of the ultimate issues which divide Plato from Aristotle" is "the question of the mode of being of [the] pure monads" ("The World of Physics and the 'Natural' World" [hereafter *WPNW*], in *LE*, 24)

4. "Giving of Accounts," 462.

5. "Giving of Accounts," 458.

6. *AI* 189; Klein is translating Aristotle, *Metaphysics* 7.1.1028b2–4, 6–7.

7. Martin Heidegger, *Being and Time* [hereafter *BT*], trans. J. Macquarrie and E. Robinson (San Francisco: HarperCollins, 1962), 19; as Heidegger states, his whole inquiry aims ultimately at offering an "Interpretation of *time* as the possible horizon for any understanding whatsoever of Being" (19). For all their differences, Klein concurs with Heidegger's judgment that the occlu-

sion of this question is one of the principal dangers of our epoch. See Klein, *GMTOA*, 117–25; note especially that Klein speaks of the moderns as obviating the central question of the ancients concerning "the mode of being of mathematical objects" (122).

8. See *BT*, 370–82, especially Heidegger's conclusion that "the proposition, 'Dasein is historical', is confirmed as a fundamental existential ontological assertion" (381). For a critical evaluation of Heidegger's undertaking, see Carl Page, "Heidegger: The Metaphysics of Finite Historicity" in *Philosophical Historicism and the Betrayal of First Philosophy* (University Park, PA: Pennsylvania State University Press, 1995), 129–56. Compare Richard Velkley, "Reason's Parochiality: On Carl Page's Critique of Historicism," *The St. John's Review* XLIII, no. 3 (1996), 89–100. On the need to deconstruct the tradition see Heidegger, *The Basic Problems of Phenomenology*, 22–23. For Heidegger's remarkable evaluation of his own project in comparison to Plato and Aristotle see *BT*, 63.

9. Plato, *Phaedo*, 99e5; *AI*, 178–80. Compare Klein, "Plato's *Phaedo*," in *LE*, 386–88, and *GMTOA*, 73.

10. As far as I am aware, save for the autobiographical references in "Giving of Accounts," Klein named Heidegger in his published writings only once. See "Speech, Its Strengths and Its Weaknesses," in *LE*, 361–74. To be sure, tacit references abound. See, for example, Klein's discussion of ἀλήθεια in Jacob Klein, *A Commentary on Plato's "Meno"* (Chicago: The University of Chicago Press, 1989), 157.

11. On the challenges of reading philosophical texts, see Klein's *A Commentary on Plato's "Meno,"* 17–20.

12. Leo Strauss, *Thoughts on Machiavelli* (Chicago: University of Chicago Press, 1978), 13.

13. Jacob Klein to Gerhard Krüger, March 14, 1930, in *The New Yearbook for Phenomenology and Phenomenological Philosophy* VI (2006): 317.

14. In Werner Marx's formulation, "when, in our day, [Heidegger] expressly poses the question of Being *no longer* as . . . a question of essence and expressly thinks *no longer* in the sense of *ousia* or substance, we must regard this attempt as a veritable revolution" (*Heidegger and the Tradition*, trans. Theodore Kisiel and Murray Greene [Northwestern University Press, 1982], 5).

15. The absence is all the more noteworthy given that the essay originally appeared in a *Festschrift* for Leo Strauss, the explicit leitmotif of whose work is the recovery of classical *political* philosophy.

16. "The Problem of Freedom," in *LE*, 124. Aristotle links λόγος closely

to our political being. See *Politics*, 1253a1–19 and *Poetics*, 1448b4–20; compare *History of Animals*, 487b33–488a13, 488b25–27, with *On Memory and Recollection*, 453a6–14, and *Physics* 199a22–30. Heidegger, in contrast, consistently diminishes the political dimension of human life. Note the absence of any reference to the human as political in Heidegger's discussion of the meaning of ζῷον λόγον ἔχον in "On the Essence and Concept of Φύσις in Aristotle's Physics B, I" (in *Pathmarks*, ed. William McNeill [Cambridge: Cambridge University Press, 1998], 212–15). Contrast Heidegger's withering critique of man as the "*animal rationale*" and his "calculative reasoning" in *The Principle of Reason*, trans. Reginald Lilly (Bloomington, IN: Indiana University Press, 1991), 128–29 and 99–105, with Klein's discussion of the connection between counting, *dianoia*, and *logos* in *GMTOA*, 71–79 and 83–87. Contrast Heidegger's "Letter on 'Humanism,'" in *Pathmarks*, ed. William McNeill (Cambridge: Cambridge University Press, 1998), 245–46, 253–54, 260–61 with Klein's attention to the etymology of λέγειν and its political dimension (*SSW*, 362–63, 368). See also Heidegger, *Introduction to Metaphysics* (hereafter *IM*), 2nd ed., trans. Gregory Fried and Richard Polt (New Haven, CT: Yale University Press, 2014), 151–53, 186–87, 219–20.

17. "The Problem and the Art of Writing," in *LE*, 144–45.

18. Klein provides an unusual gloss on ἐπαγωγή as "the way in which our teachers bring us face to face with the things to be understood." Although *induction* is an "exact" translation, the term can also mean *introduction*. Klein includes Aristotle's reliance on ἐπαγωγή as one of the decisive departures from Plato insofar as it represents a return to the first sailing rejected by Socrates in *Phaedo*. Klein says Aristotle's ἐπαγωγή is one of "two ways in which one is mastered by the εἴδη νοητά" (the other being the syllogism) (187).

19. We may contrast Klein's selection with the Aristotelian terminology Heidegger focused on in the 1924 seminar Klein attended: *Basic Concepts of Aristotelian Philosophy*. Note especially Heidegger's decision to start with οὐσία (17–30).

20. Contrast Heidegger's rejection of the view that language is "a kind of communication" ("Origin of the Work of Art," in *Poetry, Language, Thought*, trans. Albert Hofstadter [Harper Perennial, 2013], 71).

21. On how the ψυχή possessing νοῦς is affected by the νοητά, see Klein's discussion of Aristotle's second principal disagreement with the Socratic-Platonic view (*AI*, 185–87).

22. Plato, *Sophist*, 263e quoted in *SSW*, 366. After stating that διάνοια "as Plato understands it, is *not* tied to what the moderns means by the 'stream

of consciousness,'" Klein adds: "it is necessary to note that for Plato, and for Plato *alone*, this identity of thought and speech is *not* a complete one: facing the highest, all-comprehending intelligibles, thought is not able to transpose itself into suitable words" (*SSW*, 366).

23. See James Carey, "Socrates' Exhortation to Follow the *Logos*" in *Socrates in the Cave: On the Philosopher's Motive in Plato*, ed. Paul J. Diduch & Michael P. Harding (Cham: Springer Verlag, 2019), 107–39.

24. "The articulations of language correspond to the various ways of questioning which we address to ourselves and to others as beings having a primordial although not always habitable home, namely the world. For being in a world is the most elementary and the most crucial character of our existence. Aristotle was if not the first then perhaps the most careful to analyze the articulation of language and thereby to indicate the various modes of our being in a world." Jacob Klein, "The Art of Questioning and the Liberal Arts," *The College* XXX, no. 2 (1979), 2.

25. "Mostly" may allude to the fact that philosophy itself has not been mentioned in the list. Perhaps this is because philosophy does not have a special subject matter all its own but addresses the very same beings the rest of human speech is about. While this suggests a high degree of continuity between ordinary and philosophic discourse, elsewhere Klein emphasizes discontinuity: there is a rare genius who questions so thoroughly, profoundly, and in such a comprehensive manner that he finds himself compelled to fashion new words, to stretch human speech to respond to his uncovering of "the hidden articulations of the language of things" (*SSW*, 365; 373–74).

26. *SSW*, 363.

27. Klein, *GMTOA*, 192.

28. The formulation comes from *AI*, 171; see below.

29. "An Unspoken Prologue to a Public Lecture at St. John's College," in *Jewish Philosophy and the Crisis of Modernity*, 450. Strauss's judgment as well as his understatement is echoed by Klein: "Martin Heidegger . . . is the very great thinker of our time, although his moral qualities do not match his intellectual ones" ("Giving of Accounts," 458).

30. On the connection between Heidegger's philosophy and National Socialism, see Karl Löwith, *Martin Heidegger and European Nihilism*, ed. Richard Wolin, trans. Gary Steiner (New York: Columbia University Press, 1995), 211–25.

31. See for example Hannah Arendt, "Heidegger at Eighty" in *Thinking Without a Banister: Essays in Understanding, 1953–1957*, ed. Jerome Kohn (New

York: Schocken Books, 2018), 421; Hans Jonas, *Memoirs*, trans. Krishna Winston, ed. Christian Wiese (Waltham, MA: Brandeis University Press, 2008), 42.

32. Leo Strauss, "Existentialism," *Interpretation* 22, no. 3 (Spring 1995), 304.

33. Strauss, "Existentialism," 304. See also Leo Strauss, "Kurt Reizler," in *What Is Political Philosophy?* (Chicago: University of Chicago Press, 1959), 245–46.

34. "Unspoken Prologue," 450. See Klein's discussion of the roots of Greek science and the possibility and necessity of learning "to see Greek science from the point of view of . . . its 'natural' basis [*die griechische Wissenschaft von dieser ihrer 'naturlichen' Basis*]" (*GMTOA*, 118–19).

35. "Giving of Accounts," 458.

36. "Giving of Accounts," 458.

37. Jacob Klein, "The Idea of Liberal Education," in *LE*, 162.

38. "The Idea of Liberal Education," 162. Compare Plato, *Republic*, 515a–517a, with Heidegger's description of the effect of asking the fundamental question of philosophy in *IM*, 6–7, 32–33, 49. See also Michael W. Grenke, "The Question of Questions," *The St. John's Review* 54, no. 2 (2013), 115–33.

39. The "why" of metastrophic questioning "seems not to assign causes to the existence of things or to events, but rather to find *reasons* for the being of things as they are . . . to account for what is the way it is—λόγον διδόναι" ("The Art of Questioning," 4).

40. See "The Idea of Liberal Education," 162, 164–65, 167–68; "On Liberal Education," in *LE*, 263–65; "Phenomenology and the History of Science," 76–79; "History and the Liberal Arts," 130–33, 137–38; *SSW*, 372–73. Consider Jon Lenkowski, "Meno's Paradox and the Zetetic Circle," *The St. John's Review* XLIII, no. 3 (1996), 7–27.

41. "Unspoken Prologue," 450.

42. "Unspoken Prologue," 450. Regarding Strauss's estimation of Klein's preeminence among his contemporaries, in a letter to Koyré (June 19, 1956, unpublished), Strauss playfully identifies Klein and Kojève as the only other members of his generation "who still believe in Reason."

43. See Leo Strauss's references to Hegel and to Klein in "Political Philosophy and History" in *What Is Political Philosophy?*, 74–75. See also "Preface to *Hobbes' Politische Wissenschaft*," in *Jewish Philosophy and the Crisis of Modernity*, 454.

44. Compare Heidegger's remarks from the published version of these lectures: "Regarding the personality of a philosopher, our only interest is that he was born at a certain time, that he worked, and that he died" (*Basic Concepts of Aristotelian Philosophy*, 4).

45. Arendt, "Heidegger at Eighty," 424.

46. Heidegger, *Basic Concepts of Aristotelian Philosophy,* 4.

47. Heidegger, *Basic Concepts of Aristotelian Philosophy,* 5. See also Heidegger's claim that Greek philosophy comes to an end in Aristotle (*IM,* 17).

48. Martin Heidegger, "Preface" to William J. Richardson, S.J., *Heidegger: Through Phenomenology to Thought* (The Hague: Martinus Nijhoff, 1974), x–xv.

49. Heidegger does not begin to explore Aristotle's "basic concepts" by defining them; instead, he sees the logical concept of definition as a "decline" that obscures genuine "conceptuality" (*Basic Concepts of Aristotelian Philosophy,* 11). What Heidegger seeks to uncover in Aristotelian concepts is their *Bodenständigkeit,* translated as "indigenous character." In other words, the meaning of concepts is to be traced back to the ground on which they originally stood. This basis is a concrete experience of phenomena, and this "basic experience is primarily not theoretical, but instead lies in the commerce of life with its world" (12). Compare Heidegger's remarks from his 1940 lecture course, "Nietzsche: The Will to Power (II. European Nihilism)" in Martin Heidegger, *Nietzsche Vol. IV,* trans. David Farrell Krell (San Francisco: HarperCollins, 1982), 171–72.

50. Heidegger, *Contributions to Philosophy (Of the Event),* trans. Richard Rojcewicz and Daniella Vallega-Neu (Bloomington, IN: Indiana University Press, 2012), 5, 50, 67, 71–72.

51. See *Identity and Difference,* trans. Joan Stambaugh (Chicago: University of Chicago Press, 2002), 54–61. Heidegger distinguishes between "on the one hand metaphysical thought (the thinking of the Being of beings) and on the other the Being-question in the sense of the thinking of Being as such (the revealed-ness of Being)" ("Preface" to *Heidegger: Through Phenomenology to Thought,* xiv–xv).

52. "Western metaphysics, however, since its beginning with the Greeks has eminently been both ontology and theology. . . . For this reason my inaugural lecture *What Is Metaphysics?* (1929) defines metaphysics as the question about beings as such *and* as a whole. The wholeness of this whole is the unity of all beings that unifies as the generative ground. To those who can read, this means: metaphysics is onto-theo-logy" (*Identity and Difference,* 54; see also "Plato's Doctrine of Truth" in *Pathmarks,* 180–81). One might also describe this as the supplanting of the ontological problem by the cosmological problem. See Strauss, "Kurt Riezler," 247–48, 253–54.

53. See Martin Heidegger, *Plato's Sophist,* trans. Richard Rojcewicz and André Schuwer (Bloomington, IN: Indiana University Press, 1997), 5–13.

54. See Heidegger's assertion that "Aristotle's *Physics* is the hidden, and therefore never adequately studied, foundational book of Western Philoso-

phy" ("On the Essence and Concept of Φύσις," 185). See also *IM*, 18–20, and *The Principle of Reason*, 62–63.

55. Contrast Heidegger, *Phenomenological Interpretation of Kant's "Critique of Pure Reason,"* trans. Parvis Emad and Kenneth Maly (Bloomington, IN: Indiana University Press, 1997), 2–4.

56. On the implausibility of this enterprise, see Jacob Howland, "Re-Reading Plato: The Problem of Platonic Chronology" *Phoenix* 45, no. 3 (Autumn, 1991), 189–214.

57. Contrast Heidegger's assertion that "to define the fundamental metaphysical position of Aristotle" in terms of "the traditional contrast with Plato is quite insufficient." See *Nietzsche Vol. IV*, 171–72.

58. See Strauss's discussion of the importance of friendship (in contrast to recognition) in classical philosophy (*On Tyranny*, ed. Victor Gourevitch and Michael S. Roth [Chicago: University of Chicago Press, 2000], 194–204).

Modern Symbolic Unreality, or Mr. Klein's Question: Who Lives Symbolically? by David Lawrence Levine

1. This is a revised version of a lecture given at St. John's College, Santa Fe, on February 28, 2020. For the title, compare Hegel, "*Who Thinks Abstractly?*" My thanks to Eva Brann, Daniel Maher, Andrew Romiti, and Jacqueline Zeller Levine for their constructive suggestions.

2. Goethe, *Letter to Zelter*, June 6, 1825.

3. Jacob Klein, "Modern Rationalism" [hereafter *MR*], in *Lectures and Essays* [hereafter *LE*], ed. Robert Williamson and Elliott Zuckerman (Annapolis: St. John's College Press, 1985), 63.

4. Burt Hopkins, *The Origin of the Logic of Symbolic Mathematics: Edmund Husserl and Jacob Klein* [hereafter OLSM] (Bloomington: Indiana University Press, 2011), 5.

5. Goethe, Maxims and Reflections, #1119.

6. *MR* 61.

7. Jacob Klein, "The World of Physics and the 'Natural' World" [hereafter *WPhys*], in *LE*, 8.

8. *MR* 56.

9. *MR* 64.

10. Aristophanes, *The Clouds*, 348. It is hard to hold to distinctions that amalgamate over time (entropy of ideas?).

There is an ancient report that Plato kept a copy of Aristophanes' plays beside his bed. The question is whether it is ancient or modern philosophy that is lost in its ideas.

11. *Greek Mathematical Thought and the Origin of Algebra* [hereafter *GMTOA*], trans. Eva Brann (Cambridge: MIT Press, 1968), originally published as "Die griechische Logistik und die Entstehung der Algebra" [Greek Logistic and the Emergence of Algebra] (1934–6); in addition to the two essays already cited (*MR* and *WPhys*), I also rely on "The Concept of Number in Greek Mathematics and Philosophy" [*LE* 43–52, hereafter *CNGMP*] and "Phenomenology and the History of Science" [*LE* 65–84, hereafter *PhHS*]. In these essays Klein explicitly connects the mathematical developments to their philosophical presuppositions and their human consequences. See also David Levine, "Plato's Arithmological Ordering of Being" [hereafter PAOB], *The Southwestern Journal of Philosophy*, XI, (1980), 109–128.

12. See David Levine, "Four Sides of a Cube, The Way of Great Books," *The Imaginative Conservative*, October 24, 2018 (originally given as a dean's lecture, with the subtitle "Why a Certain Question Needs to be Asked Again and Again," St. John's College, Santa Fe, August 31, 2001), n. 39.

13. Like Husserl and Koyré, Klein sought to articulate the profound differences between the modern scientific mode of conceptualization and what then came to be called the "pre-scientific" outlook (decisive in understanding the ancient/modern distinction more generally). As the reader will see, we wonder whether the distinction is not miscast and should rather be conceived as the natural/post-natural distinction.

14. *MR* 55.

15. Heidegger makes explicit what is implicit in Klein's work, namely, that the revolution in mathematical conceptualization *precedes* and thus prepares the revolution in modern science. As prior, "the mathematical" (in Heidegger's more essential sense) is the more revealing. See Martin Heidegger, "Modern Science, Metaphysics and Mathematics" [hereafter *MSMM*], in *Basic Writings* [hereafter *BW*], ed. David Krell (New York: Harper and Row, 1977), 247–82, excerpted from *What Is a Thing?* [*Die Frage Nach dem Ding*, 1935–6], (Chicago: Henry Regnery Press 1967, 65–108): "We must . . . show in what sense the foundation of modern thought is essentially mathematical" (254); "In the essence of the mathematical . . . lies *a specific will to a new formation and self-grounding* of the form of knowledge as such" (272); "In what way does modern metaphysics arise out of the spirit of the mathematical?" (272); "All this happened in the midst of a period in which for a century [prior] mathematics had already been emerging more and more as the *foundation* of [the new] thought, . . . a time which . . . embarked on *a new assault of reality*" (275). Klein, Husserl and Heidegger all worked on the question of the conceptual origins of the modern project at the same time. Who learned from whom?

16. Compare Aristotle, *Nicomachean Ethics*, V.iii.1131a31.

17. Plato asks this question: What makes numbers themselves possible? His eidetic conception of number seeks to go to the ground of number. The eidetic structure of the primary ideas, in this instance, their unity and inner manyness, make unity, multiplicity, and numerability possible. See PAOB §§ 4–6.

18. *MR* 63. Italics added for emphasis.

19. *MR* 58. Compare Nietzsche's "the chamber of consciousness" ("On Truth and Lies in a Non-moral Sense" [hereafter *TLNMS*], in *Philosophy and Truth: Selections from Nietzsche's Notebooks of the Early 1870's*, trans. Daniel Breazeale [London: Humanities Press, 1979], 80).

20. It may be surprising to see Mr. Klein illustrate the philosophical foundations of the earlier conceptual or eidetic transformation begun in the fourteenth century (*MR* 54) by means of philosophical texts of the sixteenth and seventeenth. Perhaps the following might help us: "I do not overestimate the influence of scientific or philosophic books on people in general, but it seems to me that each important book of this kind is only *an expression of a certain unconscious public sentiment*, which after a certain passage of time—generally thirty years—is awakened to consciousness by those books which [the unconscious public sentiment] has inspired. From this time on, this opinion is expressed without doubt or hesitation," that is, it becomes accepted and therewith unexamined (*MR* 55; italics added). Klein's soft Hegelianism?

21. My translation from the French text: Descartes, *Meditationes de Prima Philosophia, Meditations Metaphysique*, ed. Geneviève Rodis-Lewis (Paris: Librairie Philosophique J. Vrin, 1967), 37. Descartes continues: "For without doubt if I considered the ideas *only as modes or manners (façons) of my thoughts without trying to relate them to anything exterior*, they could scarcely give me occasion for error." Only "hyperbolic doubt" dictates such a retreat to modes of thought (compare *agnosia*, discussed below).

22. The ancients knew this problem, not as alienation, but as the problem of number (twoness). They sought to understand the linkage but never doubted the original connectedness, as do the moderns. "As the Greeks put it, we receive the world in our mind by means of the λόγος. . . . [F]or the ancients world and mind are inseparable from each other, [that is] the nature of the world consists in being comprehensible. This is not just another philosophical theory but *the very premise of their whole thought*" (*MR* 58; italics added for emphasis). The world is graspable because the soul is *twinned. Logos* means *above all* inter-connectedness, correlation and communication (hence speech). And for that reason, we are inseparably *part* of the world.

23. Descartes's account is comparable, if less technically sophisticated, and involves "animal spirits" and a mechanistic account of the nerves (see *The Passions of the Soul*). Such terms may be distracting for the modern reader, hence our use of a generalized modern version. But the problem remains.

24. *MR* 56. Italics added for emphasis.

25. *MR* 56; italics added here and in the preceding quotation for emphasis.

26. Descartes himself admits that "it is *impossible* to construct any corporeal idea which shall represent to us what the act of knowing is" (*Rules for the Direction of the Mind* [hereafter *RDM*], in *Philosophical Works of Descartes*, Vol. I, trans. Elizabeth Haldane and G. R. T. Ross [New York: Dover Publications, 1955], 41).

27. Descartes, too, understands this as a serious problem. He seeks to address it with his supposition of the pineal gland (*The Passions of the Soul*). However, the pineal gland hypothesis only displaces the problem one step back, so to speak, so that it becomes minuscule, if not invisible, allowing us to lose sight of this supposed difference in kind. The problem in short is *not* solved. Klein is not alone in thinking that Descartes's solution is "obviously unsatisfactory" (*MR* 56).

28. The account of modern philosophy and science doesn't make a true "two," only, at best, a "one plus one," that is, it gives us an aggregate and not a true whole.

29. Kant has captured the incongruity: Ideas so conceived, he says, are "empirically real, but transcendentally ideal," that is, they appear *as if* they are real but they are rather the byproducts of our constitutive faculties (*Critique of Pure Reason*, B52–53). Also see Nietzsche's exploration of this problem and its implications—what he calls the "complete overleaping" from one medium to another (*TLNMS* 82). Also see this author's reflections: David Levine, "A World of Worldless Truths, An Invitation to Philosophy," in *The Envisioned Life, Essays in Honor of Eva Brann*, ed. Peter Kalkavage and Eric Salem (Philadelphia: Paul Dry Books, 2007), 155–69.

30. Epistemology thus has an historical origin. Compare Heidegger: "A theory of knowledge [epistemology] had to be erected before a theory of the world [physics]" (*MSMM* 274).

31. Compare, for example, Thomas Aquinas, *Summa Theologica*, I-II, Q. 93, A.1, R.3: "The human intellect is measured by things, so that a human concept is not true by reason of itself, but by reason of its being consonant with things." Also: "An opinion is true or false as it answers to reality."

32. "Innate ideas . . . [pre-]guarantee the possibility of a perfect knowledge of the [otherwise alien] world" (*MR* 56).

33. Compare Galileo: "reforming the human mind" (*Dialogue Concerning the Two Chief World Systems*, trans. Stillman Drake [Berkeley: University of California Press, 1967], 57). Also see Hopkins: "the total redesign of human knowledge" (*OLSM* 240).

34. Aristotle, *De Caelo*, III.vii.306a5.

35. *RDM* 46.

36. G. W. F. Hegel, *Phenomenology of Spirit* [hereafter *PhSp*], trans. A.V. Miller (Oxford: Clarendon Press, 1977), 79 (¶132).

37. John Locke, *An Essay Concerning Human Understanding* [hereafter *ECHU*], Vol. I, ed. Alexander Campbell Fraser (New York: Dover Publications, 1959), 173. Locke contends that in so saying we still think of these qualities as effects and thus presuppose a *cause* in the world of these subjective experiences. There is "in truth nothing in the objects themselves, but *powers* to produce various sensations in us; and [secondary qualities] depend on the primary qualities, viz. bulk, figure, texture, and motion of the parts" (173).

38. *ECHU* 174.

39. *ECHU* 173. Curiously, Descartes doesn't acknowledge any ultimate problem: "Is there any disadvantage, if . . . *abstracting from every other feature* except that it possess the nature of [geometric] figure, we conceive the diversity existing between white, blue, and red, etc. as being *like* the differences between [geometric] figures? . . . [F]or it is certain that the infinitude of figures *suffices to express* [re-present] *all* the differences in sensible things" (*RDM* 37). That *likeness* or *imaginative analogy* suffices for Descartes to represent *all* the differences in sensible things, not just their numberability or mathematizability, is quite telling (see also *PhHS* 82; *OLSM* 60, n. 52).

As Descartes says, "*all my physics is part of geometry*" (*Letter to Mersenne, July 27, 1638*, quoted in *Discourse on Method* [hereafter *DM*], trans. Richard Kennington, ed. Pamela Kraus and Frank Hunt [Newburyport Mass.: Focus Publishing, 2007], 75). Kennington adds: "The laws of nature [of Descartes] are . . . 'laws' [only] because they satisfy the requirement of [his] method, *not* because they can be traced to or lead to some metaphysical principle" (74–75). (See §7 "*As if* Thinking," herein). That is, Descartes knows that his distinction, if taken as an ontological one, would involve us in irresolvable paradox.

40. Descartes: "I have been in the habit of perverting the order of nature" (*Meditation* VI).

41. See, for example, Rule XII: "[W]e must *think* that that power by which we are properly said to *know* things is purely spiritual, and not less distinct from every part of the body than blood from bone, or hand from eye. It is *a single agency*" (*RDM* 38); "Now it is the *same faculty* that in cor-

respondence with those various functions is called either pure understanding, or imagination, or memory, or sense" (39). See also *Discourse on Method*, VI: "The mind is so dependent on the temperament and on the arrangement of the organs of the body that, if it is possible to find some means that generally render men more wise . . . I believe that we must seek it in [*physical*] *medicine*" (*DM* 49). Compare Leo Strauss, *Thoughts on Machiavelli* (Glencoe, Il.: The Free Press, 1958), 297.

42. Rule XII: "The senses must be *banished* and the imagination as far as possible *divested of every distinct impression*" (*RDM* 39). Here we "lose our senses," properly speaking. Once cleansed, however, the purified imagination can be "distinct" in this new non-sensuous way and thus serve to bridge the divide (see *GMTOA* 206; *OLSM* 314).

43. See, for example, Oliver Sachs, *The Man Who Mistook His Wife for a Hat and Other Clinical Studies* (New York: Simon and Shuster, 1970).

44. Compare Descartes, *Meditations*, II. Descartes's "new world" might, perhaps, be gauged by the following *thought experiment* (the psychic correlate to the melted beeswax): Withdraw from man his various senses, save some portion of his sense of *touch*, such that one would be blind, deaf, without a sense of taste, smell, hardness, or heat—in this way we would "more truly" experience the world simply as "extension" (compare the first sentence of *Meditations III*).

45. John Eckermann, *Conversations with Goethe*, trans. John Oxenford, (London: J. M. Dent and Sons, 1930, February 26, 1824) 48.

46. *ECHU* 174.

47. Galileo, "The Assayer," in *Discoveries and Opinions of Galileo*, trans. Stillman Drake (New York: Anchor Books, 1957), 238.

48. Compare "The proposition that an abstract idea like *number* is subject to historical change strikes at the heart of the most basic presupposition of the dominant conception of exact science, namely that its basic concepts are essentially a priori and therefore timeless, or at least invariant through time" (*OLSM* 5).

49. *MR* 60. "An algebraic equation as used by the *mathesis universalis* [the new universal science] cannot be simply described as a greater degree of abstraction" (62).

50. *MR* 60.

51. See Aristotle, *Posterior Analytics*, II.19.

52. My thanks to Andrew Romiti for helping me make this explicit.

53. In an endnote to his "*Talking Points on Klein's Math Book*," Richard Hassing draws our attention to an important distinction: "I don't think the

Greeks have 'concepts' [in the modern sense]. . . . [For] the most fundamental distinction between scholastic and Cartesian second-intention doctrines concerns the corresponding mind–world relations. The scholastic account is part of the 'form-receptive' . . . *realism* deriving from Aristotle; the Cartesian account [by contrast] pre-supposes mind-world *separation*" (paper presented at the 4th Jacob Klein Conference, Assumption College, Worcester, MA, May 19, 2018; for an extended discussion of this topic, see Hassing's contribution to the present volume. Also see *RDM*, Rule XII, and *GMTOA*, 202, 207).

Hassing sees the new distinction as the necessary outcome of the modern turn to subjectivity. This is insightful, for, given the fundamentality of the psycho-physical problem as presented by Klein, the first-second intention distinction can no longer be an "outside / inside" distinction, so to speak. It is a distinction within consciousness itself. Without a "world" as the ancients understood it, "first intentions" (our concepts of experience) come to have a different ontological standing that Mr. Klein seeks to elucidate.

54. *MR* 61. Heidegger too makes plain the further consequences of this incongruity: "Modern physics must resign itself ever increasingly to the fact that its realm of representation remains inscrutable and incapable of being visualized" ("*The Question of Technology*," in *BW*, 304). We are reminded of Kant's distinction between what is *thinkable* (but not exhibitable in intuition) and what is *knowable* (because it is).

55. *MR* 61.

56. For example, Vieta (PhHS 81). A number is now conceived of "*apart from the things counted* and consequently only as a 'symbol' . . . [with only] *indirectness* [because mediate] in apprehending the 'numbered assemblage'" (*GMTOA* 213; italics in original). "[T]he replacement of '2' [or any number] . . . is [now] possible because the concept of '*two' no longer refers, as it [previously] did . . . directly to an object*, viz., to two pure monads, but in itself already has a *'more general' character*" (*WPhys* 25; italics added). That is, even our current notion of "two" is the result of this intentional transformation and an example of the "characteristic modification of *every* ancient concept" (*WPhys* 8). In the ancient context, "pure monads" or "pure units" are still thought of as *objects* with an ultimate back-reference to our experience. Compare Hopkins, "Aristotelian abstractions yield 'units' that are species-neutral but *hardly indeterminate*" (*OLSM*, 524).

57. *WPhys* 25.

58. *WPhys* 23. Number is a *pros ti*: "A number is always and indissolubly *related* to that of which it is a number" (*GMTOA* 48).

59. *CNGMP* 52.

60. There might be a remnant of this kind of thinking in our continued use of different *collective nouns* to name different animal groups: a herd of sheep, a school of fish, a murder of crows, a clowder of kittens, a pride of lions, an array of hedgehogs, etc. They are not indifferently all multitudes. There are different species-defined collectivities, each "according to its own kind." To begin with, then, our experience is concrete, our "concepts" grounded.

61. Compare *Republic* VII 525d ("numbers that are attached to visible and tangible bodies"). The question is what is the net effect for our being-in-the-world of the fact that we are initially oriented by the whatness of things (their emergent kinds), then by their numerousness, for example (that is, by an "abstraction of an abstraction"), and then by these new "symbolic abstractions," in each subsequent case removing us in thought from our original experience of the natural articulation of things.

62. *As if* there are "undefined things" of no particular kind or "things in general" ("There is no 'general object'" [*WPhys* 16]).

63. Compare "For Vieta the replacement of '2' by 'a' is possible because the concept of 'two' *no longer refers*, as it did for Diophantus, *directly to an object*, viz., to two pure monads, but in itself already has a more general character" (*WPhy* 25; see also *OLSM* 57, 509–10).

64. *MSMM* 270.

65. *MR* 63. The concepts of Greek science "in each instance intend the individual objects themselves; they are . . . *intentiones primae* ['first intentions']—that is, concepts which refer immediately to individual objects." Consequently, with the single exception of the general theory of proportions, "the mode of presentation of Greek mathematics . . . is never . . . symbolic, but is always the presentation of an image [*abbildlich*], and in this way first-intentional" (*WPhys* 17; italics and brackets in original text). By contrast modern, second-intentional concepts "are not seen as mere . . . signs but as *symbols*—they do not only 'represent,' they 'are' in themselves, mathematical objects" (*GMTOA* 218; italics in original).

66. *MR* 63; italics added for emphasis.

67. The fundamental change in human thinking can be thought of as having three moments: (a) a conflation of ideas of different orders (first- and second-intentional concepts), (b) a new mode of thinking (symbolic abstraction), and (c) the consequent reprioritization of the categories on the basis of mathematical clarity as interpreted by Descartes.

68. Here we see the development of the *modern* notion of "idea" as a men-

tal entity detached from things, how our "thought about things" becomes de-objectified and self-referential.

69. The "presuppositions [of such concepts] are left unclarified" (*GMTOA* 184). Compare Hopkins, §69: "*The Inability of Mathematical Thought to Account for the Mode of Being of its Object*" (*OLSM*, 198; also see 86, 157, 262).

70. *GMTOA* 213; italics added.

71. *GMTOA* 223–24; italics added.

72. Heidegger: "The questionability is concealed by their results and the progress of scientific work" (*MSMM* 270).

73. There are different kinds of intellectual mis-inheritance or mis-transference, and thus different kinds of sedimentation. The general impression that the metaphor of sedimentation gives is that of a complete over-layering, such that one stratum of evidence is obscured by a subsequent one, but there are rather different modes of obfuscation and complexification (if that is a word). Here we see a mixing of types of conceptualization, such that the ontological status or reality of "interlaced" or "entangled" modes renders the amalgamation confused or "unclarified."

As a result, for Husserlian phenomenologists, Mr. Klein among them, it is a mistake to consider "epistemology" in isolation. It is not a distinct discipline but has to be coupled with the "history of sedimentation." For ideas are not found objects but themselves have histories with the result that their "original evidences" may not at first be simply available. As Mr. Klein says:

> [The] interlacement of original productions and 'sedimentation' of significance constitutes the true character of history. . . . [T]here is only *one* legitimate form of *history*: the history of human thought. . . . [T]he main problem of any historical research is precisely the disentanglement of all these strata of 'sedimentation,' with the ultimate goal of *reactivating the 'original foundations,'* i.e., of descending to the true beginnings, to the 'roots,' of any scientific and consequently . . . pre-scientific conceptions of mankind. . . . [A] history of this kind is the *only legitimate form of epistemology*. . . . History . . . cannot be separated from philosophy. (*PhHS* 78)

But as we've seen, the "geological" task of recovering embedded meanings by itself is only one side of the story that Mr. Klein has introduced to us. The "eidetic-geologist" him- or herself has also undergone a radical change. And lest there be an effort to un-re-constitute the mode of symbolic thinking that led to these encrusted meanings (as in Nietzsche and Heidegger), we would only see the recovered object through the same lens or "mentality" that brought us to mis-take it along the way.

The question is therefore twofold: not only whether we can reactivate the "original evidences" but also whether we can re-constitute the eidetic-geologist, so to speak, such that he or she can see with un-predisposed openness. Otherwise, correcting one tendentiousness with another partial mode of apprehension, while perhaps "better," leaves the original evidence out of view and we morph into yet another "mentality" (or cave), our modern conflationary modes of thought remaining at work.

Sedimentation occurs throughout all periods of history. But it is this new *mode* of thinking that makes us who we've become (Heidegger: modern *Dasein*). That correlative task of recovery *and* reconstitution remains (Goethe).

74. *MR* 60.

75. *MR* 64.

76. *PhHS* 84.

77. *PhHS* 78.

78. "This interlacement of original production and 'sedimentation' of significance constitutes the true character of history. . . . And the main problem of any historical research is precisely the disentanglement of all these strata of sedimentation" (*PhHS* 78).

79. *WPhys* 8.

80. Goethe, *Letter to Zelter*, June 6, 1825.

81. *MR* 57.

82. *MR* 64; italics added.

83. Heidegger introduced the compound term "being-in-the-world" (*In-der-Welt-Sein*) because we had become so inured in this new way of seeing and living that we lost sight of what is "first for us," our most immediate and familiar lived experience, the "life-world" (*Lebenswelt*). He takes this in his own direction, though.

84. Heidegger understands this and makes "the mathematical" (*ta mathêmata*) constitutive of modern thought. "The mathematical," he says, "is a projection of thingness which . . . [however] *skips* the things" (*MSMM* 267–68). It is an example of "method" (predisposition) or what we ahead of time bring to our experience ("a procedure how in general we are to pursue things decided in advance . . . what [kind of] truth we shall seek out of the things"). He rightly sees that this transformation has re-enframed us all. Klein argues, however, that it is not simply a "skipping," but, more compli-

cated, an amalgamation and conflation that, as concealing, might be construed as a skipping.

85. *MR* 64; italics added for emphasis.

86. *MR* 57.

87. Compare *MR* 59–60.

88. *PhSp* 359–60 (¶590). In other words: "the empty point of the absolutely free self" (360 [¶590]). See also David Levine, "Humanity Dehumanized: Hegel's Reflections on the Enlightenment and the French Revolution . . . and Their Other Legacy," *Imaginative Conservative*, Special Issue in Celebration of Eva Brann's 90th Birthday, January 23, 2019 (originally given as a lecture, St. John's College, Santa Fe, November 3, 2017).

89. And is the bee's wax really the same as the charred remains after submitting it to the analytical flame (compare *Meditations II*)?

90. Descartes has been more successful than we might first think. Our sense of ourselves and our world has been recast in terms of his doubly reductive epistemological (not ontological) distinction: *res extensa / res cogitans* (and the conceptual shift that brought us thereto). We thus now *live out* this abstract disjunction, with not just the world as reinterpreted by modern science (an interpretation without a text [compare Nietzsche, "On the Prejudices of the Philosophers," *Beyond Good and Evil*, §14]), but with ourselves as a "thought thing," our sense of reason reconstituted and restricted. (Needless to say, Descartes's "provisional morality" [*Discourse on Method*, III] does not help us deal with this radical revision of our being-in-the-world.)

We have a lot of work ahead of us, then, if indeed we want to reclaim *our natural inherence* (compare Goethe's effort "to restore to the human spirit, its ancient right to come face to face with nature" ["Analysis and Synthesis," in *The Collected Works*, Vol. XII: Scientific Studies, trans. Douglas Miller (Princeton: Princeton University Press, 1988), 48]).

Jacob Klein's Defense of Liberal Education by Antonio Marino López

1. Leo Strauss, *The City and Man* (Chicago: The University of Chicago Press, 1964), 1.

2. Jacob Klein, *Lectures and Essays*, ed. Robert B. Williamson and Elliott Zuckerman (Annapolis, MD: St. John's College Press, 1985). All numbers between parentheses refer to page numbers in this book.

3. Richard Kennington, review of *Lectures and Essays* in *Review of Metaphysics* 41, No. 1 (Sept. 1987): 145.

4. Fragment 18, my translation.

Jacob Klein on the Problem of History for Liberal Education by Mary Elizabeth Halper

1. Plato, *Sophist*, 246a–c, in *The Being of the Beautiful*, trans. Seth Benardete (Chicago: University of Chicago Press, 1984).

2. As will become clearer below, there are also parallels between the corporealists (Giants) and idealists (Gods) and the Humanities (reduced to history), which traffic in the concrete, and the Sciences (reduced to mathematical physics), which deal with the abstract. Klein's account thereby provides an intriguing reversal of the more common, and often polemical, descriptions of these disciplines—the Humanities usually described as soft and preoccupied with ideas to the detriment of concrete, practical value, and the Sciences usually described as hard and preoccupied with minutiae to the detriment of being meaningful.

3. All parenthetical citations refer to Jacob Klein, *Lectures and Essays*, ed. Robert B. Williamson and Elliott Zuckerman (Annapolis: St. John's College Press, 1985).

4. I follow Klein in using the term "History" (capitalized) to denote primarily the conception of history that entails a pervasive, *a priori* sense that conditions all human sense-making.

5. Jacob Klein, "The Idea of Liberal Education," in *Lectures and Essays*, 162.

6. Given Klein's word choice here, one wonders to what extent phenomenology is a liberal art, or, if not itself an art, then how it may be a condition for the possibility of the liberal arts.

7. For a thorough and more precise account of the different iterations and claims of philosophical historicism, see Carl Page, *Philosophical Historicism and the Betrayal of First Philosophy* (University Park, PA: The Pennsylvania State University Press, 1995), chapter 2. Precision in delineating the contours of philosophical historicism is less a concern here, as the object is not so much to refute historicism as to provide sufficient warrant to ignore its diagnosis of the capacities of human reason. Page himself only glancingly engages with Husserl, by way of David Carr's explication of and development on Husserl's so-called "newly acquired 'historical consciousness'"(102). Insofar as Carr's treatment of Husserl's later thought seems to me to run parallel, in essentials, to Derrida's reading of Husserl's thought, I take Burt Hopkins's case that Klein is Husserl's better reader to apply also to Carr's reading. See Burt Hopkins, "Klein and Derrida on the Historicity of Meaning and the Meaning of Historicity in Husserl's *Crisis*-Texts," *Journal of the British Society for Phenomenology* 36.2 (2005), 179–87. In other words,

I believe Husserl's account of historicity does not exclude him from pursuing first philosophy.

8. This problem of history, Klein believes, is one that "from the very outset . . . has a definite, if not the most important, place in Husserl's mind" (68). See Hopkins, "Klein and Derrida," 181–82, for an argument that on this point Klein is superior to Derrida and others who understand Husserl's concept of intentional history to be a later innovation and one that is in tension with his earlier thought on the meaning of historicity.

9. See Investigation V, section 10, in Edmund Husserl, *Logical Investigations, Volume II*, trans. J. N. Findlay, ed. Dermot Moran (New York: Routledge, 2001), 95.

10. This quotation is from Eva Brann's preface to Burt Hopkins, *The Origin of the Logic of Symbolic Mathematics* (Bloomington: Indiana University Press, 2011), xxviii. Earlier in that preface, Brann claims that "The St. John's Program is, as it were, an elementary preparation for the kind of 'intentional history' realized in Klein's book" (i.e., *Greek Mathematical Thought and the Origin of Algebra*) (xxv). I agree with Brann's point but would add that all those charged with the perpetuation of liberal education would be supported in that task by conducting Klein's kind of intentional history. The care and detail of Hopkins's work is further evidence that the work of desedimentation presupposes a hard-won intimacy with the history of ideas, and therefore belongs properly to those liberal learners who have already reflected at length and with great solicitude on this history. As for the act itself, desedimenting encompasses a range of sense-gaining routes: imaginative variation, analysis, critique, interpretation, etc. See Edmund Husserl, *The Crisis of European Sciences and Transcendental Phenomenology: An Introduction to Phenomenological Philosophy* (Chicago: Northwestern University Press, 1970), Part II, Section 14 for a brief and potent description of the work.

11. Husserl uses the term "reactivation" ("desedimentation" was coined by Derrida), which may be more fitting in this context, since here the teacher provokes the student to do the meaning-generative activity himself, not merely to appropriate it as something that has been done.

12. This account of the execution of liberal education fits beautifully with a further specification of its content, a specification to a "Great Books" curriculum. Briefly, this reservoir of eminently shareable meaning abides for both the teacher and the learner in the repository of the great works of human intelligence and endeavor. The books are the abode of the original meaning, and, in a live sense, fellow-travelers with the liberal educator and educated.

13. From Eva Brann, "Jacob Klein: European Scholar and American Teacher," originally a keynote address for the Jacob Klein Conference on Liberal Education at Providence College in March 2016, republished in the present volume.

14. Preface, *The Origin of the Logic of Symbolic Mathematics*, xxvii.

The Role of "Intentionality" in Jacob Klein's Account of the Historicity of the Concept of Number by Burt C. Hopkins

1. Jacob Klein, "Die griechische Logistik und die Entstehung der Algebra," *Quellen und Studien zur Geschichte der Mathematik, Astronomie und Physik*, Abteilung B: *Studien*, vol. 3, no. 1 (1934), 18–105 (Part I), and no. 2 (1936), 122–235 (Part II); English trans. *Greek Mathematical Thought and the Origin of Algebra*, trans. Eva Brann (Cambridge, MA: MIT Press, 1968; reprint: New York: Dover, 1992). Hereafter cited as "*GMTOA*." Parenthetical citations of this work will give page numbers of both the original and the translation, in that order. The translations given throughout this paper are the author's own modified versions of the published translation. Bracketed material inserted into quotes will include the following designations when any ambiguity might arise to specify whose addition it is: JK for Jacob Klein, EB for Eva Brann, BH for Burt Hopkins.

2. Jacob Klein, "Phenomenology and the History of Science," in *Philosophical Essays in Memory of Edmund Husserl*, ed. Marvin Farber (Cambridge, MA: Harvard University Press, 1940): 143–63; reprinted in Jacob Klein, *Lectures and Essays*, ed. Robert B. Williamson and Elliott Zuckerman (Annapolis, MD: St. John's Press, 1985): 65–84. The later version will be cited in what follows as *PHS*.

3. Klein coined this term, which is not to be found in Husserl's texts.

4. Edmund Husserl, "Die Krisis der europäischen Wissenschaften und die transzendentale Phänomenologie. Eine Einleitung in die phänomenologische Philosophie," *Philosophia* I (1936), 77–176; Edmund Husserl, "Die Frage nach dem Ursprung der Geometrie als intentional-historisches Problem," *Revue internationale de Philosophie* I (1939): 203–25. English translations of these texts are available in *The Crisis of European Sciences and Transcendental Phenomenology*, trans. with an introduction by David Carr (Evanston, IL: Northwestern University Press, 1970), where the latter German text appears as appendix VI with the title "The Origin of Geometry." Klein's *PHS* is the first discussion of these articles in the literature and thus the first discussion of the final developments of Husserl's phenomenology.

5. Hiram Caton, "Review of Jacob Klein's *Greek Mathematical Thought and the Origin of Algebra*," *Studi Internazionali di Filosofia* 3 (1971): 225.

6. "Imaginary" in the sense that they do not provide an answer to the question "how many."

7. Thus Klein writes about Greek science in general and mathematics in particular: "Its concepts in each instance intend the individual objects themselves; they are—to speak in Scholastic language—*intentiones primae* ['first intentions']—that is concepts which refer immediately to individual objects. . . . The lines drawn in the figure exhibit the object, they 'image' it. Consequently, the mode of presentation of Greek mathematics . . . is never merely representative [*stellvertretend*], never symbolic, but is always the presentation of an image [*abbildlich*]" ("The World of Physics and the 'Natural' World," in *Lectures and Essays*, 17).

8. Henk Bos, *Redefining Geometrical Exactness* (New York: Springer, 2001), Chapter 8 (145–158); Michael Mahoney, "The Beginnings of Algebraic Thought in the Seventeenth Century," in *Descartes: Philosophy, Mathematics and Physics*, ed. S. Gaukroger (Sussex: The Harvester Press/Totowa, NJ, Barnes and Noble Books, 1980); Michael Mahoney, *The Mathematical Career of Pierre de Fermat 1601–1665*, 2nd ed. (Princeton: Princeton University Press, 1994), Chapter II (26–71); Danielle Macbeth, "Viète, Descartes, and the Emergence of Modern Mathematics," *Graduate Faculty Philosophy Journal* 25, no. 2 (2004): 87–115; Marco Panza, "What is New and What is old in Viete's Analysis Restituta and Algebra Nuova," available online: https://halshs.archives-ouvertes.fr/halshs-00116725/document; Antoni Malet, "Renaissance notions of number and magnitude," *Historia Mathematica* 33 (2006), 63–81 (see pp 65–66 where he criticizes Klein); Jacqueline A. Stedall, *A Discourse Concerning Algebra: English Algebra to 1685* (Oxford: Oxford University Press, 2002), 50–52.

9. Reviel Netz, "Archimedes Transformed: The Case of a Result Stating a Maximum for a Cubic Equation," *Archive for History of Exact Sciences* 54 (1999): 1–47, here 44.

10. Reviel Netz, *The Transformation of Mathematics in the Early Mediterranean World: From Problems to Equations* (Cambridge: Cambridge University Press, 2004), 5.

11. Netz, *Transformation of Mathematics*, 6.

12. See note 17 below.

13. Because on Klein's view the ancient ἀριθμοί are precisely "*Anzahlen*," i.e., definite amounts of definite objects, in essence his point here is that the way in which Viète understood the concept of species in his "logistice speci-

osa" was still dependent on the ancient ἀρθμοί. This is reflected in the English translation, which renders "*Anzahlen*" here as "*arithmoi*."

14. 180/173. In the typography employed by the English translation of GMTOA the numeral 3 descends below the line, which may result in the erroneous appearance that the b is printed in superscript as an exponent in modern notation.

15. According to Klein, this law "says, in modern terminology, that all parts of an equation must have the same dimension" (181/173).

16. The published English version of Klein's text omits the German "meint zunächst einmal das Buchstaben-Zeichen bei Viète eben diesen *Begriff* der Anzahl als einer auf Dinge bzw. Einheiten unablöslich bezogenen Bestimmung."

17. Caton's gloss on this passage is instructive. After quoting the English translation of this passage, into which he inserts, after the word "ἀριθμός," the following in brackets: "[number sign]," he writes:

> Klein means to say, I take it, that the letter sign signifies an indeterminate number of other signs (numbers), which in turn signify things or beings (units, monads). But the main thing is to understand correctly in what way the letter signifies the number signs, for therein lies the secret of the letter as a sign of an *indeterminate magnitude* (i.e., a wholly new, un-Greek number conception), and hence as a true variable or symbol. (Caton, "Review," 223)

There are three problems with Caton's view of the matters expressed here. One, Klein nowhere associates or otherwise connects "number sign" with ἀριθμός. Indeed, his account of the non-theoretical, which is to say practical, distinction between "saying" and "thinking" rules out precisely the *separation* of the "expressive" (i.e., saying) and the "conceptual" (i.e., thinking) that is implicit in Caton's apparent equation of ἀριθμός, or the ἀριθμός concept, with "number sign." Two, Klein nowhere suggests that Viète's letter sign signifies other signs (indeed, signs that *are* numbers!), and that this, viz., the letter signifying number signs, has anything to do with the signification of an indeterminate magnitude. Klein's passage, restored to its entirety, makes this clear, since it *explicitly* states that what Viète's letter sign means is the "*concept* of an amount [*Anzahl*]," a concept moreover that is said to be "insolubly related to things or units," and therefore manifestly *not* to other signs. Finally, three, as we will see below, Viète's letter as a sign—in the novel sense of a symbol—of an indeterminate magnitude does not *signify* anything apart from itself. This (the identification of "the object represented with the means of its representation") is the "secret" of Viète's letter sign, and it means that the concept of an indeterminate magnitude, in the guise of Viète's species, collapses into his letter sign, such that what is meant by both is, *in precisely this sense*, "*symbolic* in nature" (183/176).

18. With the exception of Caton, all of the discussions (with which I am familiar) of Klein's account of the origin of symbolic cognition completely elide the "decisive turn" in connection with this origin that Klein attributes to the "direct apprehension," as the object of a "first intention," of Viète's letter sign. Thus, in the following gloss, Caton is very much to the point: "The letter sign takes on 'independence' in the sense that it becomes a *computational element* thanks to 'precise rules' for its manipulation. It thus becomes an object of the first intention, namely, as a visible sign, with which computations may be performed" (Caton, "Review," 223–24).

19. Klein's analysis here of the origin of the "meaning" of mathematical symbols, an analysis that we have shown occurs within the context of his account of the "matter-of-course acceptance within modern consciousness" (178/171) of the symbolic procedure made possible by such symbols, will remain inaccessible to anyone whose conceptual horizon is determined (and, therefore, limited) by such an acceptance of their "meaning." This is exemplified in Mahoney's account, where he writes: "what should be understood as the 'algebraic mode of thought'? It has three main characteristics: first, this mode of thought is characterized by the use of an operative symbolism, that is, a symbolism that not only abbreviates words but represents the workings of the combinatory operations, or, in other words, a symbolism with which one operates" (Mahoney, "The Beginnings of Algebraic Thought," 142). Not only is no attempt made here to define or otherwise account for what an "operative symbolism" is, but the very fact that it is explained in the manner of a logical tautology (viz., "an operative symbolism" = "a symbolism with which one operates") raises the suspicion that the author does not really see anything problematical in what a symbolism is because *what it is* apparently for him is *self-evident*.

20. Jeffrey Oaks, in "François Viète's Revolution in Algebra" (*Archive for History of Exact Sciences* [2018] 72: 245–302), critically assesses Klein's account of these conceptual presuppositions. Oaks argues that the proper historical context of Viète's innovations presents compelling evidence that the species represent the values of geometrical magnitudes and therefore not, as Klein maintains, generalized objects identical with neither of the traditional objects of mathematics (number or geometric magnitude). Moreover, Oaks argues that Klein's claim that the symbolic mode of the being of the species is determined by the syntactical rules stipulated by Viète (in ch. IV of *In Artem Analyticem Isagoge*), which "represent the first modern

axiom system" (*GMTOA*, 184/176), is mistaken. These rules "are instead an extension to higher dimensions of the well-established rules for operating on lines, planes, and bodies" (Oaks, 292). Klein's "oversight" of this extension, evident in the fact that his text "gives no indication that he was aware of Viète's higher-dimensional geometrical magnitudes," is behind his mistaken interpretation of the conceptual status of those rules in terms of modern axioms. Oaks holds, moreover, "[t]he 'being' of these magnitudes is not even a point to be addressed" and "Viète works with them simply because they are useful."

We may grant Oaks's claims that Viète's algebra functions mathematically in the exclusive service of geometrical magnitude and that the numbers involved in the arithmetical metricization of geometrical magnitude—in contrast to the numerical status of the Greek *arithmos* as a positive integer—are continuous in nature. Moreover, Oaks agrees with Klein that the rule-governed operations on letters in Viète's zetetic represents an unprecedented mathematical innovation. Klein's interpretation acknowledges that Viète understood zetetic as an auxiliary (*GMTOA*, 176/170) procedure in the service of the object of traditional geometrical analysis, which is consistent with Oaks's presentation of that object. But Oaks maintains that Viète's species ultimately represent geometric magnitude, even though they may be interpreted either numerically or figurally in the rhetic or exegetic part of *logistice speciosa*. Nevertheless, according to Klein, in the first, zetetic part of *logistice speciosa* the species function mathematically as symbolic objects that are identical with neither of the traditional objects of mathematics. And it seems to me that's enough to substantiate Klein's claim that Viète's species cannot be identified with geometrical magnitude.

21. How exactly the general concept of twoness (in the example at hand) *and* the reference to two (again, in the example at hand) entities are to be understood as belonging "at the same time" to *number*, is something that, according to Klein, modern set theory first tries to clarify. He writes: "Modern *set theory* first tries to separate these two constituents, to clarify what 'at the same time' means" ("The World of Physics," 25).

22. "The World of Physics," 25.

23. This is to say that Viète's concept of species is "numerically" indeterminate when the measure for numerical determinacy is ἀριθμοί, namely, "numbers" that are "definite amounts of definite objects," which is to say with Klein: *Anzahlen*.

24. Klein provides the following reference for his citations from Gilson: "Gilson, *Index*, p. 107" (220/207), referring to Gilson's *Index Scholastico-Cartesien* (Paris: Alcan, 1912).

25. The translator of the English edition here adds the following: "[i.e., an act the object of whose intention is already an expressly signified concept, as opposed to the object of the first intention which is a being on which the *actus exercitus* is immediately exercised]."

26. In *GMTOA* "*symbolische Abstraktion*" is rendered as "symbol-generating abstraction," in recognition of Klein's characterization of the role that Descartes's account of abstraction plays in the generation of the symbols for the *mathesis universalis*, and the translator's belief that, properly speaking, this abstraction itself is not "symbolic." Nevertheless, because it is precisely the involvement of the "pure" intellect's abstractive power in maintaining the separation that is responsible for its apprehension of the algebraic letters and geometric figures that belong to the *mathesis universalis* as "symbols" rather than as determinate images (and therefore determinate "ideas"), on my view it remains appropriate to characterize the abstraction involved as "symbolic."

27. Klein refers at this point in his text to his earlier discussion of the studies of Julius Stenzel and Oskar Becker, both of which attempt to draw the distinction between the ancient and modern number concepts on the basis of the former's "intuitability" (65/62). Klein's point, both in his earlier discussion and now, is that this basis for the misunderstanding of this distinction "is guided after all by *our* number concept [*Zahlbegriff*]," the presupposition of which obscures access to the non-conceptual, one-and-many structure of ἀριθμός.

28. The "intuition" here, of course, is *not* Descartes's "*intuitus*," which is "conceptual" or "intellectual" in a sense that rules out precisely the "intuition" as "*Anschauung*" that is involved in the opposition here between "intuition" and "concept."

29. Jacob Klein, "Modern Rationalism," in *Lectures and Essays*, 64.

Viètian Magnitudes: Is Viète's *Isagoge* an Attempt to Overcome the Euclidean Distinction between Magnitude and Multitude? by Michael Dink

1. The original version of this paper was delivered at the third Klein Conference, held at Providence College, March 11–12, 2016. Its delivery was preceded in the same session by that of a paper by Jeffrey Oaks, also on Viète. While my paper is based on a close reading of Euclid's *Elements* and of one text by Viète, Oaks's paper was based not only on a complete review of *all* of Viète's mathematical works, but also on a thorough familiarity with the work of many of Viète's predecessors and contemporaries in medie-

val mathematics who were involved in the emergence of algebra. Oaks has subsequently expanded his paper and published it: Jeffrey Oaks, "François Viète's Revolution in Algebra," *Archive for History of Exact Sciences* 72, no. 3 (May 2018): 245–302.

Since I have the greatest respect not only for Oaks's deep and broad mastery of the relevant historical material, but also for the acuteness of his judgment in assessing it, it was with some hesitation that I consented to offer my paper for inclusion in this volume. Having studied Oaks's published paper, however, I have concluded that it would be permissible for me to do so, provided that I made an effort to compare the conclusions of my paper with those of his and indicated where I think mine might need to be revised and where there might remain disagreements between us.

The present version of the paper differs from the original only in a slight revision of the title, the omission of a paragraph briefly surveying other mathematical works by Viète, the addition of footnotes referencing Oaks's paper, and the addition of an addendum reassessing its claims in the light of Oaks's article.

2. I have retained *magnitude* and *multitude* as the terms of the contrast from my original paper. These terms are, however, slightly imprecise in two ways. First, *number* may be a more specific term than *multitude* insofar as in a number each of the many must be a 'unit,' identical in some respect to every other one of the many. There might arguably be multitudes in which this is not the case, as in modern set theory. Second, insofar as *magnitude* means anything that admits of the relations "greater than," "less than," and "equal," numbers must be allowed to be magnitudes. If these two precisions are taken into account, the more precise version of the contrast would be between continuous magnitude and number.

3. All references to Euclid's *Elements* are based on the following edition: Euclid, *Euclid's Elements: All Thirteen Books Complete in One Volume*, trans. Thomas L. Heath, ed. Dana Densmore (Santa Fe: Green Lion Press, 2002).

4. Proposition XII.2, which speaks of area (*xôrion*) without specifying it as to figure, may constitute an exception to this rule.

5. Parenthetical page references in the main body of this text refer to Jacob Klein, *Greek Mathematical Thought and the Origin of Algebra*, trans. Eva Brann (Cambridge, MA: MIT Press, 1968).

6. Quotations from the *Isagoge* are taken from the translation by J. Winfree Smith, which appears as an appendix in the English translation of Klein's *Greek Mathematical Thought and the Origins of Algebra*.

7. As Klein points out, Viète seems to have transformed the ancient

distinction between two parallel forms of analysis, one used in the investigation of theorems and another in the investigation of problems, into a distinction between two parts in one sequence of analysis, although he never succeeds in giving a clear account of the boundary between the two parts in this revised, sequential form (166).

8. This agrees with the interpretation of Jeffrey Oaks: "Reading Viète's passages with numbers across all his published works shows that he regarded numbers to be the measures of geometric magnitudes" ("Viète's Revolution," 267).

9. Henry Higuera, "Multiplication Ancient and Modern: Sorting Out the Meanings" (lecture, St. John's College, Annapolis, April 17, 2009).

10. This is part of what Descartes does in the opening pages of *La Géométrie*.

11. It is this last inference that Oaks vigorously denies. His argument is that Viète treats these higher-dimensional magnitudes in the same way that his predecessors and contemporaries treated "irrational numbers," that is, as something to be accepted as practically useful, even though contrary to more or less accepted (at least verbally conceded?) theoretical principles ("Viète's Revolution," 265; see also 259, 260, 268). See the addendum below for my reply.

12. Oaks says that Viète has done neither, but that the language implying the multiplication of magnitudes was not uncommon in the preceding tradition and hence was not seen as a radical innovation or a "flagrant and reprehensible abuse" ("Viète's Revolution," 280). (I wonder if this phrase was aimed in part at my paper!)

13. Oaks denies that either Viète or his contemporaries would be bothered by either of these outcomes. Concerning the first, fractions and irrationals were widely used as numerical measures of geometric magnitudes (see "Viète's Revolution," 255, 265–68), and concerning the second, Viète seemed to make use of the higher-dimensional magnitudes only in a few restricted instances and treated them as more valuable for their utility than disturbing because of their incomprehensibility (see Oaks, 257, 259, 260, 265, 268, 280).

14. Oaks denies that anything in the *Isagoge* amounts to an axiom system defining a new mathematical object. Nonetheless, he acknowledges the following points: (1) That in allowing magnitudes of more than three dimensions, Viète is "another example of a sixteenth-century mathematician *following syntax at the expense of semantics*" ("Viète's Revolution," 280, my emphasis); (2) "They [the higher-dimensional magnitudes or all magnitudes

as objects intended by species?] attain independence from ratio and proportion by Viète's stipulation that proportions can be resolved into equalities" (Oaks, 268); (3) "Viète himself was aware that with the creation of his *logistice speciosa* he had not only developed a useful tool for calculation, but he had revolutionized both algebra and geometric analysis" (Oaks, 248).

15. Thus far, Oaks and I are in agreement with one another, against Klein.

16. Oaks denies this second point, or at least he thinks that no sharp line ought to be drawn between Euclid's and Viète's treatment of geometric magnitudes, except that the latter allowed for the existence of some such magnitudes of dimensions greater than three (see points 1 and 2 in note 14 above).

17. Here, my paper agrees with Klein, against Oaks, that the objects of Viète's analytic art are determined by the rules that govern them. See the addendum for further discussion of this issue.

18. Klein does not offer this third alternative explicitly in the Viète chapter, but he does mention "identify[ing] the object represented with the means of its representation" as one of "two things which constitute the heart of the symbolic procedure" (*Greek Mathematical Thought*, 123).

19. Strictly speaking, this would require a geometric construction of the magnitude. Oaks says that Viète himself never carries out such a construction in his published works, but some of his successors do ("Viète's Revolution," 279).

20. Oaks, "Viète's Revolution," 291.

21. Oaks, on the other hand, views Viète's "supreme stipulation" as merely "a generalization of Euclid's *Elements* VI.16, where the parameters are lines, and XI.34, where two are lines and two are planes" ("Viète's Revolution," 258). This, however, elides the fact that neither proposition mentions multiplication.

22. Oaks himself is willing to say that "Viète's adoption of higher-dimensional magnitudes *because they are useful* . . . is another example of a sixteenth-century mathematician *following syntax at the expense of semantics*" ("Viète's Revolution," 280, my emphasis).

23. Hence, Oaks claims, "it becomes clear that the rules in Chapter II are not axioms defining 'the object to which they refer'. They are instead an extension to higher dimensions of the well-established rules for operating on lines, planes, and bodies" ("Viète's Revolution," 292). What Oaks calls "well-established rules" I would characterize as an accepted practice of blurring an acknowledged distinction, without thematization or explicit justification of the practice.

24. That even this justification was regarded by an editor as insufficiently clear seems to be indicated by the insertion of additional, if not convincing, explanatory remarks by van Schooten in his edition of 1646 (see Klein, *Greek Mathematical Thought*, 315n1).

Simon Stevin and the Matter of Number by Daniel P. Maher

1. Introduction to *De Thiende*, in *Principal Works of Simon Stevin*, vol. II *Mathematical Works of Simon Stevin*, ed. D. J. Struik, with translations from Dutch into English by C. Dikshoorn (Amsterdam: C. V. Swets & Zeitlinger, 1958), 373. Many of Stevin's works are available in Dutch, French, and English in *Principal Works of Simon Stevin*, ed. Ernst Crone, E. J. Dijksterhuis, R. J. Forbes, M. G. J. Minnaert, and A. Pannekoek, 5 vols. (Amsterdam: C. V. Swets & Zeitlinger, 1955–1966). Hereafter, citations to Stevin's writings from this edition will be identified by *PW*, together with volume and page numbers. The text is available at www.dwc.knaw.nl/.

2. Jacob Klein, *Greek Mathematical Thought and the Origin of Algebra*, trans. Eva Brann (Cambridge, MA: MIT Press, 1968; reprint New York: Dover Publications, 1992): 3–4. Hereafter, this book will be cited parenthetically in the body of the paper as *GMTOA* with a page number.

3. Jacob Klein, "Phenomenology and the History of Science," in *Lectures and Essays*, ed. Robert B. Williamson and Elliott Zuckerman (Annapolis, MD: St. John's College Press, 1985), 79.

4. For more see my "Aristotle on Mathematical and Eidetic Number," *Hermathena* 190 (Summer 2011): 29–51.

5. "À une continue grandeur, correspond le continue nombre qu'on lui attribue" (Stevin, *Arithmétique*, *PW* II 502). In *PW*, Stevin's *Arithmétique* is presented in a facsimile of the 1585 edition. The editor has added an English summary and notes; some parts of the summary are direct translations, but translations from Stevin's French herein are my own. In cases where Stevin's wording deserves emphasis, I include the French in the body of the paper.

6. "We cannot find in the 16th century a theory of numbers and magnitudes that confronts the classical notions head on—not until we get to Simon Stevin's *Arithmétique* of 1585." Antoni Malet, "Renaissance Notions of Number and Magnitude," *Historia Mathematica* 33 (2006): 65.

7. Richard Kennington, "Bacon's Critique of Ancient Philosophy in *New Organon* 1," in *On Modern Origins*, ed. Pamela Kraus and Frank Hunt (Lanham, MD: Lexington Books, 2004), 17. Interestingly, Klein's notes in the

GMTOA chapter on Stevin repeatedly cite Bacon. I have found no evidence linking Bacon directly to Stevin, but there are striking affinities between these contemporaries.

8. "On a Sixteenth-Century Algebraist," in *Lectures and Essays*, 40–41.

9. Klein, "Sixteenth-Century Algebraist," 40. For more on the connection between Descartes and Stevin, see my "Simon Stevin's *Vita Politica*: Pre-provisional Morality?" *Interpretation* 43, no. 2 (Winter 2017): 215–32.

10. "Nombre est cela, par lequel s'explique la quantité de chascune chose" (*Arithmétique*, *PW* II 495). *Made known* is probably a better rendering of *s'explique*, but it's less literal. *Expressed* or *unfolded* are candidates as well.

11. "La demande est combien il y a de matière." My translation; French text available in *Les Oeuvres Mathématiques de Simon Stevin*, 6 vols., ed. Albert Girard (Leiden: Elsevier, 1634), vol. I 211. Compare *PW* II 441, where the English translation from the Dutch reads: "The question is how much the substance or matter of that pillar is."

12. "Il faut doncques sçavoir, que les Hommes i'adis voians, qu'il leur estoit mestier de parler & avoir intelligence de la quantité des choses ils nommoient chasque chose simple, un; & quand à la mesme estoit appliquée encore une autre, les appelloient ensemble deux, & quand la propose simple chose estoit divisée en deux parties egales, ils nommoient chascune partie demi, &c." (Arithmétique, PW II 497). Italics in translation added for emphasis.

13. "Et qui le nie, faict comme celui, qui nie qu'une piece de pain soit du pain" (*Arithmétique*, *PW* II 495).

14. The objection is reported by Jurgen Naets, "How to Define a Number? A General Epistemological Account of Simon Stevin's Art of Defining," *Topoi* 29 (2010), 80. See Antoine Arnauld and Pierre Nicole, *Logic or the Art of Thinking*, trans. and ed. Jill Vance Buroker (Cambridge and New York: Cambridge University Press, 1996), 244–45; original text published in 1662.

15. Arnauld and Nicole, *Logic*, 245.

16. See *Metaphysics* 8.3.1044a2–5.

17. Girard, ed., *Oeuvres Mathématiques* I 175; my translation. Consider also this claim from his *Cosmography*: "Theory is a fictitious operation without natural material, such as e.g., the theories of the theoretician Euclid, which operate by the assumption of quantities and numbers, but each of them without connection with natural material. Practice is an operation which essentially takes place with natural material, such as the measurement of land and ramparts, counting the number of rods or feet contained therein, and the like" (*PW* III 619).

18. Klein says Stevin understands the object of a second intention as if it were the object of a first intention (*GMTOA* 192). For discussion of this terminology, see essays by Hopkins, Dink, and Hassing in this volume.

19. *PW* II 403. The English translation is by Robert Norton, first published in 1608.

20. "La Disme, qui se pourroit dire par autre nom, *La Practique des Practiques*" (*La Practique d'Arithmétique* in Girard, ed., *Oeuvres Mathématiques* I 175).

21. In his introduction to *De Thiende*, D. J. Struik writes: "He did not propose anything about the nature of the unit itself: he only pointed out the advantages of a decimal subdivision" (*PW* II 383).

22. In Dutch: *ghevonden* (*Thiende*, *PW* II 402); the French has *inventée* (Girard, ed., *Oeuvres Mathématiques* I 208).

23. The English text prints *invention*, which I have corrected here. The Dutch uses *voornemen* (*Thiende*, *PW* II 422), and the French has *intention* (Girard, ed., *Oeuvres Mathématiques* I 210).

24. Stevin's notation is expressed here inexactly. Stevin draws complete circles around the numerals that indicate the position of the numerals we would place to the right of the decimal point; I have used parentheses. By *whole number* Stevin means what we call a positive integer: "Definition vii: Nombre entier est unité, ou composée multitude d'unitez" (*Arithmétique*, *PW* II 505); "Definition vii: A whole number is a unit or a multitude composed of units."

25. George Sarton, "The First Explanation of Decimal Fractions and Measures (1585)," *Isis* 23, no. 1 (June 1935): 174–75. See E. J. Dijksterhuis: "By the introduction of a unit which is one hundredth of the original one, the fraction is transformed into a whole number." *Simon Stevin: Science in the Netherlands around 1600* (The Hague: Martinus Nijhoff, 1970), 19.

26. "Puis considerans que un, deux, trois, demi, tiers, &c. estoient noms propres, & convenables, pour l'explication de ladicte quantité, ils ont veu qu'il estoit necessaire de comprendre toutes ces especes soubs un genre (car telle est leur maniere de faire en tous autres semblables comme bled, orge, avoine, ils le nomment en genre Grain; aigle, tourterelle, rosignol, en genre Oseau) lequel genre ils appelloient nombre" (*Arithmétique*, *PW* II 497).

27. "À une continue grandeur, correspond le continue nombre qu'on lui attribue, & telle discontinuité que puis apres reçoit la grandeur par quelque division, semblable discontinuité reçoit aussi son nombre" (*Arithmétique*, *PW* II 502).

28. To provide just one text in support: "For either the dyad is not one or there is not a monad in it actually (ἐντελεχείᾳ)" (Aristotle, *Metaphysics*

7.13.1039a13–14). If the dyad is not one but two, this will be because two monads are present actually; "for actuality divides" (7.13.1039a7; my translation). For further discussion, see my "Mathematical and Eidetic Number."

29. "Et à fin d'en parler par exemple, le nombre est quelque chose telle en grandeur, comme l'humidité en l'eau, car comme cette ci s'estend par tout & en chasque partie de sa grandeur : Item comme à une continue eau correspond une continue humidité, ainsi à une continue grandeur correspond un continue nombre : Item comme la continue humidité de l'entiere eau, souffre la mesme division & disioinction que son eau, Ainsi le continue nombre souffre la mesme division & disioinction que sa grandeur ; De sorte que ses deux quantitez ne se peuvent distinguer par continue & discontinue" (*Arithmétique*, *PW* II 502).

30. For more on that difference, see Richard F. Hassing, "History of Physics and the Thought of Jacob Klein," *The New Yearbook for Phenomenology and Phenomenological Philosophy* 11 (2011): 214–48, especially 239–46.

31. Antoni Malet, "Renaissance Notions of Number," 76–77. Malet goes on to say, "This is the key argument that appears in his attack on the old belief that unity is not a number but only its first principle or origin" (77), but that is inaccurate. The analogy supports Stevin's thesis that number is not discontinuous quantity.

32. "Them" refers to being a man and being indivisible. *Metaphysics* 13.3.1078a23–28; translation (with modifications) from Julia Annas, *Aristotle's* Metaphysics: *Books M and N* (Oxford: Clarendon Press, 1976).

33. Naets, "How to Define a Number?" 80.

34. *Dialectike ofte Bewysconst* (Leiden: Christoffel Plantijn, 1585); see https://www.dbnl.org/tekst/stev001dial01_01/. At this writing, Marius Buning is preparing a critical edition of the text and a translation into English, which will be the first into any language. See Marius Buning, "The Art of Demonstration in the Work of Simon Stevin: Linguistic and Mathematical Innovation," *Rethinking Stevin, Stevin Rethinking: Constructions of a Dutch Polymath*, ed. Karel Davids, Fokko Jan Dijksterhuis, Rienk Vermij, and Ida Stamhuis (Leiden: Brill, 2020), 123–54.

35. In a note Naets quotes Stevin's *Bewysconst*, 120–21: "De Definitie is een Reden, aenwijsende het wesen der saecken door hare Wesentlickheden; Dese woorden, Door hare Wesentlickheden, legghen sy uyt, Door haer Gheslachte ende Differentie."

36. Naets, "How to Define a Number?" 78. Naets adds a note quoting Stevin's *Bewysconst*, 121: "weynich saecken ja beter gheseyt gheen ter werelt, en souden connen Ghedefiniert worden."

37. Naets, "How to Define a Number?" 78.
38. Naets, "How to Define a Number?" 79.
39. Naets writes:

> Due to Stevin's inclusion of one in the number domain, the numbers lose their natural origin, and so too their original ontological content. . . . Also the unit loses its original integrity as a monad. From now on, its representational value depends wholly on a pregiven continuum, abstracted from the process of measurement. From that point onwards, the new unit finds its equivalence in the metric unit, which resulted from the comparison of two commensurable magnitudes, i.e. their greatest common divisor. Since there are innumerable ways in which we can cut a continuum into equal parts, it was a unit in a totally arbitrary sense. The unit no longer referred to an external realm, instead, it was in every case the product of an arbitrary or discretionary choice to regard one quantity as the unit relative to which other quantities can be measured. The origin of the metric unit, and of any unit in general, was an operation, namely the activity of comparison ("How to Define a Number?" 82).

40. For a connection between Descartes and Ramist sources, see Riccardo Pozzo, "Ramus and Other Renaissance Philosophers on Subjectivity," *Topoi* 22 (2003): 5–13.

41. See *De Wysentyt*, *PW* III 593. The Dutch original and an English translation of this text are printed in *PW* under this title (*The Age of Sages* in English). It is not an independent work, but merely an excerpt from Stevin's *Vant Eertclootschrift* (*Geography* in English), which is one of several works incorporated into his two-volume *Wisconstighe Ghedachtenissen*, published in 1605 and 1608. Most of these texts were translated into French by Jean Tuning and published by Stevin as *Memoires Mathématiques* (Leiden: Jan Paedts Jacobsz, 1608). In 1634, after Stevin's death, Albert Girard published many of these texts along with French versions of other works by Stevin in *Oeuvres Mathématiques* (see note 11). In *GMTOA* Klein relies on Girard's edition, and he cites the French version of the passage quoted above under the title *Geographie* (*GMTOA* 187). I use the title *Geography* for this and other excerpts from the same source published in *PW* under various titles. The complicated relation of these texts is explained by E. J. Dijksterhuis, *Simon Stevin*, 134–39; see also *GMTOA* 285–86n283.

42. The discourse appears in *Elements of the Art of Weighing*; see *PW* I 59.

43. See the concluding sentence of the first book of his *Geography* (*PW* III 623).

44. Francis Bacon, *Advancement of Learning*, ed. G. W. Kitchin (London and Melbourne: J. M. Dent & Sons, 1973), II.vii.1, 90; see also *Novum Organum* II, 9 and 51.

45. *Advancement of Learning* II.viii.3, 101. Just as Bacon uses *magic* according to an ancient rather than a then-contemporary meaning, so he feels free "to retain the ancient terms, though I sometimes alter the uses and definitions;" indeed, "wheresoever my conception and notion may differ from the ancient, yet I am studious to keep the ancient terms" (*Advancement* II.vii.2, 92, 91). Bacon rejects inquiry into substantial forms as "a vain pursuit" (*Advancement* II.vii.5, 95), and he means by the term *form* rather the law of action or motion according to which a simple nature (i.e, an attribute or quality such as color, density, malleability, and so on) comes to be in matter. See the passage in *Advancement* just cited but also *New Organon*, especially I.51 and II.1–5. Accordingly, Bacon's appeal to form is not fundamentally opposed to Stevin's rejection of form.

46. By contrast, Klein shows, for example, how "theoretical logistic arises from practical logistic when its practical applications are neglected" (*GMTOA* 23).

47. See his short supplement to *The Art of Weighing* called *The Pressure of the Bridle* (*PW* I 575–607).

48. See *Metaphysics* 1.2.983a12–21.

49. George Sarton, "Simon Stevin of Bruges (1548–1620)," *Isis* 21, no. 2 (July 1934), 275. See also Dijksterhuis's "General Introduction" to Stevin's life and works: "In the same book (*Art of Weighing*), he proves in a most ingenious and interesting way the law of equilibrium on an inclined plane, basing himself on the conviction of the impossibility of perpetual motion. From this theorem the rule for composition and decomposition of a force acting on a point is deduced" (*PW* I 17).

50. Richard F. Hassing, "Modern Natural Science and the Intelligibility of Human Experience," in *Final Causality in Nature and Human Affairs*, ed. Richard F. Hassing (Washington, D.C.: The Catholic University of America Press, 1993), 221–22.

51. "Since by means of the tongue, lips, teeth, palate, and throat we can utter an almost infinite variety of monosyllabic sounds, it is fit that we should assign to every single thing a monosyllabic sound (for less is impossible, and more is useless), and of such a nature that they are fit for composition, so that we may pleasingly and intelligibly represent by them not only

ordinary things, but also the strange things which Nature creates daily" (*Art of Weighing*, *PW* I 89; italics in original). Dutch is the language "which is capable of describing Nature's properties most thoroughly" (*Art of Weighing*, *PW* I 93).

52. For a much more developed version of the argument in this paragraph, see my "Simon Stevin's *Vita Politica*."

53. See Simon Stevin, *Civic Life*, ed. Annie Romein-Verschoor, in *PW* V 465–581. This provides a facsimile of Stevin's Dutch text with a facing English translation. The text quoted comes from the sixth chapter, *Whether Religion Is Necessary*, 551.

54. In an appendix (unpublished during his lifetime) to his *Vita Politica* Stevin treats Machiavelli and the question of whether the prince should mix virtue with vice or, rather, he should keep virtue pure. See *Simon Stevin: De la vie civile, 1590*, ed. Catherine Secretan and Pim den Boer (Lyon: ENS Éditions, 2005), 72–86.

Two Reflexivities: Scholastic and Cartesian Second Intentions in Klein's *Greek Mathematical Thought and the Origin of Algebra* by Richard F. Hassing

1. The following abbreviations are used throughout: *GMTOA*: Jacob Klein, *Greek Mathematical Thought and the Origin of Algebra*, trans. Eva Brann (Cambridge, MA: M.I.T. Press, 1968). Numbers in parenthesis without an abbreviation refer to this text by the pages and (after a colon, when needed) lines; e.g., (206:5) means *GMTOA*, page 206, line 5; (198:–3) means page 198, third line from the bottom. *GL*-II: Jacob Klein, "Die griechische Logistik und die Entstehung der Algebra, Teil II," *Quellen und Studien zur Geschichte der Mathematik, Astronomie und Physik*, Abteiling B, Band 3, Heft 2 (Berlin: Julius Springer, Berlin: Julius Springer, 1936): 122–235. The German is cited only where there are small but significant differences between it and Brann's English translation, especially concerning the word 'object.' *WPNW*: Jacob Klein, "The World of Physics and the 'Natural' World," in *Lectures and Essays*, ed. Robert B. Williamson and Elliott Zuckerman (Annapolis, MD: St. John's College Press, 1985), 1–34. *MR*: Jacob Klein, "Modern Rationalism," in *Lectures and Essays*, 53–64. *OP*: Jacob Klein, "On Precision," in *Lectures and Essays*, 289–308. *OLSM*: Burt Hopkins, *The Origin of the Logic of Symbolic Mathematics: Edmund Husserl and Jacob Klein* (Bloomington, IN: Indiana University Press, 2011). *RI*: Burt Hopkins, "The Role of 'Intentionality' in Jacob Klein's Account of the Historicity of the Con-

cept of Number," in the present volume. *CM*: Andrew Romiti, *Cartesian Mind and Its Concept of Space: A Contribution to the Project of Jacob Klein*, Ph.D. dissertation, Catholic University, 2016. *ECM*: Joseph Owens, *An Elementary Christian Metaphysics* (Houston, TX: Center for Thomistic Studies, 1985). AT: *Oeuvres de Descartes*, ed. Charles Adam and Paul Tannery, 11 vols. (Paris: Vrin, 1996). Citations are to AT, volume and page number, and where full precision is required, a colon and line number; e.g., AT X 435:22. CSM: *The Philosophical Writings of Descartes*, trans. John Cottingham, Robert Stoothoff, and Dugald Murdoch, 2 vols. (Cambridge: Cambridge University Press, 1985).

2. Comment made at the 2nd Jacob Klein Conference, St. John's College, Annapolis, June 5, 2013. It refers to Klein, *GMTOA* 208, as discussed in Section V of this paper.

3. When we calculate, we combine two mathematical objects to make a third, e.g., by addition or multiplication: $2 + 3 = 5$, $2 \times 3 = 6$. We then generalize from the simple binary operations of the arithmetic of whole numbers to abstract rules ("axioms"), e.g., both addition and multiplication are *commutative*, $a + b = b + a$, $a \times b = b \times a$, multiplication is *distributive* over addition, $a \times (b + c) = a \times b + a \times c$, but addition is not distributive over multiplication, $a + (b \times c) \neq (a + b) \times (a + c)$. All objects of syntactically based axiomatic mathematics must be quantities, or qualities with quantitative aspects (like rotations around certain axes), not substances, in the sense that any two members of the relevant set are either equal or unequal, unlike substances. *The equation* is thus the basic object on which we work in mathematics and any science based on mathematics, e.g., physics. Algebraic letter signs in equations are analogous to syllables and words in sentences. By "the elevation of syntax" in equations (a phrase I owe to Robert Sokolowski) new operations and objects are created, e.g., imaginary numbers, whose squares are negative, and matrices, whose products in general do not commute. (Can we do the same thing with sentences and thereby make new realities?)

4. Significant texts, discussed in the following, also appear in Chapter 11 on Viète (174–75), and in Chapter 12A on Stevin (192).

5. See, on this score, *OLSM* 312–13, also *RI* (final paragraph of the Introduction): "[Klein] employs the scholastic distinction between first and second intentions in a non-scholastic way, in order to capture what he maintains is distinctive about the mathematical symbol's specific mode of being."

6. See Aristotle, *De Anima* 3.8, 431b20–432a4.

7. How to translate Klein's key term *symbolische Abstraktion*? Brann uses "symbol-generating abstraction" to avoid the implication that the abstrac-

tion by pure intellect is itself symbolic ("Preface" to *OLSM* xxvii, n. 3). Hopkins finds "symbolic abstraction" still appropriate; see *OLSM* 306–7n165. I use the latter; there are arguments pro and con for both translations.

8. *Veram partem corporis* (AT X 414:20); *nihil aliud . . . quam verum corpus reale extensum et figuratum* (AT X 441:12–13); see also Descartes's *Optics*, Discourse 5 and 6. See note 13 for the problem with Descartes's insistence that the imagination is purely corporeal, part of the body-machine.

9. *Se applicat, applicet se* (AT X 415:18 and 28); see also Descartes's Fifth Replies, AT VII 387:13.

10. *Entia abstracta separandi* (AT X 444:23).

11. AT X 445:25

12. See also "indeterminate manyness" (201; "*bloße*" (*unbestimmte*) *Vielheit*—*GL*-II 211); "multiplicity in general," "'naked' multiplicity" (202; *Vielheit überhaupt*, "*bloße*" *Vielheit*—*GL*-II 211); "'mere manyness'," "multitudinousness as such" (207; *bloße Vielheit, Mengenhaftigkeit als solche*—*GL*-II 221).

13. Klein refers (more clearly in the German) to Descartes's imagination in its intellect-active function as the "power of imagination" or "imaginative power" (201, 202; *Einbildungskraft, imaginative Kraft*, also *Einbildungsvermögen, Vorstellungsvermögen*—*GL*-II 209, 210, 211). In Rules 12–14, Descartes consistently uses *imaginatio* or *phantasia*; *vis* [power] is reserved exclusively to the intellect (*vis cognoscens*—AT X 415:23). We do have "*vis . . . imaginandi*" at *Meditation* 2, AT VII 29:9–10, which seems to be a faculty of the *vis cognoscens* while the existence of all body is doubted. (Or is it? See Sixth Replies, AT VII 435:18–22, referring to the model of vision in *Optics*, Discourse 5 and 6, as tacitly presupposed for the argument of *Meditation* 2.) See Hopkins, *OLSM* 302–6 and 510n163, in support of Klein's usage. Salient for Klein's attribution of an imaginative *power* is simply that a true Cartesian body part (shaped, mobile extension) cannot have a power. Therefore, to the extent that Descartes's own account of intellect and imagination in Rule 14 in fact requires an imaginative power separate from the intellectual power (and I give Klein and Hopkins the benefit of the doubt), it reminds of Aristotle on powers of the soul, some of which (not imagination) are exercised through corresponding bodily organs (see, e.g., *De Anima* 2.1, 412a10), which organs thus cannot be mere Cartesian (inert) body parts. In other words, isn't Descartes putting a power in a power-less body part? The point is that, despite the value of Descartes's attempt to account for symbolic abstraction ("perhaps novel in the history of science"; 200), his model of pure intellect and corporeal imagination is not fully coherent. But this is hardly news: "How this mediation [by the imagination between the mind and the world] is to be understood

is, as is well known, *the* insoluble problem of Cartesian doctrine" (203). See *OLSM* §207, for a phenomenological account independent of psychophysics.

14. I thank Blaise Blain for this metaphor. Calculating with symbols is the analogy to feeding and petting. Accordingly, the disanalogy is that we don't need a *set* of animals for feeding and petting (one will do) whereas there must be a set of symbols, equal and unequal, and at least one binary operation by which to combine two elements of the set into a third. See note 3, above.

15. Symbols are imaginable (we see them on the paper in front of us) but they are not *images* of intelligible ideal originals or *signs* pointing to a number of pure intelligible units (such as Moγ, three units, in Diophantine notation) as were the numbers and diagrams of premodern mathematics. An algebraic symbol, unlike an image or sign, does not acquire its meaning from what it points to or images; rather (description 1, above), it acquires its meaning only within the symbol set as a whole with its rules of calculation. A symbol in physics has, in addition, a physical dimension (e.g., mass, length, area, volume, time, charge) and is thus related to a procedure of measurement whereby we can assign a number of kilograms to mass m, kilometers to distance x, seconds to time t, etc.

16. Is this the notorious Cartesian metaphysical (two-substance) dualism of *Discourse* 4 and *Meditation* 6? Romiti, *CM* 53–57, argues that Cartesian mind-world separation consists in a metaphysically neutral operational or functional dualism (in doing so, he follows Pamela Kraus, "*Mens Humana: Res Cogitans* and the Doctrine of Faculties in Descartes' *Meditations*," *International Studies in Philosophy* 18 [1986]: 4–13). More generally, the relation of mind and world in Descartes's science is a central theme of *CM*. Suffice to say that Descartes's conceiving of mind and world as separate in the *Rules* is not a scientific or philosophic discovery; it is a deliberate, willful decision, like his radical doubt. The intellectual simple natures of the *Rules* include cognition *and volition* (see Rules 6, 8 and 12; AT X 383, 399, 419). The thinking thing is also the willing thing.

17. The bracketed [not originally but] is Klein's. A question for Eustachius: If privation, for example, appertains to something in its own mode before any operations of the intellect, then why is a privation a being of reason? Perhaps in this sense: Consider the privation of sight in a cat. By nature (for the most part—see Aristotle's *Physics*, 196b11) cats have the power of vision, which is thus not a being of reason. There is no power of blindness. But blindness "appertains" to cats in that sight does belong to their feline mode of being. Privation is the lack of something in a being that, in its own mode, has the potency for it.

18. First intention is mentioned by Klein but only after second intention, and in connection with symbol, the goal of the account on page 208 of *GMTOA*: The letter sign is a sensible particular: we calculate with it, and thus deal with it as a "first intention" (*GL*-II 222). The word for "object" (208:23), *Gegenstand*, does not appear in the German.

19. Klein follows this order in *MR* (60–63) but he does not there discuss reflexivity.

20. See Aristotle, *Metaphysics* 7.13, 1039a4–6: one substance cannot be composed of many substances.

21. See, especially, Sixth Replies, point 9, AT VII 436–37 (CSM II 294–95), as well as Rule 8, "very much foreign"—AT X 398:13 (CSM I 31), Rule 12, AT X 412–17 (CSM I 40–43), *The World*, AT XI 3–15 (CSM I 81–85), *Principles of Philosophy* 2.23, AT VIIIA 52–53 (CSM I 232–33), *Passions of the Soul*, article 13, AT XI 338 (CSM I 333). From his early writings (*Rules* and *World*) to his late (*Principles* and *Passions*), Descartes rejects any notion of the irreducible wholeness of an organic being (e.g., a cat) in favor of universal corpuscular reductionism: the cat and the fire is a cloud of corpuscles (of three kinds) colliding in the plenum under the (hypothetical) three laws of nature. The mind can know figure, extension, motion because the corporeal imagination is extended, shaped, mobile.

22. See also 122 and 213.

23. More needs to be said. Didn't the ancient materialists (e.g., the atomists, Democritus and Lucretius) propose pre-symbolic-algebraic models? Yes, for example, the generation of a new offspring is, despite appearances, just a rearrangement in the void of swirling Democritean atoms. But the materialists did not have mathematical laws that enabled prediction and control of certain phenomena and thereby inspired belief in a comprehensive worldview entailing unlimited mastery of nature. See *GMTOA* 175 and 185; *WPNW* 30–34; *OP* 305 ("matching," as discussed in note 39 below).

24. See Aristotle, *Physics* 2.1–2.

25. Robert Sokolowski, in a private conversation, noted that the term *intention* here blurs the distinction between the intend*ing* activity and the target intend*ed*, and is a potential source of confusion. Where needed in the following, I try to state which is meant, the intend*ing* or the intend*ed*.

26. A precision: for Aristotle, a nature in the sense of *Physics* 2.1 belongs to the species of the informed substance, e.g., man, not to the genus, animal (see also *Metaphysics* 7.4, 1030a12–13). In the Thomistic account, animal as belonging to a man is called a "common nature" (see Owens, *ECM* 239n13).

27. More than one unit is needed for an *arithmos*, the first of which is accordingly two. The question of the unity of an *arithmos* is disputed

between Plato and Aristotle (see *GMTOA* 105–7), but any putative unity of an *arithmos* would presumably also be first-intentional, irreducible to but also inseparable from the determinate amount of units.

28. Aristotle, *De Anima* 3.8, 431b20–432a2. I believe this remains the case despite the reification of concepts characteristic of late (sixteenth and seventeenth century) scholasticism, about which Descartes complains in Rule 14, paragraphs 9–12 (AT X 443–45; CSM I 59–61). In *WPNW*, Klein says that the conceptuality (*Begrifflichkeit*) of the late scholastics was the same as that of the founders of the new science (6). However true this may be, the scholastic account of second intention and reflexivity in Eustachius (*GMTOA* 207) is not the same as what Klein finds (by adapting Eustachius) in Descartes (*GMTOA* 208), namely, *cogito*-like reflexivity, as discussed in Part V.

29. "[For the ancients,] though there is a clear distinction between mind and world, there is no separation between them, but rather mind is very emphatically the receiving of the world and nothing but that. . . . This is not just another philosophical theory but the very premise of their whole thought" (*MR* 58).

30. On Descartes's *cogito* ("I think therefore I am"; *locus classicus Disc.* 4, AT VI 32) as well as the distinctive *cogito*-like reflexivity, see the following from *Meditation* 2: "At last I have discovered it—thought; this alone is inseparable from me. I am, I exist. . . . [f]or as long as I am thinking. . . . I am, then, in the precise sense only a thing that thinks. . . . which is real and which truly exists" (AT VII 27; CSM II 18). "And here is the point, the perception I have of it [the wax] <or rather the act whereby it is perceived> is a case not of vision or touch or imagination—but of purely mental scrutiny. . . . the scrutiny of the mind alone" (AT VII 31–32, AT IXA 24; CSM II 21, and note 2 for the French).

31. The term *object* here can be either scholastic (it's in the intellect) or Cartesian (it's the target of the intellect's intending).

32. In the realist account, the unity of things as known (the unity of intentional beings) originates from, and remains rooted in, the unity of substances. "In general, those things are one in the highest degree if the thinking of their essence is indivisible . . . and of these the substances above all." Aristotle, *Metaphysics*, 1016b1–4. See also *Physics*, 192b33–35 and *Metaphysics*, 1052a30–34.

33. Aristotle, *De Anima* 3.8, 431b20–432a3, also *Nic. Ethics* 6.1, 1139a9–11. The concept here seems to be *of* the conceiving of a many without regard to how many. Any many can be combined (by +, −, ×, ⁄) with any other many to make a third many, given appropriate consideration to units and dimensions.

34. Aristotle, *Categories*, 4b26–33 & 5a1–5; *Physics* 5.3, 227a21–22 & 6.1; *Metaphysics* 5.13, 1020a7 & 12.10, 1075b28–30. Note that ratio—crucial for the development of modern mathematics—is not included in the category of the quantified but in that of relation (*pros ti*). Note also that the seven per se quantities (number, line, surface, solid, speech, time, place) are sorted by Aristotle according to three different divisions: discrete vs. continuous, having vs. not having relative position in the parts, having vs. not having permanence in the parts. In view of these additional divisions (beyond discrete and continuous), it is in fact unlikely that the category of quantity possesses the unity of a genus; it is too cut up and lacks ratio.

35. See Stevin's syllogism, *GMTOA* 191–92: "[Stevin] understands [*numerus* as 'a multitude . . . of units'] . . . as the 'material' of the thing to be defined, in the same sense in which one speaks of the material . . . of water or bread."

36. The problem, divide a square into two equal squares, would have a solution in magnitudes but not in numbers; due to incommensurability, there would be no univocal mathematical object, *x*, such that *x*2 = 2.

37. On Viète's "Cartesian" self-reflexivity, see *OLSM* 521. According to Klein, the general theory of proportions meets "half-way" "Vieta's conception of a . . . '*general*' algebra which will be equally applicable to geometric magnitudes and numbers" (158). For example, proportions can be alternated for numbers, magnitudes, and times: if $a : b :: c : d$, then $a : c :: b : d$, in general. Proclus comments that "a certain common nature" of numbers, magnitudes, and times permits this (*GMTOA* 160). But, as Klein says, the Euclidean general theory of proportions only got halfway to a general object: proportions involving heterogeneous magnitudes or involving magnitudes and numbers cannot be alternated. In Greek mathematics, operations remain limited by objects. In contrast, in the species logistic of Viète's analytic art (see his *Introduction to the Analytic Art*, Chapter II, stipulations 14 and 15—*GMTOA* 323–34), proportions involving heterogeneous magnitudes can be resolved into equations with quotients and products of heterogeneous magnitudes, e.g., a magnitude with dimension cm3 (volume) can be divided by a magnitude with dimension cm2 (area) to yield a magnitude of dimension cm (length), in accordance with Viète's calculational axioms ("Precepts") and "law of homogeneity" (see *GMTOA* 324–38). Vietan magnitudes are thus numerical and dimensional, like quantities in physics. I submit that Euclidean magnitudes are non-numerical and dimensional (lines, not lengths; surfaces, not areas; solids, not volumes); Cartesian magnitudes are numerical and dimensionless, but can take any dimensions needed for problem-solving application. Prior to Viète, generality of method in the theory of propor-

tions did not imply generality of object: "on this above all Aristotle, *Posterior Analytics* A 24, 85a31–b3" (*GMTOA* 124).

38. Could we calculate with the genealogical tree or the triangle and square in Rule XIV (AT X 450–451, CSM I 64)?

"As 'arithmetician' Stevin no longer deals with numbers of units which are determinate in each case but with the *unlimited possibility of combining ciphers* according to definite rules of calculation'" (193). "[Stevin] thus once and for all fixes the ordinary understanding of the nature of number, for which being able 'to count' is tantamount to knowing how to handle 'ciphers'" (197).

39. On the final sentence of this quotation, see Klein, *OP* 304–6: equations and the models built on them make possible the "matching" of calculated numerical predictions and experimentally measured numerical results; it's as if modern number—ultimately the length of the digit string on which theory matches experiment—replaces *logos* for the understanding of the world. As Heidegger says, "[P]hysics . . . will never be able to renounce this one thing: that nature reports itself in some way or other that is identifiable through calculation and that it remains orderable as a system of information [e.g., 0's and 1's]" (*The Question concerning Technology*, trans. William Lovitt [New York: Harper and Row, 1977], 23). For the link between the calculability of symbols and their first-intentional status see the paragraphs immediately following.

40. See *CM* 118–33.

41. Eva Brann, "Immediacy: The Ways of Humanity," *The Imaginative Conservative*, November 1, 2014 (originally given as a lecture, St. John's College, Santa Fe, October 2014).

The Symbolic Space of Descartes's *Geometry* and Its Symbolic Mathematical Underpinnings by Andrew Romiti

1. Jacob Klein, "The World of Physics and the 'Natural' World," in *Lectures and Essays*, ed. Robert B. Williamson and Elliott Zuckerman (Annapolis: St. John's College Press, 1985), 3.

2. Jacob Klein, *Greek Mathematical Thought and the Origin of Algebra*, trans. Eva Brann (Cambridge: M.I.T. Press, 1968; reprint, New York: Dover Publications, 1992), 210–11.

3. Klein, "World of Physics," 21.

4. This conflation in Descartes's concept of extension mirrors part of the conceptual structure of the symbolic concept of number, which according

to Klein entails the conflation of the individual and determinate multitudinousness of a number with the general and indeterminate property of being a multitude—a general property he refers to as "multitudinousness as such" (*Greek Mathematical Thought*, 207).

5. It is perhaps surprising that Klein claims the modern understanding of "Euclidean space" is actually this symbolically conceived domain of extension which is only mistakenly read back onto ancient geometry. To unpack this claim, let alone argue for it, is beyond the scope of the present investigation, as a careful study of Euclid's *Elements* would be necessary to address the issue. David Lachterman has provided some starting-points for such a project in his book *The Ethics of Geometry*, which contains an analysis of the difference between Euclid and Descartes's geometry that is largely an extension of Klein's analysis of the difference between the ancient and modern concepts of number. Lachterman cautions that "[t]he locale of Greek geometry may be foreign to the modern conceptions of extension and space," and later points out that "there is no term corresponding to or translatable as 'space' in [the] generalized sense anywhere to be found in Euclid's *Elements*" (*The Ethics of Geometry: A Genealogy of Modern Thought* [New York: Routledge, 1989], 28 & 80). These comments serve as a warning that in seeking Descartes's concept of space in the *Geometry*, we cannot assume there is some univocal understanding of space that governs all geometrical works; instead, we must examine the concept of space as it emerges from the proceedings of this particular work itself. Given Klein's establishment of the non-symbolic character of ancient mathematics, however, we can conclude that the establishment of the symbolic character of Cartesian space in the present essay entails that this space cannot be the domain of Euclid's geometry.

6. While Klein points to Newton in both of the quotations above, he makes no effort to explain the relationship between the Cartesian and Newtonian concepts of space, leaving his suggestion of a connection between the two in need of investigation.

7. Klein does discuss "analytical geometry" under the names of Descartes and Fermat, but he does not employ an example drawn from the mathematical procedure of the *Geometry* itself, and he continually uses circumlocutions that are careful to avoid attributing mathematical methods to Descartes that are not his own ("World of Physics," 12–19). In conjunction with this, it should be noted in particular that the Cartesian coordinate grid is not found in Descartes's *Geometry* but is rather a later development of his mathematics. (Descartes's "principal lines," which are central to the pres-

ent analysis, are the precursor to the coordinate axes, as will be highlighted below.) Accordingly, I take Klein's reference to a "coordinate system" in the quotation above as part of the evidence that his comments about the modern concept of space are meant generally, while he is only pointing to the roots of that concept in the thought of Descartes.

8. In this way, the present study is limited to examining the symbolic-mathematical aspect of the modern concept of space established in the *Geometry*, without taking up its connection to the physical world. One must distinguish the mathematical and physical concepts of space even in the thought of Descartes. While his concept of extension connects the two realms, it is only a particular and well-defined subset of extended bodies that is permitted into the domain of Descartes's geometry (as discussed in detail below); in other words, all body is extension for Descartes but not all extended body is mathematical. Accordingly, his mathematical space is also confined to a particular subset of the extension that makes up the entire physical world on his account. To completely unpack Klein's suggestions about the Cartesian roots of the modern concept of space requires connecting Descartes's mathematical and physical concepts of space, which would entail following up on the delineation of the mathematical concept of space contained in the present analysis by investigating Descartes's physical concept of space in other works (most notably his *Principles of Philosophy* and *The World*). In my own attempt to do that I found that while the two concepts of space cannot be simply equated, their conceptual structures allow for them to be brought together such that a physical space can be turned into and treated as a symbolic mathematical one, thereby making the mathematical and physical domains convertible but not identical (*Cartesian Mind and Its Concept of Space: A Contribution to the Project of Jacob Klein*, Ph.D. dissertation [The Catholic University of America, 2016], Ch. 4). I take it that part of the reason Klein points to later developments in his comments on the modern concept of space is that it is only in the later employment of what is set up as a possibility by Descartes that this concept reaches its mature form. Thus, as I understand it, Descartes's contribution to the development of the symbolic concept of space is confined to the fact that he laid the conceptual groundwork of that concept. To fully trace the genealogy of this concept, then, one would not only need to connect Descartes's mathematical and physical understandings of space but also trace the later development and employment of the form of the concept that combines the two.

9. Parenthetical citations refer to page numbers in Volume VI of the standard Adam-Tannery edition of the complete works of Descartes: *Oeuvres*

de Descartes, 11 vols., ed. Charles Adam and Paul Tannery, 2nd ed. (Paris: Vrin, 1964–76). All translations are my own, made in consultation with the following published translations: *Discourse on Method, Optics, Geometry, and Meteorology*, trans. Paul J. Olscamp, rev. ed. (Indianapolis: Hackett Publishing Company, 2001); *The Geometry of René Descartes with a facsimile of the first edition*, trans. David Eugene Smith and Marcia L. Latham (Mineola, N.Y.: Dover Publications, Inc, 1954).

10. Note that this is a non-Euclidean understanding of multiplication, as Euclid's definition of multiplication only covers the multiplication of two numbers (*Elements* VII, Definition 15). Definitions 4 and 5 of Book V imply an understanding of multiplying a line by a number, but this only confirms the necessity of the multiplier itself being a number. Thus the multiplication of one line by another is meaningless on Euclidean grounds.

11. Henry Higuera, in a helpful lecture on various historical understandings of multiplication, points out that Descartes has here redefined the unit "as the '*multiplicative identity* "1,"' such that for all *a*, 1 · *a* = *a*" ("Multiplication, Ancient and Modern: Sorting Out the Shifts in Meaning" [lecture, St. John's College, Annapolis, April 17 2009—available in the St. John's College Library and Bookstore], 8).

12. While the particular example at hand is fleshed out further in the following paragraph, for Klein's full analysis of the nature of algebraic symbols and the abstraction that underlies them see *Greek Mathematical Thought*, Chapters 11 and 12, especially pages 174–76 and 198–208.

13. As Klein says, "Descartes does not, as is often thoughtlessly said, identify 'arithmetic' and 'geometry'—rather he identifies 'algebra' understood as symbolic logistic with geometry *interpreted by him for the first time as symbolic science*" (*Greek Mathematical Thought*, 206).

14. Or, in more properly Euclidean language, the square on LM is equal to the rectangle with sides OM and PM (see Euclid *Elements* Book III, Proposition 36). Note that Descartes here implicitly takes the multiplication of two lines to make a rectangle as equivalent to multiplying them algebraically.

15. Here we have an indication that these principal lines are the original version of coordinate axes, although we can also see that they differ from the later form commonly known today. For one, it is clear here that the two axes need not be at right angles to each other, but more importantly they are a part of the given diagram itself rather than a separate frame of reference into which the mathematical object is placed.

16. This is the case because there will be at most three lines being multiplied together on one side of the equation, but *x* is not used in the expres-

sion of one of the lines (namely, the first, which is simply *y*), so that there will only ever be two *x*'s entering into one multiplication.

17. An example of such a curve mentioned by Descartes is the quadratrix, whose construction depends upon a combination of straight and curvilinear motion, which makes it unknowable—and thus not geometrical— to Descartes because he believes that "the proportion that exists between straight and curved lines is not known." He continues: "and I even believe that it is not able to be known by men, such that one can conclude nothing about this that is exact and assured" (412).

18. The account of this connection occupies Descartes throughout the *Geometry* and we cannot consider the arguments for it here. For a good discussion of the relationship between the different aspects of Descartes's criterion of admissibility, see Henk J. M. Bos, *Redefining Geometrical Exactness: Descartes' Transformation of the Early Modern Concept of Construction* (New York: Springer, 2001), Ch. 24 (for a concise presentation, see Table 24.1 on page 337).

19. As highlighted earlier, Descartes's principal lines are always a part of the diagram under consideration; they are never posited as a frame of reference separate from the rest of the figure, within which that figure exists. In other words, Descartes never begins with coordinate axes and then places objects into the frame of reference marked out by those axes, as is done with the coordinate grid in later developments of Cartesian geometry. While the symbolic representation of space may be seen more clearly in these separated coordinate axes, the foregoing analysis is meant to show that this symbolic representation is already present in Descartes's use of the principal lines.

20. Klein, "World of Physics," 21.

Klein and Einstein on Cartesian Space by Joseph Cosgrove

1. Jacob Klein, *Greek Mathematical Thought and the Origin of Algebra*, trans. Eva Brann (Cambridge, MA: MIT Press, 1968; reprint: New York: Dover, 1992), 3. Subsequent citations to this text are given hereafter as "*GMTOA*" followed by the page number of the Brann translation.

2. Hereafter, "The Problem of Space, Ether, and the Field in Physics" will be identified as *PS*, and "Physics and Reality" will be designated as *PR*. Both essays appear in *Ideas and Opinions: Albert Einstein*, trans. Sonja Bargmann (New York: Crown Publishers, 1954, 1982), 276–85 (*PS*) and 290–323 (*PR*).

3. Klein's own focus in *Greek Mathematical Thought* is not the origin of concepts in direct experience or immediate "intuition" per se, something

that more defines Husserl's orientation than Klein's, but rather the way concepts intend or are related to their objects. Indeed, in his discussion of the difference between the Greek and modern modes of concept formation, Klein specifically rejects framing the issue in terms of the supposedly "intuitive" character of Greek concepts:

> However, one fundamental objection is to be raised immediately against stressing the 'intuitive' character of the *arithmos* concept, namely that it arises from a point of view whose criteria are taken not from Greek, but from modern, symbolic mathematics. . . . Greek scientific arithmetic and logistic are founded on a 'natural' attitude to everything countable as we meet it in daily life. This closeness to its natural basis is *never* betrayed in ancient science. It follows that, strictly speaking, it is not possible to call *arithmoi* 'numbers'. The peculiarity of the Greek concept of 'number' lies therefore less in an 'archaic' or 'intuitive' character (which is not at all its primary property) than in the *kind of relation* it has to the 'thing' it intends (*GMTOA* 63).

4. *Rules for the Direction of the Mind*, in *The Philosophical Writings of Descartes*, vol. 1, trans. John Cottingham, Robert Stoothoff, and Dugald Murdoch (Cambridge: Cambridge University Press, 1985), 60. Subsequent citations to this text are given hereafter as "*Rules*" followed by the page number of the Cottingham (et al.) translation.

5. On the English translation of Klein's *symbolische Abstraktion* as "symbol-generating abstraction" see Burt C. Hopkins, *The Origin of the Logic of Symbolic Mathematics* (Bloomington and Indianapolis: Indiana University Press, 2011), 306–7n165.

6. See the perceptive remarks of John A. Schuster:

> The imagination and the patterns in it are corporeal entities bearing the same ontological certification as the mechanical deliverances of sensation registered in the common sense. Then, the argument moves forward in two well-planned stages. First [Descartes] says that any particular sort of magnitude may be chosen to depict in the imagination the conditions of the problem previously construed in terms of magnitude in general. His point is that any sort of magnitude depicted in the imagination will be ontologically certified as corporeally present, and, in addition, it will be susceptible to the same sort of manipulations as would have applied to the original quantity from which magnitude in general was abstracted. Next, a

criterion of intuitive simplicity specifies the sort of magnitude to be used—'figures'. But simplicity is not merely a heuristic condition. The point about clear and simple intuition is, as always, that it is self-verifying. The aim of representing magnitude in general by figures is to lend ontological grounding to the objects, and logical certainty to the manipulations, which in this case are immediate acts of comparison. ("Descartes' *Mathesis Universalis* 1619–28," in *Descartes: Philosophy, Mathematics and Physics*, ed. Stephen Gaukroger [Sussex: The Harvester Press, 1980], 64–65.)

7. On Klein's interpretation of Cartesian "symbolic abstraction" in terms of the logic of first and second intentions in the contemporary scholastic literature, see *GMTOA* 206–8.

8. "Thirdly, the 'common' sense functions like a seal, fashioning in the phantasy or imagination, as if in wax, the same figures or ideas which come, pure and without body, from the external senses. The phantasy is a genuine part of the body . . ." (*Rules* 41–42).

9. As already emphasized above, Klein notes that Descartes's ever-increasing concern over method is primarily motivated by the need to justify the identification thesis (*GMTOA* 294n310). The same concern likewise determines Descartes's metaphysics, in which, Klein observes, the "actual points of departure of his 'system' came to be increasingly assigned to oblivion" (*GMTOA* 294n308). From this point of view, Descartes's justification of the identification thesis in terms of the imagination's mediation between real and symbolic extension is less important for the subsequent history of mathematical physics than the way the identification thesis is operationalized, so to speak, in Descartes's *Geometry*.

10. In Jacob Klein, *Lectures and Essays*, ed. Robert W. Williamson and Elliott Zuckerman (Annapolis, MD: St. John's College Press, 1985), 1–34. Citations to this text are given hereafter as "*WPNW*".

11. Descartes's *Geometry* does not itself employ "Cartesian coordinates" in the sense we use the term today (i.e., perpendicular axes detached from the figure). Nevertheless, Descartes's use of reference lines in the *Geometry* to coordinatize points in terms of algebraic variables is equivalent for our (and for Klein's) purposes. Klein has updated his example in terms more familiar to us. Nor does Klein actually use the term "graph," but his observation that, instead of "imaging" the geometrical object under study, Descartes's curve expresses generalized algebraic relations amounts to calling the figure the graph of an equation. The ellipse of Apollonius is a plane fig-

ure, whereas a Cartesian ellipse is a locus of coordinatized points (a symbolic curved line).

12. In Rule 14, Descartes defines a "dimension" as a "mode or aspect in respect of which some [extended] subject is considered to be measurable," and lists, in addition to "length, breadth, and depth," also weight and speed (*Rules* 62)

13. Hopkins, *Logic of Symbolic Mathematics*, 313n173.

14. I addressed briefly Einstein's reflections on Cartesian space in *Relativity without Spacetime* (Palgrave Macmillan, 2018), 94–96.

15. With his reference, in the last sentence of the quotation, to a "definite state of motion, which yet did not appear to be fully determined by the phenomena of mechanics," Einstein is evidently adverting to the fact that absolute rest cannot be identified empirically in Newtonian mechanics, but only rest relative to an inertial reference body, which may itself still be in motion relative to space. Today most philosophers of science regard Newtonian absolute space as inessential to Newtonian absolute acceleration, since absolute acceleration can be defined relative to inertial frames of reference without a concept of absolute rest. Such a space (and time) is often called "neo-Newtonian." Einstein's general point remains unaffected, though, since what is required for Newtonian physics is an absolute background space and time relative to which inertia and acceleration can be determined absolutely.

16. Descartes, *Principles of Philosophy*, in *Philosophical Writings of Descartes*, vol. 1, 240. Descartes's law of inertia differs from Newton's in that (1) Cartesian inertia does not exert resistance and (2) inertia of speed and inertia of direction are treated independently (that is, in our terms, Cartesian inertial motion does not carry momentum). But this difference is irrelevant for present purposes. Descartes's concept of inertia first appears in writing in the suppressed treatise *The World*, Chapter 7, written 1629–1633.

17. Descartes's "relativistic" definition of motion as change of position with respect to contiguous bodies (*Principles*, Part Two, #25), which allows him to deny that his Copernicanism entails the motion of the earth, can be disregarded here.

18. This is not strictly true, since the general group of coordinate transformations is larger than those associated with the arbitrary motion of coordinate systems. Although Einstein realized this, he generally did not distinguish between coordinate systems (the assignment of coordinate labels to points or "events") and reference frames (physical systems in definite states of motion relative to which measurements are carried out). For

the less mathematically adept reader, a coordinate transformation reassigns the numerical coordinates of points according to a definite law expressible in a transformation equation. A simple case, for example, is a transformation from a coordinate system using English units to the metric system. Einstein was particularly interested in coordinate transformations effected through the motion of a reference body.

19. There exists an enormous body of literature on the hole argument and its implications. Two basic accounts are John Norton, "Einstein, the Hole Argument and the Reality of Space," in *Measurement, Realism and Objectivity*, ed. J. Forge (Dordrecht: D. Reidel, 1987), 153–88, and John Stachel, "Einstein's Search for General Covariance, 1912–1915," in *Einstein and the History of General Relativity*, ed. Don Howard and John Stachel (Boston: Birkhäuser, 1989), 63–100.

20. In technical terms, we speak of the "diffeomorphism invariance" of the gravitational field equation. The mathematics is beyond the scope of the present essay.

21. The reader familiar with the polemics between Leibniz and Newton's defender Samuel Clarke will be reminded of the former's argument to the effect that nothing would be altered in a physical sense if we moved two bodies in a given relative configuration to some other location in Newtonian absolute space.

22. Einstein to Michele Besso, January 3, 1916, in *The Collected Papers of Albert Einstein*, vol. 8, *The Berlin Years 1914–1918* (English Translation Supplement), trans. Ann M. Hentschel (Princeton: Princeton University Press, 1998), 172 (document no. 178). Einstein here employs the unconventional symbolism $G(x)$ and $G'(x)$ for our $g_{\mu\nu}(x_i)$ and $g'_{\mu\nu}(x_i)$ respectively. The physical equivalence of the two solutions today is often called "diffeomorphism equivalence" or, in the philosophical literature, "Leibniz equivalence" after an influential paper against the doctrine of spacetime substantivalism by John Earman and John Norton, "What price spacetime substantivalism: the hole story," *British Journal for the Philosophy of Science* 38 (1987): 515–25.

23. In his theory of gravity, Einstein no longer conceives a "coordinate system" as a rigid physical frame subject to particular states of motion, but as the purely mathematical assignment of unique numerical coordinates to points of space and time.

24. *Relativity: The Special and General Theory*, trans. Robert W. Lawson (New York: Random House, 1961), 176.

Published Writings of Jacob Klein

"Das Problem der Wahrheit." *Philosophische Blätter der Kant-Gesellschaft* (Landesgruppe Westdeutsches Industriegebiet) no. 6 (1924): 3–8.

"Die griechische Logistik und die Entstehung der Algebra, Teil I." *Quellen und Studien zur Geschichte der Mathematik, Astronomie und Physik*, Abteilung B, 3, no. 1 (Berlin, 1934): 18–105.

"Die griechische Logistik und die Enstehung der Algebra, Teil II." *Quellen und Studien zur Geschichte der Mathematik, Astronomie und Physik*, Abteilung B, 3, no. 2 (Berlin, 1936): 122–235.

Review (in French) of Erwin Straus, *Vom Sinn der Sinne: Ein Beitrag zur Grundlegung der Psychologie* (Berlin: Julius Springer, 1935). *Recherches philosophiques* V (1935–1936): 431–33.

"Phenomenology and the History of Science." In *Philosophical Essays in Memory of Edmund Husserl*, edited by Marvin Farber, 143–63. Cambridge, MA: Harvard University Press, 1940. Reprinted in *Lectures and Essays*, 65–84.

"The Idea of Liberal Education." In *The Goals of Higher Education*, edited by Willis D. Weatherford, Jr., 26–41. Cambridge, MA: Harvard University Press, 1960. Reprinted in *Lectures and Essays*, 157–70.

"Aristotle, an Introduction." In *Ancients and Moderns: Essays on the Tradition of Political Philosophy in Honor of Leo Strauss*, edited by Joseph Cropsey, 50–69. New York: Basic Books, 1964. Reprinted in *Lectures and Essays*, 171–95.

A Commentary on Plato's "Meno." Chapel Hill, NC: University of North Carolina Press, 1965. Reprint, Chicago and London: University of Chicago Press, 1989.

"On Dante's Mount of Purgation." *Cesare Barbieri Courier* VII, no. 2 (Spring 1965): 24–33. Reprinted in *Lectures and Essays*, 241–60.

"On Liberal Education." *Bulletin of the Association of American Colleges* 52, no. 2 (1966): 133–43. Reprinted in *Lectures and Essays*, 261–268.

"A Note on Plato's *Parmenides*." In *Orbis Scriptus: Dimitrij Tschizewskij zum 70. Geburtstag*, edited by Dietrich Gerhardt, Wiktor Weintraub, and

Hans-Jürgen zum Winkel, 431–32. Munich: Wilhelm Fink, 1966. Reprinted in *Lectures and Essays*, 285–87.

Greek Mathematical Thought and the Origin of Algebra. Translated by Eva Brann. Cambridge, MA: MIT Press, 1968. Reprint, New York: Dover, 1992.

"The Problem of Freedom." *The College* XXI, no. 4 (December 1969): 4–8. Reprinted in *Lectures and Essays*, 117–26.

"A Giving of Accounts." With Leo Strauss. *The College* XXII, no. 1 (April 1970): 1–5. Reprinted in *Jewish Philosophy and the Crisis of Modernity*, edited by Kenneth Hart Green, 457–65. Albany: State University of New York Press, 1997.

"The Myth of Virgil's *Aeneid*." *Interpretation: A Journal of Political Philosophy* 2, no. 1 (Summer 1971): 10–20. Reprinted in *Lectures and Essays*, 269–84.

"On Precision." *The College* XXIII, no. 3 (October 1971): 1–8. Reprinted in *Lectures and Essays*, 289–308.

"Discussion as a Means of Teaching and Learning." *The College* XXIII, no. 4 (December 1971): 1–2.

"About Plato's Philebus." *Interpretation: A Journal of Political Philosophy* 2, no. 3 (Spring 1972): 157–82. Reprinted in *Lectures and Essays*, 309–43.

"Plato's *Ion*." *Claremont Journal of Public Affairs* 2 (Spring 1973): 23–37. Reprinted in *Lectures and Essays*, 345–60.

"Speech, Its Strength and Its Weaknesses." *The College* XXV, no. 2 (July 1973): 1–6. Reprinted in *Lectures and Essays*, 361–74.

Memorial to Leo Strauss. *The College* XXV, no. 4 (January 1974): 2.

"Plato's *Phaedo*." *The College* XXVI, no. 4 (January 1975): 1–10. Reprinted in *Lectures and Essays*, 375–93.

Plato's Trilogy: "Theaetetus," "The Sophist," and "The Statesman." Chicago and London: University of Chicago Press, 1977.

"The Art of Questioning and the Liberal Arts." *The College* XXX, no. 2 (January 1979): 1–5.

"The Copernican Revolution." *The College* XXX, no. 2 (January 1979): 6–16. Reprinted in *Lectures and Essays*, 85–115.

"On a Sixteenth-Century Algebraist." *The College* XXX, no. 2 (January 1979): 17–19. Reprinted in *Lectures and Essays*, 35–42.

"On the Nature of Nature." *Independent Journal of Philosophy* III (1979): 101–9. Reprinted in *Lectures and Essays*, 219–39.

"The World of Physics and the 'Natural' World." Translated by David R. Lachterman. *The St. John's Review* XXXIII, no. 1 (Autumn 1981): 22–34. Reprinted in *Lectures and Essays*, 1–34.

"Left and Right." Translated by Eva Brann and Beate Ruhm von Oppen. *The St. John's Review* XXXV, no. 2 (Spring 1984): 60–63.

"The Frame of Plato's *Timaeus*." English and German. Translated and annotated by Laurence Berns, Gisela Berns, Eva Brann, and Robert Williamson. *The St. John's Review* XXXV, no. 2 (Spring 1984): 63–65.

"The Problem and the Art of Writing." *The St. John's Review* XXXV, no. 3 (Summer 1984): 16–22. Reprinted in *Lectures and Essays*, 139–55.

Lectures and Essays. Edited by Robert B. Williamson and Elliott Zuckerman. Annapolis, MD: St. John's College Press, 1985.

"On the *Republic*." In *Essays in Honor of Robert Bart*, edited by Cary Stickney, 131–39. Annapolis, MD: St. John's College Press, 1993. Also printed (with minor differences) as "Plato's *Republic*: An Address." *The New Yearbook for Phenomenology and Phenomenological Philosophy* VII (2007): 297–308.

"Korrespondenz: Leo Strauss—Jacob Klein." In Leo Strauss, *Gesammelte Schriften* III: *Hobbes' politische Wissenschaft und zugehörige Schriften—Briefe*, 2nd ed., edited by Heinrich Meier, 455–605. Stuttgart: J. B. Metzler, 2001.

"On the Platonic *Meno* in Particular and Platonic Dialogues in General." *The New Yearbook for Phenomenology and Phenomenological Philosophy* I (2001): 357–67.

"The Problem of Truth." Translated by Marcus Brainard. *The New Yearbook for Phenomenology and Phenomenological Philosophy* II (2002): 367–74.

"Aristotle (I)." Edited by Burt C. Hopkins. *The New Yearbook for Phenomenology and Phenomenological Philosophy* III (2003): 295–313.

"History and Dialectics." *The New Yearbook for Phenomenology and Phenomenological Philosophy* VI (2006): 161–67.

Review of Erwin Straus, *Vom Sinn der Sinne: Ein Beitrag zur Grundlegung der Psychologie* (Berlin: Julius Springer, 1935). Translated by Emmanuel Patard. In *The New Yearbook for Phenomenology and Phenomenological Philosophy* VI (2006): 305–6.

"Selected Letters from Jacob Klein to Gerhard Krüger." German and English. Edited and translated by Emmanuel Patard. *The New Yearbook for Phenomenology and Phenomenological Philosophy* VI (2006): 308–29.

"The Logical and Historical Element in Hegel's Philosophy." Translated by Jerome Veith. *The New Yearbook for Phenomenology and Phenomenological Philosophy* XII (2012): 243–85.

Selected Bibliography

The following is a selected bibliography of works in English that touch on or relate to Klein in some significant capacity; it is meant as a resource for those interested in further pursuing the study of Klein or Kleinian themes. It also includes works referenced in the present volume that are related to Klein or thinkers that Klein discusses.

Allen, W. B. Critical notice of Jacob Klein, *Plato's Trilogy: "Theaetetus," "The Sophist," and "The Statesman." Review of Metaphysics* 32, no. 3 (1979): 553–54.

Anastaplo, George. "Jacob Klein of St. John's College." *The Newsletter* III, no. 1. Politics Department of the University of Dallas (1979): 1–9.

Angus, Ian. "Jacob Klein's Revision of Husserl's *Crisis*: A Contribution to the Transcendental History of Reification." *Philosophy Today* 49 (2005): 204–11.

Baratelli, Gabriele. "How Letters become Symbols: Jacob Klein's Genealogy of Formalization." *The New Yearbook for Phenomenology and Phenomenological Philosophy* XVIII (2021): 407–45.

Black, Deborah. "Intentionality in Medieval Arabic Philosophy." *Quaestio* 10 (2010): 65–81.

Bos, Henk J. M. *Redefining Geometrical Exactness: Descartes' Transformation of the Early Modern Concept of Construction*. New York: Springer, 2001.

Brann, Eva. "Depth and Desire." *The St. John's Review* 39, no. 3 (1989–90): 83–92.

——. "'The Math Book' Remembering Klein's Seminal Work." *The College* 35, no. 3 (2010): 32–33.

——. "Jacob Klein's Two Prescient Discoveries." *The St. John's Review* 52, no. 1 (2010): 5–19. Reprinted in *The New Yearbook for Phenomenology and Phenomenological Philosophy* XI (2011): 144–53.

——. "Immediacy: The Ways of Humanity." *The Imaginative Conservative*, November 1, 2014. https://theimaginativeconservative.org/2019/03/immediacy-ways-of-humanity-eva-brann-90.html.

——. "Jacob Klein: European Scholar and American Teacher." *The St. John's Review* 59, no. 1–2 (2017–2018): 22–34.

Buning, Marius. "The Art of Demonstration in the Work of Simon Stevin: Linguistic and Mathematical Innovation." In *Rethinking Stevin, Stevin Rethinking: Constructions of a Dutch Polymath*, edited by Karel Davids, Fokko Jan Dijksterhuis, Rienk Vermij, and Ida Stamhuis, 123–54. Leiden: Brill, 2020.

Carey, James. "Socrates' Exhortation to Follow the *Logos*." In *Socrates in the Cave: On the Philosopher's Motive in Plato*, edited by Paul J. Diduch & Michael P. Harding, 107–139. Springer Verlag, 2019.

Carter, Richard B. *Descartes' Medical Philosophy: The Organic Solution to the Mind-Body Problem*. Baltimore and London: The Johns Hopkins University Press, 1983.

Caton, Hiram. *The Origins of Subjectivity*. New Haven: Yale University Press, 1973.

——. "Review of Jacob Klein's *Greek Mathematical Thought and the Origin of Algebra*." *Studi Internationali di Filosofia* 3 (1971): 222–26.

Cifoletti, Giovanna C. "'New' Early Modern Evidence for Jacob Klein's Theses." *The New Yearbook for Phenomenology and Phenomenological Philosophy* XVIII (2021): 488–533.

Coquard, Jean-Marie. "Stevin's Mathesis and Number." *The New Yearbook for Phenomenology and Phenomenological Philosophy* XVIII (2021): 459–87.

Cosgrove, Joseph. "Husserl, Jacob Klein, and Symbolic Nature." *Graduate Faculty Philosophy Journal* 29, no. 1 (2008): 227–51.

——. "On the Mathematical Representation of Spacetime: A Case Study in Historical-Phenomenological Desedimentation." *The New Yearbook for Phenomenology and Phenomenological Philosophy* XI (2011): 154–86.

——. *Relativity Without Spacetime*. Cham: Palgrave Macmillan, 2018.

Dorter, Kenneth. Review of Jacob Klein, *Plato's Trilogy*. *Dialogue* 19, no. 4 (1980): 717–18.

Ferrier, Richard. "Viète on the Solution of Equations and the Constructions of Problems." *The St. John's Review* 48, no. 1 (2004): 115–36.

Flaumenhaft, Harvey. "Why We Won't Let You Speak of the Square Root of Two." *The St. John's Review* 48, no. 1 (2004): 7–41.

——. *Insights and Manipulations: What Classical Geometry Looked Like At Its Peak, and How It Was Transformed—A Guidebook*. South Bend: St. Augustine's Press, 2020.

Fowler, David. *The Mathematics of Plato's Academy: A New Reconstruction.* Oxford: Clarendon Press, 1999.

Fried, Michael N. "A Note on the Opposite Sections and Conjugate Sections in Apollonius of Perga's *Conica.*" *The St. John's Review* 48, no. 1 (2004): 91–113.

German, Andy. "From Intermediates through Eidetic Numbers: Plato on the Limits of Counting." *Plato Journal* 18 (2018): 111–24.

Gonda, Joseph. "On Jacob Klein's *Greek Mathematical Thought and the Origin of Algebra.*" *Interpretation* 22, no. 1 (1994): 111–28.

Gould, Josiah B. "Klein on Ethological Mimes, for Example, the *Meno.*" *Journal of Philosophy* 66, no. 9 (1969): 253–65.

Grenke, Michael. "The Question of Questions." *The St. John's Review* 54, no. 2 (2013): 115–133.

Halper, Edward C. "Klein on Aristotle on Number." *The New Yearbook for Phenomenology and Phenomenological Philosophy* XI (2011): 271–81.

Hassing, Richard F. "Modern Natural Science and the Intelligibility of Human Experience." In *Final Causality in Nature and Human Affairs,* edited by Richard Hassing, 211–56. Washington, D.C.: The Catholic University of America Press, 1993.

——. "The Exemplary Career of Newton's Mathematics." *The St. John's Review* 44, no. 1 (1997): 73–93.

——. "History of Physics and the Thought of Jacob Klein." *The New Yearbook for Phenomenology and Phenomenological Philosophy* XI (2011): 214–48.

Heeffer, Albrecht. "The Symbolic Model for Algebra: Functions and Mechanisms." In *Model-Based Reasoning in Science and Technology,* edited by L. Magnani, W. Carnielli, and C. Pizzi, 519–32. Berlin and Heidelberg: Springer, 2010.

——. "On the Curious Historical Coincidence of Algebra and Double-Entry Bookkeeping." In *Foundations of the Formal Sciences VII,* edited by K. François, G. Löwe, T. Müller, and B. Van Kerkhove (London: College Publications, 2011), 109–30.

Higuera, Henry. "Multiplication, Ancient and Modern: Sorting Out the Shifts in Meaning." Lecture, St. John's College, Annapolis, April 17 2009.

Hopkins, Burt. "Jacob Klein and the Phenomenology of History, Part I." *The New Yearbook for Phenomenology and Phenomenological Philosophy* I (2001): 67–110.

——. "The Phenomenological Project of Desedimenting the Formalization of Meaning: Jacob Klein's Contribution." *Philosophy Today* 46 (2002): 168–77.

——. "Crisis, History, and Husserl's Phenomenological Project of Desedimenting the Formalization of Meaning: Jacob Klein's Contribution." *Graduate Faculty Philosophy Journal* 24, no. 1 (2003): 75–102.

——. "Jacob Klein and the Phenomenology of Formal Systems." In *Analysis of Systems on the Edge of the Millennia: Theory and Practice*, edited by V.V. Leschenko, 108–122. Moscow: Institute of Control Sciences, 2003.

——. "Jacob Klein and The Phenomenological Project of Desedimenting the Formalization of Meaning." *The St. John's Review* 47, no. 2 (2003): 51–68.

——. "The Husserlian Context of Klein's Mathematical Work." *The St. John's Review* 48, no. 1 (2004): 43–71.

——. "Jacob Klein on Francois Vieta's Establishment of Algebra as the General Analytical Art." *Graduate Faculty Philosophy Journal* 25, no. 2 (2004): 51–85.

——. "Klein and Derrida on the Historicity of Meaning and the Meaning of Historicity in Husserl's Crisis-Texts." *The Journal of the British Society for Phenomenology* 36, no. 2 (2005): 179–87.

——. "Meaning and Truth in Klein's Philosophico-Mathematical Writings." *The St. John's Review* 48, no. 3 (2005): 57–87.

——. "Husserl's Psychologism, and Critique of Psychologism, Revisited." *Husserl Studies* 22, no. 2 (2006): 91–119.

——. "Eva Brann and the Philosophical Achievement of Jacob Klein." In *Essays in Honor of Eva Brann*, edited by Eric Salem and Peter Kalkavage, 106–19. Philadelphia: Paul Dry Books, 2007.

——. "Klein and Gadamer on the *Arithmos*-Structure of Platonic Eidetic Numbers." *Philosophy Today* 52 (2008): 151–57.

——. "Jacob Klein on the Myth of Learning." *The St. John's Review* 51, no. 1 (2009): 5–39.

——. "The Philosophical Achievement of Jacob Klein." *The New Yearbook for Phenomenology and Phenomenological Philosophy* XI (2011): 282–96.

——. *The Origin of the Logic of Symbolic Mathematics: Edmund Husserl and Jacob Klein*. Bloomington: Indiana University Press, 2011.

——. "Manifold, Intuition, and Synthesis in Kant and Husserl: The Problem of Collective Unity in Transcendental Philosophy." *Logical Analysis and History of Philosophy* 16 (2013): 264–307.

——. "Prolegomenon to a Critique of Symbolic Reason." *Research in Phenomenology* 44, no. 3 (2014): 362–83.

——. "Husserl and Jacob Klein." *The European Legacy* 21, nos. 5–6 (2016): 535–55.

——. "Phenomenology and Ancient Greek Philosophy: Methodological Protocols and Two Specimens of Interpretation: Part I." *The New Yearbook for Phenomenology and Phenomenological Philosophy* XV (2017): 222–246.

———. "Husserl and Jacob Klein on Unity and Multiplicity." In *Phenomenology and the Problem of Meaning in Human Life and History,* edited by Ľubica Učnik and Anita Williams, 19–44. Nordhausen: Verlag Traugott Bautz, 2017.

———. "Husserl and Jacob Klein on Arithmetical Unity." In *Essays on Husserl's Logic and Philosophy of Mathematics,* edited by Stefania Centrone, 461–84. Dordrecht: Springer, 2017.

———. "Jacob Klein." In *The Routledge Handbook of Phenomenology and Phenomenological Philosophy,*" edited by Daniele de Santis, Claudio Majolino, and Burt Hopkins, 533–42. London and New York: Routledge, 2021.

———. "Jacob Klein on François Viète and the Birth of the Modern Symbolic Concept of 'Number'." *The New Yearbook for Phenomenology and Phenomenological Philosophy* XVIII (2021): 446–58.

Jannsens, David. "Back to the Roots. The Correspondence Between Leo Strauss and Jacob Klein." *Philosophical Readings* IX, no. 1 (2017): 25–30.

Kane, Robert H. Critical notice of Jacob Klein, *Greek Mathematical Thought and the Origin of Algebra. Review of Metaphysics* 23, no. 1 (1969): 132.

Kates, Joshua. "Philosophy First, Last, and Counting: Edmund Husserl, Jacob Klein, and Plato's Arithmological *Eide.*" *Graduate Faculty Philosophy Journal* 25, no. 1 (2004): 67–96.

———. "Modernity and Intentional History: Edmund Husserl, Jacob Klein, and Jacques Derrida." *Philosophy Today* 49 (2005): 193–203.

———. "Two Versions of Husserl's Late History: Jacob Klein and Jacques Derrida and the Problems of Modernity." *The New Yearbook for Phenomenology and Phenomenological Philosophy* V (2005): 245–75.

Kennington, Richard. Review of Jacob Klein, *Lectures and Essays. Review of Metaphysics* 41, no. 1 (1987): 144–49.

———. *On Modern Origins,* edited by Pamela Kraus and Frank Hunt. Lanham, MD: Lexington Books, 2004.

Koochesfahani, Arian. "On Jacob Klein's Greek Mathematical Thought and the Origin of Algebra." *The St. John's Review* 57, no. 2 (2016): 47–69.

Kraus, Pamela A. "*Mens Humana: Res Cogitans* and the Doctrine of Faculties in Descartes' Meditationes." International Studies in Philosophy 18 (1986): 1–18.

Kutler, Samuel S., Eva Brann, Robert B. Williamson, J. Winfree Smith, and Elliott Zuckerman, eds. *Essays in Honor of Jacob Klein.* Annapolis, St. John's College Press: 1976.

Lachterman, David. Review of Jacob Klein, *Plato's Trilogy: "Theatetus," "The Sophist," and "The Statesman." Nous* 13 (1979): 106–12.

———. *The Ethics of Geometry: A Genealogy of Modernity.* New York: Routledge, 1989.

Larsen, Kristian. "Counting (on) Being: On Jacob Klein's Return to Platonic Dialectic." In *Phenomenological Interpretations of Ancient Philosophy*, edited by Kristian Larsen and Pål Rykkja Gilbert, 202–28. Leiden: Brill, 2021.

Lenkowski, Jon. "Meno's Paradox and the Zetetic Circle." *The St. John's Review* 43, no. 3 (1996): 2–27.

Levine, David. "Plato's Arithmological Ordering of Being: A Review of Jacob Klein's *Plato's Trilogy*." *The Southwestern Journal of Philosophy* XI, no. 2 (1980): 109–128.

——. "A World of Worldless Truths, An Invitation to Philosophy." In *The Envisioned Life, Essays in Honor of Eva Brann*, edited by Peter Kalkavage and Eric Salem, 155–169. Philadelphia: Paul Dry Books, 2007.

——. "Four Sides of a Cube, The Way of Great Books." *The Imaginative Conservative*, October 24, 2018. https://theimaginativeconservative.org/2018/10/four-sides-cube-great-books-david-levine.html.

——. "Humanity Dehumanized: Hegel's Reflections on the Enlightenment & the French Revolution." *The Imaginative Conservative*, January 23, 2019. https://theimaginativeconservative.org/2019/01/humanity-hegel-enlightenment-french-revolution-david-lawrence-levine.html.

Macbeth, Danielle. "Viète, Descartes, and the Emergence of Modern Mathematics." *Graduate Faculty Philosophy Journal* 25, no. 2 (2004): 87–117.

Manca, Danilo. "Naturalness and Historicity: Strauss and Klein on the Quarrel between the Ancients and the Moderns." *Philosophical Readings* IX, no. 1 (2017): 44–49.

Majolino, Claudio. "Splitting the *Monas*: Jacob Klein's *Math Book* reconsidered (Part I)." *The New Yearbook for Phenomenology and Phenomenological Philosophy* XI (2011): 187–213.

Maher, Daniel. "Aristotle on Mathematical and Eidetic Number." *Hermathena* 190 (2011): 29–51.

——. "Simon Stevin's *Vita Politica*: Pre-provisional Morality?" *Interpretation: A Journal of Political Philosophy* 43, no. 2 (2017): 215–32.

Mahoney, Michael. "The Beginnings of Algebraic Thought in the Seventeenth Century." In *Descartes: Philosophy, Mathematics and Physics*, edited by S. Gaukroger, 141–56. Sussex: The Harvester Press/Totowa, N.J., Barnes and Noble Books, 1980.

——. *The Mathematical Career of Pierre de Fermat 1601–1665*. Princeton: Princeton University Press, 1994.

Malet, Antoni. "Renaissance notions of number and magnitude." *Historia Mathematica* 33 (2006): 63–81.

Miller, J. Philip. *Numbers in Presence and Absence: A Study of Husserl's Philosophy of Mathematics*. The Hague: Nijhoff, 1982.

Naets, Jurgen. "How to Define a Number? A General Epistemological Account of Simon Stevin's Art of Defining." *Topoi* 29 (2010): 77–86.

Netz, Reviel. "Archimedes Transformed: The Case of a Result Stating a Maximum for a Cubic Equation." *Archive for History of Exact Sciences* 54, no. 1 (1999): 1–47

——. *The Transformation of Mathematics in the Early Mediterranean World: From Problems to Equations*. Cambridge: Cambridge University Press, 2004.

Oaks, Jeffrey. "François Viète's Revolution in Algebra." *Archive for History of Exact Sciences* 72, no. 3 (2018): 245–302.

O'Grady, William. "About Jacob Klein's Books About Plato." *The College* XXX, no. 2 (1979): 32–33.

O'Neill, John. *Worlds without Content: Against Formalism*. London: Routledge, 1991.

Owens, Joseph. *An Elementary Christian Metaphysics*. Houston: Center for Thomistic Studies, 1985.

Page, Carl. *Philosophical Historicism and the Betrayal of First Philosophy*. University Park, PA: The Pennsylvania State University Press, 1995.

——. "Symbolic Mathematics and the Intellect Militant: On Modern Philosophy's Revolutionary Spirit." *Journal of the History of Ideas* 57, no. 2 (1996): 233–53.

Panza, Marco. "What is New and What is old in Viete's Analysis Restituta and Algebra Nuova." 2007. https://halshs.archives-ouvertes.fr/halshs-00116725/document.

Polansky, Ronald M. Review of Jacob Klein, *Plato's Trilogy*. *Journal of the History of Philosophy* 19, no. 3 (1981): 377–80.

Pozzo, Riccardo. "Ramus and Other Renaissance Philosophers on Subjectivity." *Topoi* 22 (2003): 5–13.

Pritchard, Paul. *Plato's Philosophy of Mathematics*. Sankt Augustin, Germany: Academia Verlag, 1995.

Romiti, Andrew. "Jacob Klein on the Dispute Between Plato and Aristotle Regarding Number." *The New Yearbook for Phenomenology and Phenomenological Philosophy* XI (2011): 249–70.

——. *Cartesian Mind and Its Concept of Space: A Contribution to the Project of Jacob Klein*. PhD. diss. The Catholic University of America, 2016.

Rosen, Stanley. *Plato's "Sophist": The Drama of Original & Image*. New Haven: Yale University Press, 1983.

Sachs, Joe. "Introduction" to *Socrates and The Sophists: Plato's "Protagoras," "Euthydemus," "Hippias Major," and "Cratylus"*. Indianapolis: Focus Publishing, 2011.

Sarton, George. "Simon Stevin of Bruges (1548–1620)." *Isis* 21, no. 2 (July 1934): 241–303.

——. "The First Explanation of Decimal Fractions and Measures (1585)." *Isis* 23, no. 1 (1935): 153–244.

Schuster, John A. "Descartes' *Mathesis Universalis* 1619–28." In *Descartes: Philosophy, Mathematics and Physics*, edited by S. Gaukroger, 41–96. Sussex: The Harvester Press/Totowa, N.J., Barnes and Noble Books, 1980.

Scriba, C. Review of *Greek Mathematical Thought and the Origin of Algebra.* Isis 61 (1970): 132–33.

Sedeyn, Olivier. "The Wisdom of Jacob Klein." Translated by Brother Robert Smith. *The St. John's Review* 47, no. 2 (2003): 5–10.

Smith, J. Winfree. *A Search for the Liberal College: The Beginning of the St. John's Program.* Annapolis: St. John's College Press, 1983.

Stedall, Jacqueline A. *A Discourse Concerning Algebra: English Algebra to 1685.* Oxford: Oxford University, 2002.

Strauss, Leo. "An Unspoken Prologue to a Public Lecture at St. John's [In Honor of Jacob Klein, 1899–1978]." *Interpretation* 7, no. 3 (1978): 1–3. Reprinted in *The College* XXX, no. 2 (1979): 30–31. Reprinted in *Jewish Philosophy and the Crisis of Modernity*, edited by Kenneth Hart Green, 449–52. Albany: State University of New York Press, 1997.

Unguru, Sabetai. "On the Need to Rewrite the History of Greek Mathematics." *Archive for History of Exact Sciences* 15, no. 1 (1975): 67–114.

——. "Words, Diagrams, and Symbols: Greek and Modern Mathematics, or 'On the Need to Rewrite the History of Greek Mathematics' Revisited." *The St. John's Review* 48, no. 1 (2004): 71–90.

Velkley, Richard. "Reason's Parochiality: On Carl Page's Critique of Historicism." *The St. John's Review* 43, no. 3 (1996): 89–100.

Waerden, B. L. van den. *A History of Algebra: From al-Khwārizmī to Emmy Noether.* Berlin: Springer-Verlag, 1980.

Wilson, Curtis A. "Jacob Klein at 75." *The College* XXVI, no. 1 (1974): 1–4. Reprinted as the Preface to *Essays in Honor of Jacob Klein*, edited by Samuel S. Kutler et al., vii–x. Annapolis, St. John's College Press: 1976.

Wilson, Curtis A., Simon Kaplan, Samuel S. Kutler, Brother Robert Smith, J. Winfree Smith, Robert S. Bart, Robert G. Hazo, Barbara Dvorak Winiarski, Elliott Zuckerman, and Eva T. H. Brann. "Memorial Service for Jacob Klein." *The College* XXX, no. 2 (1979): 20–30.

Contributors

Andrew Romiti is a Tutor at St. John's College in Annapolis, MD, where he also did his undergraduate studies. He earned his doctorate in Philosophy from the Catholic University of America, where he wrote a dissertation on Jacob Klein and Descartes.

Daniel P. Maher is Professor of Philosophy at Assumption University in Worcester, MA, where he is also Director of the Core Texts & Enduring Questions Program. He earned his doctorate at Boston College with a dissertation on Aristotle's understanding of counting and number, which was inspired by Klein's work.

Eva Brann has been a member of the faculty at St. John's College in Annapolis, MD for more than sixty years, serving as Dean of the College from 1990 to 1997. She is the author of numerous books and essays and is translator of *Greek Mathematical Thought and the Origin of Algebra*, by Jacob Klein, her colleague at St. John's until his death in 1978.

Julia Klein is an alumna of the undergraduate program at St. John's College in Santa Fe, NM. She holds an M.A. in Humanities from Duke University and an M.A. in Philosophy from The Catholic University of America, where she is also a Doctoral Candidate.

Paul T. Wilford is Assistant Professor of Political Science at Boston College. He graduated from St. John's College in Annapolis, MD, and then earned a second B.A. in Classics and an M.Phil. in Intellectual History and Political Thought from King's College at Cambridge University, followed by a doctorate in Philosophy from Tulane University. He is the co-editor with Samuel A. Stoner of *Kant and the*

Possibility of Progress (PENN, 2021) and with Kate Rozansky of *Athens, Arden, Jerusalem* (Lexington, 2017).

David Lawrence Levine taught for twenty-seven years at St. John's College in Santa Fe, NM, where he served as both Dean of the College and Director of the Graduate Institute. He has written and lectured broadly on Plato, Aristotle, Plutarch, Rousseau, Goethe, Tocqueville, Nietzsche, Husserl, and the Great Books Program at St. John's.

Antonio Marino Lopez is Professor of Greek Philosophy at Facultad de Estudios Superiores of the Universidad Nacional Autónoma de México. He was a student of Jacob Klein's at St. John's College in Annapolis, MD.

Mary Elizabeth Halper is Dean of the Humanities at Hertog program and, since 2021, a Tutor at St. John's College in Annapolis, MD. She holds a B.A. in Philosophy and Classics from the University of Dallas and a doctorate in Philosophy from The Catholic University of America.

Burt C. Hopkins, PhD., is affiliated with the University of Lille, France (UMR-CNRS 8163 STL), and the Faculty of Humanities, Charles University, Prague (Czechia). He is the author of *The Origin of the Logic of Symbolic Mathematics: Edmund Husserl and Jacob Klein*, along with numerous articles on Klein's thought as it relates to Ancient Greek philosophy and mathematics, early modern mathematics, and the tradition of phenomenology inaugurated by Husserl early in the twentieth century.

Michael Dink is a Tutor at St. John's College in Annapolis, MD, where he also served as Dean of the College and Director of the Graduate Institute in Liberal Education. He is an alumnus of St. John's College in Annapolis, where he was a student of Jacob Klein's in a preceptorial on Plato's *Sophist*. He earned his doctorate from the School of Philosophy at The Catholic University of America.

Richard F. Hassing is Research Associate Professor in the School of Philosophy at The Catholic University of America, where he has taught since 1990. He holds M.A. degrees from The Catholic University of America (Philosophy) and from University of Toronto (Political Theory), and he earned his doctorate in Theoretical Physics from Cornell University.

Joseph Cosgrove is Associate Professor of Philosophy at Providence College. His recent scholarship focuses on the philosophy of science, with a particular interest in the implications of Jacob Klein's account of the origin of algebra to modern mathematical physics.

www.ingramcontent.com/pod-product-compliance
Lightning Source LLC
Jackson TN
JSHW022203020325
79869JS00001B/1
9781589881976